People and Culture in Ice Age Americas

People and Culture in Ice Age Americas

New Dimensions in Paleoamerican Archaeology

Edited by
Rafael Suárez and Ciprian F. Ardelean

THE UNIVERSITY OF UTAH PRESS
Salt Lake City

The Defiance House Man colophon is a registered trademark
of The University of Utah Press. It is based on a four-foot-tall
Ancient Puebloan pictograph (late PIII) near Glen Canyon, Utah.

LIBRARY OF CONGRESS CATALOGING-IN-PUBLICATION DATA

Names: Suárez, Rafael, editor. | Ardelean, Ciprian F. (Ciprian Florin),
    editor. | Society for American Archaeology. Annual Meeting (79th : 2014 :
    Austin, Tex.)
Title: People and culture in Ice Age Americas : new dimensions in
    Paleoamerican archaeology / edited by Rafael Suárez and Ciprian F.
    Ardelean.
Description: Salt Lake City : The University of Utah Press, [2018] | Includes
    bibliographical references and index. |
Identifiers: LCCN 2018032170 (print) | LCCN 2018041042 (ebook) | ISBN
    9781607816461 | ISBN 9781607816454 (cloth : alk. paper)
Subjects: LCSH: Paleo-Indians—America. | Social archaeology—America. |
    Human settlements—America—History. | America—Antiquities.
Classification: LCC E61 (ebook) | LCC E61 .P423 2018 (print) | DDC
    970.01—dc23
LC record available at https://lccn.loc.gov/2018032170

Printed and bound in the United States of America.

Contents

Figures

Tables

An Upside-Down View

Rafael Suárez and Ciprian F. Ardelean

It is hard to identify another topic in world archaeology still as hot, controversial, mysterious, shifting, and continuously conflictive as the Ice Age archaeology of Americas. For decades, passions have surged, egos have clashed, academic politics have boiled, and paradigms have risen and changed. Now, almost a century since the initial discoveries that began to challenge the thick ice of preconceptions, we are living in a new era of exciting finds that show us that archaeological knowledge is never definitive.

America's two hemispheres have lived these experiences in separate manners and from relatively divergent positions. To the north, the more homogenous Anglo world (principally, the United States) was long haunted by the conservative theories of single-route recent human arrival on the continent. Scholars developed a culture of caution and skepticism around the strongholds of tough paradigms such as Clovis-first. To the south, the more rebel and eclectic Latin world traditionally stood apart from the northern postures and felt freer to sustain out-of-the-box ideas, often constructed upon expedient conjectures, and frequently cemented by their own regional paradigms. Between the two, dialogue and constructive communication were not the rule, and the creation of models upon the particular archaeological records of the North and the South manifested as parallel, rarely compatible interpretations of the past. The causes behind such a geocultural dichotomy were diverse and many, including tense historical backgrounds, meta-academic and transcontinental political stress, self-taught para-xenophobic and nationalistic postures, and generational attitudes.

Yet the ambience has changed considerably. International collaborations are more frequent and normal, the interchange of data has become easier and is actively promoted, while the national academic barriers within the Americas have turned less cold and more permeable due to a change in the mentality of the old and the internationalizing postures of the young. Nevertheless, we should ask ourselves at this point: is the scientific environment in today's American Pleistocene archaeology really more collaborative and communicative than before, beyond the mere organization of meetings and symposia and the publication of contributed volumes? Do we display true dialogue or only politically correct alternating monologues?

This book is a cautious attempt to test for potential answers to these questions. It is part of a project meant to generate our own environment of discussion in which researchers from different countries may find a place to present and debate a variety of topics related to the early peopling of America. This process started in 2012 with a symposium on lithic technology, chaired by César Méndez and Kurt Rademaker, at the 77th Annual Meeting of the Society for American Archaeology in Memphis, Tennessee, which culminated in the publication of volume 47, no. 1, of *Chungara: Revista Chilena de Antropología*. Later, in 2014, we organized the symposium "Early Human Occupation during the Ice Age in Americas: New Directions and Advances" at the SAA's 79th Annual Meeting in Austin, Texas, and invited a diversity of contributors from different countries and academic backgrounds as means to obtain the pulse of modern Pleistocene–Early Holocene archaeology. The book you are holding now is the result of that symposium.

Even more recently, in the year 2016, Rafael Suárez and Cesar Méndez organized another symposium, "Mobility and Use of Space in Late Pleistocene South America: Is It Possible to Discuss Early Human Regionalization Ranking?" at the 81st Annual SAA Meeting in Orlando, Florida, seeking to provide a proper space for looking more deeply into the issues of mobility, use of space, and regional differences during the peopling of South America (since published as a special volume of *Quaternary Journal*, 473 Part B, 2018). We are hopeful that in the future new challenges may lead to more concrete and solid collaborations and spaces for discussion.

The present volume of contributions looks at areas where new knowledge is being produced. Of course, many relevant regions and a bounty of crucial specific topics could not be represented, so the content may not satisfy everybody. Like most books based on previously held symposia, this one cannot offer an absolutely thorough coverage of geographical zones and topics. Rather, it depends on the diversity of subjects presented by the people who actually attended the meeting in Austin a few years ago. In our consideration, that participation was important and the spectrum of themes diverse enough, covering most of the significant geographical areas across the hemisphere. However, a few colleagues preferred not to be part of this volume; others withdrew their papers in the early stages of the project. To compensate, we invited other contributors who had not been present in Austin. The apparent lack of "geographical equilibrium" is simply the natural result of those dynamics.

Our book seeks a balance between papers coming from South and North America, leaving evident gaps for Central American regions where new studies are surely about to present new and interesting results. The cover of this volume itself and the arrangement of chapters "backwards," from south to north, were inspired by the work of Joaquín Torres García, an Uruguayan constructivist painter, who drew South America upside down. In this way, we express the need for rethinking and reevaluating our views and paradigms about the last expansion and colonization process undertaken by ancient *Homo sapiens*.

There are several terminological and conceptual ambiguities that require attention if we want to go ahead with a much better and fruitful transcontinental academic communication. Among such words and syntagms that (in English and Spanish alike) lack a properly established significance while allowing a rather promiscuous employment are: "*peopling* of America," "human *occupation*," "*first*" (people, Americans), and "*early*" (early occupation, early people, etc.). What do they mean in the context of American prehistoric archaeology and under the light of evidently shifting paradigms? Because if used indiscriminately in relationship to the arduous problem of the original human presence on the continents, they may reach very different meanings and communicate unsustained realities.

Let us start with the concept of "peopling." The term is widely used in the kind of studies alluded to in this book, freely employed in reference to any sort of "Paleoindian" archaeological records radiocarbon dated to a chronological interval of pristine human presence. But not every trace of cultural activity indicates a peopling process, properly speaking. The human peopling of a territory means a complexity of sociocultural dynamics, a certain degree of permanence, and a gradual occupation and involvement with the landscape, followed by a successful demography and a legacy passed on to subsequent generations. It is hard to tell whether the discovery of an archaeological context showing early human presence speaks of a real peopling of that territory, region, or continent. We believe that we have not achieved yet a sufficient degree of refinement in our studies to be able to discern, in every case, between actual colonization of a territory and ephemeral contexts of cultural presence. Peopling a segment of land as pioneers means that one remains there for a considerable amount of time, leaves descendants, and passes culture along.

Of course, for nomadic hunter-gatherers, the absolute values of such variables would necessarily be different from those expected for more sedentary societies. However, the peopling of a geographical extension of any size is a process that must involve the assumption of success and stability, positive demographic statistics, and certain regularity of contact between people and the "peopled" landscapes. Transitory populations, or the ephemeral presence of a small exploratory band at a specific location, does not mean peopling. Thus, we should be careful not to use this term as a convenient and expedient cover. We humans went to the moon several times, but that does not mean we were peopling or colonizing it. Such is the case with the "early peopling of America."

Certainly, many of the archaeological finds we read and write about—especially those accumulating in the last decades after a veritable boom of "older-than-Clovis" discoveries—do not yet reflect an actual peopling or settling process. They may be remnants of failed colonizing episodes that left no long-standing legacy, of populations in transit heading to far more distant places, or just meteoric instants in the life of small exploratory groups that passed by just once, only to disappear into the shadows. But it is clear that when viewed from our present perspective and at a very low resolution, the great puzzle we try to articulate from an assortment of disconnected discoveries across the hemisphere is the pale reflection of a long-lasting and diffuse colonization/peopling process that eventually left descendants and a large diversity of human societies by the beginning of the Holocene.

Clovis and Folsom cultures, spreading across their territories and sharing a complex culture over a vast geography, definitely were signs of a successful peopling. But what about humans before them? When can we actually start talking about a true peopling and not mere isolated incursions? Today, all over the western hemisphere, we are facing an increasing wave of archaeological sites whose scientifically obtained ages challenge the new conservative visions and even the liberal ones. Sites giving strange archaeological signals display "dangerously" old dates. Before they become accepted and are integrated in the paradigms of future decades, we can ask ourselves, somewhat rhetorically: if people arrived in America a really long time before Clovis, were they *peopling* this new world? Did their presence last long enough and over wide enough space to be considered proper peopling? Or did they just step on the continent and vanish without trace after a few years, decades, or generations? How many failed entries were there before the archaeological record began to keep track of them? It thus becomes clear that the semantic relevance and the ontological coverage under the term "peopling" now increase in importance, as the antiquity of "pre-Clovis" and "pre-Fishtail" populations recedes farther and farther in time.

The same discussion is valid for the concept of "occupation." We are all familiar with books and articles whose titles speak of human occupations during the Pleistocene and Early Holocene. Occupation actually means that people *occupied* an area: they moved over specific territories with certain regularity and exploited the natural resources in a deeper way than with mere transit or exploratory visit. So, speaking of an actual human occupation implies that the archaeological record entitles us to confirm a recurrence in the involvement of a determined human group with the landscape on a larger chronological and spatial scale. A hearth and a few tools in a rockshelter, do they tell us about an actual occupation by humans who were peopling a region, or are they only ephemeral signals of a small band that moved through, never looking back? Overcoming the biases in our field explorations, developing systematic and sustained regional explorations, and investing in refined absolute dating programs are a few ways to define the difference between true human occupations and simple human *presence* at a specific locality.

To summarize the discussion so far, there are three levels of early cultural visibility in the Pleistocene archaeological record:

a) "presence": this is the most acceptable and broadest of the terms we can use, especially when we are unsure of the chronological depth and spatial extension of the indicators;

b) "occupation": when people interacted with a territory more than once; when recurrence and permanence are comparable in more than one site and for longer than a single moment; then we can speak of an actual occupation of an area beyond a mere incidental visit;

c) "peopling": when human groups extended and lasted over wider territories and passed their culture on to subsequent generations that continued to live in the same regions and expanded outward.

We should be able to define which of these categories best suit our archaeological indicators in order to communicate an adequate message to our colleagues and the public.

It is also very common to say that we study the "first" people on the continent, the "first inhabitants," or the "first Americans." Again, what does "first" mean today? Two or three decades ago, the valid paradigm of the moment gave the "first inhabitants" a face and a name. For a long time, the Clovis culture's title was almost unchallenged by emerging "heretical" discoveries within and outside the United States. But today the situation has changed radically, and the 13,500 cal BP barrier has long been broken, both on the field and in the minds of scholars. Time's doors opened on an immensity of possibilities, and America's prehistory will soon be rewritten. So, who are "The First" now? For none of us can deny that The Site bearing the oldest human presence in the hemisphere still represents an absolute Holy Grail in our hearts and dreams. And first means first—not the second, not the third. Clovis people, although forever retaining the special aura of those who thrived over a vast diversity of landscapes, are not the first anymore,

and for most archeologists working on this topic in Latin America they never were. Under these circumstances, perhaps we should stop talking about the "first Americans" for a while—at least until the whirling waters of this new epoch of exploration settles down and brings us a new apparent "truth."

But then, if the first are no longer the first, are the early sites early? The archaeological semantics of "early" and "old" vary from continent to continent, from region to region, and from topic to topic. What does "old" mean today in American prehistory? How old should an archaeological find be in order to be "old enough" to be accepted as a valid discovery by the defenders of one or another of the modern paradigms?

"Old" and "early" are related but not entirely coincident conceptualizations, for both bear significant burdens of relativity. In the archaeological vocabulary, the lexical distinction between the two is easier to note in English than in Spanish. "Early" should be applied to those cultural contexts that belong to the Pleistocene and Early Holocene in general. Ergo, "early" means older than the terminus point of the Early Holocene, according to the chronological scheme in use—let us say, older than 8,200 cal BP. This way, we can at least defend our professional ego and distinguish ourselves from those doing a "later archaeology." On the other hand, "old" seems to be more like a Golden Apple of Discord, feeding the disputes within our own elitist guild.

In the newly fashioned behavior inside the "Paleoindian academia"—conveniently resettled on the fundaments of a wide and politically corrected acceptance of "pre-Clovis" or "older-than-Clovis"—the absolute age of the site matters more than an outsider could possibly imagine. If a few decades ago it was inconceivable to speak of pre-Clovis radiocarbon dates and remain accepted by the highly paradigmatic cloud of peers, the situation has not changed much. It has only adapted and moved a little bit back along the continuum of the "acceptable" range of dates. Today, it seems that a pre-Clovis or pre-Fishtail date must fall within a decent range of "pre-Clovisness" in order to be mentioned, let alone accepted. If "too old" (the absolute values of reference varying themselves according to the personal taste of detractors), it definitely causes problems and faces similar aggressions from the naysayers. The gravitational attraction of the "Clovis milestone" produces the same powerful effect on the new wave of non-conventional discoveries as it did decades ago, just in a different direction. From the point of view of the open and relaxed scientific attitudes we should adopt in the twenty-first century, *that* is a harmful situation.

These first pages are not quite the usual foreword. The reader should not expect a summary of the included papers. The last chapter, written by Tom Dillehay himself—one of the most noted celebrities in archaeology today—fulfills precisely that function, from a wiser and much more professional perspective. But there are some technical aspects that do need attention, especially the abbreviations we employ to refer to absolute dating. As it has become evident in the previous pages, this book uses the form "RCYBP" to refer to "radiocarbon or ¹⁴C years before present," the age measurements as received from radiocarbon laboratories. The calibration of the dates into calendar years is expressed as cal BP, per the SAA/LAA. We have tried to maintain continuity across the volume, speaking in calibrated years whenever possible, to facilitate easy comparison between regions. The dates obtained by other methods, such as luminescence of sediment grains (OSL) are given as "ka" (kilo annum, or thousands of years before present).

So, does this book pretend to bring new, revolutionary, and yet acceptable evidence to the eager reader? What is "acceptable evidence," after all? Can we ask such a question today from an objective position? That is very hard to answer and even harder to adapt to our times, if we want to avoid another epoch of academic police and Procrustean beds for other peoples' work. Scientific ethics, objectivity, and good data control during fieldwork and in the lab are what we need in our daily work and when we seek to evaluate the relevance of the discoveries emerging around us. Most authors in this volume address these issues from their own theoretical stances and in relationship to their particular geographies and historiographies. But as simple human beings or ambitious scientists, we cannot do more than our own science empowers us to do.

This volume is not a new gospel for a revolutionary movement. In fact, the reader may find it rather "decent" and "unharmful." What, then, should readers expect? Certain diversity, before all. A diversity of approaches and a fairly large geographical coverage spanning the entire Western Hemisphere. It is not something new in itself but something that should become noted in American Pleistocene archaeology. In fact, this volume pretends to change—at least a little bit and at least for a moment—the predominant north-centric view in Pleistocene–Early Holocene archaeological studies and to invert that polarity for the sake of equilibrium.

Fascinating stuff is being done right now in Latin America, and many maps drawn in the North continue to leave our regions blank. The new chronological revolution in Ice Age archaeology is accompanied by an evident geographical boost of discoveries rising from southern latitudes. And there will always be space for surprises.

CHAPTER 1

The Cave at the End of the World

Cueva del Medio and the Early Colonization of Southern South America

Fabiana M. Martin, Dominique Todisco, Joel Rodet, Francisco J. Prevosti,
Manuel San Román, Flavia Morello, Charles Stern, and Luis A. Borrero

The early history of the human exploration and colonization of Fuego-Patagonia is based on evidence obtained from four different and widely separated regions: the Central Plateau (Miotti 1998), the Pali Aike Lava Field (Bird 1988), Ultima Esperanza (Nami 1987; Prieto 1991; Jackson and Prieto 2005), and northern Tierra del Fuego (Massone 2004). In this chapter we will review the data from one of the sites that produced crucial evidence for our understanding of this process: Cueva del Medio. This is a large exogenous cave located in Ultima Esperanza, Chile, at the Cerro Benítez (51°34.209 S, 72°36.161 W), oriented toward the southwest (Figure 1.1). Cueva del Milodón and several other caves and rock-shelters containing Late Pleistocene faunas are situated within a radius of 4 km around Cueva del Medio (Jackson 2007), all formed in the Upper Cretaceous conglomerates of the Cerro Toro Formation (CTF; Hubbard et al. 2008).

Hugo Nami studied Cueva del Medio intensively. His archaeological discoveries firmly established its importance for the Late Pleistocene peopling of southern Patagonia (Nami 1987). In this chapter, we present results of new excavations at the cave and also discuss some previous interpretations. Nami noted the presence of Late Pleistocene carnivore remains (1987, 1993), and recent chronological results show that *Smilodon* and Felidae cf. *Panthera* were deposited by the time of human arrival (Prieto et al. 2010; Martin 2008, 2013). This information, together with the chronological range of herbivore remains recovered by Nami, dictated a taphonomic approach. Accordingly, we discuss the different agents involved in the accumulation of the bone assemblages at the end of the Pleistocene. This presentation will focus on geoarchaeological and chronological issues, with an emphasis on Nami's distinction of two early archaeological components. The existence of a Late Holocene component is also relevant. Finally, the archaeological evidence will be evaluated and compared with nearby sites.

The presence of carnivore and herbivore remains not associated with the human occupations (Nami 1987, 1993, 1994a; Prieto et al. 2010; Martin 2013) makes it necessary to discuss in more detail which bones are behaviorally associated with humans. Recent taphonomic developments in the study of Fuego-Patagonian cave assemblages suggest caution in attributing agency to the different materials found in physical association, particularly bones (Borrero 2009; Martin 2013). There are many ways bones accumulate, not all necessarily implying human agency. Under these conditions, it is no easy task to separate which of the available radiocarbon dates are relevant for the study of early human occupation and which are not (Martin 2012). Many radiocarbon dates were considered relevant on the exclusive basis of physical association with archaeological remains (Borrero 2009). However, this is not sufficient to justify

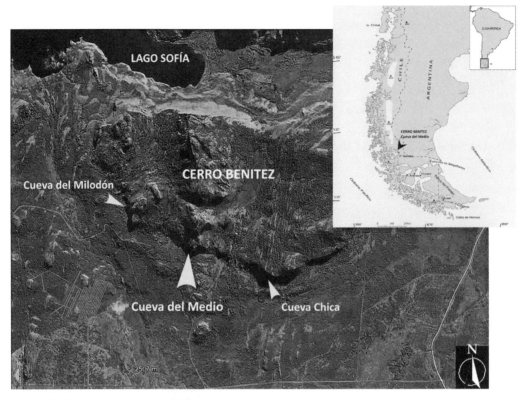

Figure 1.1a. Cueva del Medio. Location map.

Figure 1.1b. Cueva del Medio. View of the cave entrance.

TABLE 1.1. Cueva del Medio. Bones recovered in the Fell III component (Nami and Menegaz 1991:121).

Species	Elements
Lama sp.	Phalanx I, Phalanx II
Lama guanicoe	Metapodial epyphysis, rib*
Hippidion	M3 sup. right
Mylodon	Unguial phalanx, two osteoderms

*Nami and Nakamura 1995

FIGURE 1.2. Fell Cave projectile point recovered in deposits below the rockfall near the western wall.

contemporaneity. Our criteria for chronological evidence of human presence are radiocarbon dates from bones with cut marks or charcoal from hearths (Martin 2012).

Antecedents

A surface sample was initially recovered in the 1980s in a disturbed area of the cave. This sample indicated the presence of extinct Late Pleistocene fauna there (Nami 1987; Borrero et al. 1988). Nami was able to find sediments not perturbed by the activities of amateurs, which he separated into five stratigraphic units. His excavations displayed a short but important sequence on the upper 40 cm of the sediment pile that comprised the full Late Pleistocene occupation series (Nami 1985–1986:106). Importantly, he defined what he called the Fell III component in Unit 3, a brown-reddish sand with clasts found only in the central squares of his excavation grid. Unit 4, below, formed by sand, contains his Fell I component (Nami 1993:126). A thin layer of clastic material resulting from the disintegration of the conglomerate of the roof separates both components.

Recovered faunal remains include rodents, Rheidae, camelids (*Lama* morphotype *Lama owenii*, *Lama guanicoe*, and *Lama gracilis*), Cervidae, *Hippidion saldiasi*, *Mylodon*, *Smilo-*

don, and Felidae cf. *Panthera* (Nami 1987; Nami and Menegaz 1991; Nami 1994a, 1994b; Prieto et al. 2010). Remains of *Lycalopex culpaeus* were also found on the modern cave surface (Borrero et al. 1988:140). The fauna found associated with his Fell III component is not abundant but limited to eight elements (Table 1.1). In contrast, 76 *Lama* sp., 27 *Hippidion*, and five *Mylodon* elements were assigned to his Fell I component (Nami and Menegaz 1991:121). Most of the extinct fauna bones from Nami's collection were recovered from the surface on the west side of the cave. Among his important Late Pleistocene findings were Fishtail (or Fell Cave) projectile points (Figure 1.2), which are widely accepted as markers for early populations in South America (Flegenheimer et al. 2013). These points were stratigraphically associated with hearths and both extinct and modern fauna that produced Late Pleistocene radiocarbon dates (Table 1.2; Nami and Menegaz 1991; Nami and Nakamura 1995). Those points and other tools were found exclusively within his Fell I component.

The Fell III component, on the other hand, is characterized by stemless triangular projectile points and other tools that Nami compares with the so-called Toldense industry (Nami 1987:102; Gradín et al. 1979). These points are also associated with extinct and modern fauna (Nami 1987:87). It is this distinction between both components that we want to discuss, together with the character of its association with the bone assemblage.

In conclusion, Nami's stratigraphic work between 1986 and 1993 recovered excellent archaeological and chronological information (Nami 1987, 1989–1990; Nami and Menegaz 1991; Nami 1992) and was unanimously recognized

TABLE 1.2. Cueva del Medio. Radiocarbon dates attributed to Fell I component (Nami and Nakamura 1995; Martinic 1996). Calibration curve: IntCal13 (Reimer et al. 2013).

Dated material	RCYBP	cal BP (2σ)	Lab no.
Charcoal (hearth)	9595 ± 115	10,595–11,215	PITT 0344
Averaged sample (bones several spp.) (Nami 1989–1990: 127)	9770 ± 70	10,809–11,329	Beta 40281
Charcoal (hearth)	10,310 ± 70	11,825–12,404	Gr-N 14913
Undetermined burned bone (hearth)	10,350 ± 130	11,647–12,592	Beta 58105
Charcoal (hearth)	10,430 ± 80	12,039–12,564	Beta 52522
cf. *Lama owenii,* Fg. Metapodial (hearth)	10,430 ± 100	11,988–12,619	NUTA- 1734
Undetermined burned bone (hearth)	10,550 ± 120	12,099–12,709	Gr-N 14911
H. saldiasi, vertebra	10,710 ± 100	12,421–12,767	NUTA- 1811
H. saldiasi, tibia (hearth)	10,860 ± 160	12,432–13,084	NUTA- 2331
Undetermined bone (Martinic 1996)	10,885 ± 90	12,672–12,996	(A-7242) AA-13018
Charcoal (hearth)	10,930 ± 230	12,240–13,300	Beta 39081
cf. *Lama owenii,* phalanx	10,960 ± 150	12,639–13,114	NUTA- 2330
cf. *Lama owenii,* undetermined diaphysis (hearth)	11,040 ± 250	12,430–13,432	NUTA- 2197
cf. *Lama owenii.* Metapodial epiphysis	11,120 ± 130	12,726–13,206	NUTA-1737
Undetermined bone (Martinic 1996)	11,570 ± 100	13,187–13,585	(A-7421) AA-12578
Undetermined bone (Martinic 1996)	11,990 ± 100	13,579–14,083	(A-7240) AA-12577
Undetermined burned bone (hearth) [rejected by Nami]	12,390 ± 230	13,778–15,239	PITT 0343

as a proof for Late Pleistocene occupation of the south of the continent (Dillehay 2000; Borrero 2012). Nami's research also produced evidence for Late Holocene occupations at the site, basically at the back of the cave.

Results

The Geomorphological Context of the Cave

Geoarchaeological research was an integral component of our project and offered a better understanding of the formation processes acting at Cueva del Medio and the other caves (Martin et al. 2013). The landscape underwent Late Pleistocene glaciation, paraglacial/periglacial conditions, and finally interglacial (Holocene) environmental dynamics. Consequently, the cave can be viewed as a specific underground geomorphological system whose formation and evolution were influenced by different physical forces during the Last Glacial Period. Processes including both karstic and nonkarstic (especially glacial) dynamics, probably acting at different spatial and temporal scales, were involved.

Cueva del Medio is located on the south side

of Cerro Benitez, on the lee side of the Andes, southeast of the South Patagonian Ice Field (Figure 1.1). During the Last Glacial Maximum (LGM), outlet glaciers from the Patagonian Ice Sheet coalesced and nourished the Ultima Esperanza piedmont lobe, which flowed eastward toward the extra-Andean plains in Argentina. This ice lobe overrode Cerro Benitez sometime during or prior to the local LGM, as suggested by ice modeling of its summits (Sagredo et al. 2011). In the Puerto Natales region, at least two major LGM advances are documented between about 17,500 and 40,000 cal BP (calendar yr BP), the most recent of which corresponds to the Dos Lagunas moraines and the Arauco Moraine Complex (Sagredo et al. 2011). The Last Glacial Termination in the Ultima Esperanza area started shortly before ca. 17,500 cal BP, when the piedmont lobe abandoned these moraines. A near-minimum age for ice recession from the final local LGM advance is given by the chronology from Vega Benitez, suggesting enough ice thinning/recession in Cerro Benitez just prior to 17,500 cal BP (Sagredo et al. 2011).

Glacial recession gave rise to the develop-

TABLE 1.3. Cueva del Medio. Paleontological samples recovered by Nami (Nami and Nakamura 1995; Prieto et al. 2010). Calibration curve: IntCal13 (Reimer et al. 2013)

Dated material	RCYBP	cal BP (2σ)	Lab no.
Smilodon, incisor	11,100 ± 80	12,770–13,101	Ua-37622
Mylodon sp., bone.	12,720 ± 300	14,050–15,991	NUTA 2341

ment of an ice-dammed proglacial lake, the Lago Puerto Consuelo. This lake reached elevations between 125 and 150 meters above sea level (m a.s.l.), with its highest level dated between about 16,200 and 16,900 cal BP. A regressive phase occurred after the Ultima Esperanza ice lobe abandoned its stabilized position, exposing sectors with elevations below 125 m a.s.l. (Sagredo et al. 2011; Stern et al. 2011; García et al. 2014).

The local paleoecological information obtained by Moreno and colleagues (2012) marks changes in deglacial climate conditions. The analysis of two columns (Pantano Dumestre and Eberhard) indicates that southwesterly winds (SWW) drove changes in hydrologic balance and precipitation throughout the Last Glacial Termination. Such changes may have affected water circulation in the karst network and amounts and pattern of rain/snow precipitation on Cerro Benitez, with consequences for cave sedimentation. Another factor that may have influenced cave sedimentation and affected stratigraphy is the evolution of glacial cryogenic conditions in relation to past temperature fluctuations. It is hypothesized that permafrost may have formed on the recently deglaciated land of Cerro Benitez and then in cave sediments. During periods of warmer climate (paraperiglacial), permafrost thaw-degradation may have provided water or enhanced water infiltration and circulation in the karst network, therefore influencing cave sedimentation.

Excavations

The limits of Nami's excavations were identified as a basis for our main excavations. We dug a surface of 15 m² in the central part of the cave. Approximately the first meter was already excavated by Nami, and we reached a maximal depth of about 5 m. Two squares adjacent to Nami's main excavation were completely excavated, including the archaeological layers, and used as a comparative reference between our work and that of Nami. Also, on the basis of the previously recorded presence of megafaunal remains on the surface and on a profile (Table 1.3), a new locus was selected for excavation near the west wall of the cave. Rocks fallen from the ceiling were sealing those deposits and had to be destroyed with a jackhammer. This excavation proceeded toward a maximal depth of 2 m, uncovering archaeological and paleontological deposits.

Our excavations at the center of the cave revealed a stratigraphy that partially covers the Last Glacial Termination. The archaeological information that we recovered in the upper part of the sequence is basically comparable to that obtained by Nami, including a *Hippidion* astragalus dated to ca. 10,860 RCYBP, which displays cut marks (Table 1.4), and a baciform hearth dated to 10,410 ± 50 RCYBP [Beta 39538]. This falls well within the range of the hearths previously dated by Nami (Table 1.2). A much more recent hearth, dated to 2970 ± 30 RCYBP, was found nearby. Also, two camelid bones—one with cut marks—were dated as 3820 ± 30 and 3830 ± 30 RCYBP, respectively. They may have belonged to the same individual but confirm the presence of Late Holocene occupations in the area. An important conclusion here is that both Late Pleistocene and Late Holocene components are found in physical contact.

The deepest part of the excavation revealed large weathered rocks, covering *Mylodon* bones, which were dated to 13,790 ± 60 and 13,670 ± 50 RCYBP (Table 1.4), the oldest ages for the site. These rocks are interpreted as the result of debris fall and were included within a clay matrix linked to water movement. Above that layer, there was a postglacial clayey sediment. With abundant *Mylodon* remains, this stratum

TABLE 1.4. Cueva del Medio. Radiocarbon dates Project FONDECYT 1100822. Calibration curve: IntCal13 (Reimer et al. 2013).

Dated Taxon/element	RCYBP	cal BP (2σ)	Lab no.	Observations
Charcoal (hearth)	2,970 ± 30	3007–3229	Beta 344433	
Camelidae, metapodial	3,820 ± 30	4093–4397	Beta 344431	
Camelidae, rib	3,830 ± 30	4101–4405	Beta 344432	
L. guanicoe, rib	3,900 ± 30	4247–4418	Beta 341900	West Wall; cut marks
Camelidae, rib	4,230 ± 30	4649–4856	Beta 344429	West wall
Charcoal (hearth)	10,410 ± 50	12,073–12,524	Beta 319538	Center of cave
Hippidion, first phalanx	10,680 ± 40	12,571–12,711	Beta 344428	West wall
Canidae, tibia	10,710 ± 50	12,577–12,724	Beta 341903	West wall
Felidae cf., *Panthera*	10,860 ± 40	12,692–12,798	Beta 344430	West wall
H. saldiasi, astragalus	10,860 ± 110	12,595–13,008	AA 100235	Center of cave; cut marks
P. o. mesembrina, mandible	11,410 ± 80	13,096–13,415	Ua-24687 AMS	Center of cave; coll. Nami (Martin 2008)
Mylodon, scapula	11,830 ± 130	13,416–13,997	AA 100228	Center of cave; carnivore marks
Felidae, rib	12,490 ± 50	14,301–15,041	Beta 344434	Center of cave
Mylodon, vertebra	12,760 ± 140	14,586–15,725	AA 100232	Center of cave
Mylodon, mandible	12,990 ± 50	15,307–15,751	Beta 344435	Center of cave; brown clay
Mylodon, bone frag.	13,100 ± 50	15,466–15,953	Beta 319539	Center of cave; clays
Mylodon, rib	13,670 ± 50	16,264–16,737	Beta 344436	Center of cave; brown-reddish clay
Mammalia, frag.	13,670 ± 50	16,264–16,737	Beta 341901	Center of cave; weathered blocks, bottom
Mylodon, osteoderm	13,790 ± 60	16,413–16,946	Beta 341902	Center of cave; weathered blocks, bottom

can be defined as a matrix-supported diamicton. The diamicton showed evidences of waterlogged conditions of sedimentation. This layer was overlain by irregularly stratified autochthonous and allochthonous sediments, mostly water-laid local sands and pyroclastic airfall deposits (tephra), with bedrock-derived coarse materials including debris fall deposits. Irregularly strati-fied sediments revealed reworked medium sand and diffuse tephra; color variations suggest that tephra is more or less mixed with local sand. The stratigraphy is characterized by: (a) sandy beds more or less rich in coarse elements (pebbles, cobbles); (b) clast-supported materials (re-worked conglomerate slabs); (c) fine-textured thin laminations mostly dipping northward and westward; (d) microchannels suggesting west-ward paleoflows; (e) deformed structures with reworked tephra/sand; and (f) diffuse redoxi-morphic features (Fe/Mn concentrations).

Geochemical studies indicate that the tephra derives from the large late-glacial explosive R1 eruption of the Reclus volcano and corresponds to an event dated to 12,670 ± 240 RCYBP (Stern 2008; Stern et al. 2011; Sagredo et al. 2011). Following that event, the deposition of sand/reworked tephra would have begun at or shortly after 12,500 RCYBP and seems to have continued until the beginning of the Holocene. A *Mylodon* vertebra embedded in the tephra but lying on the clays was dated 12,760 ± 140 RCYBP, which is in line with the age for the tephra. Scarce mammal remains were retrieved in stratified re-worked sand/tephra sediments above the diam-icton, whereas archaeological deposits were only present in the upper part of the stratigraphy.

FIGURE 1.3. *Mylodon* scapula with scoring and crenulated marks, recovered by Nami.

FIGURE 1.4. *Mylodon* vertebra with carnivore marks, recovered by Nami.

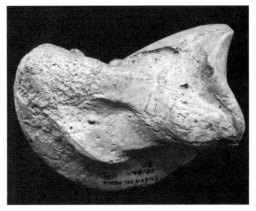

FIGURE 1.5a. *Hippidion saldiasi* astragalus with cut marks.

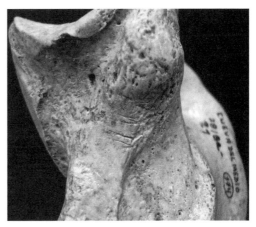

FIGURE 1.5b. Detail of Figure 1.5a.

The presence of human occupations in the sands of Nami's layer 4 was confirmed by our excavations both in the central part and near the west wall of the cave. Late Holocene occupations were also identified.

Discussion
Carnivores

Nami noted the presence of carnivores, and some herbivore bones (mostly *Mylodon*) present carnivore punctures and pits (Figures 1.3, 1.4). The evidence suggests a complex taphonomic panorama. Remains of *Felidae* and *Cervidae* are found only in sediments deposited before the human occupation (Nami and Menegaz 1991:

126). In contrast, bones corresponding to *Lama* and *Lama guanicoe* are found only in archaeological assemblages or physically associated with them. However, they do not always display marks of human exploitation. Bones of *Hippidion* (horse) also appear in cultural contexts, and at least one of them, dated to 10,860 ± 110 RCYBP (Table 1.4), displays cut marks (Figure 1.5). The range of radiocarbon dates for *Hippidion* at Cueva del Medio is 10,860–10,680 RCYBP.

We must recall that two radiocarbon dates of ca. 11,990 and 11,570 RCYBP, published by Martinic (1996), are older than those informed by Nami and Nakamura (1995) for the early human occupations of the cave. Nami does not include those results in a recent list of archaeological dates for Cueva del Medio (Nami 2007). Also, Nami recovered a panther mandible below the archaeological layers (Nami 1985–1986:106–7; Nami and Menegaz 1991:126) that we dated to 11,410 RCYBP (Martin 2008). This date overlaps both dates published by Martinic, and we think that these ages should all be treated as unrelated to humans (Tables 1.2, 1.3). We also have an age of 11,830 RCYBP for a juvenile *Mylodon* scapula with carnivore marks recovered by Nami, who ascribed it to his Fell I component (Nami and Menegaz 1991:121; Table 1.4). Other bones with similar ages are physically associated with the archaeological remains but without published evidence of human exploitation (Martinic 1996). In this context, the existence of another depositional agent—carnivores—is an invitation to caution.

Using all the available radiocarbon ages, a range between 10,930–9535 RCYBP is evident for the Late Pleistocene occupation of the cave. Alternatively, if we only used AMS radiocarbon dates, the chronological range would shorten to 10,860–10,410 RCYBP. The second alternative appears to be preferred, since not only is it difficult to assess the cultural meaning of some of the standard dates, but at least one of the most recent radiocarbon values (9770 ± 70 RCYBP) had resulted from dating splinters and fragments of *Mylodon* sp., *Hippidion* sp., and *Lama* (Nami 1989–1990:127). In other words, this is an averaged date.

In conclusion, indicators of use of the cave by both carnivores and humans are concentrated within a short period. There are three Late Pleistocene radiocarbon dates on bones of horse, panther, and canid obtained below the blocks near the western wall. The horse remains were close to a fragment of a Fell Cave projectile point and other tools. The panther and canid bones were found some 30 and 66 cm below the archaeological evidence. Panthers and canids are potential accumulating and bone-modifying agents, while horse is the only extinct animal for which we have evidence of human exploitation in the form of cut marks. The date of the panther at 10,860 RCYBP (Table 1.4) suggests that humans

and carnivores may have alternated use of the cave. Thus, using both Nami's and our own data, the best evidence for human occupations lies in radiocarbon dates obtained on charcoal recovered from hearths and cut-marked bones (Tables 1.2, 1.4).

The Fell I and III Components

Bird describes Fell I and Fell III as two separate and nonoverlapping periods at the Pali Aike Lava Field (Bird 1946; Nami 1987). Nami recognizes the presence of both components at Cueva del Medio. According to Nami and Menegaz (1991), the Fell III component was found above the Fell I component in the north sector of the excavation, confined to a few squares. The limited distribution of tools attributed to this component was confirmed, since our work in other parts of the cave failed to recover any other tools ascribed to Fell III. In contrast, the Fell I component was found all over the surface excavated by Nami, as well as in our excavations. It is characterized by the presence of hearths, fishtail projectile points, sidescrapers, endscrapers, knives, debitage, and faunal remains (Nami and Menegaz 1991). Anthropic marks on bones are mentioned, including cut marks, fracture patterns, and burning (Nami and Menegaz 1991:119, 122; Nami 1994a:150), but the evidence was not published (Nami and Nakamura 1995:132; Menegaz et al. 1994:35). A horse skull fractured on a sagittal plane is mentioned (Nami and Menegaz 1991:120), as well as a pile of *Hippidion* bones (Nami 1994a:123; Nami 2013).

According to Bird, his Fell I component was associated with extinct fauna, while Fell III was only found associated with modern animals (Bird 1946, 1988). However, at Cueva del Medio both components were physically associated with modern and extinct fauna. Nami explains that his use of Bird's nomenclature is only nominal (Nami 1987:83), but he immediately asks if humans were synchronic with megamammals during the early Holocene and makes stratigraphic and chronological comparisons with Pali Aike (Nami 1987:88). In some cases, the characterization of his Fell I or III components was based on chronology (Nami 1989–1990:127;

TABLE 1.5. Cueva del Medio. Radiocarbon dates attributed to Fell III component (Nami and Nakamura 1995). Calibration curve: IntCal13 (Reimer et al. 2013).

Taxa	Dated element	RCYBP	cal BP (2σ)	Lab no.
Lama guanicoe	phalanx	10,450 ± 100	12,020–12,637	NUTA- 1735
Lama guanicoe	rib	10,710 ± 190	12,077–13,017	NUTA- 2332
Lama guanicoe	phalanx	10,850 ± 130	12,560–13,037	NUTA- 1812

Nami and Nakamura 1995:130) or directly on the shape of the projectile points (Nami 1993:127). Nami considered the possibility of Holocene survival of extinct fauna (Nami 1987; Nami and Menegaz 1991:126), or that the bones migrated due to postdepositional processes (Nami and Menegaz 1991:126). Results of his NUTA radiocarbon series support the second alternative (Nami and Nakamura 1995:126, 130; Table 1.5). Effectively, three of the bones recovered at the Fell III component, two *Lama* sp. phalanges— now attributed to *Lama guanicoe*—and a *Lama guanicoe* rib, were dated and produced results indistinguishable from those of Fell I (Table 1.5). The distinction made by Nami, then, is not temporally clear cut, since all radiocarbon dates assigned to both components were associated with Pleistocene faunas and temporally overlapping (Martin 2013). Either the bones associated with the Fell III component were differentially destroyed—a situation very difficult to substantiate—or there is basically only one bone assemblage associated with the remains attributed to both components.

It is clear that the bone assemblage assigned to Fell III cannot be separated from the bones assigned to Fell I. Since it is a fact that triangular projectile points were found segregated from the earlier levels, even though one of the points was recovered on the surface (Nami 1987:84), it must be said that their chronology at the cave is still unknown. If the chronological sequence recorded by Bird in the Pali Aike region is reproduced here, then those points may belong to the Early Holocene. However, there isn't a shred of chronological evidence supporting this. If the association between the dated specimens and the triangular projectile points is correct, then these might be the oldest triangular points in the whole of Patagonia (cf. Gradín et al. 1979), even

inviting the idea that it was a southern innovation. The existence of a long depositional gap between the Late Holocene occupations and the Late Pleistocene layers at the cave implies that a much later date cannot be excluded. Even when the differences in the shape of projectile points are clear, the limited distribution of Nami's Fell III component and the lack of chronological differentiation make it preferable not to separate these occupations. Indeed, this was done in the study of the lithic tools (Huidobro 2016). The existence of depositional gaps of the magnitude noted in this chapter indicates that it is better to treat both early components as part of a continuum of short human visits to the cave.

Conclusion

We are interested in an occupational gap of at least 6,000 radiocarbon years between ca. 4200 and 10,400 RCYBP in both excavation loci at Cueva del Medio. What is extremely important from a formational point of view is that the older occupations are recorded in very close vertical and horizontal proximity to the late Holocene occupations. Obviously, occupational gaps affect our interpretation of the human use of the cave. Thus, the different human occupations are not clearly segregated and constitute palimpsests very difficult to disentangle. It is hard to separate tools and debris corresponding to different human visits. This is the reason why we are so exacting in accepting or rejecting associations between faunal remains and human evidences.

Regardless, the Late Pleistocene archaeological signal at the site is strong. It includes projectile points and other stone tools widely recognized as old and bones of extinct faunas— at least one of them with cut marks—and basin-shaped hearths. However, we lack the means to establish a precise list of tools or bones associated with the Late Pleistocene or Late Holocene occupations. We strongly believe that this is also the case at many other archaeological sites, but only when time and efforts are devoted to understanding the involved formation processes and palimpsests are recognized as such (i.e., Politis et al. 2014).

There is no evidence of the exploitation of *Mylodon* nor even a temporal overlap between them and humans at the cave. The *Mylodon* remains were deposited before the arrival of humans. Although ground sloths were living in the region at the same time as humans (Borrero and Martin 2012), they were not recorded in the cave during the period of human occupation. As noted, there is limited evidence for the exploitation of horse at Cueva del Medio, which confirms data already obtained at Cueva Lago Sofía 1 and Cueva del Milodón (Alberdi and Prieto 2000; Martin 2013). It was earlier postulated that horses were quantitatively important as subsistence items at Cueva del Medio (Nami 1993: 131), but our observations do not support this.

Three different problems for the interpretation of the evidence at Cueva del Medio were discussed. First, the difficulties in separating the activities of carnivores and humans. Second, the difficulties in separating Nami's components Fell I and Fell III, and finally the difficulties in telling Late Pleistocene from Late Holocene occupations.

The most important conclusion is that it is no longer useful to maintain the separation in two components suggested by Nami. All the available indicators suggest that it is better to treat them as a single component. Moreover, not all physically associated remains within that component can be securely ascribed to the Late Pleistocene human occupation. Some of the bones result from carnivore activity, and some could even be the product of Late Holocene human activity. But the presence of averaged samples at Cueva del Medio is a reality that does not affect the fact that a strong Late Pleistocene human occupation was recovered.

Acknowledgments

We thank Rafael Suárez and Ciprian F. Ardelean for their kind invitation to participate in this volume. This research was conducted with support from Projects FONDECYT 1100822, 1150845 and CD MAG0901.

References

Alberdi, María T., and Alfredo Prieto
2000   *Hippidion* (Mammalia, Perissodactyla) de las cuevas de las provincias de Magallanes y Tierra del Fuego. *Anales del Instituto de la Patagonia* (Serie Ciencias Humanas) 28:147–171.

Bird, Junius B.
1946   The Archaeology of Patagonia. In *The Marginal Tribes*, edited by Julian H. Steward, pp. 17–29. Handbook of South American Indians, Vol. 1., Julian H. Steward, general editor. Smithsonian Institution, Washington, D.C.
1988   *Travels and Archaeology in South Chile*, edited by John Hyslop. University of Iowa Press, Iowa City.

Borrero, Luis A.
2009   The Elusive Evidence: The Archeological Record of the South American Extinct Megafauna. In *American Megafaunal Extinctions at the End of the Pleistocene*, edited by Gary Haynes, pp. 145–168. Springer, Berlin.
2012   The Human Colonization of the High Andes and Southern South America during the Cold Pulse of the Late Pleistocene. In *Hunter-Gatherer Behavior: Human Response during the Younger Dryas*, edited by Metin Eren, pp. 57–78. Left Coast Press, Walnut Creek, CA.

Borrero, Luis A., and Fabiana M. Martin
2012   Taphonomic Observations on Ground Sloth Bone and Dung from Cueva del Milodón, Ultima Esperanza, Chile: 100 years of Research History. *Quaternary International* 278:3–11.

Borrero, Luis A., José L. Lanata, and Florencia Borella
1988   Reestudiando huesos: nuevas consideraciones sobre sitios de Última Esperanza. *Anales*

del Instituto de la Patagonia (Serie Ciencias Sociales) 18:133–155.

Dillehay, Tom D.

2000 *The Settlement of the Americas: A New Prehistory*. Basic Books, New York.

Flegenheimer, Nora, Laura Miotti, and Natalia Mazzia

2013 Rethinking Early Objects and Landscapes in the Southern Cone: Fishtail-Point Concentrations in the Pampas and Northern Patagonia. In *Paleoamerican Odyssey*, edited by Kelly Graf, Caroline V. Ketron, and Michael R. Waters, pp. 359–376. Texas A&M University Press, College Station, TX.

García, Juan L., Brenda L. Hall, Michael R. Kaplan, Rodrigo M. Vega, and Jorge A. Strelin

2014 Glacial Geomorphology of the Torres del Paine Region (Southern Patagonia): Implications for Glaciation, Deglaciation and Paleolake History. *Geomorphology* 204:599–616.

Gradín, Carlos J., Carlos A. Aschero, and Ana M. Aguerre

1979 Arqueología del área río Pinturas. *Relaciones de la Sociedad Argentina de Antropología* 13:183–227.

Hubbard, Stephen M., Brian W. Romans, and Stephen A. Graham

2008 Deep-Water Foreland Basin Deposits of the Cerro Toro Formation, Magallanes Basin, Chile: Architectural Elements of a Sinuous Basin Axial Channel Belt. *Sedimentology* 55(5):1333–1359.

Huidobro, Consuelo

2016 Fabricación de instrumentos líticos en cueva del Medio, Última Esperanza, Patagonia Austral. In *Arqueología de la Patagonia: de mar a mar*, edited by Francisco Mena, pp. 189–199. Ediciones CIEP/Ñire Negro, Santiago, CL.

Jackson, Donald

2007 Estructura, intensidad y reiteración en las ocupaciones paleoindias en cuevas y aleros de Patagonia meridional (Chile). *Revista Cazadores-recolectores del Cono Sur. Revista de Arqueología* 2:65–85.

Jackson, Donald, and Alfredo Prieto

2005 Estrategias tecnológicas y conjunto lítico del contexto paleoindio de cueva de Lago Sofía 1, Última Esperanza, Magallanes. *Magallania* (Chile) 33:115–120.

Martin, Fabiana M.

2008 Bone Crunching Felids at the End of the Pleistocene in Fuego Patagonia, Chile. *Journal of Taphonomy* 6(3–4):337–372.

2012 Human-Carnivore Interaction at the End of the Pleistocene in Southern Patagonia, Chile. *Journal of Taphonomy* 10 (3–4): 561–574.

2013 *Tafonomía de la transición Pleistoceno–Holoceno en Fuego-Patagonia. Interacción entre humanos y carnívoros y su importancia como agentes en la formación del registro fósil*. Ediciones de la Universidad de Magallanes, Punta Arenas, CL.

Martin, Fabiana M., Manuel San Román, Flavia Morello, Dominique Todisco, Francisco J. Prevosti, and Luis A. Borrero

2013 Land of the Ground Sloths: Recent Research at Cueva Chica, Última Esperanza, Chile. *Quaternary International* 305:56–66.

Martinic, Mateo

1996 La cueva del Milodón: historia de los hallazgos y otros sucesos. Relación de los estudios realizados a lo largo de un siglo (1895–1995). *Anales del Instituto de la Patagonia* 24:43–80.

Massone, Mauricio

2004 *Los cazadores después del hielo*. Ediciones de la Dirección de Bibliotecas, Archivos y Museos, Santiago, CL.

Menegaz, Adriana N., Hugo G. Nami, and María X. Senatore

1994 Alteraciones de los restos faunísticos óseos de cueva del Medio: un análisis preliminar. In *Actas y Memorias del 11º Congreso Nacional de Arqueología Argentina*. Resúmenes, San Rafael, Revista del Museo de Historia Natural de San Rafael, 13–1/4:35–36.

Miotti, Laura

1998 *Zooarqueología de la meseta central y costa de Santa Cruz: un enfoque de las estrategias adaptativas aborígenes y los paleoambientes*. Museo Municipal de Ciencia Natural de San Rafael, Mendoza, AR.

Moreno, Patricio, Rodrigo Villa-Martinez, Macarena L. Cárdenas, and Esteban A. Sagredo

2012 Deglacial Changes of the Southern Margin of the Southern Westerly Winds Revealed by Terrestrial Records from SW Patagonia (52°S). *Quaternary Science Reviews* 41:1–21.

Nami, Hugo G.

1985–1986 Excavación arqueológica y hallazgo de una punta cola de pescado Fell 1 en la cueva del Medio. *Anales del Instituto de la Patagonia* (Serie Ciencias Sociales) 16:103–109.

1987 Cueva del Medio: perspectivas arqueológicas para la Patagonia austral. *Anales del Instituto de la Patagonia* (Serie Ciencias Sociales) 17:73–106.

1989–1990 Avances en las investigaciones arqueológicas en el área del Cerro Benitez (Última Esperanza, Magallanes). *Anales del Instituto de la Patagonia* (Serie Ciencias Sociales) 18:125–132.

1992 Resumen de las actividades y nuevos datos obtenidos en la quinta campaña de investigaciones arqueológicas en Última Esperanza, Chile. Palimpsesto. *Revista de Arqueología* 2:123–132.

1993 Las excavaciones arqueológicas y los hallazgos de fauna extinta en el Seno de Última Esperanza, Chile. In *Explotación de recursos faunísticos en sistemas adaptativos americanos 4*, edited by José L. Lanata, pp. 123–133. *Arqueología Contemporánea* (edición especial). Buenos Aires, AR.

1994a Reseña sobre los avances de la arqueología finipleistocénica del extremo sur de Sudamérica. *Chungara: Revista Chilena de Antropología* 26:145–163.

1994b Paleoindio, cazadores-recolectores y tecnología lítica en el extremo sur de Sudamérica continental. *Arqueología Contemporánea* 5:89–103.

2007 Research in the Middle Negro River Basin (Uruguay) and the Paleoindian Occupation of the Southern Cone. *Current Anthropology* 48(1):164–174.

2013 Archaeology, Paleoindian Research, and Lithic Technology in the Middle Negro River, Central Uruguay. *Archaeological Discovery* 1(1):1–22.

Nami, Hugo G., and Adriana N. Menegaz

1991 Cueva del Medio: aportes para el conocimiento de la diversidad faunística hacia el Pleistoceno-Holoceno en Patagonia Austral. *Anales del Instituto de la Patagonia* (Serie Ciencias Sociales) 20:117–132.

Nami, Hugo G., and Takeshi Nakamura

1995 Cronología radiocarbónica con AMS sobre muestras de huesos procedentes del sitio cueva del Medio. *Anales del Instituto de la Patagonia* (Serie Ciencias Sociales) 32: 125–133.

Politis, Gustavo, María A. Gutiérrez, and Clara Scabuzzo, eds.

2014 *Estado actual de las investigaciones en el sitio arqueológico Arroyo Seco 2 (partido de Tres Arroyos, provincia de Buenos Aires, Argentina).* INCUAPA Serie Monográfica 5, Olavarría, AR.

Prieto, Alfredo

1991 Cazadores tempranos y tardíos en cueva de Lago Sofía 1. *Anales del Instituto de la Patagonia* (Serie Ciencias Sociales) 20: 75–99.

Prieto, Alfredo, Rafael Labarca, and Victor Sierpe

2010 New Evidence of the Sabertooth Cat *Smilodon* (Carnivora: Machairodontinae) in the Late Pleistocene of Southern Chilean Patagonia. *Revista Chilena de Historia Natural* 83(2):299–307.

Reimer, Paula J., Edouard Bard, Alex Bayliss, J. Warren Beck, Paul G. Blackwell, Christopher Bronk Ramsey, Caitlin E. Buck, et al.

2013 IntCal13 and MARINE13 Radiocarbon Age Calibration Curves 0–50000 Years Cal BP. *Radiocarbon* 55(4):1869–1887. doi.org/10.2458/azu_js_rc.55.16947.

Sagredo, Esteban A., Patricio I. Moreno, Rodrigo Villa-Martinez, Michael R. Kaplan, Peter W. Kubik, and Charles R. Stern

2011 Fluctuations of the Última Esperanza Ice Lobe (52°S), Chilean Patagonia, during the Last Glacial Maximum and Termination 1. *Geomorphology* 125(1):92–108.

Stern Charles

2008 Holocene Tephrochronology: Record of Large Explosive Eruptions in the Southernmost Patagonian Andes. *Bulletin of Volcanology* 70(4):435–454.

Stern, Charles R., Patricio I. Moreno, Rodrigo Villa-Martinez, Esteban A. Sagredo, Alfredo Prieto, and Rafael Labarca

2011 Evolution of Ice-Dammed Proglacial Lakes in Última Esperanza, Chile: Implications from the Late-Glacial R1 Eruption of Reclús Volcano, Andean Austral Volcanic Zone. *Andean Geology* 38(1):87–97.

CHAPTER 2

Lithics and Early Human Occupations
at the Southern End of the Deseado Massif
(Patagonia, Argentina)

Nora Viviana Franco and Lucas Vetrisano

The earliest occupations of the southern end of the Deseado Massif have been identified in La Gruta 1, a small rockshelter on a cliff next to a lagoon. They date to the Pleistocene–Holocene transition (Franco et al. 2010). Archaeological remains are scarce, and the archaeological sequence is discontinuous (Brook et al. 2015). The site has been characterized as a logistic one, taking into account its location and the characteristics of the artifacts recovered (Franco et al. 2012b). The area where the site is located is an ancient volcanic landscape with abundant natural depressions frequently occupied by shallow, mostly seasonal lagoons (Figures 2.1 and 2.2). Water levels depend on rainfall, with almost all of the lagoons showing evidence of higher water levels in the past (Brook et al. 2015).

Rockshelters and caves are rare in this area but are the type of locations that have yielded most of the earliest human occupations in Patagonia. The relevance of caves and rockshelters as resources for hunter-gatherers has been discussed by some researchers (i.e., Borrero 1989), who point out that there is a strong bias in archaeological fieldwork toward such sites though they represent only a part of hunter-gatherer activities—a position we agree with. In the case of the La Gruta area, human occupation of rockshelters is highly discontinuous, which has been linked to the existence of erosive episodes during arid periods (Brook et al. 2013, 2015), when humans may have abandoned the area

or exploited it from residential sites located in nearby spaces.

Sedimentary sequences are short (30–60 cm deep), both in rockshelters within ignimbrites (Bahía Laura group) and in fossiliferous sandstones (Monte León formation; Panza and Marin 1998). In contrast, between 20 to 30 km north-northeast of the La Gruta area—at Viuda Quenzana, La Martita, and El Verano areas (Figure 2.3)—rockshelters and caves are more abundant. They are in the same ignimbrites but with less compaction and silicification, which makes them prone to erosion (Claudio Iglesias, personal communication 2014). This may be the reason why sedimentary sequences are thicker in these areas, in some cases more than 2 m deep (for example, Aguerre 2003; Durán et al. 2003).

In addition, we should mention that at La Martita, Viuda Quenzana, and El Verano there is more evidence of human occupation, as shown by the quantity of lithic and faunal remains, as well as rock-art motifs (Franco et al. 2013). In Viuda Quenzana, more than 45 sites with rock art have been identified within 2.5 km² (Acevedo, personal communication 2014), which is in sharp contrast with La Gruta where only six sites with rock art were identified along outcrops extending for 1.5 km. Of course, differences in archaeological remains can also be attributed to different site functions and continuity in their occupation.

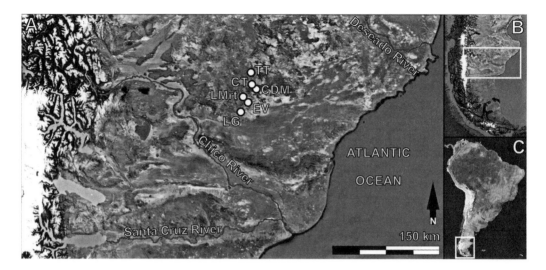

FIGURE 2.1. Main archaeological localities mentioned in the text (*a*); location within Patagonia (*b*); and South America (*c*). LG: La Gruta; TT: Cerro Tres Tetas; CT: Cueva Túnel; CDM: Casa del Minero; LMrt: La Martita; EV: El Verano. Images modified from Google Earth.

FIGURE 2.2. La Gruta area: earliest archaeological site and surface artifacts attributed to early occupations. LG1: La Gruta 1; LG: surface finding; Eng: El Engaño; LEsc: Laguna Escondida.

FIGURE 2.3. Archaeological sites in the southern end of the Deseado Massif corresponding to the Pleistocene–Holocene transition and the Early Holocene. LG1: La Gruta 1; LG2: La Gruta 2; EV: El Verano; LM: La Martita.

Another important difference is that in the spaces located to the north there are seasonal streams and bogs or springs, locally known as *mallines* (Franco et al. 2013). These include one that is more than 3 m deep, recently sampled during paleoenvironmental work in the area (Mancini, personal communication 2014). If this were also the case in the past, it would make the northern area more predictable in terms of water availability than La Gruta.

To the south and southeast of La Gruta, open-air spaces extend to the Chico River. To the southwest, olivinic basaltic plateaus can be found (Panza and Marin 1998). This change in the environment probably implies utilization of different hunter-gatherer strategies.

General Background and Methodology

The results presented here were achieved within projects that focus on the relationship between human behavior and environmental variables. Paleoenvironmental work was carried out in

various areas in order to understand changes in humidity and water availability in the past (Brook et al. 2013, 2015; Mancini et al. 2012, 2013). Along with water predictability, these variables are important for hunter-gatherer groups in arid environments (e.g. Borrero 2005; Veth 2005).

Recent archaeological work at La Gruta 1 included widening the previous excavation and the identification and sampling of raw material sources in order to understand lithic utilization strategies and their changes through time (Figure 2.4). Our knowledge of the regional lithic resource base (sensu Ericson 1984) is still preliminary, mainly due to the high variability found across the space explored. The La Gruta area is rich in primary (sensu Luedtke 1979) and secondary potential sources of siliceous rocks coming from the Chon Aike and La Matilde Formations (Echeveste 2005; Panza and Haller 2002; Panza and Marin 1998). Generally, these rocks are of lower quality and less abundant than those available to the north (Franco et al. 2011)

FIGURE 2.4. La Gruta 1 archaeological site.

in Viuda Quenzana and El Verano, where there are also rocks of the Bajo Grande and Baqueró Formations, including petrified and silicified wood (Panza and Marin 1998). To the west of La Gruta, the presence of veins and stockworks was identified in Manantial Espejo, with siliceous infills, including quartz, chalcedony, and opal (Zubia 1998). Also, at Manantial Espejo there are laminated jasperoids entirely formed of chalcedony, with silicification occurring at a later stage during the intense hydrothermal alteration accompanying the formation of the quartz veins carrying gold and silver (Echeveste 2005). Manantial Espejo is currently under mining exploitation, which prevented sampling of raw materials there.

Fluvial and glacial processes were important in Patagonia, especially in certain places and periods. Such processes left wide deposits of cobbles and pebbles. It is likely that during humid periods some watercourses held more importance, as may have been the case with the Chico River, south of the La Gruta area (Fig-

ure 2.1). Occasional and seasonal flooding of lagoons could also expose raw materials. Such secondary sources were an important part of our work in the area.

The recovered artifacts were analyzed following Aschero's morpho-technological classifications (1975, 1983), widely used in Patagonia. In addition, artifacts were sorted into 5 mm grids. Results were checked against expectations developed within a framework of technological organization (sensu Nelson 1991).

Archaeological Expectations

People entering a new environment have to acquire knowledge of available resources, a process that takes time (e.g. Borrero 1994–1995; Kelly 1988; Kelly and Todd 1988; Rockman 2003). On the basis of what we already know about hunter-gatherer behavior, the artifact characteristics, raw materials, and prioritized design variables can all be expected to vary through time, not only in relationship with the activities at different spaces but also with the increase in the knowledge of available local resources (Nelson 1991). In the case of Patagonia, expectations for lithic artifacts related to the early exploration of new spaces have been derived from the ecological model for peopling this region (Borrero 1994–1995), as well as from ethnoarchaeological data and design variables (Borrero and Franco 1997; Franco 2004, 2012). In the cases of short-scale initial movements of people into new, unknown spaces within the environment they are inhabiting, some differences could be anticipated between the initial occupations and the following ones. Of course, artifact types would vary according to activities and length of stay. In general, the following traits can be expected for initial occupations:

a) Low utilization indexes of immediately available raw materials (except in cases when they are abundant and easily located). Their utilization would increase through time if people decided to stay at those locations.

b) Transport of raw materials from nearby spaces. Their characteristics will vary according to the distance involved, expectations of returning to the base camp, and variations within environments. In the case of hunter-gatherer groups, the transportation of projectile points, fire accessories, as well as resin can be expected. Transportation of artifacts for further work can also be assumed. In this case, the archaeological record would probably show the presence of broken artifacts, resharpening flakes, and bifacial flakes made on raw materials not immediately available.

Results

We focus here on the earliest evidence of occupation of the La Gruta area, corresponding to the Pleistocene–Holocene transition. To the north and northeast of La Gruta, the earliest evidence of human occupation dates from the Early Holocene (Aguerre 2003; Durán et al. 2003; Franco et al. 2013).

Raw Material Availability

During surface surveys, localized sources of siliceous raw materials were identified, distinguishable by variations in visual characteristics (mainly size, color, and shape) from their surroundings.

In the case of La Gruta, we identified *sinters*—stone outcrops originating from the deposition of siliceous materials in a hydrothermal environment—of chalcedony of good to very good quality (Figures 2.5 and 2.6; Schalamuk et al. 2002). To the west, there is also a reddish siliceous sinter of very good quality at the La Alianza locality (Figure 2.5). These sinters appear as outcrops with a distinctive shape that distinguishes them from other outcrops, as they vary in color, texture, and quality.

Other sources include the La Barda outcrop (Figures 2.5 and 2.7). Due to the amount of quartz it contains, its colors and brightness make it visible from the near distance. However, its coarse grain and high quartz content also make it of poorer flintknapping quality.

In contrast, the Viuda Quenzana locality yielded a highly localized hot spring (Figures 2.5 and 2.8), with a dispersion of high-quality chalcedony and siliceous rocks extending on a low hill over a surface of about 100 m². This source cannot be seen from the vicinity, and it would be necessary to walk over it in order to see the rocks.

Secondary sources have been previously characterized, showing variability between the Viuda Quenzana and La Gruta areas. In Viuda Quenzana, cobbles and pebbles recovered in streams are of high quality (Franco et al. 2011, 2012b). On the contrary, in La Gruta, raw materials are dispersed along the lagoons and are of lower quality (Franco et al. 2012b. Recently, a secondary source of black obsidian has been identified at a location named 17 de Marzo in open spaces south of La Gruta (Franco et al. 2017). Geochemically, it cannot be distinguished from Pampa del Asador, the main source of black obsidian in Patagonia (Stern 1999).

This information allows us to characterize the environment as highly heterogeneous in terms of the quantity, size, quality, and visibility of available rocks. Understanding this variation will help us to better measure the incorporation rates of different environments. For example, the utilization of highly localized sources with

FIGURE 2.5. Map showing localized raw-material lithic sources. Af: outcrop; LG: La Gruta; VQ: Viuda Quenzana.

FIGURE 2.6. View of La Gruta sinter.

Figure 2.7. View of La Barda outcrop.

Figure 2.8. Viuda Quenzana hot spring.

FIGURE 2.9. View of La Gruta 2 archaeological site.

low visibility—such as the Viuda Quenzana hot spring—would not be expected within initial human occupation.

Stratigraphic Information

Excavations carried out in this region revealed the presence of short sedimentary sequences reaching bedrock, with discontinuous evidence of occupation, both by animals and humans. In the case of La Gruta 1, the shortness of the sedimentary sequence (ca. 50 cm of depth) can be explained by the silicified nature of the ignimbrites that form the outcrop where the site is located and its low contribution of sediments due to its hardness. This is not, however, the case of La Gruta 2 (Figure 2.9) and La Gruta 3, both located in a sandstone rockshelter. In La Gruta 2, a date of ca. 7,700 years RCYBP (Franco et al. 2013) was obtained from a guanaco bone bearing cultural marks at ca. 30 cm of depth, just immediately above bedrock. In La Gruta 3, a sedimentary sequence about 60 cm thick pro-

vided a range of ages between approximately 32,000 RCYBP (above bedrock) and 290 RCYBP at the top (Brook et al. 2015). La Gruta 3 is located very close to the level of the present-day lagoon, and sedimentological and historical evidence points to extensive periodic flooding (Brook et al. 2015).

The earliest human occupations of this area correspond to a wet period (Brook et al. 2015). Recent widening of the excavation at LG1 provided an additional date of ca. 10,500 years RCYBP, and two more between about 9,300 and 9,000 RCYBP (Table 2.1).

The charcoal concentrations are small in the earliest deposits. Dated samples come from these well-defined charcoal concentrations. Larger charcoal concentrations were identified in deposits dating to the Early Holocene. At present, we cannot discard the possibility that these thicker hearths may have continued to be used later. More dates should be obtained in order to evaluate this possibility.

TABLE 2.1. New dates obtained at La Gruta 1 and dates prior to 10,2 ka years BP available in the southern Deseado Massif arranged in chronological order. Dates were calibrated at the 2σ probability level in calendar years BP (cal BP) using CALIB 7.0 (Stuiver and Reimer 1993) and the Southern Hemisphere (SHcal13) atmospheric calibration curve of Hogg et al. (2013).

Site	Lab no.	RCYBP	cal BP	Sample Material	Reference and Comments
Cerro Tres Tetas	LP-525	11,560 ± 140	13,162–13,333	charcoal	Frank and Paunero 2009. Date rejected according to new dates (Steele and Politis 2009).
Cerro Tres Tetas	OXA-9244	10,915 ± 65	12,680–12,914	charcoal, for redating LP-525	Steele and Politis 2009
Cerro Tres Tetas	OXA-10745	11,145 ± 60	12,800–13,088	charcoal	Steele and Politis 2009
Cerro Tres Tetas	AA-22233	11,100 ± 150	12,701–13,188	no data	Frank and Paunero 2009
Cerro Tres Tetas	AA-39368	11,015 ± 66	12,717–13,005	charcoal	Frank and Paunero 2009
Casa del Minero	AA-37207	10,999 ± 55	12,716–12,980	charcoal	Paunero 2000, 2003
Casa del Minero	AA-37208	10,967 ± 55	12,704–12,952	charcoal	Paunero 2000, 2003
Cerro Tres Tetas	OXA-9244	10,915 ± 65	12,680–12,914	charcoal	Frank and Paunero 2009
Cerro Tres Tetas	AA-39366	10,853 ± 70	12,570–12,831	charcoal, for redating LP-525	Steele and Politis 2009
Cerro Tres Tetas	LP-781	10,850 ± 150	12,427–13,048	no data	Frank and Paunero 2009
La Gruta 1		10,845 ± 61	12,653–12,799	charcoal	Franco et al. 2010
La Gruta 1		10,840 ± 62	12,650–12,801	charcoal	Franco et al. 2010
La Gruta 1		10,790 ± 30	12,663–12,730	charcoal	Franco et al. 2010
La Gruta 1		10,656 ± 54	12,434–12,692	charcoal	Franco et al. 2010
La Gruta 1	UGAMS-17353	10,520 ± 30	12,388–12,554	charcoal	this chapter
Cueva Túnel	AA-82496	10,510 ± 100	12,026–12,650	bone	Skarbun et al. 2015. No indication of taxon.
La Gruta 1		10,477 ± 56	12,049–12,549	charcoal	Franco et al. 2010
Cueva Túnel	LP-1965	10,420 ± 180	11,601–12,690	bone	Paunero 2009. No indication about taxon.
Cueva Túnel	AA-71147	10,408 ± 59	11,989–12,425	charcoal	Skarbun 2012
Cueva Túnel	AA-71148	10,400 ± 100	11,819–12,551	Hippidium bone	Skarbun 2012
Cerro Tres Tetas	LP-800	10,260 ± 110	12,404–11,591	no data	Frank and Paunero 2009
Casa del Minero	AA-45705	10,250 ± 110	12,299–11,401	no data	Paunero et al. 2007
La Gruta 1	UGAMS-18362	9330 ± 30	10,372–10,582	charcoal	this chapter
La Gruta 1	UGAMS-18361	9020 ± 30	10,231–10,123	charcoal	this chapter

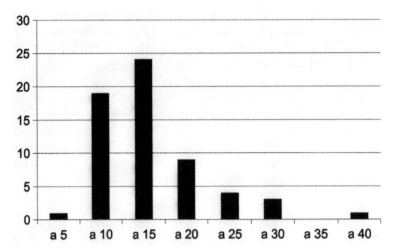

Figure 2.10. La Gruta 1. Size and number of artifacts recovered in deposits corresponding to the Pleistocene–Holocene transition. *a5*: sizes from 0.1–5 mm; *a10*: 5.1–10 mm; *a15*: 10.1–15 mm; *a20*: 15.1–20 mm; *a25*: 20.1–25 mm; *a30*: 25.1–30 mm; *a35*: 30.1–35 mm; *a40*: 35.1–40 mm.

Only 62 artifacts were recovered from deposits corresponding to the Pleistocene–Holocene transition, most of them flakes of chalcedony and siliceous rocks. Only one flake is obsidian, and only two are made from a coarse-grain rock. A total of 21 flakes (34 percent of the sample) are unbroken; and 30 (49 percent) have percussion platforms. If we take into account calibrated dates, the sediment accumulated over a span of 413 years, and the artifacts were recovered from a surface of 2 m². This would yield a discard rate of 3.63 artifacts per each 100 years, considering only the artifacts with proximal ends, or 7.51, if we considered all of them.

Artifact sizes range between 5 and 40 mm, the largest corresponding to a conjoint flake. Most of the sample (70 percent) displays sizes between 5.1 and 15 mm (Figure 2.10).

The majority of the artifacts are flakes (90 percent), although a blade, a chunk (polyhedral, indeterminate piece, without ventral and dorsal surfaces, probably resulting from hard-hammer percussion), and waste were also recorded. With only one exception, they are all internal (tertiary) flakes, corresponding to stages of advanced manufacture (Figure 2.11). If we consider only the complete flakes, most are multi-directional (43 percent), although there are also bladelike flakes (21 percent), bifacial reduction

flakes (18 percent), resharpening flakes (7 percent), and other flakes corresponding to final manufacturing stages (7 percent). Most of the bladelike flakes are probably the result of bifacial reduction. However, a true blade was recognized. If we consider the complete sample, there are also two external flakes. In the case of the coarse-grain raw materials, we do not have enough information to infer its mode of utilization, although they could be related to initial stages of manufacture of groundstone artifacts.

The characteristics of the artifacts (lipped platforms and curvature) suggest that soft hammers were used, at least in some cases. The presence of a chunk and the pronounced bulb of percussion in another case would suggest that there was also some utilization of hard hammerstones at the site. The angle and characteristics of the retouch in the case of one resharpening flake suggests that it was probably obtained from a large, thick end-scraper.

Prepared platforms are the most abundant (Figure 2.12), including punctiform (35 percent; in some cases, isolated), linear (23 percent), faceted (10 percent), and dihedral (6 percent). Only 23 percent of the sample corresponds to flat platforms. Such platforms are consistent with the last stages of flintknapping activity at the sites, also indicated by the size of complete

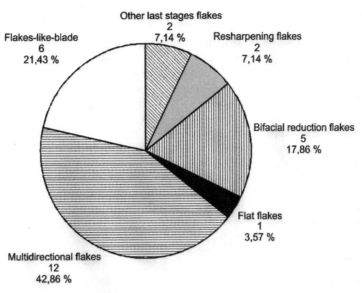

FIGURE 2.11. La Gruta 1. Classes of flakes (taking into account only flakes with proximal ends) recovered in deposits corresponding to the Pleistocene–Holocene transition.

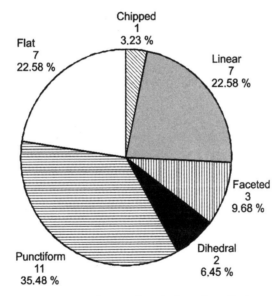

FIGURE 2.12. La Gruta 1. Types of percussion platforms in artifacts recovered in deposits corresponding to the Pleistocene–Holocene transition.

flakes recovered. The presence of a chipped platform can also suggest the utilization of hard hammerstones.

Regarding the raw materials employed, at least 24 percent of the sample does not come from the La Gruta area. This is the case in the bladelike flakes, bifacial reduction flakes, last-stage manufacturing flakes, and multidirectional flakes. At the moment, there is no evidence of utilization of the sinters present at La Gruta, which were immediately available for the occupants. There is also a black obsidian flake

FIGURE 2.13. Surface findings corresponding to early designs in La Gruta area. LG: La Gruta 1; Eng: El Engaño; LEsc: Laguna Escondida.

that, according to its size, could have been obtained either from the 17 de Marzo or Pampa del Asador sources.

Surface Information

As mentioned, not all hunter-gatherer activities took place in rockshelters or caves. Test pits made in open spaces for geomorphological and archaeological purposes have shown the hardness of sediments and the lack of organic remains in the La Gruta area.

It is very difficult to estimate the date of surface findings, especially because there are not enough stratigraphical sequences in Patagonia able to provide a good chronological and technological framework. Some tools, however, have always been attributed to early human occupations. This is the case of the so-called "Fishtail" or "Fell 1" projectile points (e.g., Bird 1938, 1969; Flegenheimer et al. 2010, 2013; Hermo and Terranova 2013; Massone and Prieto 2004; Méndez et al. 2010; Miotti et al. 2010; Nami 2003; Suárez 2006, 2010), dated between ca. 11,000 and 9,500

RCYBP in Central and South America. Most researchers recognize that the type embraces great morphological and technological variability (Bayón and Flegenheimer 2003; Mayer Oakes 1986; Nami 2003, 2013, 2014; Flegenheimer and Zárate 1989; Flegenheimer et al. 2013; Politis 1991; Weitzel et al. 2014).

Three preforms displaying technological and morphological similarities to early designs were discovered in La Gruta and nearby areas (Figure 2.13). The first one is an unfinished stem of a Fishtail projectile point recovered from the same outcrop as La Gruta 1, close to the site (Figures 2.14 and 2.15). It is made of chalcedony, with a maximal width of 16 mm and a thickness of 5.3 mm. Both faces show laminar parallel retouch, which on one face reaches the center of the stem. The base of the stem, worked by marginal retouch, is concave. If we consider the measurements of several projectile points originally defined as Fishtails by Bird (1969), the mean width of the stem is 15.5 mm in the cases present both at El Inga (northern South

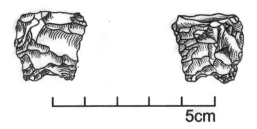

FIGURE 2.14. La Gruta. Unfinished stem of Fishtail projectile point (drawing).

America) and Fell Cave (southern Patagonia). The mean thickness recorded is 4.59 mm in El Inga and 5.66 mm in Fell.

The second case is a fragmented bifacial preform manufactured in chalcedony recovered from El Engaño (Figures 2.13–18), an outcrop located 6.5 km southwest of La Gruta 1. One of its edges was retouched as a knife. The width of the blade, which is fragmented, measures 68 mm, and its thickness is 11.5 mm. Given its size, it may correspond to an early-age design, as later projectile points in the area are considerably smaller. The mean width of the blades of Fishtail projectile points is 28.4 mm in the case

FIGURE 2.15. La Gruta. Unfinished stem of Fishtail projectile point (photo).

of El Inga, and 29 mm in the case of Fell Cave. The mean thickness of the blade is 4.6 mm in El Inga and 5.6 in Fell.

The last case is a bifacially flaked preform of a projectile point made out of chalcedony, found at Laguna Escondida, north of La Gruta (Figures 2.13, 2.19 and 2.20). The piece still holds some

FIGURE 2.16. View of El Engaño.

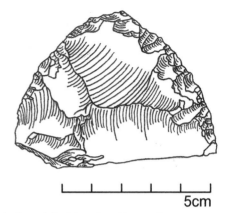

5cm

FIGURE 2.17. El Engaño. Knife on a preform of a large bifacial artifact (drawing).

FIGURE 2.18. El Engaño. Knife on a preform of a large bifacial artifact (photo).

cortex on one edge. It is slightly asymmetrical, and the concave-based stem shows a more advanced manufacture stage than the blade where hinge terminations can be observed.

The width of the blade is 37.5 mm, its thickness is 10 mm, while the width and thickness of the stem are 22 and 7 mm, respectively. Although a preform, its dimensions do not seem to correspond to Fishtail points, especially considering the relationship between the length of the stem

and the blade, as can be seen in illustrations published by different researchers (e.g. Bird 1969; Massone and Prieto 2004; Méndez et al. 2010). It shows strong similarities with a preform from Tres Arroyos (Jackson 2002), more than 450 km away, on the island of Tierra del Fuego, reached by pedestrian hunter-gatherers during the Pleistocene–Holocene transition (Massone and Prieto 2004). This preform, according to Jackson, is a Fishtail point manufactured by an apprentice. It was recovered in proximity to the stem of a Fishtail point and the preform of a bifacial blade.

The differences between the Laguna Escondida preform and the one attributed to an apprentice in Tres Arroyos, as well as other projectile points classified as Fishtails, speaks to the great variability included within this category (Flegenheimer and Zárate 1989; Flegenheimer et al. 2010; Mayer Oakes 1986; Nami 2014). This may suggest that there was more than one early design used by hunter-gatherers (e.g. Nami 2014; Suárez 2010), which would not be surprising considering ethnoarchaeological evidence.

Discussion and Final Remarks

The different characteristics of the environments located within the southern Deseado Massif (including the La Gruta, Viuda Quenzana, El Verano, and La Martita areas), the open spaces to the south, and the basaltic plateaus to the southwest would indicate their complementary use in the past.

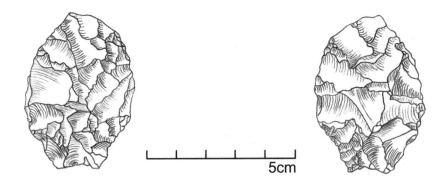

FIGURE 2.19. Laguna Escondida. Preform of projectile point (drawing).

As rockshelters and caves are generally scarce in the La Gruta area, they had more chances to be used and reoccupied by humans and, in this way, provide better opportunities to find signs of early human occupation. If their use was continuous, there would be more probability of mixed deposits (see for example Bailey 2007). This does not seem to have been the case for La Gruta 1. The earliest radiocarbon dates from the site show some overlapping, when calibrated (Figure 2.21). But taken together, the discontinuous nature (both spatially and vertically) of the small charcoal concentrations, their size, and the quantity of lithic materials do not stand for any continuity of human occupation. This fact can probably be related to water unpredictability in time and space. During arid periods, it could have been temporarily abandoned or exploited from other areas (see also Brook et al. 2013, 2015; Mancini et al. 2013), a pattern that has been observed in ethnographic cases in places with patchy and unpredictable resources (see for example Gould 1991; Kelly 1992, 1995, 2013; Veth 2005). Low redundancy in the use of La Gruta 1 could result in a relatively high integrity of deposits (see also Borrero 2005).

Humans who used the La Gruta area were probably coming from northern territories, where we have earlier evidence of human presence, at a minimal distance of ca 50 km (Figure 2.21 and Table 2.1; Paunero et al. 2007; Paunero 2009). Only one of these sites, Casa del Minero, is thought to be a place where multiple activities

FIGURE 2.20. Laguna Escondida. Preform of projectile point (drawing).

were performed (Paunero 2009). In the other sites, only specific activities seem to have taken place during the Pleistocene–Early Holocene transition (see for example Cueva Túnel in Paunero 2009).

La Gruta 1 is a logistical site. In this case, at least 24 percent of the artifacts are made of nonlocal rocks, which is consistent with our expectations for the initial occupation of spaces. Tools brought to the site include bifaces as well as bladelike flakes. Tool resharpening also took place there, seemingly including a thick endscraper. Such scrapers were used in the area until about 7,500 RCYBP, according to evidence

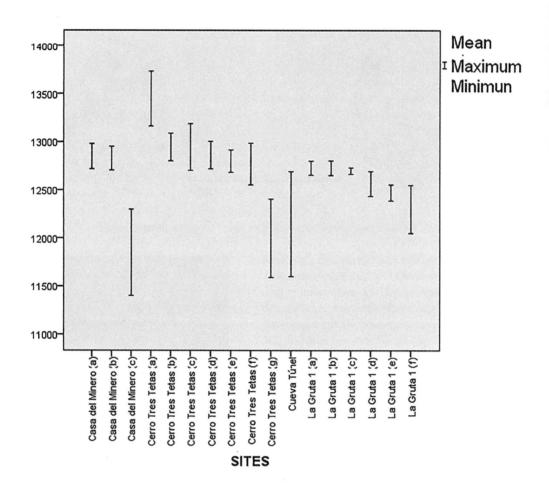

FIGURE 2.21. Comparison of earliest calibrated radiocarbon dates from the southern Deseado Massif, considering mean and two standard deviations. Only dates that could be replicated have been included.

from El Verano and La Martita (Aguerre 2003; Durán 1986–1987; Durán et al. 2003) and in agreement with regional information (e.g., Gradin et al. 1981).

Stone flaking activities could have taken place while watching for game. According to available evidence from a nearby rockshelter (La Gruta 3), both guanaco (*Lama guanicoe*) and Mylodontidae were available, although no clear evidence of human exploitation of the latter has been identified yet in the area. There are no indicators for the use of the immediately available sinter outcrops (sensu Meltzer 1989), which conforms to expectations. In this sense, we do not expect highly localized sources to be exploited

during the initial colonization of environments, which is indeed the case with this outcrop and the hot spring of Viuda Quenzana.

Obsidian, as well as translucent chalcedony, were raw materials brought into La Gruta area. Macroscopically similar chalcedonies were found in locations approximately 30 km to the north, a distance that is well within home range estimates for hunter-gatherers living at those latitudes (Binford 2001; Kelly 1995, 2013). The obsidian, originally thought to have been obtained in the Pampa del Asador primary source or its vicinity, could also have been obtained in the recently discovered secondary source of 17 de Marzo (Franco et al. 2017).

As mentioned, siliceous rocks of excellent quality are more abundant to the north (Franco et al. 2011), including the La María locality, where both Casa del Minero and Cueva Túnel are located (Skarbun 2009). In the case of Cueva Túnel, the Pleistocene occupations show the use of nonlocal translucent opal and evidence of first manufacturing stages of high-quality local flints, possibly transported as tools to other areas (Skarbun 2012). Although the margin of error associated with the date of Cueva Túnel is high (three errors that range from 100–180 years, one error of 59 years, see Table 2.1), its occupation seems to be partially contemporaneous to that of La Gruta, as may also be the case for Cerro Tres Tetas and Casa del Minero (Figure 2.21), suggesting that movement between these spaces could have occurred during that time.

Although the faunal availability may not have changed within the Deseado Massif itself, people moving into those environments for the first time—either in short or longer migrations—would have found places where high-quality rocks or suitable rockshelters and caves were less availabile. Thus, more activities would have been performed in open spaces. In the La Gruta area, at least some projectile point manufacture took place in areas with good visibility, close to rockshelters (La Gruta 1), and in places relatively higher than their surroundings (El Engaño) or near ponds (Laguna Escondida).

South of La Gruta, the Deseado Massif ends and the environment changes. We think it is probable that these open spaces and the basaltic plateaus to the southwest were incorporated into the hunter-gatherer home ranges during daily activities. In the open areas to the south, early cultural materials would be scarce and difficult to find, due to the lack of specific places that could have attracted human beings. Possible exceptions are lagoons such as the one located at 17 de Marzo. The presence of preforms of projectile points or stems in the extreme south of the Deseado Massif can also be related to the fact that high-quality siliceous rocks suitable for making relatively large projectile points are very scarce (Franco et al. 2015).

We believe that the archaeological record is better understood when we consider the different lines of evidence, as well as the time involved in the learning process. In order to do so, a good understanding of environmental variability—in relation to the availability of water and lithic raw materials—at short and long scales is needed, implying the joint efforts of different researchers.

Acknowledgments

This research was funded by projects PIP 0447 (CONICET), Cooperation Project CONICET-National Science Foundation (Res.1838/13), and PICT 2015-2038. We wish to thank Dr. Rafael Suárez for his invitation to participate in this symposium at the Society for American Archaeology Meeting and in its publication. Minera Triton Argentina S. A. and Piedra Grande S. A. supported our field work. Dr. George Brook, University of Georgia, provided support for AMS radiocarbon ages. We also wish to thank Dr. Claudio Iglesias, of Piedra Grande S. A., the Dirección de Cultura and Dirección de Turismo of Gobernador Gregores, and especially Pablo Ramírez. Our thanks also go to researchers A. Aguerre and V. Durán, and to the owners of Hotel Cañadón León and Cardiel Chico, Gobernador Gregores. Finally, we thank all the people who participated in the fieldwork.

References

Aguerre, Ana M.
2003   La Martita: ocupaciones de 8000 años en la Cueva 4. In *Arqueología y paleoambiente en la Patagonia Santacruceña Argentina*, edited by A. Aguerre, pp. 29–61. Ediciones del Autor, Buenos Aires, AR.

Aschero, Carlos A.
1975   *Ensayo para una clasificación morfológica de artefactos líticos aplicada a estudios tipológicos comparativos.* Report to CONICET, Buenos Aires, AR.

1983   *Ensayo para una clasificación morfológica de artefactos líticos aplicada a estudios tipológicos comparativos.* Report to CONICET, Buenos Aires, AR.

Bailey, Geoff
2007   Time Perspectives, Palimpsests, and the Archaeology of Time. *Journal of Anthropological Archaeology* 26(2):198–223.

Bayón, Cristina, and Nora Flegenheimer
2003   Tendencias en el estudio del material lítico. In *Análisis, interpretación y gestión en arqueología de Sudamérica*, edited by R. Curtoni and M. L. Endere, pp. 65–90. INCUAPA, Facultad de Ciencias Sociales, UNICEN, Olavarría, Buenos Aires, AR.

Binford, Lewis R.
2001   *Constructing Frames of Reference: An Analytical Method for Archaeological Theory Building Using Ethnographic and Environmental Data Sets.* University of California Press, Berkeley, CA.

Bird, Junius
1938   Antiquity and Migrations of the Early Inhabitants of Patagonia. *Geographical Review* 28(2):250–275.
1969   A Comparison of South Chilean and Ecuadorean Fishtail Projectile Points. *Kroeber Anthropological Society Papers* 40:52–71.

Borrero, Luis A.
1989   Replanteo de la arqueología Patagónica. *Interciencia* 14(3):127–135.
1994–1995 Arqueología de la Patagonia. *Palimpsesto. Revista de Arqueología* 4:9–69.
2005   The Archaeology of the Patagonian Deserts. Hunter-Gatherers in a Cold Desert. In *Desert Peoples: Archaeological Perspectives*, edited by P. Veth, M. Smith, and P. Hiscock, pp. 142–158. Blackwell Publishing, Oxford, UK.

Borrero, Luis A., and Nora V. Franco
1997   Early Patagonian Hunter-Gatherers: Subsistence and Technology. *Journal of Anthropological Research* 53(2):219–239.

Brook, George A., Nora V. Franco, Pablo Ambrústolo, María V. Mancini, and Pablo Fernandez
2015   Evidence of the Earliest Humans in the Southern Deseado Massif (Patagonia, Argentina), Mylodontidae, and Changes in Water Availability. *Quaternary International* 363:107–125.

Brook, George A., María V. Mancini, Nora V. Franco, Florencia Bamonte, and Pablo Ambrústolo
2013   An Examination of Possible Relationships between Paleoenvironmental Conditions during the Pleistocene–Holocene Transition and Human Occupation of Southern Patagonia (Argentina) East of the Andes, between 46° and 52°S. *Quaternary International* 305:104–118.

Durán, Víctor A.
1986–1987 Estudio tecno-tipológico de los raspadores del sitio El Verano-Cueva 1. Patagonia centro meridional, Santa Cruz, Argentina. *Anales de Arqueología y Etnología* 41–42: 129–163.

Durán, Víctor, Adolfo Gil, Gustavo Neme, and Alejandra Gasco
2003   El Verano: ocupaciones de 8900 años en la Cueva 1 (Santa Cruz, Argentina). In *Arqueología y paleoambiente en la Patagonia Santacruceña Argentina*, edited by A. Aguerre, pp. 93–120. Ediciones del Autor, Buenos Aires, AR.

Echeveste, Horacio
2005   Travertinos y jasperoides de Manantial Espejo, un ambiente de hot spring Jurásico. Macizo del Deseado, provincia de Santa Cruz, Argentina. *Latin American Journal of Sedimentology and Basin Analysis* 12(1): 33–48.

Ericson, Jonathan E.
1984   Toward the Analysis of Lithic Reduction Systems. In *Prehistoric Quarries and Lithic Production*, edited by J. Ericson and B. Purdy, pp. 11–22. Cambridge University Press, Cambridge, UK.

Flegenheimer, Nora, and Marcelo Zárate
1989   Paleoindian Occupation at Cerro El Sombrero Locality, Buenos Aires Province, Argentina. *Current Research in the Pleistocene* 6:12–13.

Flegenheimer, Nora, Jorge G. Martínez, and Mariano Colombo
2010   Una experiencia de lanzamiento de puntas cola de pescado. In *Mamül Mapu: pasado y presente desde la arqueología pampeana*, edited by Mónica Berón, Leandro Luna, Mariano Bonomo, Claudia Montalvo, Claudia Aranda, and Manuel Carrera Aizpitarte, pp. 215–236. Editorial Libros del Espinillo, Buenos Aires, AR.

Flegenheimer, Nora, Laura Miotti, and Natalia Mazzia.
2013   Rethinking Early Objects and Landscapes in the Southern Cone: Fishtail-Point Concentrations in the Pampas and Northern Patagonia. In *Paleoamerican Odyssey*, edited by Kelly E. Graf, Caroline V. Ketron, and Michael Watters, pp. 359–376. Texas A&M University Press, College Station, TX.

Franco, Nora V.
2004   La organización tecnológica y el uso de escalas espaciales amplias. El caso del sur y oeste de Lago Argentino. In *Temas de arqueología, análisis lítico*, edited by A. Acosta,

D. Loponte, and M. Ramos, pp. 101–144. Universidad Nacional de Luján, Buenos Aires, AR.

2012 Binford and Ethnoarchaeology, a View from the South. Reflections on His Contributions to Hunter-Gatherer Archaeology and Lithic Analysis. *Ethnoarchaeology* 4(1):79–99.

Franco, Nora V., Pablo Ambrústolo, Agustín Acevedo, Natalia Cirigliano, and Miriam Vommaro

2013 Prospecciones en el sur del Macizo del Deseado (provincia de Santa Cruz). Los casos de La Gruta y Viuda Quenzana. In *Tendencias teórico-metodológicas y casos de estudio en la arqueología de la Patagonia*, edited by A. F. Zangrando, R. Barberena, A. Gil, G. Neme, M. Giardina, L. Luna, C. Otaola, S. Paulides, L. Salgán, and A. Tívoli, pp. 371–378. Museo de Historia Natural de San Rafael, Altuna Impresores, Buenos Aires, AR.

Franco, Nora V., Pablo Ambrústolo, and Natalia Cirigliano

2012a Disponibilidad de materias primas líticas silíceas en el extremo sur del Macizo del Deseado: los casos de La Gruta y Viuda Quenzana. *Magallania* 40(1):279–286.

Franco, Nora V., Pablo Ambrústolo, Natalia. Cirigliano, and Luis A. Borrero

2012b Initial Human Exploration at the Southern End of the Deseado Massif, In *Southbound: Late Pleistocene Peopling of Latin America*, edited by L. Miotti, M. Salemme, N. Flegenheimer, and T. Goebel, pp. 159–163. Center for the Study of the First Americans, Texas A&M University, College Station, TX.

Franco, Nora V., Pablo Ambrústolo, Marilina Martucci, George Brook, María V. Mancini, and Natalia Cirigliano

2010 Early Human Occupation in the Southern Part of the Deseado Massif (Patagonia, Argentina). *Current Research in the Pleistocene* 27:13–16.

Franco, Nora V., Pablo Ambrústolo, Fabiana Skarbun, Natalia Cirigliano, and Marilina Martucci

2011 El Macizo del Deseado como fuente de aprovisionamiento de rocas silíceas. Variaciones en disponibilidad y circulación: algunos ejemplos. *Cazadores recolectores del Cono Sur. Revista de Arqueología* 5: 81–95.

Franco, Nora V., George Brook, Natalia Cirigliano, Charles Stern, and Lucas Vetrisano

2017 17 de Marzo (Santa Cruz, Argentina): A New Distal Source of Pampa del Asador Type Black Obsidian and Its Implications for Understanding Hunter-Gatherer Behavior in Patagonia. *Journal of Archaeological Science: Reports* 12:232–243.

Franco, Nora V., Natalia Cirigliano, Lucas Vetrisano, and Pablo Ambrústolo

2015 Raw Material Circulation at Broad Scales in Southern Patagonia (Argentina): The Cases of the Chico and Santa Cruz River Basins. *Quaternary International* 375:72–83.

Frank, Ariel D., and Rafael Paunero

2009 Análisis de la alteración térmica de los restos óseos del componente temprano de Cerro Tres Tetas (meseta central de Santa Cruz). Evidencia arqueológica y estudios experimentales. In *Arqueología de la Patagonia. Una mirada desde el último confín*, pp. 750–772. Editorial Utopías, Ushuaia, Tierra del Fuego, AR.

Gould, Richard A.

1991 Arid Land Foraging as Seen from Australia: Adaptive Models and Behavioral Realities. *Oceania* 62(1):12–33.

Gradin, Carlos, Carlos Aschero, and Ana M. Aguerre

1981 Arqueología del área del Río Pinturas, provincia de Santa Cruz. *Relaciones de la Sociedad Argentina de Antropología* 13:183–227.

Hermo, Dario, and Enrique Terranova

2012 Formal Variability in Fishtail Points of the Amigo Oeste Archaeological Site, Somuncurá Plateau, Río Negro. In *Southbound: Late Pleistocene Peopling of Latin America*, edited by Laura Miotti, Mónica Salemme, Nora Flegenheimer, and Ted Goebel, pp. 121–126. Center for the Study of the First Americans, Texas A&M University, College Station, TX.

Hogg, Alan C., Quan Hua, Paul G. Blackwell, Caitlin E. Buck, Thomas P. Guilderson, Timothy J. Heaton, Mu Niu, et al.

2013 SHCal13 Southern Hemisphere Calibration, 0–50,000 Years cal BP. *Radiocarbon* 55(4). https://doi.org/10.2458/azu_js_rc.55.16783.

Jackson, Donald

2002 *Los instrumentos líticos de los primeros cazadores de Tierra del Fuego*. Ediciones de la Dirección de Bibliotecas, Archivos y Museos, Santiago, CL.

Kelly, Robert L.

1988 The Three Sides of a Biface. *American Antiquity* 53(4): 717–734.

1992 Mobility/Sedentism: Concepts, Archaeological Measures, and Effects. *Annual Review of Anthropology* 21:43–66.

1995 *The Foraging Spectrum. Diversity in Hunter-Gatherer Lifeways.* Smithsonian Institution, Washington, D.C.

2013 *The Lifeways of Hunter-Gatherers: The Foraging Spectrum.* Cambridge University Press, New York.

Kelly, Robert L., and Lawrence C. Todd
1988 Coming into the Country: Early Paleoindian Hunting and Mobility. *American Antiquity* 53(2):231–244.

Luedtke, Barbara E.
1979 The Identification of Sources of Chert Artifacts. *American Antiquity* 44(4):744–756.

Mancini, María V., Nora V. Franco, and George A. Brook
2012 Early Human Occupation and Environment South of the Deseado Massif and South of Lake Argentino. In *Southbound: Late Pleistocene Peopling of Latin America*, edited by L. Miotti, M. Salemme, N. Flegenheimer, and T. Goebel, pp. 197–200. Center for the Study of the First Americans, Texas A&M University, College Station, TX.

2013 Palaeoenvironment and Early Human Occupation of Southernmost South America (South Patagonia, Argentina). *Quaternary International* 299:13–22.

Massone, Mauricio, and Alfredo Prieto
2004 Evaluación de la modalidad cultural Fell 1 en Magallanes. *Chungara: Revista de Antropología Chilena* 36 (Special Supplement) 1:303–315.

Mayer Oakes, William
1986 El Inga, a Paleo-Indian Site in the Sierra of Northern Ecuador. *Transactions of the American Philosophical Society* 76(4):1–235.

Meltzer, David J.
1989 Was Stone Exchanged among Eastern North American Paleoindians? In *Eastern Paleoindian Lithic Resource Use*, edited by C. J. Ellis and J. Lothrop, pp. 11–39. Westview Press, Boulder, CO.

Méndez, César, Donald Jackson, Roxana Seguel, and Amalia Nuevo Delaunay
2010 Early High-Quality Lithic Procurement in the Semiarid North of Chile. *Current Research in the Pleistocene* 27:19–27.

Miotti, Laura, Darío Hermo, and Enrique Terranova
2010 Fishtail Points, First Evidence of Late-Pleistocene Hunter-Gatherers in Somuncurá Plateau (Rio Negro Province, Argentina). *Current Research in the Pleistocene* 27:22–24.

Nami, Hugo
2003 Experimentos para explorar la secuencia de reducción Fell de la Patagonia Austral. *Magallania* 31:107–138.

2013 Archaeology, Paleoindian Research and Lithic Technology in the Middle Negro River, Central Uruguay. *Archaeological Discovery* 1(1):1–22.

2014 Observaciones para conocer secuencias de reducción bifaciales paleoindias y puntas Fell en el valle del Ilaló, Ecuador. In *Población de América del Sur: la contribución de la tecnología lítica. Proceedings of the 16th World Congress International Union of Prehistoric and Protohistoric Sciences.* Archéo-éditions, Lormont, FR.

Nelson, Margaret C.
1991 The Study of Technological Organization. In *Archaeological Method and Theory*, Vol. 3, edited by M. Schiffer, pp. 57–100. University of Arizona Press, Tucson.

Panza, José L., and M. J. Haller
2002 El volcanismo Jurásico. In *Relatorio del 15º congreso geológico Argentino: geología y recursos naturales de Santa Cruz*, Actas 1, edited by M. Haller, pp. 89–101. Buenos Aires, AR.

Panza, José L., Graciela Marín, and Mario Zubia
1998 Geología. In *Hoja geológica 4969-I, Gobernador Gregores, provincia de Santa Cruz.* Servicio Geológico Minero Argentino, Boletín 239.

Paunero, Rafael S.
2000 Localidad arqueológica Cerro Tres Tetas. La Plata. In *Guía de Campo de la visita a las localidades arqueológicas*, edited by L. Miotti, R. Paunero, M. Salemme, and R. Cattáneo, pp. 89–100. INQUA, La Plata, AR.

2003 The Presence of a Pleistocene Colonizing Culture in La María Archaeological Locality, Casa del Minero 1. In *Where the South Winds Blow: Ancient Evidences of Paleo South Americans*, edited by R. Bonnichsen, L. Miotti, M. Salemme, and N. Flegenheimer, pp. 127–132. Center for the Study of the First Americans and Texas A&M University Press, College Station, TX.

2009 *El arte rupestre milenario de Estancia La María, Meseta Central de Santa Cruz.* Estudio Denis, La Plata, AR.

Paunero, Rafael S., Ariel D. Frank, Fabiana Skarbun, G. Rosales, Manuel Cueto, G. Zapata, M. Paunero, N. Lunazzi, and Manuel Del Giorgio
2007 Investigaciones arqueológicas en sitio Casa

del Minero 1, estancia La María, meseta central de Santa Cruz. In *Arqueología de Fuego-Patagonia. Levantando Piedras, desenterrando huesos y develando arcanos*, edited by F. Morello, M. Martinic, A. Prieto, and G. Bahamonde, pp. 577–588. Ediciones CEQUA, Punta Arenas, CL.

Politis, Gustavo
1991   Fishtail Projectile Points in the Southern Cone of South America: An Overview. In *Clovis. Origins and Adaptations*, edited by Rob Bonnichsen and Karen Turnmire, pp. 287–301. Center for the Study of the First Americans and Texas A&M University Press, College Station, TX.

Rockman, Marcy
2003   Knowledge and Learning in the Archaeology of Colonization. In *Colonization of Unfamiliar Landscapes: The Archaeology of Adaptation*, edited by M. Rockman and J. Steele, pp. 3–24. Routledge, London.

Schalamuk, Isidro B., Raùl E. De Barrio, Mario A. Zubia, Adolfo Genini, and J. Valdano
2002   Mineralizaciones auro-argentíferas del Macizo del Deseado y su encuadre metalogénico. In *Relatorio del 15º congreso geológico Argentino: geología y recursos naturales de Santa Cruz*, Actas 4, edited by M. Haller Geología y recursos naturales de Santa Cruz. Relatorio del 15º Congreso Geológico Argentino, pp. 679–713. Buenos Aires, AR.

Skarbun, Fabiana
2009   *La organización tecnológica en grupos cazadores-recolectores desde las ocupaciones del Pleistoceno final al Holoceno Tardío en la meseta central de Santa Cruz*. PhD dissertation, Facultad de Ciencias Naturales y Museo, Universidad Nacional de La Plata, La Plata, AR.
2012   Variability in Lithic Technological Strategies of Early Human Occupations from the Central Plateau, Santa Cruz, Argentina. In *Southbound: Late Pleistocene Peopling of Latin America*, edited by L. Miotti, M. Salemme, N. Flegenheimer, and T. Goebel, pp. 143–148. Center for the Study of the First Americans, Texas A&M University, College Station, TX.

Skarbun, Fabiana, Manuel Cueto, Ariel Frank, and Rafael Paunero
2015   Producción, consumo y espacialidad en

Cueva Túnel, meseta central de Santa Cruz, Argentina. *Chungara: Revista Chilena de Antropología* 47(1):85–99.

Steele, James, and Gustavo Politis
2009   AMS ^{14}C Dating of Early Human Occupation of Southern South America. *Journal of Archaeological Science* 36(2):419–429.

Stern, Charles R.
2000   Sources of Obsidian Artifacts from the Pali Aike, Fell's Cave, and Cañadón La Leona Archaeological Sites in Southernmost Patagonia. In *Desde el país de los gigantes. Perspectivas arqueológicas en Patagonia*, vol. I, edited by J. B. Belardi, F. Carballo Marina, and S. Espinosa, pp. 43–55. Unidad Académica Río Gallegos, Universidad Nacional de la Patagonia Austral. Río Gallegos, AR.
1993   Extended ^{14}C Database and Revised CALIB 3.0 ^{14}C Age Calibration Program. *Radiocarbon* 35(1):215–230.

Suárez, Rafael
2006   Comments on South America Fishtail Points: Design, Reduction Sequences, and Function. *Current Research in the Pleistocene* 23:69–72.
2010   Arqueología durante la transición Pleistoceno–Holoceno: componentes Paleoindios, organización de la tecnología lítica y movilidad de los primeros americanos en Uruguay. PhD dissertation, Facultad de Ciencias Naturales y Museo, Universidad de La Plata, La Plata, AR.

Veth, Peter
2005   Cycles of Aridity and Human Mobility. Risk Minimization among Late Pleistocene Foragers of the Western Desert, Australia. In *Desert Peoples: Archaeological Perspectives*, edited by P. Veth, M. Smith, and P. Hiscock, pp. 100–115. Blackwell Publishing, Oxford, UK.

Weitzel, Celeste, Nora Flegenheimer, Jorge Martínez, and Mariano Colombo
2014   Breakage Patterns on Fishtail Projectile Points: Experimental and Archaeological Cases. *Ethnoarchaeology* 6(2):81–102.

Zubia, Mario A.
1998   Recursos Minerales. In *Hoja geológica 4969-I, Gobernador Gregores, provincia de Santa Cruz*. Servicio Geológico Minero Argentino, Boletín 239.

CHAPTER 3

A Systematic Strategy for Assessing the Early Surface Archaeological Record of Continental Aisén, Central Western Patagonia

César Méndez, Amalia Nuevo Delaunay, Omar Reyes,
Antonio Maldonado, and Juan-Luis García

The identification of localities with evidence of human occupation for the Pleistocene–Holocene transition in South America—particularly in Patagonia—has not usually been targeted within guided search programs. Rather, most new evidence has been conditioned by the formation processes that exposed them, or their discovery resulted from excavations at caves and rockshelters where their occurrence was unanticipated (Jackson and Méndez 2004). Consequently, in Patagonia, the vast majority of human evidence dated to the Pleistocene–Holocene transition has been identified in the latter type of sites (Borrero and Franco 1997; Massone 1999, Jackson 2007), despite the fact that human beings must have performed quite a significant proportion of their activities at open-air locations. These circumstances entail a limited potential for new findings that may embrace variability in temporal, spatial, and/or functional scales.

A substantial proportion of the archaeological record in Patagonia is on the surface of open-air locations, thereby posing difficulties for constraining it within a credible chronological range. In particular, the primary means of addressing the surface record of earliest human evidence in Patagonia has been through typological considerations of formal tool types, chiefly Fishtail projectile points and, to a lesser extent, discoidal stones (Figure 3.1). Junius Bird first recognized these two archaeological types

during the 1930s while excavating sites north of the Magellan Strait, especially at Fell's Cave (Bird 1938, 1970, 1993). The most reliable dates for these tool types in cave sites suggest a range between ca. 12,980 and 11,820 cal BP (Nami and Nakamura 1995; Jackson and Méndez 2007; Méndez 2013; Prates et al. 2013). On the surface, these artifacts have been generally found isolated (e.g. Nami 1994, Jackson 2004, Bahamondes and Jackson 2006, Jackson and Méndez 2007, Méndez et al. 2013). Only recently have Fishtail points been located with higher frequency and in denser concentration, at Los Dos Amigos Oeste (Miotti et al. 2010, 2012).

This chapter addresses recent research conducted to elucidate the contextual characteristics of the surface archaeological record of continental Aisén (Chile) in order to provide clues for understanding the initial occupation of the region. Essential to this endeavor was the reconstruction of environmental conditions during the last glacial–postglacial transition (18,000–11,500 cal BP) through the integration of paleoecological and geomorphological analyses, thereby providing a broad environmental context for the archaeological record. We develop a research program at mesospatial (river basin, landform) and microspatial (site) scales (Dincauze 2000) in two river basins of western Patagonia—Cisnes and Ñirehuao—where glacial features signal the potential for recording Late Pleistocene–Early Holocene physiographic changes. Surface and

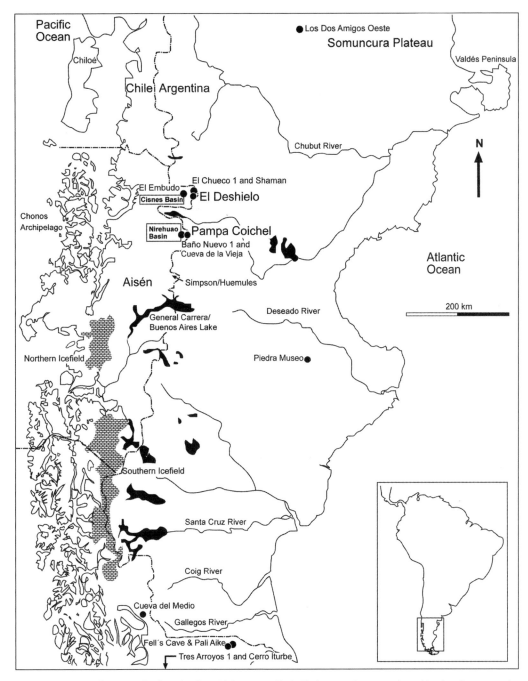

Figure 3.1: Map of Patagonia showing late Pleistocene–Early Holocene sites mentioned in the chapter and locations with Fishtail projectile points.

stratigraphic surveys at these scales were used to constrain the temporal expression of the archaeological record, either by identifying former glacial features (i.e. proglacial lake shorelines) or by dating paleosols. Findings at the easternmost areas within Cisnes and Ñirehuao valleys (i.e. the El Deshielo site and Pampa Coichel) provided insight to a type of open landscape where Terminal Pleistocene/Early Holocene open-site occupations were located.

Regional Setting

The study area corresponds to the continental northern Aisén region (ca. 44°25'–45°20' S), specifically the upper sections of two formerly glaciated valleys, Ñirehuao and Cisnes, east of the Andes Mountains. The study areas expose extensive last-glacial period moraine belts and glaciolacustrine depositional beds that were reworked by postglacial fluvial erosion. At Ñirehuao, Tertiary glacially molded volcanic constructions are widespread (Suárez et al. 2007). The vegetation distribution is mainly controlled by a marked west-to-east precipitation gradient shaped by the Andes, which produces semiarid conditions within the eastern rain shadow where the study areas are situated (Garreaud 2009). For instance, temperate deciduous forests of *Nothofagus pumilio* and *Berberis ilicifolia* are present on the eastern Andean foothills, gradually changing into an open Mediterranean steppe with *Festuca pallescens* and *Mulinum spinosum* in an ecotonal manner (Luebert and Pliscoff 2006).

The eastern steppes and the forest/steppe ecotone of the Cisnes and Ñirehuao upper basins provide sensitive areas for the identification of changes in the landscape and human records at the Pleistocene–Holocene boundary. Deglaciation, after ice occupied Cisnes and Ñirehuao basins during the Last Glacial Maximum (LGM), was characterized by ice-front stabilizations and the formation of regional-scale glacial lakes draining eastwards to the Atlantic Ocean. We mapped lake shorelines standing approximately 900 to 600 m a.s.l. within the valleys. All point to a steady lake recession during deglaciation. The available main records for glacial/postglacial environmental conditions come from the sedimentary columns of El Shaman and El Embudo sites located inboard of the LGM and glacial moraine belts, respectively, within the Cisnes Valley (De Porras et al. 2012, 2014). Whereas the easternmost Lake Shaman record starts at about 19,000 cal BP, the El Embudo stratigraphic sequence, closer to the western ice source, starts at ca. 13,000 cal BP. The pollen records show a transition from a low-precipitation, open grass–dominated environment toward a higher forest expansion associated with higher precipitation as a consequence of the shifting of the westerlies influence between 13,000–8500/7600 cal BP, a period in which the actual forest/steppe ecotone distribution was established (De Porras et al. 2012, 2014). In Patagonia, several climatic records suggest a cold reversal phase synchronous with the Antarctic Cold Reversal (Strelin et al. 2011; García et al. 2012), while others indicate a reversal occurred during the Younger Dryas chronozone (Bennett et al. 2000; Glasser et al. 2012). Regardless, independent pollen records from Aisén indicate that the warming trend during the Pleistocene–Holocene transition manifested as a stepped rather than continuous process (De Porras et al. 2012, 2014; Villa-Martínez et al. 2012).

Regional Archaeological Trends at the Pleistocene–Holocene Transition

The earliest archaeological evidence in the Aisén region of southern Chile has been recorded at El Chueco 1 (44°29'37" S), which coincides with general trends in Patagonia: it corresponds to a cave site in the upper Cisnes River basin (Reyes et al. 2007a) and yielded stratigraphic deposits with human occupations starting at 11,500 cal BP. This initial occupational event shows a minimal human signal consisting of isolated charcoal particles in association with a multifunctional, expedient flaked stone tool (Méndez et al. 2009). Averaged radiocarbon dates at the site resulted in at least 13 occupational events, which suggest that this area of the upper Cisnes basin was visited intermittently, and with low intensity occupations, from the onset of the Holocene until the last centuries (Méndez et al. 2011).

Within this same period, the first occupations

appear in the neighboring valley of Ñirehuao, as shown by the stratigraphic deposits of Cueva de la Vieja (45°16'27" S) starting at 12,000 cal BP (Méndez et al. 2018). Expedient tools, chipping debris and one hearth indicate a brief, low intensity initial occupation. As with El Chueco 1, averaged radiocarbon dates at the site showed at least twelve occupational events throughout the Holocene. Just 2 km away, the Baño Nuevo 1 site (45°17'36" S) provided pooled radiocarbon dates of at least 15 occupational events when it was used as a transitory shelter from 11,100 to 3000 cal BP (Mena et al. 2003). Remarkably, the site yielded the burials of ten individuals whose dates overlap, at a 2σ range, between 10,200 and 9700 cal BP (Mena and Stafford 2006; Reyes et al. 2012). Combined ICP-MS data of obsidian artifacts from both El Chueco 1 and Baño Nuevo 1 suggest that different patterns of long-distance procurement of this exotic stone resource were already occurring by the Early Holocene (Méndez et al. 2012). Seemingly, the results from stable isotope analyses on the bioarchaeological assemblage of Baño Nuevo 1 have been interpreted as dietary choices that, although relying on guanaco (*Lama guanicoe*, the largest extant artiodactyl), probably targeted other smaller omnivorous taxa (Méndez et al. 2014). Furthermore, combined radiocarbon data of these three sites underscores temporal discontinuities, as expected for marginal regions (Veth 1993), thus supporting the idea of a peripheral settlement linked to population nuclei east in Patagonia (Borrero 2004).

Methods

This study is based upon defining a multiscalar approach following exponential spatial scales suggested by Dincauze (2000). These include a meso-regional scale between 10^2 and 10^4 km², a meso-local scale between 1 and 10^2 km², and a microscale of <1 km². Different field techniques were applied in approaching surface archaeological data and the environmental information at these varying scales. The discussion of the results seeks to understand the transit between the different spatial scales (Moran 1995).

For the broader geographic scale, available geological maps signaled the existence of late Quaternary glacio-lacustrine deposits (Suárez et al. 2007). Given that the upper course of the Ñirehuao basin had remained without systematic surveys (Méndez et al. 2012), it was selected for a targeted surface search guided by landforms. In order to determine key geomorphological features, mapping relied on a stereoscopic analysis of aerial photos and extensive ground coverage. Photographic interpretation was rectified using ArcGIS and ENVI 4.0 software, information provided by the L7123091_09120051212 Landsat satellite image, and elevation data from the Shuttle Radar Topography Mission (s46w072; Ortega 2011). Comprehensive mapping suggestive of the extent of LGM glacial landforms provided a hypothetical indicator for areas outside the realm of glaciers and proglacial lakes, thereby allowing an archaeological survey avoiding major sectors that were either covered by water or barren lands during deglaciation.

The meso-local scale was approached through systematic surface surveys of selected landscapes. These followed predetermined parallel transects (separated by 25 m) aiming to provide a thorough coverage of eroded surfaces where the archaeological record of potential interest was presumably located. Such a survey was conducted at Pampa Coichel area, a wind-deflated high plain immediately next to a small lake body near the Chile–Argentina border in the upper Ñirehuao valley (Figure 3.2). Survey techniques included the geopositioning of all visible artifacts (mainly lithics), determining discrete concentrations, and performing selective collections. Taphonomic observations on lithic material arose as a key feature for studying erosion on surfaces that may be indicative of exposure history, hypothetically from different broad time frames (Borrazzo 2006, 2007).

At microscale, the surface archaeological record was carefully piece-plotted in order to provide specific locations, useful in the resolution of site-scale formational questions (Méndez et al. 2010). Selected artifacts were collected at two specific sites, which we chose to include in this study: El Deshielo and Vega Coichel, in the Cisnes and Nirehuao basins, respectively. The

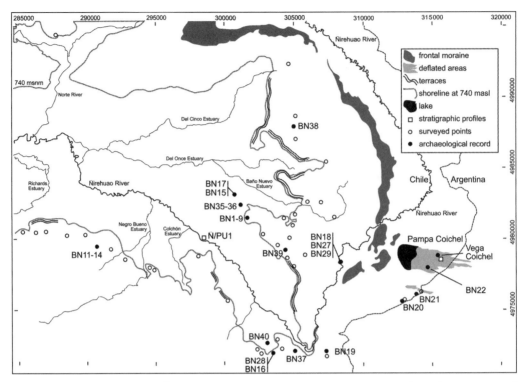

FIGURE 3.2. Detailed map of the Ñirehuao River basin showing current rivers and creeks and past margins of the 740 m a.s.l. paleolake phase, along with selected surveyed points and archaeological findings. Ñ/PU1: Ñirehuao River stratigraphic section; BN1: Baño Nuevo 1 site; BN15: Cueva de la Vieja site.

main aim within the microscale approach was to understand the general stratigraphy of the locale as a means to provide a reasonable comprehension of the depositional units (stratigraphical) for the artifacts. Thereafter, efforts were made to determine the age of the stratigraphic units of interest, either by dating organic material from soil profiles or organic remains enveloped in the sediments. Although these procedures do not provide direct ages for the archaeological materials or occupation levels where they were discarded (for instance, discrete features), the aim was to bracket the human activities in order to discuss broad sedimentary processes.

All age determinations discussed here were obtained from radiocarbon AMS analyses and were calibrated using Calib 7.0.0 program (Stuiver et al. 2013) at a 2σ range using the ShCal13 curve (Hogg et al. 2013) and are expressed in calibrated years (cal BP), unless specified otherwise.

Results and Discussion
The Ñirehuao Proglacial Shoreline Lake Survey (Meso-Regional Scale)

The upper course of the Ñirehuao basin exposes a complex assemblage of glacial and proglacial landforms deposited during the LGM and subsequent deglaciation. Glacial geomorphic units include multigenerational moraine belts, kame terraces on the valley sides, paleolake shorelines, of which the 810, 770, and 740 m a.s.l levels encompass prominent landforms, paleodrainages, and lake outlets (Figure 3.2). Most of this glacial geomorphology remains undated. However, based on dates obtained on stratified basal deposits of glacio-lacustrine origin at Baño Nuevo 1 (ca. 740 m a.s.l.), Mena and Stafford (2006) suggested that a 740 m a.s.l. lake existed before 16,500 cal BP. We chose this level as a guideline for a pedestrian archaeological survey (Méndez et al. 2013). Despite the fact that evidence from Baño Nuevo 1 does not provide a precise time framework within which to establish the paleolake at 740 m a.s.l., nor any assurance that human beings were contemporaneous with this landform, it does set a tentative limit for the areas to be surveyed by excluding significant sectors within its boundaries. Other excluded sectors were those that may have been obliterated and/or covered by Holocene deposit mass removals. Additionally, and considering the multiple lake levels produced by a dynamic deglaciation, the survey also included locations in areas more distant from the boundaries of this level in order to explore sectors that may have always been available for human occupation during the last glacial–interglacial transition.

A total of 46 ground positions were defined to guide the survey: 17 at 740 m a.s.l.; 15 at 770 m a.s.l.; and 14 at or above 810 m a.s.l., the highest recorded paleo-shore level. Among the latter, seven positions were situated north, three to the south, and four to the east in the area of Pampa Coichel. Another limit meant to establish the distribution of survey positions was the Chile–Argentina border. Determination of survey positions included open-air locations, as well as formations where rockshelters were potentially available. At each position, surveys covered an approximate 0.5 km radius, within which major landforms and occasional archaeological findings were systematically described.

This survey did not seek to provide a complete distributional picture of the surface archaeological record of the upper Ñirehuao basin but instead sought to sample locations of potential interest through a guided search. As such, the archaeological material was recorded in low frequencies for a total of 31 loci of interest (Méndez et al. 2013). These should be added to another nine found before our work in the area (F. Mena, personal communication 2013). In sum, these loci include 17 proper sites (either rockshelters with evidence of human occupation, or lithic surface scatters), 15 isolated finds, and eight rockshelters with undetermined potential for archaeological record. Only 19 (10 sites and 9 isolated findings) were identified in association with the predefined ground positions that guided the survey (within the radius or at close

range). Among these, a Fishtail-type projectile point was recorded in the area of Pampa Coichel (BN22, 45°19'47.1" S, 71°21'36.39" W, 851 m a.s.l.).

The Fishtail-type projectile point was manufactured on a siliceous white/black rock, currently of unknown origin, since there are no available raw material regional characterizations yet. Measurements following the parameters suggested by Morrow and Morrow (1999) place this artifact within the expected ranges (Méndez et al. 2013). The thinning flake scars are mainly oriented diagonally and tend to surpass the longitudinal axis. Macroscopic signs of hafting wear on the stem edges suggest that the tool was in an operational stage (Rots 2003). Additionally, the piece shows two fractures in its distal part, with attributes presumably produced by an impact against a hard substrate (e.g., Titmus and Woods 1986; Weitzel 2012). It is logical to assume that discard of such pieces would occur during hunting activities (e.g., replacement, Andrefsky 2010) or may correspond to an occasional loss (Schiffer 1996; Borrero 2001), since there is no indication of subsequent resharpening. Finally, slightly higher erosion was observed on the face exposed upwards than on the one facing the ground, indicating exposure time to wind deflation. Lichens were recorded on the lee margin of the piece. Just 2 m away from this artifact, we recorded a core with use-wear traces and heavy erosion on its faces.

Although the majority of Fishtail projectile points in South America come from assemblages lacking a known chronology, those associated with dated deposits belong to the Pleistocene–Holocene transition (Politis 1991; Flegenheimer et al. 2003). In Patagonia, this type of projectile point was recorded at Fell's Cave, Pali Aike (Bird 1993), Cueva del Medio (Nami 1985–1986), Tres Arroyos 1 (Jackson 2002; Massone 2004), and Piedra Museo (Miotti 1995) and isolated in the Pali Aike ranch (Nami 1994), Cerro Iturbe (Jackson 2004), and in museum collections (Bahamondes and Jackson 2006). In the Aisén region, only two basalt bifacial artifacts had been previously described as blanks for this tool type—both from private collections obtained at the headwaters of the Simpson–Huemules river

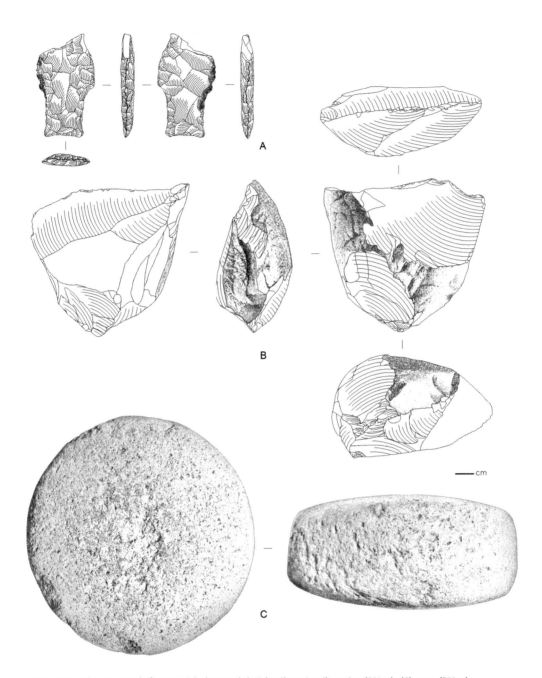

FIGURE 3.3. Lithic materials from Coichel area: (*A*) Fishtail projectile point (BN22); (*B*) core (BN22); (*C*) discoidal stone (BN75).

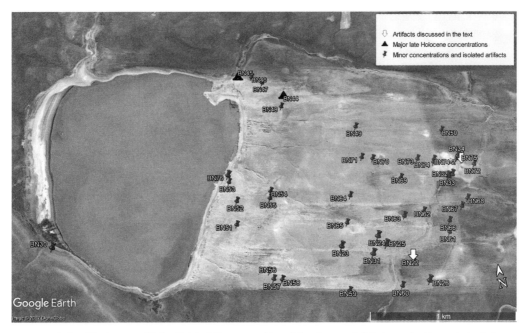

FIGURE 3.4. Satellite image of Lake Coichel (820 m a.s.l.) and the Pampa Coichel area to the east depicting the location of the surface archaeological record (Google Earth Pro 2014).

(Bate 1982; Sade 2007). Since this particular tool type has yielded no reliable dates younger than 11,820 cal BP[1] elsewhere in Patagonia (Méndez 2013; Prates et al. 2013), it is possible to consider it an appropriate temporal marker on which to build hypotheses about the spaces available for the first inhabitants of the region.

The Pampa Coichel Intensive Survey (Meso-Local Scale)

Considering the earlier findings, plus the fact that the area of Pampa Coichel yielded an above-average frequency of surface lithic material, an intensive survey was initiated in order to characterize its distributional record (Dunnell and Dancey 1983). It was based on the idea that areas subjected to strong wind deflation, where previous landscape analyses indicate potential access to Late Pleistocene–Early Holocene surfaces, may provide ideal settings for intercepting an early archaeological record. Pampa Coichel corresponds to an approximately 4 km² area at a mean altitude of 850 m a.s.l., where a deflated dune system composed of sands, silts, and fine selected clays occur between a dry-

ing, topographically closed shallow lake body (sediment source) close to the Chile–Argentina border (Suárez et al. 2007). High wind activity produces coarse lag deposits with surface archaeological material and the occasional exposure of small stratigraphic sections exhibiting paleosols.

A total of 30 parallel transects provided a systematic coverage of the area. Forty-three loci with archaeological materials were recorded, including the location where the surface projectile point was observed (Figure 3.4). Among these loci only two were major lithic scatters (BN44 [45°19'3.01" S, 71°22'4.32" W, 782 m a.s.l.] and BN45 [45°18'55.47" S, 71°22'18.72" W, 823 m a.s.l.]), while the rest were either isolated artifacts, or minor concentrations (i.e., <3 lithic units). The two primary concentrations were located adjacent to the shore of Lake Coichel and composed of abundant lithic debitage on various raw materials. One (BN45) yielded a distinctive assemblage of formal tools that included triangular broad-stemmed projectile points, bifacial knives, frontal scrapers, grinding stones, and discrete large-pebble concentrations. All

TABLE 3.1. Radiocarbon ages used to constrain timing of surface archaeological record and stratigraphic units in the study area. Dates were calibrated with CALIB 7.0.0 using the ShCal13 curve.

Lab code	Spatial and stratigraphic references	pMC** (1σ)	RCYBP	δ¹³C (‰)	cal BP (2σ)	Material
D-AMS 007521	Vega Coichel PU1.SU2-A	61.34 ± 0.22	3926 ± 29	−22.4	4230–4420	charred material
D-AMS 005063	Vega Coichel PU3.SU2-C*	91.79 ± 0.57	688 ± 50	−25.0	550–670	organic sediment
D-AMS 005064	Vega Coichel PU3.SU2-E*	43.34 ± 0.31	6716 ± 57	−25.0	7440–7620	organic sediment
AA 103407	El Deshielo (CIS 083) SU1		1287 ± 46	−20.2	1060–1270	bone (*Lama guanicoe*)
D-AMS 007522	El Deshielo (CIS008) SU3	31.28 ± 0.16	9336 ± 41	−20.5	9930–10,230	charred material
BETA 381095	El Deshielo (CIS008) SU3		9020 ± 30	−25.1	10,300–10,590	organic sediment
UGAMS 8374	Cisnes headwaters, clay/sand contact		16,400 ± 50	−26.9	19,550–19,960	organic sediment

* Submitted samples were mostly inorganic, accurate δ¹³C were not obtained, and radiocarbon dates were calculated using the −25.0‰ standard.
** The fraction of modern charcoal is quoted for informative reasons. D-AMS: Direct AMS Lab.; BETA: Beta Analytic Inc.; AA: NSF-Arizona AMS Laboratory; UGAMS: CAIS lab., University of Georgia; PU: profile unit; SU: stratigraphic unit.

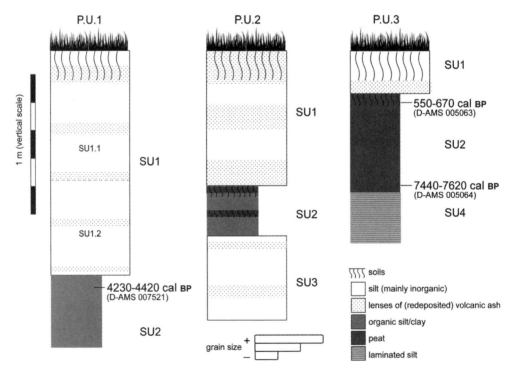

FIGURE 3.5. Schematic stratigraphy of Vega Coichel and dates used to constrain buried soils. PU: profile unit; SU: stratigraphic unit.

were consistent with late Holocene campsites (ca. 1500/1000–650 cal BP), as dated elsewhere in the Aisén region (Velásquez et al. 2007; Reyes et al. 2007b; Méndez and Reyes 2008).

The erosion visible on the surface of the lithic materials from sites BN44 and BN45 provides a distinctive local measure for recently exposed and/or recently flaked artifacts subjected to strong aeolian agents. As such, the degree of differential erosion on the lithic surfaces produced by blown sand particles (Borrazzo 2006) represents a relative dating approach for "late" (i.e., less eroded) artifacts. Since a measure like this is comparable throughout materials with analog lithological properties, it is safe to claim that most of the artifacts composed of siliceous rocks (which dominate the Pampa Coichel assemblage) are either comparable in time of exposure or in age of manufacture. However, lithics also display varying degrees of erosion on their surfaces, thereby indicating—as a whole—at least two independent, recognizable manufacture and/or exposure intervals. While the Fishtail projectile point exhibits slightly higher erosion on one face, the above-mentioned core shows distinctive traces of erosion across the entire piece, probably due to higher exposure rates and instability (Borrazzo 2006, 2007) rather than an earlier deposition. Other scattered artifacts with similar higher level of erosion comprise both evident artifacts, as well as other nondiagnostic pieces whose anthropogenic character is still under study.

At the easternmost sector of the surveyed area, a series of stratigraphic profiles revealed buried soils that hold the potential for understanding the chronology of the sedimentary deposition of the locality and hypothetically provide reference ages for the archaeological record in the immediate vicinity. Laying on the surface, ten meters away from one of the profiles, we recorded a discoidal stone (BN75, 45°19'28.28" S, 71°21'9.92" W, 838 m a.s.l.). The discoidal stones, although not so precisely constrained within a time scale as the Fishtail projectile points, serve to consider the possibility of an ice- and water-free landscape at the Pleistocene–Holocene transition also. Based on available dates associated

with this tool type for Pampas and Patagonia, it is possible to establish their occurrence between 12,900 and 8270 cal BP (Jackson and Méndez 2007).

Vega Coichel and El Deshielo
Site-Specific Approach (Microscale)

The site-specific approach was conducted at locations where the following characteristics were met: (a) presence of surface archaeological material; (b) potential association with immediate stratigraphic information; and (c) availability of buried organic material, either paleosols or enveloped samples (e.g., bone or charcoal). Considering the above-mentioned lithic findings at the Pampa Coichel area, we selected a sector with the remnants of stratigraphic sections for further study. We have named it Vega Coichel, because of the buried organic deposits suggestive of a former wetland (*vega*) present in the area. This sector corresponds to a small (48,900 m²) basin enclosing a lag deposit with only minor artifact concentrations (N = 2) and isolated artifacts (N = 4).

As observed on the exposed profiles, the general stratigraphy includes a top silty unit (SU1) with thin volcanic ash layers deposited in a shallow subaquatic environment (Figure 3.5). The topsoil is immature, mainly exposing an organic A-horizon. This unit overlies in sharp contact by normal grading a second unit that yields organic silt, clayey silt, and peat facies (SU2), suggestive of a wetland environment. In turn, SU2 overlies either inorganic silts with volcanic ash lenses (SU3) or a localized laminated silt stratum (SU4) occurring only at the southwest area, closer to a former drainage, where topography reaches the lowest elevation. The base of SU2 yielded a radiocarbon date of 7620–7440 cal BP, which should be considered a minimum age, based on the fact that the sample was constituted of organic sediments (Table 3.1). However, the top of this unit yielded a 4420–4230 cal BP age on charcoal, which should be regarded as a reliable date for the change in sedimentation regimes. Although this paleo-wetland is a highly localized feature, it is noteworthy that the available ages are coincidental with the period of

FIGURE 3.6. Lag deposit at El Deshielo site.

highest effective moisture experienced during the Holocene, as suggested by the combined pollen profiles from El Shaman Lake and Mallín El Embudo in the neighboring valley of Cisnes (De Porras et al. 2012, 2014).

The discoidal stone was on the surface, 10 m away from profile unit 1, on top of the stratigraphic unit buried by the organic silt layer (SU2). We think that the radiocarbon date from the base of SU2 at Vega Coichel provides a minimum age (i.e., *terminus ante quem*) for this artifact, as well as for the surface on which it laid. This also should be regarded as a potential surface for open-air activities during the Early Holocene and perhaps for the Pleistocene–Holocene transition.

On the basis of the information gathered at Vega Coichel, we selected another site, El Deshielo (CIS008, 44°36'16.12" S, 71°13'46.12" W, 930 m a.s.l.), because it met the above-mentioned criteria. Lithic material at this site was not only recorded on a lag deposit (Figure 3.6), thereby providing a complex interpretive scenario, but differential erosion as a consequence of abrasion from small particles blown by heavy winds was characteristic of the artifact surfaces (sandblasted artifacts). This fact underpinned earlier assessments of lithic taphonomy (Méndez et al. 2010).

Two lithic scatters comprise the assemblage recorded at El Deshielo. They show an atypically high proportion of core tools, predominantly planes and denticulates, which are interpreted as a technology oriented toward wood processing (Méndez et al. 2006). Most artifacts were identified in concentration 1, showing distinctive degrees of erosion on their surfaces. Therefore, initial assessments at the site questioned the potential early age for the production of such tools. On one hand, the lower degree of erosion in concentration 2, compared to concentration 1, was interpreted as a potentially more recent age of production and/or exposition. However, surface piece plotting suggested that internal differences in the degree of surface erosion within concentration 1 were higher in those artifacts placed windward (to the west). Rather than indicating different ages of production, the evidence signaled the location as the main factor responsible for the taphonomic properties of the artifacts. In this case, therefore, higher erosion was attributable to an earlier exposition (Méndez et al. 2010). If the age of artifact manufacture was undistinguished after analysis, then we can

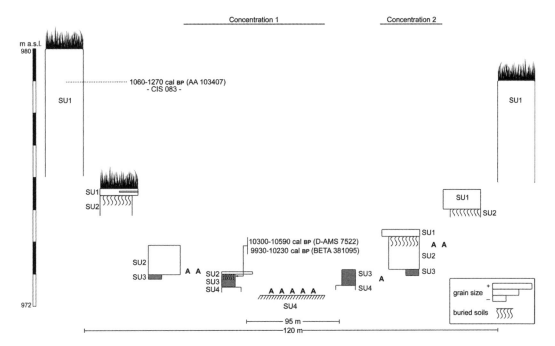

FIGURE 3.7. Schematic stratigraphy of El Deshielo and dates used to constrain buried soils and inorganic strata. SU: stratigraphic unit; A: artifacts.

assume relative contemporaneity of the assemblage and begin questioning the age of the stratigraphic deposit(s) from which these sandblasted artifacts originally eroded.

The general stratigraphy at El Deshielo comprises four units that overlie older Late Glacial–Holocene sediments exposed after the incision of the Cisnes River, as suggested by the 19,550–19,960 cal BP age obtained from the contact of sand and clays in the profile midsection (Table 3.1). In the archaeological site, the top unit consists of massive coarse sands (SU1) exceeding 4 m of depth (Figure 3.7). This unit overlies in sharp contact a second unit yielding compact silty sands with pedogenetic structures (SU2). In turn, SU2 overlies an approximately 30-cm-thick, dark organic, highly compacted clay layer (SU3). Unit SU3 represents a possible localized wetland environment, which also presents a paleosol in the upper part of the unit. The final stratigraphic unit (SU4) is composed of inorganic, oxidized, compact sandy clay. No evident erosional contacts were observed in this stratigraphic section.

Since SU1 was basically inorganic, we dated a sample of a guanaco (*Lama guanicoe*) mandible, located some 380 m southwest of the site (CIS083, 44°36'24.87" S, 71°13'55.69" W, 927 m a.s.l.), in the same sediment unit. This analysis resulted in an age of 1270–1060 cal BP (2σ range), thereby constraining the end of sand deposition with a minimum date for the top section. This date does not indicate a relative age for the initial dune formation. Two additional radiocarbon dates were obtained from the top of SU3 at El Deshielo: 10,230–9930 cal BP (bulk sediment) and 10,590–10,300 cal BP (charcoal; 2σ range). Although relatively coincidental, the dates on a charcoal speck provide a more reliable maximum age for the top of the unit than the results from sediment organic content, therefore placing the end of the deposition closer to the latter value.

The field observations allowed us to locate most of the lithic material on top of SU4 in the center of the lag deposit, which showed the most severe sandblasting. Moreover, these observations also permitted us to distinguish some of

the recently exposed artifacts at the surface between profiles in positions suggesting that they
had once belonged to SU2, possibly near the
contact with SU3. Although these results do not
provide a well-constrained chronological range
for the archaeological assemblage, they serve as
a *terminus post quem* and allow us to exclude
the lithic material at El Deshielo site as Late
Pleistocene–Early Holocene in age, possibly
indicating deposition during the Early–Middle
Holocene. While we still do not know the basal
age for SU3, the date on the top section suggests
that the Late Pleistocene–Early Holocene surface was probably the top of SU4 and that it predates the wetland formation.

Final Remarks

Various research teams in South America have
addressed the search for Late Pleistocene—Early
Holocene archaeological evidence through the
reconstruction of potential environments and
conditions that would enable their recognition
(e.g., Richardson 1980; Lynch 1986; Núñez et al.
2005; Jackson et al. 2007; Sandweiss and Rademaker 2011; Santoro et al. 2011; Latorre et al.
2013; Rademaker et al. 2014). In Patagonia,
the recognition of potential surfaces for Early
Holocene occupations in Tierra del Fuego
(McCulloch and Morello 2009; Morello et al.
2009) or the search for evidence in localities
prone to accumulate paleontological/archaeo-
logical record, such as the volcanic traps in Pali
Aike (Martin and San Román 2010), are two
ways in which locating new evidence has been
guided by targeted search. The implementation
of such methodology illustrates that by recognizing formational processes of the archaeological
record and the geographical and environmental
aspects in a particular region, it is feasible to aim
for the human evidence at particular chronological blocks. Assessing human evidence at
the Pleistocene–Holocene transition is a more
complex challenge than in later periods since
it entails a higher probability of destruction of
geomorphological features and taphonomic loss
of certain lines of archaeological evidence.

This chapter seeks to address the surface archaeological record of the steppe in the northern
part of continental Aisén as a means to discuss

potential ways to recognize early human evidence. It summarizes preliminary results obtained through a program specifically designed
to target Pleistocene–Holocene transition landscapes as a means to distinguish the surfaces that
the earliest inhabitants must have used in open-
site activities. The study area was selected based
on previous archaeological work securely dating
humans in cave sites (Méndez et al. 2009, 2018;
Mena and Stafford 2006), thus providing independent lines of evidence that those areas were
explored during the Pleistocene–Holocene transition. The methodology includes recognition of
different approaches to the surface archaeological record at exponential spatial scales, either by
modeling glacial-originated features, identifying
potential occupation surfaces where such a record would be expectable, and understanding
localized environments (e.g., paleo-wetlands)
that may be used as chronostratigraphic markers
of local and regional significance. Each scale is
related to specific survey methods in which spatial location and formational processes at artifact
level informed potential ages for the recorded
assemblages. In this study, typological considerations are included as means of orienting the
research in a hypothetical way, not as the primary line of argument themselves.

The study on three different scales in the
Ñirehuao Valley and only on a site scale in
Cisnes Valley revealed landscapes and surfaces
potentially utilized by past societies. Two specific
locales, Pampa/Vega Coichel and El Deshielo,
are the distinctive locations where we chose to
focus our efforts. Radiocarbon dates at these
two sites are still insufficient, and these remarks
must be considered preliminary. Also, based on
the work summarized here, it is mandatory to
conduct additional surveys and excavations, in
order to continue solving specific research questions such as differential landscape use. In both
cases studied here, paleo-wetlands appear to be
appropriate markers for chronostratigraphic
recognition of specific environments but not
necessarily as preferred landscapes for settlement. The timing for such features needs further
study in collation with regionally available environmental records to assess their significance in
terms of climate conditions and changes.

By dating buried soils and/or enveloped organic samples, we have managed to provide localized indications for excluding or including particular lithic assemblages within broad chronological blocks. In this sense, the dated events, or those dated with a chronometric technique, differ greatly and should not be regarded as the target events or processes of archaeological interest (Nash 2009). Further work in this direction will provide answers to directed questions, such as the role of such assemblages within their own time frame and not just as undatable surface material. By recognizing the degree of wind erosion on sandblasted artifact surfaces, as in the case of Pampa Coichel, we can follow indications on specific lithic clusters that may guide us to distinct times of use

and discard. However, focusing on a site-based strategy has also allowed for a more general and perhaps an even more significant result of providing chronological basis for recognizing surfaces, nonetheless local, that may signal where early inhabitants must have set foot and that are potential environments where activities were conducted.

We believe that such an approach, although sometimes slow or occasionally unrewarding, may provide solid new evidence in the long run. The benefit is that this type of evidence moves beyond an approach to early human occupations that focuses on caves and rockshelters, one that has provided a yet incomplete view of the earliest inhabitants of Patagonia.

Acknowledgments

This research was funded by FONDECYT grant #1130128 and National Geographic grant HJ-150R-17. We thank NSF Arizona AMS Facility, University of Arizona, for the support in one ^{14}C date. We are indebted to Estancia Cisnes and Estancia Baño Nuevo for the kind permissions and help provided in our research. We thank our colleagues and students who participated in four fieldwork seasons since 2011, particularly: Kurt Rademaker, Valentina Trejo, Pablo González, Francisco Mena, Héctor Velásquez, Ismael Martínez, Catalina Contreras, María Luisa Gómez, Sara Brauer, Natalie Hormazábal, Sebastián Grasset, Ricardo Labra, and Paulina Chávez for the drawings of lithics.

Note

1. Based on an averaged age of 10,222 ± 141 BP by pooling radiocarbon dates labeled as I5146 and W915 from Fell's Cave (following Méndez 2013).

References

Andrefsky, William.
2010   Human Land Use Strategies and Projectile Point Damage, Resharpening and Discard Patterns. *Human Evolution* 25(1–2):13–30.

Bahamondes, Francisco, and Donald Jackson
2006   Hallazgo de una punta "cola de pescado" en Magallanes, Chile. *Magallania* 34(2):115–118.

Bate, Luis F.
1982   *Los orígenes de la comunidad primitiva en Patagonia*. Escuela Nacional de Antropología e Historia, Editorial Cuicuilco, México, DF.

Bennett, Keith D., Simon G. Haberle, and Susie H. Lumley
2000   The Last Glacial–Holocene Transition in Southern Chile. *Science* 290(5490):325–328.

Bird, Junius B.
1938   Antiquity and Migrations of the Early Inhabitants of Patagonia. *Geographical Review* 28(2):250–275.

1970   Paleoindian Discoidal Stones from South American. *American Antiquity* 35(2): 205–208.

1993   *Viajes y arqueología en Chile austral.* Ediciones de la Universidad de Magallanes, Punta Arenas, AR.

Borrazzo, Karen
2006   Tafonomía lítica en dunas: una propuesta para el análisis de los artefactos líticos. *Intersecciones en Antropología* 7:247–261.

2007   Aporte de la tafonomía lítica al estudio de distribuciones artefactuales en ambientes lacustres: el caso del sistema lacustre al sur del Lago Argentino (Santa Cruz, Argentina). *Comechingonia Virtual* 3:132–153.

Borrero, Luis A.
2001   *El Poblamiento de la Patagonia: toldos, milodones y volcanes.* Emecé Editores, Buenos Aires, AR.

2004   The Archaeozoology of Andean "Dead Ends" in Patagonia: Living near the

Continental Ice Cap. In *Colonisation, Migration and Marginal Areas. A Zooarchaeological Approach*, edited by Mariana Mondini, Sebastián Muñoz, and Stephen Wickler, pp. 55–61. Oxbow Books, Oxford, UK.

Borrero, Luis A., and Nora V. Franco
1997   Early Patagonian Hunter-Gatherers: Subsistence and Technology. *Journal of Anthropological Research* 53(2):219–239.

De Porras, María Eugenia, Antonio Maldonado, Ana M. Abarzúa, Macarena L. Cárdenas, Jean P. François, Alejandra Martel-Cea, Charles R. Stern, César Méndez, and Omar Reyes
2012   Postglacial Vegetation, Fire and Climate Dynamics at Central Chilean Patagonia (Lake Shaman, 44°S). *Quaternary Science Reviews* 50:71–85.

De Porras, María Eugenia, Antonio Maldonado, Flavia Quintana, Alejandra Martel-Cea, Omar Reyes, and César Méndez
2014   Environmental and Climatic Changes at Central Chilean Patagonia since the Late Glacial (Mallín El Embudo, 44°S). *Climate of the Past* 10(3):1063–1078.

Dincauze, Dena F.
2000   *Environmental Archaeology: Principles and Practice*. Cambridge University Press, Cambridge, UK.

Dunnell, Robert C., and William S. Dancey
1983   The Siteless Survey: A Regional Scale Data Collection Strategy. In *Advances in Archaeological Method and Theory*. vol. 6, edited by Michael B. Schiffer, pp. 267–287. Academic Press, New York.

Flegenheimer, Nora, Cristina Bayón, Miguel Valente, Jorge Baeza, and Jorge Femenías
2003   Long Distance Tool Stone Transport in the Argentine Pampas. *Quaternary International* 109–110:49–64.

García, Juan L., Michael R. Kaplan, Brenda L. Hall, Joerg M. Schaefer, Rodrigo M. Vega, Roseanne Schwartz, and Robert Finkel
2012   Glacier Expansion in Southern Patagonia throughout the Antarctic Cold Reversal. *Geology* 40(9):859–862.

Garreaud, René
2009   The Andes Climate and Weather. *Advances in Geosciences* 22:3–11.

Glasser, Neil F., Stephan Harrison, Christoph Schnabel, Derek Fabel, and Krister N. Jansson
2012   Younger Dryas and Early Holocene Age Glacier Advances in Patagonia, *Quaternary Science Reviews* 58:7–17.

Hogg, Alan G., Quan Hua, Paul G. Blackwell, Mu Niu, Caitlin E. Buck, Thomas P. Guilderson, Timothy J. Heaton, et al.
2013   SHCAL13 Southern Hemisphere Calibration, 0–50,000 Years cal BP. *Radiocarbon* 55(4):1889–1903.

Jackson, Donald
2002   *Los instrumentos líticos de los primeros cazadores de Tierra del Fuego. Ensayos y Estudios*. DIBAM, Santiago, CL.
2004   Hallazgo de una punta "cola de pescado" en Patagonia meridional. *Magallania* 32(2): 221–223.
2007   Estructura, intensidad y reiteración en las ocupaciones paleoindias en cuevas y aleros de Patagonia meridional (Chile). *Cazadores Recolectores del Cono Sur* 2:67–87.

Jackson, Donald, and César Méndez
2004   Hallazgo o búsqueda de sitios paleoindios: problemas de investigación en torno a los primeros poblamientos. *Werken* 5:9–14.
2007   Litos discoidales tempranos en contextos de Patagonia. *Magallania* 35(1):75–84

Jackson, Donald, César Méndez, Roxana Seguel, Antonio Maldonado, and Gabriel Vargas
2007   Initial Occupation of the Pacific Coast of Chile during Late Pleistocene times. *Current Anthropology* 48(5):725–731.

Latorre, Claudio, Calogero M. Santoro, Paula Ugalde, Eugenia Gayó, Daniela Osorio, Carolina Salas-Egaña, Ricardo De Pol-Holz, Delphine Joly, and Jason A. Rech
2013   Late Pleistocene Human Occupation of the Hyperarid Core in the Atacama Desert, Northern Chile. *Quaternary Science Reviews* 77:19–30.

Luebert, Federico, and Patricio Pliscoff
2006   *Sinopsis bioclimática y vegetacional de Chile*. Editorial Universitaria, Santiago, CL.

Lynch, Thomas F.
1986   Climate Change and Human Settlement around Late Glacial Laguna de Punta Negra, Northern Chile: The Preliminary Results. *Geoarchaeology* 1(2):145–162.

Martin, Fabiana M., and Manuel San Román
2010   Explorando la variabilidad del registro arqueológico y tafonómico en Pali-Aike (Chile) a través de la búsqueda de registros Pleistocenos a cielo abierto. *Magallania*, 38(1):199–215.

Massone, Mauricio
1999   Aproximación metodológica al estudio de las ocupaciones tempranas de los cazadores

terrestres en la región de Magallanes. In *Soplando en el viento. Actas de las Terceras Jornadas de Arqueología de la Patagonia*, edited by Juan B. Belardi, Pablo Fernández, Rafael Goñi, Ana G. Guráieb, and Mariana De Nigris, pp. 99–112. Instituto Nacional de Antropología y Pensamiento Latino-americano and Universidad Nacional de Comahue, Neuquén and Buenos Aires, AR.

2004 *Los cazadores después del hielo*. Centro de Investigaciones Barros Arana, DIBAM, Santiago, CL.

McCulloch, Robert D., and Flavia Morello

2009 Evidencia glacial y paleoecológica de ambientes tardiglaciales y del Holoceno temprano. Implicaciones para el poblamiento temprano de Tierra del Fuego. In *Arqueología de Patagonia: una mirada desde el último confín*, edited by Mónica Salemme, Fernando Santiago, Myriam Álvarez, Ernesto Piana, Martín Vázquez, and Estela Mansur, pp. 119–133. Editorial Utopías, Ushuaia, AR.

Mena, Francisco, and Thomas W. Stafford Jr.

2006 Contexto estratigráfico y fechación directa de esqueletos humanos del Holoceno Temprano en Cueva Baño Nuevo 1 (Patagonia central, Chile). In *Segundo simposio internacional del hombre temprano en América*, edited by José C. Jiménez, Silvia González, José A. Pompa, and Francisco Ortíz, pp. 139–54. INAH, México, DF.

Mena, Francisco, Omar Reyes, Thomas W. Stafford Jr., and John Southon

2003 Early Human Remains from Baño Nuevo-1 Cave, Central Patagonian Andes, Chile. *Quaternary International* 109–110:113–121.

Méndez, César

2013 Terminal Pleistocene/Early Holocene [14]C Dates from Archaeological Sites in Chile: Discussing Critical Chronological Issues for the Initial Peopling of the Region. *Quaternary International* 301:60–73.

Méndez, César, and Omar Reyes

2008 Late Holocene Human Occupation of Patagonian Forests: A Case Study at Cisnes River Basin (44°S, Chile). *Antiquity* 82(317): 560–570.

Méndez, César, Ramiro Barberena, Omar Reyes, and Amalia Nuevo Delaunay

2014 Isotopic Ecology and Human Diets in the Forest-Steppe Ecotone, Aisén Region, Central-Western Patagonia, Chile. *International Journal of Osteoarchaeology* 24(2): 187–201.

Méndez, César, Amalia Nuevo Delaunay, Omar Reyes, Ivana Laura Ozán, Carolina Belmar, and Patricio López

2018 The Initial Peopling of Central Western Patagonia (Southernmost South America): Late Pleistocene through Holocene Site Context and Archaeological Assemblages from Cueva de la Vieja Site. *Quaternary International* 473(B):261–277.

Méndez, César, Omar Reyes, Antonio Maldonado, and Jean Pierre François.

2009 Ser humano y medio ambiente durante la transición Pleistoceno Holoceno en las cabeceras del río Cisnes (~44°S, Aisén norte). In *Arqueología de Patagonia: una mirada desde el último confín*, edited by Mónica Salemme, Fernando Santiago, Myriam Álvarez, Ernesto Piana, Martín Vázquez, and Estela Mansur, pp. 75–83. Editorial Utopías, Ushuaia, AR.

Méndez, César, Omar Reyes, Amalia Nuevo Delaunay, and Catalina Contreras

2010 Criterios para evaluar ocupaciones tempranas en sitios arqueológicos superficiales, Aisén norte, Chile. In *Arqueología Argentina en el bicentenario de la revolución de Mayo*, Tomo 1, edited by Roberto Bárcena and Horacio Chiavazza, pp. 85–90. Sociedad Argentina de Antropología, Mendoza, AR.

Méndez, César, Omar Reyes, Amalia Nuevo Delaunay, and Pablo González

2013 Programa de búsqueda sistemática de evidencias tempranas y hallazgo de una punta de proyectil tipo cola de pescado en alto río Ñirehuao. *Magallania* 41(2):187–196.

Méndez, César, Omar Reyes, Amalia Nuevo Delaunay, Valentina Trejo, Ramiro Barberena, and Héctor Velásquez

2011 Ocupaciones humanas en la margen occidental de Patagonia central: eventos de poblamiento en alto río Cisnes. *Magallania* 39(2):223–242.

Méndez, César, Omar Reyes, Valentina Trejo, and Amalia Nuevo Delaunay

2012 Ocupación humana de alto río Simpson, Aisén (margen occidental de la estepa de Patagonia central) como caso para medir la intensidad de uso de espacios. In *Tendencias teórico-metodológicas y casos de estudio en la arqueología de la Patagonia*, edited by

Atilio F. Zangrando, Ramiro Barberena, Adolfo Gil, Gustavo Neme, Miguel Giardina, Leandro Luna, Clara Otaola, Salvador Paulides, Laura Salgán, and Angélica Tivoli, pp. 193–201. Museo de Historia Natural de San Rafael, Sociedad Argentina de Antropología, Instituto Nacional de Antropología y Pensamiento Latinoamericano, Buenos Aires, AR.

Méndez, César, Omar Reyes, and Héctor Velásquez
2006   Tecnología lítica en el alto río Cisnes (estepa extra andina de la XI Región de Aisén): primeros resultados. *Boletín de la Sociedad Chilena de Arqueología* 39:87–101.

Miotti, Laura
1995   Piedra Museo Locality: A Special Place in the New World. *Current Research in the Pleistocene* 12:37–40.

Miotti, Laura, Dario Hermo, and Enrique Terranova
2010   Fishtail Points, First Evidence of Late-Pleistocene Hunter-Gatherers in Somuncurá Plateau (Río Negro Province, Argentina). *Current Research in the Pleistocene* 27: 22–24.

Miotti, Laura, Enrique Terranova, Ramiro Barberena, Dario Hermo, Martin Giesso, and Michael D. Glascock
2012   Geochemical Sourcing of Obsidian Fishtail Points: Studies for the Somuncurá Plateau (Río Negro, Argentina). In *Southbound: Late Pleistocene Peopling of Latin America*, edited by Laura Miotti, Monica Salemme, Nora Flegenheimer, and Ted Goebel, pp. 127–131. Center for the Study of the First Americans, College Station, TX.

Moran, Emilio F.
1995   Levels of Analysis and Analytical Shifting: Examples from Amazonian Ecosystem Research. In *The Ecosystem Approach in Anthropology*, edited by Emilio F. Moran. University of Michigan Press, Ann Arbor.

Morello, Flavia, Luis A. Borrero, Jimena Torres, Mauricio Massone, Manuel Arroyo, Robert D. McCulloch, Elisa Calás, Marcela J. Lucero, Ismael Martínez, and Gabriel Bahamonde
2009   Evaluando el registro arqueológico de Tierra del Fuego durante el Holoceno temprano y medio. In *Arqueología de la Patagonia: una mirada desde el último confín*, Vol. 2, edited by Mónica Salemme, Fernando Santiago, Myriam Álvarez, Ernesto Piana, Martín Vázquez, and Estela Mansur, pp. 1031–1047. Editorial Utopías, Ushuaia, AR.

Morrow, Juliet E., and Toby A. Morrow
1999   Geographic Variation in Fluted Projectile Points: A Hemispheric Perspective. *American Antiquity* 64(2):215–231.

Nami, Hugo G.
1985–1986 Excavación arqueológica y hallazgo de una punta de proyectil "Fell I" en la Cueva del Medio, seno de Última Esperanza, Chile. Informe Preliminar. *Anales del Instituto de la Patagonia. Serie Ciencias Humanas* 16: 103–109.
1994   Reseña sobre los avances de la arqueología finipleistocénica del extremo sur de Sudamérica. *Chungara: Revista de Antropología Chilena* 26(2):145–163.

Nami, Hugo G., and Toshio Nakamura
1995   Cronología radiocarbónica con AMS sobre muestras de hueso procedentes del sitio Cueva del Medio. *Anales del Instituto de la Patagonia, Serie Ciencias Humanas* 23:125–133.

Nash, Stephen E.
2009   Introduction. In *Readings in Chronometric Analysis: Selections from American Antiquity and Latin American Antiquity, 1935–2006*, edited by Stephen E. Nash, pp. 1–8. SAA Press, Washington, D.C.

Núñez, Lautaro, Martin Grosjean, and Isabel Cartajena
2005   *Ocupaciones humanas y paleoambientes en la puna de Atacama*. Universidad Católica del Norte, Taraxacum, San Pedro de Atacama, CL.

Ortega, Cristina
2011   Geomorfología del área Ñirehuao–Baño Nuevo–Coyhaique Alto. In *Informe proyecto FONDECYT 1090027 año 3*, compiled by César Méndez and Omar Reyes. Report on file, CONICYT, Santiago, CL.

Politis, Gustavo
1991   Fishtail Projectile Points in the Southern Cone of South America: An Overview. In *Clovis: Origins and Adaptations*, edited by Robson Bonnichsen and Karen L. Turnmire, pp. 287–301. Center for the Study of the First Americans, and Oregon State University Press, Corvallis.

Prates, Luciano, Gustavo Politis, and James Steele
2013   Radiocarbon Chronology of the Early Human Occupation of Argentina. *Quaternary International* 301:104–122.

Rademaker, Kurt, Gregory Hodgins, Katherine Moore, Sonia Zarrillo, Christopher Miller,

Gordon R.M. Bromley, Peter Leach, David A. Reid, Willy Yépez Álvarez, and Daniel H. Sandweiss
2014   Paleoindian Settlement of the High-Altitude Peruvian Andes. *Science* 346(6208):466–469.

Reyes, Omar, César Méndez, Francisco Mena, and Mauricio Moraga
2012   The Bioanthropological Evidence of a ca. 10,000 cal BP Ten-Individual Group from Central Patagonia. In *Southbound: Late Pleistocene Peopling of Latin America*, edited by Laura Miotti, Monica Salemme, Nora Flegenheimer, and Ted Goebel, pp. 39–43. Center for the Study of the First Americans, and Texas A&M University Press, College Station, TX.

Reyes, Omar, César Méndez, Valentina Trejo, and Héctor Velásquez
2007a   El Chueco 1: un asentamiento multicomponente en la estepa occidental de Patagonia central (11400 a 2700 años cal. AP., ~44° S). *Magallania* 35(1):61–74.

Reyes, Omar, César Méndez, Héctor Velásquez, and Valentina Trejo
2007b   Ocupaciones humanas tardías en la transición bosque estepa: la localidad de Winchester (curso alto del río Cisnes, XI región de Aisén). *Magallania* 35(2):145–150.

Richardson, James B., III
1981   Modeling the Development of Sedentary Maritime Economies on the Coast of Peru: A Preliminary Statement. *Annals of the Carnegie Museum* 50:139–150.

Rots, Veerle
2003   Towards an Understanding of Hafting: The Macro- and Microscopic Evidence. *Antiquity* 77(298):805–815.

Sade, Kémel
2007   *Cazadores extintos de Aysén continental: propuesta de poblamiento.* Ediciones Ñire Negro, Coyhaique, CL.

Sandweiss, Daniel H., and Kurt Rademaker
2011   El poblamiento del sur peruano: costa y sierra. *Boletín de Arqueología PUCP* 15:275–293.

Santoro, Calogero M., Paula Ugalde, Claudio Latorre, Carolina Salas, Daniela Osorio, Donald Jackson, and Eugenia M. Gayó
2011   Ocupación humana Pleistocénica en el desierto de Atacama. Primeros resultados de la aplicación de un modelo predictivo de investigación interdisciplinaria. *Chungara: Chungara: Revista de Antropología Chilena* 43(número especial 1):357–366.

Schiffer, Michael B.
1996   [1987] *Formation Processes of the Archaeological Record.* University of Utah Press, Salt Lake City.

Strelin, Jorge A., George H. Denton, Marcus J. Vandergoes, Ulysses S. Ninnemann, and Aaron E. Putnam
2011   Radiocarbon Chronologies of the Late Glacial Puerto Bandera Moraines, Southern Patagonian Icefield, Argentina. *Quaternary Science Reviews* 30(19–20):2551–2569.

Suárez, Manuel, Rita de la Cruz, and Michael Bell
2007   *Geología del área Nireguao-Baño Nuevo. Región Aisén del General Carlos Ibáñez del Campo. Carta Geológica de Chile. Serie Geología Básica.* SERNAGEOMIN, Santiago, CL.

Stuiver, Minze, Paula J. Reimer, and Ron W. Reimer
2013   CALIB 7.0.0. Program and electronic document, http://calib.qub.ac.uk/calib/, accessed 13 October 2014.

Titmus, Gene L., and James C. Woods
1986   An Experimental Study of Projectile Point Fracture Patterns. *Journal of California and Great Basin Anthropology* 8(1):37–49.

Velásquez, Héctor, César Méndez, Omar Reyes, Valentina Trejo, Lorena Sanhueza, Daniel Quiroz, and Donald Jackson
2007   Campamentos residenciales tardíos a cielo abierto en el alto río Cisnes (XI Región de Aisén): Appeleg 1 (CIS 009). *Magallania* 35(1):85–98.

Veth, Peter M.
1993   *Islands in the Interior: The Dynamics of Prehistoric Adaptations within the Arid Zone of Australia.* International Monographs in Prehistory, Archaeological Series 3, Ann Arbor, MI.

Villa-Martínez, Rodrigo, Patricio I. Moreno, and Marcela A. Valenzuela.
2012   Deglacial and Postglacial Vegetation Changes on the Eastern Slopes of the Central Patagonian Andes (47°S), *Quaternary Science Reviews* 32:86–99.

Weitzel, Celeste
2012   Broken Stone Tools from Cerro El Sombrero Cima (Tandilia Range, Argentina). In *Southbound: Late Pleistocene Peopling of Latin America*, edited by Laura Miotti, Monica Salemme, Nora Flegenheimer, and Ted Goebel, pp 111–115. Center for the Study of the First Americans, and Texas A&M University Press, College Station, TX.

CHAPTER 4

Early Human Occupation in the Southeastern Plains of South America

Rafael Suárez

Discussion of models for the peopling of the Americas in recent decades has seen the collapse of the Clovis-first model and the emergence of various new attempts to reorganize the scenario (Amick 2017; Borrero 2016; Goebel et al. 2008; Miotti 2006; Stanford and Bradley 2012). Several South American sites have contributed to this change, with conclusive arguments suggesting that human occupation of the Americas precedes 14,200 cal BP (Dillehay 1997; Dillehay et al. 2012; Politis 2008; Suárez 2014). Other researchers have suggested ages exceeding 20,000 cal BP (Collins et al. 2014; Gruhn 1991, 2004, 2005, 2007; Miotti 2006; Stanford and Bradley 2012).

Present evidence suggests that human presence in the Southern Cone of South America was consolidated by approximately 18,000–15,000 cal BP (Miotti 2006; Dillehay et al. 2008, 2015; Politis 2008; Politis et al. 2014, 2016). Current data also show that the initial human dispersal in the Atlantic coast and Uruguay river regions occurred shortly after 14,000 cal BP. Later, between 12,900 and 10,065 cal BP, a Paleoamerican stemmed bifacial tradition emerged on the grasslands with three different techno-complexes, represented by the Fishtail, Tigre, and Pay Paso groups. These groups were adapted to the extensive plains and fluvial environments and are characterized by the presence of wide-stemmed projectile points. During the postglacial, the Pleistocene–Holocene transition, and the Early Holocene, significant climatic, ecological, environmental, and faunistic changes occurred (Behling et al. 2005; Iriondo 1999; Kerber et al. 2014; Prieto 2000; Ubilla et al. 2004; Zárate 2003). These changes directly affected the humans who colonized this region of the continent (Suárez 2003, 2011a, 2015a, 2017; Bueno et al. 2013).

There are two early archaeological sites in the southern region of South America that provide data on human presence during the postglacial period and the Late Pleistocene: Monte Verde (Chile) and Arroyo Seco 2 (Argentina, Figure 4, #1–2). Recently, data from Uruguay have been incorporated in the discussion of sites exceeding 13,200 cal BP.

One of the best-known Paleoamerican sites in South America is Monte Verde (Figure 4.1, #1), in coastal central Chile (Dillehay 1997; Dillehay et al. 2008, 2015; Meltzer et al. 1997). Initial work in the 1980s and 1990s found human evidence dating to 14,600 cal BP (Dillehay 1997; Dillehay et al. 2008). Recently, new excavations in other sectors of the Monte Verde site, as well as in other sites in the area, yielded human artifacts from about 18,000 cal BP (Dillehay et al. 2015). An even earlier occupation (Monte Verde I), dated to approximately 33,000 RCYBP, is presented with reservation and caution by Dillehay (1997:774).

The evidence from Monte Verde is contrary

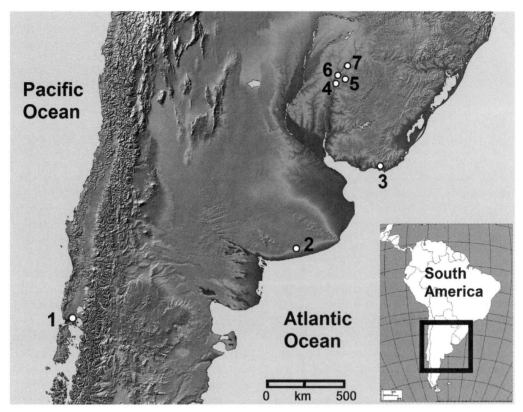

FIGURE 4.1. Main sites cited in the text: (*1*) Monte Verde, Chile; (*2*) Arroyo Seco 2, Argentina; (*3*) Urupez 2, Uruguay; (*4*) Tigre (K87), Uruguay; (*5*) Pay Paso 1, Uruguay; (*6*) Laguna Canosa, Uruguay; (*7*) RS-I-69 Laranjito (Brazil).

to the long-standing paradigm of Late Pleisto-cene archeology and proposed models for ini-tial peopling through North America (Gruhn 2004:31, 2005:202; Dillehay et al. 2008). The very good preservation is quite unusual for an archeological site from the Late Pleistocene. At Monte Verde, researchers recovered perishable objects of wood and bone, chewed and burned medicinal herbs, as well as remains of a num-ber of species of edible land plants and algae (Dillehay et al. 2008). This site has continued to provide important data on previously unknown aspects of human occupation that took place during the end of the Last Glacial Maximum (LGM) and the postglacial, which are poorly known at a continental level.

Presenting research conducted at Arroyo Seco 2, Politis and colleagues (2014) discuss

different issues related to the initial occupation of Pampa for the period between about 14,000 and 13,100 cal BP (Figure 4.1, #2). Their detailed information expands insight into the initial human regional dispersion and includes func-tional analysis of artifacts, faunal and taxonomic studies, environmental evolution, lithic tech-nology, economic use, and chronology. Arroyo Seco 2 is located in the Argentinian Pampa, adja-cent to a stream and lagoon (Politis et al. 2004). The site has been interpreted as a basecamp for multiple activities (Politis 2008; Politis et al. 2016). It is open-air with evidence of multiple occupations (i.e., multicomponent) and con-tains evidence of humans, dated to 14,145–13,812 cal BP, 13,598–13,426 cal BP, and 13,105–12,828 cal BP (Politis and Steele 2014:64–65). A low frequency of artifacts (N = 47) was recovered in

TABLE 4.1. Ages of pre-Fishtail occupations recovered from stratigraphic buried contexts in Uruguay. Calibrated with CALIB 7.0, SHCAL13 (Hogg et al. 2013).

Site	RCYBP	cal BP	Lab. Number	Reference
Urupez	12,000 ± 40	13,998–13,627	Beta 394639	Meneghin 2015
Urupez	11,690 ± 80	13,708–13,292	Beta 211938	Meneghin 2015
Tigre	11,355 ± 30	13,256–13,078	UCIAMS 145430	Suárez 2018
Tigre	11,320 ± 30	13,236–13,057	UCIAMS 145429	Suárez 2017
Tigre	11,315 ± 30	13,208–13,060	UCIAMS 145428	Suárez 2018

the S/Z stratigraphic unit containing the oldest archaeological material (Leipus and Landini 2014).

Bones recovered at the site were of modern fauna such as *Lama guanicoe, Ozotoceros bezoarticus, Rhea americana*, and extinct fauna, including *Megatherium americanum, Equus neogeus, Hippidion sp., Toxodon platensis, Glossotherium robustus*, and *Paleolama wedelli* (Steele and Politis 2009). Pleistocene fauna of nine extinct genera came from five different taxa: *Meghaterium, Glossotherium, Toxodon, Hippidion*, and *Equus* (Salemme 2014). It has been suggested that during the initial period of site occupation, the capture and/or scavenging of large mammals supplemented a diet of rhea, armadillo, and *vizcacha* (Salemme 2014).

The archaeological data from excavations, and chronological evidence over 13,000 cal BP, of buried contexts of early Uruguayan sites was uncertain until a few years ago. However, as it has been recently summarized and discussed (Suárez 2014), it will not be detailed here. Recently, two archaeological sites located in the plains of Uruguay have provided evidence of human occupation between approximately 14,000 and 13,060 cal BP (Table 4.1). The oldest archaeological sites are Urupez 2, with ages of 13,998–13,627 cal BP and 13,708–13,292 cal BP (Figure 4.1, #3; Meneghin 2006, 2015), and the Tigre (K87) site, with three ages between 13,256 and 13,060 cal BP (Figure 4.1, #4; Table 4.1). Such data integrate new information about archaeological sites that exceed 13,060 cal BP in South America (Suárez 2014).

These human occupations are still little known on a regional level, yet they represent a promising starting point in the integration of new data for this period from the plains of Uruguay (Politis et al. 2014; Suárez 2014). Preliminarily, the new chronological and archaeological evidence shows that humans were exploiting the Uruguay River at least around 13,200 cal BP and southern Uruguay at around 14,000 cal BP. The ages of the Urupez 2 and Tigre sites suggest that contemporary human populations occupied the Pampas of Argentina and Uruguay plains after 14,000 cal BP.

Other sites had assorted validation problems and were rejected as evidence for an occupation prior to 13,000 cal BP. For example, the Y58 Isla de Arriba site, excavated during an archaeological salvage project, yielded an age of 11,200 ± 500 RCYBP (Gif 4412; MEC 1989). However, the charcoal used to determine the age and the corresponding archaeological material were not associated within the same archaeological context on a horizontal level. A "series of inferior lithic levels" was recovered at 5.37 m deep, formed by three assemblages of flaking remains, while the charcoal was obtained at 5.69 m deep. There is, therefore, a difference of 0.37 m between the archaeological material and the charcoal. In addition, the excavation was done at arbitrary levels of 10 cm. On the other hand, the age was obtained from scattered charcoal fragments, and the degree of uncertainty is too high. Thus, Y58 Isla de Arriba should be considered only with extreme caution, as the evidence from the site does not meet the high standards of modern research for the early prehistory of America.

Two other sites, RS-I-50 and RS-Q-2 in southern Brazil (Miller 1987), were rejected as pre-Fishtail sites because of the inconsistency of the data originally presented to support them (Suárez 2014). The association of artifacts and

FIGURE 4.2. The grasslands of Uruguay.

Glossotherium robustum in RS-I-50 was not demonstrated in an archaeological excavation. Rather, it derived from the stratigraphic profile in a natural exposure in a ravine. Several Brazilian authors have questioned the association of artifacts with extinct fauna at the RS-I-50 site. Dias (2004:258) argues that the remains of Pleistocene megafauna are derived from fluvial entrainment, and the stone material is the product of "flaking by natural processes" and are actually geofacts, not products of human activity. Something similar may have happened at the RS-Q-2 site (Paso de la Cruz 2), on the Quaraí or Cuareim river, where a date of 15,584 cal BP (12,690 ± 100 RCYBP, SI-2351) would not be associated with cultural material or lithic artifacts (Dias 2004: Dias and Jacobus 2001; Milder 1994).

It has been recently suggested that there was human presence in southern Uruguay prior to the onset of the LGM, that is, about 32,000 cal BP (Fariña et al. 2014, Fariña 2015). Similar ages were proposed more than 50 years ago for sites and lithic materials recovered in the Uruguay plains (Ibarra Grasso 1964; Campá 1962).

Both past and current proposals have serious methodological and interpretative errors because all are based on false assumptions. One proponent describes Mousterian artifacts made by Neanderthal-like hominids (Ibarra Grasso 1964).

More recently, the simple dating of bones from Pleistocene fauna with purported cut marks—in a paleontological site in Arroyo Vizcaíno—is used to situate human presence at 32,000 cal BP (Fariña 2015). The Vizcaíno site has a number of problems, both methodological and interpretative. The main problem in relation to human presence at the site is related to formation processes and alteration of the archaeological record, ambiguity of the record, weakness of the evidence presented, and interpretation of natural marks as anthropogenic (Suárez et al. 2014; Borrero 2015, 2016). The context is a hydraulic concentration of bones in clay-like sediments with boulders, cobblestone, and pebbles at the bottom of the current stream bed where fluvial processes occur. Such processes include traction, friction, mixing, fragmentation, sedimentation, and resedimentation of different particles, including bones and lithic material (Suárez et al. 2014). On the site, bones of the following fauna were recovered: *Lestodon* sp., *Glossotherium robustum, Mylodon darwinii, Glyptodon* cf. *clavipes, Panochthus tuberculatus, Doedicurus clavicaudatus, Toxodon platensis, Hippidion principale, Stegomastodon* sp., one adult deer (*Cervidae* indet.), and *Smilodon populator*. Meanwhile, a single lithic artifact about 2.5 cm long was recovered (Fariña et al. 2014).

Of course, anyone conducting work on an early archaeological site should make every effort to recover as much evidence of human presence as possible. In that sense, the work conducted at Arroyo Vizcaíno was unsystematic in collecting lithic material, which reveals larger methodological errors and biases. The researchers themselves make this qualification: "Although during the fieldwork no systematic effort was made to collect lithic material...." (Fariña et al. 2014:5). The presence of more than 1,000 bones and 27 individuals does not fit the models of differential transport of vertebrate bones by humans, despite the fact that selection by humans is supposed to be the cause of accumulation. The bone collection from the Vizcaíno site includes many from one species (*Lestodon*) and few from many other species, which makes little sense in terms of human hunting activities. Either most of the *Lestodon amaratus* bones were transported to the site, which is absurd, or most of the other two species of ground sloths and other large animals represented by a few bones were transported elsewhere, which is also absurd (Suárez et al. 2014). Thus, the ages around 30,000 cal BP from the Vizcaíno site are not the problem, for it is not an issue of chronology. Rather, the main problem with this site is one of archaeological deficiency and misinterpretation (Borrero 2015; Suárez et al. 2014).

Technological and Cultural Reorganization during the Late Pleistocene

To date, our own research in Uruguay has provided a new understanding about different chronological, stratigraphic, archaeological, and paleoenvironmental aspects of the initial human occupations and about how they faced the sudden climatic changes during the unstable climate at the end of the Pleistocene and the beginning of the Holocene (Suárez 2011a, 2015a, 2017; Suárez et al. 2018). Methodologically, we have focused on obtaining data from archaeological excavations using strict stratigraphic controls making it possible to generate a dataset of 52 radiocarbon ages for different early sites in northern Uruguay (Suárez 2011a; Suárez et al. 2018). This has allowed us to distinguish a degree of cultural diversity not previously registered, with at least three human groups for the period between approximately 12,900 and 10,200 cal BP (Tables 4.2–4). Thus, the archaeological record of the plains of southeastern South America reveals a "tradition" of Paleoamerican stemmed points composed of at least three cultural groups: Fishtail, Tigre, and Pay Paso.

Today, we know that the colonization of southeastern South America presented a greater cultural diversity, with a succession of human groups interacting throughout that landscape during post-Fishtail times (Suárez 2015a, 2017). The archaeological excavation conducted at the Pay Paso 1 and Tigre sites (Figure 4.1, #5–6) identified a succession of at least three human discrete occupations situated chronologically during the Pleistocene–Holocene transition (Suárez 2011a, 2015b). While progress has been made in the definition of new projectile point forms, such as Tigre and Pay Paso, there are still gaps in relation in our understanding, namely, the group economy, fauna and/or prey hunted, and other vegetal resources that may have been used by such people. The same applies to the Fishtail groups from the Uruguayan plains: we still ignore basic aspects of their culture such as the economic resources they employed. Future research should be aimed at bridging these gaps.

Fishtail Groups

The Fishtail groups (ca. 12,900–12,200 cal BP) are widely distributed across the Southern Cone, from the Pacific to the Atlantic coast of South America. In the twentieth century, Fishtail points in South America were considered reliable evidence of the oldest human groups. How-

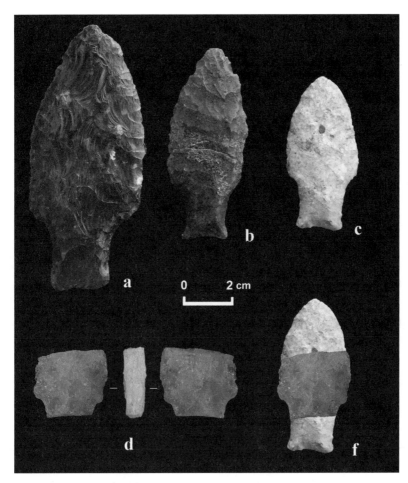

FIGURE 4.3. Fishtail points: (*a–c*) Fishtail point from surface sites; (*d*) midsection of a Fishtail point from excavations at the Tigre site, dated 12,640–12,077 cal BP (10,595, 10,580, and 10,510 RCYBP, see Table 4.2); (*f*) overlay of a complete Fishtail and midsection of another Fishtail (*d*) recovered in excavations at the Tigre site.

ever, we know today that they were neither the first nor the only ones. Ever since Fishtail points were found in association with Pleistocene fauna in stratigraphy at the Fell Cave (Bird 1938), they have been an icon of ancient human occupation throughout South America (Bird 1969; Flegenheimer et al. 2014; Mayer-Oakes 1986; Bosh et al. 1980, Suárez 2000, 2009, Nami 1987; Politis 1991). But Fishtail groups were not the first to scatter across South America. Although they adapted very successfully to various ecosystems and environments, other groups were exploring different regions even before the Fishtail groups appeared and dispersed.

Fishtail points (Figure 4.3) exhibit a large variety of sizes and morphology, not only between different regions of South America, such as Ecuador, Pampa-Patagonia, Uruguay, and Brazil (Mayer-Oakes 1986; Flegenheimer et al. 2003, 2014; Suárez 2011a) but also within same regions (Suárez 2001; Flegenheimer et al. 2014). In Uruguay, radiocarbon dated stratified sites with Fishtail points are very scarce (Table 4.2). At the Tigre site, I have recently recovered a midsection of a Fishtail point (Figure 4.3, d) dated by three radiocarbon (AMS) ages between 12,640–12,555 cal BP (10,595, 10,580, and 10,510 RCYBP; Table 4.2). At the Urupez site, another

TABLE 4.2. Ages of Fishtail points recovered from stratigraphic buried contexts in Uruguay. Calibrated with CALIB 7.0, SHCAL13 (Hogg et al. 2013). All ages obtained from charcoal samples.

Site	RCYBP	cal BP	Lab. Number	Reference
Urupez	10,800 ± 30	12,733–12,667	Beta 380727	Meneghin 2015
Urupez	10,800 ± 40	12,736–12,659	Beta 381967	Meneghin 2015
Urupez	10,680 ± 60	12,713–12,436	Beta 165076	Meneghin 2006
Tigre	10,595 ± 25	12,640–12,431	UCIAMS 125379	Suárez 2017b
Tigre	10,580 ± 50	12,658–12,320	UCIAMS 125393	Suárez 2017b
Tigre	10,510 ± 40	12,555–12,101	UCIAMS 145434	Suárez 2017b

FIGURE 4.4. Recycled Fishtail points. Note the rounded shape of the blade, not suitable for use as a weapon.

Fishtail point found in a buried context was dated by three samples at 12,733–12,436 cal BP (Meneghin 2004, 2015). In contrast with the limited presence of these points in stratigraphy, approximately one hundred points were found on the surface in various archaeological sites (Nami 2007; Politis 1991; Suárez 2000, 2001, 2006, 2009, 2011a, 2015a).

Five blades and blades cores (one pyramidal) were recovered at the base of stratum U2a of Component 1 of the Pay Paso 1 site, dated by four samples to 12,800–12,700 cal BP (Suárez 2015b). A detailed description of these artifacts has been presented in other publications (Suárez 2011a, 2011b, 2015a). In another archaeological surface context from northern Uruguay, macroblade tools have been recovered as well (Suárez 2015a:Figure 5).

The Fishtail technology can be defined as a versatile technology, whose artifacts could have been repurposed and had further use beyond hunting weapons (Suárez 2006, 2015a, 2017). Many so-identified points have a very rounded blade tip and asymmetric blade edges that would have been ineffective in penetrating the hide and connective tissues of prey animals. In some instances, once projectile points were no longer effective in hunting activities, they may have been modified to other functional forms such as stemmed knives (Figure 4.4). In other cases, large Fishtail points, originally designed as hafted knives (Suárez 2015a:Figure 9A), could be easily transformed into weapons meant for hunting, depending on task requirements. Conversely, some weaponry points that had lost their effectiveness as projectile points likely finished their utile lives as knives or cutting artifacts.

The research conducted in the Middle Uru-

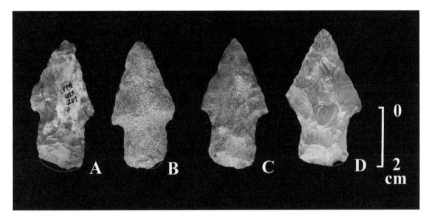

FIGURE 4.5. Tigre points from northern Uruguay: (*A*) Pay Paso 1, component 2, 12,008–11,700 cal BP; (*B–C*) Pay Paso 1 (surface); (*D*) Laguna Canosa site, 11,200 cal BP.

guay River basin, at the Pay Paso 1 and Tigre sites (Figure 4.1), suggests—based on stratigraphic, chronological, and techno-morphological observations of artifacts—the existence of two point designs during the Pleistocene–Holocene transition (Suárez 2011a). This allows us to distinguish two human groups that explored the region during the initial stages of occupation (Suárez 2015a, 2017). The names Tigre and Pay Paso for the points refer directly to the sites where the artifacts were first dated by ¹⁴C.

Tigre Groups

During the Pleistocene–Holocene transition, when regional climate changed from cold/arid to more humid/warmer conditions (Markgraf 1989; Prieto 2000) and the fauna of the Pleistocene began its decline toward extinction in the early Holocene (Politis et al. 2003; Suárez and Santos 2010), changes in the weaponry of human groups are recorded for this part of the continent. Thus, Fishtail technology is replaced by Tigre technology. The rapid climatic, ecological, and faunal changes apparently coincide with the emergence of the new Tigre points and indicate a technological reorganization in the design of weaponry and associated technology. The points continue to have a wide stem. However, blade shape becomes triangular, while the contour of the edges and the base of the stem are modified. Tigre points (Figure 4.5) have a wide stem, straight or slightly convex stem sides, usually very well-defined shoulders and can be barbed, with a short or long triangular blade, a convex base, thinned by retouch, and complete bifacial thinning.

They were discovered buried at four stratified and dated sites (Tigre, Pay Paso 1, Laguna de Canosa in Uruguay, and Laranjito in southern Brazil; Figure 4.1, #7). Most points were reshaped and renewed. In Uruguay and southern Brazil, radiocarbon ages place the Tigre points between 12,000 and 11,100 cal BP (Table 4.3; Suárez 2017; Suárez et al. 2018). These points have been found on the surface in northern and central Uruguay and in different states of southern Brazil (Santa Catarina, Rio Grande do Sul, and Paraná). The mouth of the Uruguay River was apparently the southern boundary for the territory of the Tigre groups in southeastern South America.

Pay Paso Groups

Before the year 11,000 cal BP, Pay Paso groups emerged in the region of the Uruguay River. Stratigraphic, chronological, and archaeological evidence of the multicomponent Pay Paso 1 site enabled identification of a type of projectile point in use around the Uruguay River basin between 11,081 and 10,200 cal BP (Table 4.4). Pay Paso points were found buried at Tigre and Pay Paso 1. More than forty such points were recovered in other archaeological sites along the middle Uruguay and Cuareim Rivers. Such

TABLE 4.3. Chronology of Tigre cultural techno-complex. Ages of Tigre points recovered from stratigraphic buried contexts in Uruguay. Note: n/i = no information. Calibrated with CALIB 7.0, SHCAL13 (Hogg et al. 2013). All ages are on charcoal.

Site	RCYBP	cal BP	Lab. Number	Reference
Pay Paso 1	10,205 ± 35	12,008–11,697	UCIAMS 21632	Suárez 2011a
Pay Paso 1	10,180 ± 20	11,974–11,859	UCIAMS 21634	Suárez 2011a
Pay Paso 1	10,115 ± 25	11,795–11,785	UCIAMS 21633	Suárez 2011a
Tigre (K87)	10,075 ± 30	11,747–11,336	UCIAMS145431	Suárez et al. 2018
Pay Paso 1	9890 ± 90	11,700–11,671	n/i	Austral 1995
Laguna Canosa	9730 ± 30	11,213–11,071	UCIAMS 27739	Suárez 2011a
Tigre (K87)	9710 ± 130	11,313–10,592	UCIAMS145435	Suárez et al. 2018
Tigre (K87)	9615 ± 20	11,089–10,749	UCIAMS125385	Suárez et al. 2018

FIGURE 4.6. Pay Paso points: (A) Río Tacuarembó Grande (surface); (B) from component 3 of Pay Paso 1, 11,081–10,065 cal BP; (C) middle Río Negro archaeological region.

points also appear on the middle Negro River, the Tacuarembó Grande River, and in archaeological collections of central Uruguay and southern Brazil (Corteletti 2008).

The design and main techno-morphological characteristics of the Pay Paso points (Figure 4.6) include a short stem, deeply concave stem base, divergent concave stem sides expanded toward the base, convex or straight blade edges, regular laminar blade retouch, and careful basal thinning of the stem shown by triangular and short flake scars. The Pay Paso points, like the earlier Fishtail and Tigre points, underwent intensive maintenance and renewal. Ten AMS dates place these points in the Early Holocene, between 11,081 and 10,065 cal BP (Table 4.4).

Recent Advances

Identification of different groups in southeastern South America between 14,000 and 10,000 cal BP can initiate a discussion about cultural diversity. As noted, recent evidence has shown human occupation between 14,000 and 13,000 cal BP in the north and south of Uruguay. We have only started to obtain chronological and cultural data about these groups. Very little is known about basic aspects of their material and technological culture. Neither do we know the economic base and possible relations and connections they might have maintained with contemporaneous human groups from other regions of southern South America, such as those implied by the evidence found at Arroyo Seco 2

TABLE 4.4. Chronology of Pay Paso cultural techno-complex. Ages of Pay Paso points recovered from stratigraphic buried contexts in Uruguay. Calibrated with CALIB 7.0, SHCAL13 (Hogg et al. 2013). All samples were charcoal.

Site	RCYBP	cal BP	Lab. Number	Location
Pay Paso 1	9585 ± 25	11,081–10,928	UCIAMS 21641	Río Cuareim
Pay Paso 1	9555 ± 25	11,070–10,951	UCIAMS 21642	Río Cuareim
Pay Paso 1	9550 ± 20	11,069–10,953	UCIAMS 21647	Río Cuareim
Pay Paso 1	9545 ± 20	11,068–10,954	UCIAMS 21635	Río Cuareim
Pay Paso 1	9545 ± 20	11,068–10,954	UCIAMS 21646	Río Cuareim
Pay Paso 1	9525 ± 20	11,064–11,024	UCIAMS 21640	Río Cuareim
Pay Paso 1	9525 ± 20	11,064–11,024	UCIAMS 21638	Río Cuareim
Pay Paso 1	9280 ± 200	11,124–9,901	Uru-248	Río Cuareim
Pay Paso 1	9120 ± 40	10,298–10,176	Beta-156973	Río Cuareim
Pay Paso 1	8570 ± 150	10,119–10,065	Uru 246	Río Cuareim

and Monte Verde. While this preliminary data needs confirmation by further research, it opens a new phase in the study of early occupations in southeastern South America, showing that prior to the dispersion of Fishtail groups, people were already present here. Also, this new information shows that, methodologically, the research path is through systematic work and archaeological excavation, regardless of the data that can be obtained from archaeological collections. It can be suggested that about 1,000 years before Fishtail groups emerged, humans were already exploring this region of South America.

The wide distribution of Fishtail bifacial technology throughout virtually all of South America, from the Atlantic to the Pacific coast (Nuñez et al. 1994; Méndez and Jackson 2015; Flegenheimer et al. 2014; Politis 1991; Suárez 2015a) and from Ecuador to Tierra del Fuego (Jackson 2002; Mayer-Oakes 1986; Massone 2004), could have been facilitated by earlier, preexisting populations that rapidly adopted this new technology. This may partly explain the wide range of environments with records of Fishtail occupations. We have no data regarding the technology used by the pre-Fishtail groups that would allow us to assess the costs of abandoning their technology. Still, if that were so, we should expect that during the initial Fishtail period (ca. 12,900–12,700 cal BP) there would be evidence for an earlier technology. Later, between 12,900 and 10,000 cal BP, the record indicates the presence of different human groups—groups with

bifacial technology, including stemmed projectile points, preforms, knives, and different types of bifacial artifacts.

Therefore, we do not really know what we are looking for. The extraregional evidence may help us. If we consider that the points of Monte Verde II were dated to 14,600–14,200 cal BP (Dillehay et al. 2008) and Monte Verde is 1,500 km away from Uruguay, we can guide the search toward similar artifacts in Uruguay. Dates from the Urupez 2 site would be just 200 years later than the most recent ages obtained for the Monte Verde artifacts.

The Andes were not a barrier for the people of Monte Verde. They were able to cross into the Patagonian steppes in Argentina, and those people themselves came from distant places, as already suggested (Dillehay et al. 2015:22). The exploration of southern Patagonia and Tierra del Fuego has been linked to human groups related to Monte Verde (Borrero 1999). Thus, there might have been a network of groups that circulated over long distances and transmitted knowledge and technology at an extraregional level during this period (ca. 14,600–13,200 cal BP), as happened with the emergence of the Fishtail groups. In this sense, different groups from the Patagonian steppe could have made it into periglacial areas (such as Monte Verde; Dillehay et al. 2015) and also into the Pampas of Argentina (such as Arroyo Seco 2). Eventually, these networks expanded into areas where resources abounded such as present-day Uruguay.

There is a significant change in technology with the emergence of the Fishtail techno-complex when a new design of projectile points begins to expand across the Southern Cone around 13,000 cal BP. The evidence of high residential mobility during this period is associated with a larger number of sites, indicating an increase in population. These human groups shared technological knowledge such as bifacial reduction and the same design of the stem and blade as that of Fishtail points. Furthermore, people began to use colorful and better-quality raw materials, including translucent agate, jasper, opal, chalcedony, chert, and silicified sandstone, with different transport strategies from sources to residential camps (Flegenheimer et al. 2003; Suárez 2011b). Fishtail technology features high-maintenance recycling, retooling, resharpening, and hafting (Politis 1991; Suárez 2003, 2011a).

The emergence of the Fishtail complex, increase in population density, and technological innovation (stemmed points) is reflected in the increase in the number of sites for this period. Fishtail points become frequent in widespread regions of South America, such as Ecuador, northern Peru, southern Brazil, northern and southern Chile, and the Pampa and Patagonia in Argentina and Uruguay. Technological innovation also diversifies in the preexisting human populations in these regions, which also coincides with an improvement in climatic conditions. In Uruguay and southern Brazil, the post-Fishtail occupations are represented by two other different types of projectile points: Tigre and Pay Paso.

Final Remarks

The most reliable and well-known ancient sites are located on the Pacific and the Atlantic watersheds: Monte Verde and Arroyo Seco 2. Both have good datasets. For more than 50 years, it has been argued that the Fishtail complex was the earliest evidence of the first Americans in the Southern Cone. Now we know that the southern region of the continent was populated before the emergence of the Fishtail complex in South America and the Clovis complex in North America. There are also post-Fishtail occupations emerging in Uruguay. At approximately 12,000–11,200 cal BP, on the middle Uruguay River, a social and technological reorganization occurred, along with the emergence of the Tigre techno-complex. The advent of the Tigre groups coincided with the advent of warmer and wetter climatic conditions and the beginning of the Holocene. By 11,080 cal BP, weaponry transformations had occurred in the region, including the production of the Pay Paso points, a regionally distinctive point style for the Early Holocene. The makers of Tigre and Pay Paso points are two examples of early cultures that adapted to the environmental changes of the Pleistocene–Holocene transition in southeastern South America.

Therefore, current evidence indicates that small populations, with an unsophisticated flaked stone technology and a foraging economy, were exploiting different ecosystems in the Southern Cone around 15,000 years ago. The areas related to the Pacific coastal plain, the open plains of the Pampa, and the Patagonia steppe are all highly productive regions, which would have attracted people roaming the Southern Cone during the Late Pleistocene.

The appearance of the pre-Fishtail, Fishtail, Tigre, and Pay Paso groups indicates that there was a regional reorganization and demonstrates consecutive cultural changes during the postglacial, the Pleistocene–Holocene transition, and the Early Holocene in present-day Uruguay, southern Brazil, and possibly west Argentina. Cultural readjustments are associated with the emergence of different styles of projectile points and technologies during the early prehistory of the region.

References

Amick, D.
2017 Evolving Views on the Pleistocene Colonization of North America. *Quaternary International* 431(B):125–151.

Austral, A.
1995 Los Cazadores del sitio Pay Paso hace 10,000 años. In *Arqueología del Uruguay*, edited by M. Consens, J. López, and C. Curbelo, pp. 212–218. AUA, Montevideo, UY.

Behling, H., V. Pillar V., and S. G. Bauermann
2005 Late Quaternary Grassland (Campos), Gallery Forest, Fire and Climate Dynamics, Studied by Pollen, Charcoal and Multivariate Analysis of the São Francisco de Assis Core in Western Rio Grande do Sul (Southern Brazil). *Review of Palaeobotany and Palynology* 133(3–4):235–248.

Bird, J.
1969 A Comparison of South Chilean and Ecuadorian "Fishtail" Projectile Points. *Kroeber Society Anthropological Papers* 40:52–71.

Borrero, L.
1999 The Prehistoric Exploration and Colonization of Fuego-Patagonia. *Journal of World Prehistory* 13(3):321–355.
2015 Con lo mínimo: los debates sobre el poblamiento de América del Sur. *InterSecciones en Antropología* 16(1):5–14.
2016 Ambiguity and Debates on the Early Peopling of South America. *PaleoAmerica* 2(1):11–21.

Bosch, A; J. Femenías, and A. Olivera
1980 [1974] Dispersión de las puntas de proyectil líticas pisciformes en el Uruguay. In *Actas del tercer congreso nacional de arqueología. Cuarto encuentro de arqueología del litoral*, pp. 245–261. Centro Estudios Arqueológicos. Montevideo, UY.

Bueno, L., A. Dias, and J. Steele
2013 The Late Pleistocene/Early Holocene Archaeological Record in Brazil: A Geo-Referenced Database. *Quaternary International* 301:74–93.

Campá, R.
1962 La industria lítica más antigua de América del sur. *Amerindia* 1:107–113.

Collins, Michael B., Dennis J. Stanford, Darrin L. Lowery, and Bruce A. Bradley
2014 North America before Clovis: Variance in Temporal/Spatial Cultural Patterns, 27,000–13,000 cal yr BP. In *Paleoamerican Odyssey*, edited by Kelly E. Graf, C. V. Ketron, and Michael R. Waters, pp. 521–539. Center for the Study of the First Americans and Texas A&M University Press, College Station, TX.

Corteletti, Rafael
2008 *Patrimonio arqueológico de Caxias do Sul.* Editora Nova Prova, Porto Alegre, BR.

Dias, Adriana
2004 Diversificar para poblar: el contexto arqueológico brasileño en la transición Pleistoceno–Holoceno. *Complutum* 15:249–263.

Dias, Adriana, and André Jacobus
2001 The Antiquity of the Peopling of Southern Brazil. *Current Research in the Pleistocene* 18:17–19.

Dillehay, Tom
1997 *Monte Verde: A Late Pleistocene Settlement in Chile*, Vol. 2. Smithsonian Institution, Washington, D.C.

Dillehay, Tom, D. Bonavia, S. Goodbred, M. Pino, V. Vasquez, T. Tham, W. Conklin, et al.
2012 Chronology, Mound-Building and Environment at Huaca Prieta, Coastal Peru, from 13,700 to 4,000 Years Ago. *Antiquity* 86:48–70.

Dillehay, Tom, Carlos Ocampo, José Saavedra, Andre Oliveira Sawakuchi, Rodrigo M. Vega, Mario Pino, Michael B. Collins, et al.
2015 New Archaeological Evidence for an Early Human Presence at Monte Verde, Chile. *PLoS One* 10(11):e0141923. doi:10.1371/journal.pone.0141923.

Dillehay, Tom, C. Ramírez, M. Pino, J. Rossen, and D. Pino-Navarro
2008 Monte Verde: Seaweed, Food, Medicine, and the Peopling of South America. *Science* 320(5877):784–786.

Fariña, Richard
2015 Bone Surface Modification, Reasonable Certainty, and Human Antiquity in the Americas: The Case of the Arroyo del Vizcaíno Site. *American Antiquity* 80(1):193–200.

Fariña, Richard, P. S. Tambusso, L. Varela, A. Czerwonogora, M. Di Giacomo, M. Musso, R. Bracco, and A. Gascue
2014 Arroyo del Vizcaíno, Uruguay: A Fossil-Rich 30-ka-Old Megafaunal Locality with Cut-Marked Bones. *Proceedings of the Royal Society B* 281(1774):1–6.

Flegenheimer, N., C. Bayón, M. Valente, J. Baeza, and J. Femenías
2003   Long Distance Tool Stone Transport in the Argentine Pampas. *Quaternary International* 109–110:49–64.

Flegenheimer, Nora, Laura Miotti, and Natalia Mazzia
2014   Rethinking Early Objects and Landscapes in the Southern Cone: Fishtail-Point Concentrations in the Pampas and Northern Patagonia. In *Paleomaerican Odyssey*, edited by K. Graf, C. Ketron, C., and M. Waters, pp. 359–376. Center for the Study of the First Americans and Texas A&M University Press, College Station, TX.

Goebel, Ted., Michael Waters, and Dennis H. O'Rourke
2008   The Late Pleistocene Dispersal of Modern Humans in the Americas. *Science* 319(5869): 1497–1502.

Gruhn, Ruth
1991   Stratified Radiocarbon-Dated Archaeological Sites of Clovis Age and Older in Brazil. In *Clovis Origins and Adaptations*, edited by R. Bonnichsen and K. L. Turnmire, pp. 283–287. Center for the Study of the First Americans, Oregon State University, Corvallis.
2004   Current Archaeological Evidence of Late-Pleistocene Settlement of South America. In *New Perspectives on the First Americans*, edited by B. T. Lepper and R. Bonnichsen, pp. 27–34. Center for the Study of the First Americans and Texas A&M University Press, College Station, TX.
2005   The Ignored Continent: South America in Models of Earliest American Prehistory. In *Paleoamerican Origins: Beyond Clovis*, edited by R. Bonnichsen, B. T. Lepper, D. Stanford, and M. Waters, pp. 199–208. Center for the Study of the First Americans and Texas A&M University Press, College Station, TX.
2007   The Earliest Reported Archaeological Sites in South America. *Mammoth Trumpet* 23(1):14–18.

Ibarra Grasso, Dick E.
1964   Las culturas paleolíticas Suramericanas. *Amerindia* 2:21–36.

Iriondo, Martín
1999   Climatic Changes in the South American Plains: Records of a Continent-Scale Oscillation. *Quaternary International*, 57–58:83–86.

Jackson, Donald
2002   *Los instrumentos líticos de los primeros cazadores de Tierra del Fuego*. Colección Ensayos y Estudios. Ril Editores, Santiago, CL.

Kerber, L., V. Gregis-Pitana, A. M. Ribeiro, A. Schmaltz-Hsiou, and E. V. Oliveira
2014   Late Pleistocene Vertebrates from Touro Passo Creek (Touro Passo Formation) Southern Brazil: A Review. *Revista Mexicana de Ciencias Geológicas* 31(2):248–259.

Leipus, María S., and Marcela C. Landini
2014   Materias primas y tecnología: un estudio comparativo del material lítico. In *Estado actual de las investigaciones en el sitio Arroyo Seco 2*, edited by G. Politis, M. A. Gutiérrez, and C. Scabuzzo, pp. 179–227. Serie Monográfica INCUAPA 5. Olavarría, AR.

Markgraf, V.
1989   Paleoclimates in Central and South America since 18,000 BP Based in Pollen and Lake Levels Records. *Quaternary Science Reviews* 8:1–24.

Massone, M.
2004   *Los cazadores después del hielo*. Dirección de Bibliotecas, Archivos y Museos, Santiago, CL.

Mayer-Oakes, W. J.
1986   El Inga: A Paleoindian Site in the Sierra of Northern Ecuador. *Transactions of the American Philosophical Society* 76(4).

MEC (Ministerio de Educación y Cultura)
1989   *Misión de rescate arqueológico de Salto Grande*, Vol. 2. Montevideo, UY.

Meltzer, David J., Donald K. Grayson, Gerardo Ardila, Alan Barker, Dena Dincauze, Vance Haynes, Franciso Mena, Lautaro Núñez, and Dennis J. Stanford
1997   On the Pleistocene Antiquity of Monte Verde, Southern Chile. *American Antiquity* 62(4):659–663.

Méndez, César, and Donald Jackson
2015   Terminal Pleistocene Lithic Technology and Use of Space in Central Chile. *Chungara: Revista de Antropología Chilena* 47(1):53–65.

Meneghin, Ugo
2004   Urupez. Primer registro radiocarbónico (C-14) para un yacimiento con puntas líticas pisciformes del Uruguay. *Orígenes* 2. Fundación Arqueología Uruguaya, Montevideo.
2006   Un nuevo registro radiocarbónico (C-14) en el yacimiento Urupez II, Maldonado, Uruguay. *Orígenes* 5. Fundación Arqueología Uruguaya, Montevideo.

2015   Secuencia cronoestratigráfica de Urupez II. Nuevas dataciones radiométricas. *Orígenes* 13. Fundación Arqueología Uruguay, Montevideo.

Milder, Saul
1994   A fase Ibicuí: uma revisão arqueológica, cronológica e estratigráfica. Master's thesis. Instituto de Filosofia e Ciências Humanas, PUCRS, Porto Alegre, BR.

Miller, E.
1987   Pesquisas arqueológicas paleoindígenas no Brasil ocidental. *Estudios Atacameños* 8:37–61.

Miotti, Laura
2006   La fachada Atlántica como puerta de ingreso alternativa de la colonización de América del Sur durante la transición Pleistoceno/Holoceno. In *2° Simposio Internacional el hombre temprano en América*, edited by J. C. Jiménez et al., pp. 156–188. INAH, México, D.F.

Nami, Hugo
1987   Cueva del Medio: perspectivas arqueológicas para la Patagonia austral. *Anales del Instituto de la Patagonia* 25:151–185.
2007   Research in the Middle Río Negro Basin (Uruguay) and the Paleoindian Occupation of the Southern Cone. *Current Anthropology* 48(1):164–174.

Núñez, Lautaro, Jaime Varela, R. Casamiquela, V. Schippacasse, H. Niemeyer, and C. Villagran
1994   Cuenca de Taguatagua en Chile: el ambiente del Pleistoceno superior y ocupaciones humanas. *Revista Chilena de Historia Natural* 64(4):503–519.

Politis, G.
1991   Fishtail Projectile Points in the Southern Cone of South America: An Overview. In *Clovis: Origins and Adaptations*, edited by R. Bonnichsen and K. Turnmire, pp. 287–301. Center for the Study of the First Americans, Oregon State University, Corvallis.
2008   The Pampas and Campos of South America. In *Handbook of South American Archaeology*, edited by H. Silverman and W. Isbell, pp. 235–260. Springer, New York.

Politis, Gustavo, and James Steele
2014   Cronología radiocarbónica. In *Estado Actual de las investigaciones en el sitio Arroyo Seco 2*, edited by G. Politis, M. Gutiérrez, and C. Scabuzzo, pp. 57–66. Serie Monográfica 5. INCUAPA, Universidad Centro de la Provincia, Buenos Aires, AR.

Politis, Gustavo, Eileen Johnson, María Gutierrez, and William T. Hartwell
2003   Survival of Pleistocene Fauna: New Radiocarbon Dates on Organic Sediments from La Moderna (Pampean Region, Argentina). In *Where the South Winds Blow: Ancient Evidence for Paleo South Americans*, edited by L. Miotti, M. Salemme, and N. Flegenheimer, pp. 45–50. Center for the Study of the First Americans and Texas A&M University Press, College Station, TX.

Politis, Gustavo, María Gutiérrez, D. J. Rafuse, and A. Blasi
2016   The Arrival of *Homo sapiens* into the Southern Cone at 14,000 Years Ago. *PloS One* 11(9):e0162870. doi:10.1371/journal.pone .0162870.

Politis, Gustavo, María Gutiérrez, and Clara Scabuzzo (editors)
2014   *Estado actual de las investigaciones en el sitio Arroyo Seco 2*. Buenos Aires, Universidad del Centro de la Provincia de Buenos Aires, AR.

Politis, Gustavo, Pablo G. Messineo, and Cristian A. Kaufmann
2004   El poblamiento temprano de las llanuras pampeanas de Argentina y Uruguay. *Complutum* 15:207–224.

Prieto, Aldo
2000   Vegetational History of the Late Glacial–Holocene Transition in the Grassland of Eastern Argentina. *Palaeogeography, Palaeoclimatology, Palaeoecology* 157:167–188.

Salemme, Mónica
2014   Zooarqueología y paleoambientes. In Estado Actual de las investigaciones en el sitio Arroyo Seco 2, edited by G. Politis, M. Gutiérrez, and C. Scabuzzo, pp. 67–96.. Serie Monográfica 5. INCUAPA, Universidad Centro de la Provincia, Buenos Aires, AR.

Stanford, D., and B. Bradley
2012   *Across Atlantic Ice: The Origin of America's Clovis Culture*. University of California Press, Berkeley.

Steele, James, and Gustavo Politis
2009   AMS ^{14}C Dating of Early Human Occupation of Southern South America. *Journal of Archaeological Science* 36(2):419–429.

Suárez, Rafael
2000   Paleoindian Occupations in Uruguay. *Current Research in the Pleistocene* 17:78–80.
2001   Technomorphological Observations on Fishtail Projectile Points and Bifacial

Artifacts from Northern Uruguay. *Current Research in the Pleistocene* 18:56–58.

2003 Paleoindian Components of Northern Uruguay: New Data for Early Human Occupations of the Late Pleistocene and Early Holocene. In *Where the South Winds Blow: Ancient Evidence for Paleo South Americans*, edited by L. Miotti, M. Salemme, and N. Flegenheimer, pp. 29–36. Center for the Study of the First Americans and Texas A&M University Press, College Station, TX.

2006 Comments on South American Fishtail Points: Design, Reduction Sequences, and Function. *Current Research in the Pleistocene* 23:69–72.

2009 Unifacial Fishtail Points and Considerations about the Archaeological Record of South Paleoamericans. *Current Research in the Pleistocene* 26:12–15.

2011a *Arqueología durante la transición Pleistoceno Holoceno en Uruguay. Componentes paleo-indios, organización de la tecnología lítica y movilidad de los primeros Americanos.* British Archaeological Reports International Series 2220. Archaeopress, Oxford, UK.

2011b Movilidad, acceso y uso de ágata traslucida por los cazadores-recolectores tempranos durante la transición Pleistoceno Holoceno en el norte de Uruguay (ca. 11,000–8500 AP). *Latin American Antiquity* 22(3): 359–383.

2014 Pre-Fishtail Settlement in the Southern Cone ca. 15,000–13,100 yr cal. BP: Synthesis, Evaluation, and Discussion of the Evidence. In *Pre-Clovis in the Americas: International Science Conference Proceedings Held at the Smithsonian Institution, Washington, D.C.*, edited by D. Stanford and A. Stenger, pp. 153–191. Smithsonian Institution, Washington, D.C.

2015a The Paleoamerican Occupation of the Plains of Uruguay: Technology, Adaptations, and Mobility. *PaleoAmerica* 1(1):88–104.

2015b Tecnología lítica y conjunto de artefactos utilizados durante el poblamiento temprano de Uruguay. *Chungara: Revista de Antropología Chilena* 47(1)67–84.

2017 The Human Colonization of the Southeast Plains of South America: Climatic Conditions, Technological Innovations, and the Peopling of Uruguay and South of Brazil. *Quaternary International* 431(part B): 181–193.

Suárez, Rafael, and Guaciara Santos
2010 Cazadores-recolectores tempranos, supervivencia de fauna del Pleistoceno (Equus sp. y Glyptodon sp.) y tecnología lítica durante el Holoceno temprano en la frontera Uruguay–Brasil. *Revista de Arqueología* 23(2):22–42.

Suárez Rafael, Luis Borrero, Karen Borrazzo, Martín Ubilla, Sergio Martínez, and Daniel Perea
2014 Archaeological Evidences are Still Missing: A Comment on Fariña et al. Arroyo del Vizcaíno Site, Uruguay. *Proceedings of the Royal Society B* 281(1795). doi:10.1098/rspb .2014.0449.

Suárez, Rafael, Piñero Gustavo, and Flavia Barceló
2018 Living on the River Edge: The Tigre Site (K-87) New Data and Implications for the Initial Colonization of the Uruguay River Basin. *Quaternary International* 473:242–260.

Ubilla, Martín, Daniel Perea, César Goso, and Nicolás Lorenzo
2004 Late Pleistocene Vertebrates from Northern Uruguay: Tools for Biostratigraphic, Climatic, and Environmental Reconstruction. *Quaternary International* 114:129–142.

Zárate, Marcelo
2003 Loess of Southern South America. *Quaternary Science Reviews* 22:1987–2006.

CHAPTER 5

Mobility and Human Dispersion during the Peopling of Northwest South America between the Late Pleistocene and the Early Holocene

Francisco Javier Aceituno-Bocanegra and Antonio Uriarte

Because of its geographical position and high environmental diversity, the region defined by present-day Colombia is crucial to the understanding of the peopling of South America. Considering the arrival of the first human groups and their entry routes, there are more questions than answers. Details are still scarce due, in no small part, to a lack of research during the last twenty years. Thus, there are currently just four sites in Colombia with radiocarbon dates before 11,000 RCYBP, all concentrated in the Andean region. Other possible routes, such as the Caribbean coast or Pacific coast, remain unexplored.

These sites are Pubenza 3, El Jordán, El Abra II, and Tibitó (Tables 5.1, 5.2; Figure 5.1). It is unnecessary to go into much detail regarding the characteristics of each because all have detailed publications (Correal 1981; Salgado 1998; van der Hammen and Correal 2001). Nevertheless, these sites are located in different environments and evidence various lithic industries with singular characteristics. Pubenza 3 is in the lowlands of the Magdalena River valley and contains remains of mastodon (*Cuvieronius* sp.), turtles, and rodents associated with a few flakes, one of obsidian (Correal 1993). El Jordán is in the Cordillera Central at about 2,400 m a.s.l. and contains only a few unifacial tools (Salgado 1998:114). El Abra II and Tibitó are located in the Sabana de Bogotá (Cundiboyacan High Plateau), at about 2,600 m a.s.l. The deep levels at el Abra II contain flakes belonging to the Abriense class associated with remains of deer and small rodents (Correal 1986). At Tibitó—an open butchering site—more Abriense stone tools were recovered associated with faunal remains of mastodon (*Haplomastodon* and *Cuvieronius*), American horse (*Equus*), and deer (*Odocoileus virginianus*; Correal 1982).

Viewed together, these sites are too few and too scattered in space and time to allow the development of an occupation model for the period before 11,000 RCYBP. Even at the continental level, the chronological range and the lack of dates makes it difficult to establish regional relationships with any clarity. Some publications have proposed, in a very speculative way, the relationship between the sites of the Sabana de Bogotá and the Jobo tradition of the Venezuelan coast (Aceituno et al. 2013).

In international debates, dates older than 11,000 RCYBP have been criticized, directly ignored, or rejected as in the case of Pubenza 3 (Politis 1999). Dates from the Sabana de Bogotá (El Abra II and Tibitó), although traditionally considered the earliest in the Colombian region, have also received criticism for allegedly presenting discontinuous distribution and being isolated cases, given the scarce number of dates obtained at that time (Delgado et al. 2015). Yet together, these dates support the idea of human presence in South America before 13,000 cal BP (Dillehay 2009; Dillehay et al. 2015). Moreover, new dates obtained in Monte Verde, ranging

TABLE 5.1. Sites in northwest South America, Late Pleistocene–Early Holocene, with associated lithic tradition.

No.	Site	Phase	Lithic Tradition	Region
1	Cueva de los Murciélagos/Gloria Bay	Late Pleistocene	Middle Magdalena/Fishtail	Isthmus of Panama
2	PIIIOI-52	Late Pleistocene	Middle Magdalena	Middle Porce
3	PIIIOP-59	Early Holocene	Tropical Forest Archaic	
4	Sitio 021	Early Holocene	Tropical Forest Archaic	
5	Sitio 045	Early Holocene	Tropical Forest Archaic	
6	La Morena	Pleistocene–Holocene transition	Tropical Forest Archaic	Medellín River
		Early Holocene	Tropical Forest Archaic	
7	Torre 46 (Nare)	Late Pleistocene	Middle Magdalena	Middle Magdalena
8	La Palestina 1	Early Holocene	Middle Magdalena	
9	La Palestina 2	Late Pleistocene	Middle Magdalena	
10	San Juan de Bedout	Late Pleistocene	Middle Magdalena	
11	Peñones de Bogotá	Early Holocene	Middle Magdalena	
12	39 El Recreo Cancha	Early Holocene	Tropical Forest Archaic	Middle Cauca
13	La Selva	Early Holocene	Tropical Forest Archaic	
14	El Antojo	Early Holocene	Tropical Forest Archaic	
15	El Jazmín	Late Pleistocene	Tropical Forest Archaic	
		Early Holocene	Tropical Forest Archaic	
16	La Pochola	Early Holocene	Tropical Forest Archaic	
17	San Germán II	Early Holocene	Tropical Forest Archaic	
18	La Chillona	Early Holocene	Tropical Forest Archaic	
19	La Montañita	Early Holocene	Tropical Forest Archaic	
20	Nuevo Sol	Early Holocene	Tropical Forest Archaic	
21	66PER001	Early Holocene	Tropical Forest Archaic	
22	La Trinidad I	Early Holocene	Tropical Forest Archaic	
23	La Trinidad II	Early Holocene	Tropical Forest Archaic	
24	El Guatín	Late Pleistocene	Tropical Forest Archaic	
25	Génova	Early Holocene	Tropical Forest Archaic	
26	Salento 21	Early Holocene	Tropical Forest Archaic	
27	Salento 24	Early Holocene	Tropical Forest Archaic	
28	Neusa	Early Holocene	Abriense	Sabana de Bogotá
29	Checua	Early Holocene	Abriense	
30	Gachalá	Early Holocene	Abriense	
31	Sueva I	Pleistocene–Holocene transition	Abriense	
32	El Abra II	Late Pleistocene	Abriense	
		Early Holocene	Abriense	
33	Tibitó	Late Pleistocene	Abriense	
34	Galindo I	Early Holocene	Abriense	
35	Tequendama I	Late Pleistocene	Tequendamiense	
		Early Holocene	Abriense	
36	Pubenza	Late Pleistocene	Unifacial	Cundinamarca
37	El Jordán	Late Pleistocene	Unifacial	Cordillera Central
		Early Holocene	Tropical Forest Archaic	
38	Sauzalito	Early Holocene	Tropical Forest Archaic	Calima River
39	El Recreo	Early Holocene	Tropical Forest Archaic	
40	San Isidro	Pleistocene–Holocene transition	Tropical Forest Archaic	Popayán Plateau
		Early Holocene	Tropical Forest Archaic	
41	Peña Roja	Early Holocene	Tropical Forest Archaic	Caquetá River

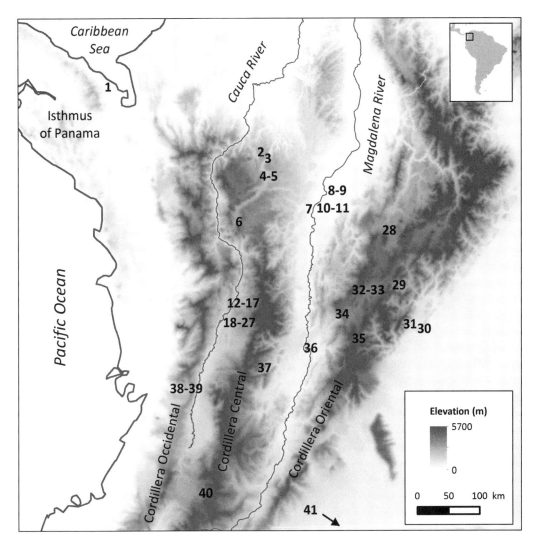

FIGURE 5.1. Archaeological sites: (*1*) Cueva de los Murciélagos (Gloria Bay); (*2*) PIII0I-52; (*3*) PIII0P-59; (*4*) Sitio 021; (*5*) Sitio 045; (*6*) La Morena; (*7*) Torre 46 (Nare); (*8*) La Palestina 1; (*9*) La Palestina 2; (*10*) San Juan de Bedout; (*11*) Peñones de Bogotá; (*12*) 39 El Recreo Cancha; (*13*) La Selva; (*14*) El Antojo; (*15*) El Jazmín; (*16*) La Pochola; (*17*) San Germán II; (*18*) La Chillona; (*19*) La Montañita; (*20*) Nuevo Sol; (*21*) 66PER001; (*22*) La Trinidad I; (*23*) La Trinidad II; (*24*) El Guatín; (*25*) Génova; (*26*) Salento 21; (*27*) Salento 24; (*28*) Neusa; (*29*) Checua; (*30*) Gachalá; (*31*) Sueva I; (*32*) El Abra II; (*33*) Tibitó; (*34*) Galindo I; (*35*) Tequendama I; (*36*) Pubenza; (*37*) El Jordán; (*38*) Sauzalito; (*39*) El Recreo; (*40*) San Isidro; (*41*) Peña Roja.

between 18,500 and 14,500 cal BP, validate the oldest date from Pubenza 3. After 10,000 RCYBP, the volume of data increases considerably, coinciding with the Pleistocene–Holocene transition, which allows us to propose hypotheses about dispersion routes (Aceituno et al. 2013).

Based on these assumptions (developed in the next section), this chapter suggests poten-

tial routes of communication between regions and proposes a mobility model for the expansion and occupation of northwestern South America between the Late Pleistocene and the Early Holocene. We will implement GIS tools to contrast the hypotheses or models proposed to date regarding human dispersion and occupation during the earliest settlement of Colombia.

TABLE 5.2. Radiocarbon dates, northwest South America, Late Pleistocene–Early Holocene.

No.	Site	Dated Material	RCYBP	cal BP	References
2	PIIIOI-52	Charcoal	10,260 ± 50	10,225–9818	Otero and Santos 2006, 2012
3	PIIIOP-59	Charcoal	8340 ± 40	7520–7313	Cardona et al. 2007; Cardona 2012
4	Sitio 021	Charcoal	8990 ± 80	8380–7935	Castillo and Aceituno 2006
5	Sitio 045	Charcoal	9120 ± 90	8616–8202	Castillo and Aceituno 2006
6	La Morena	Charcoal	10,090 ± 60	9881–9366	Santos 2010
		Charcoal	9680 ± 60	9275–8837	
7	Torre 46 (Nare)	Charcoal	10,400 ± 40	10,473–10,125	López 2008
		Charcoal	10,400 ± 60	10,488–10,095	
		Charcoal	10,350 ± 60	10,472–10,016	
8	La Palestina 1	Charcoal	9820 ± 115	9698–8837	CAIN OCENSA 1997, in López 2008
9	La Palestina 2	Charcoal	10,400 ± 90	10,613–10,025	López 2008
		Charcoal	10,300 ± 70	10,448–9872	
		Charcoal	10,260 ± 70	10,435–9806	
		Charcoal	10,230 ± 80	10,293–9670	
10	San Juan de Bedout	Charcoal	10,350 ± 90	10,581–9980	López 1989
11	Peñones de Bogotá	Charcoal	8480 ± 40	7586–7497	López 2008
12	39 El Recreo Cancha	Charcoal	8550 ± 60	7683–7497	Herrera et al. 2011
		Charcoal	8480 ± 40	7586–7497	
		Charcoal	8030 ± 80	7177–6686	
13	La Selva	Charcoal	8680 ± 60	7871–7586	Aceituno and Loaiza 2007
		Charcoal	9490 ± 100	9221–8556	Rodríguez 2002
		Charcoal	8712 ± 60	7943–7596	Dickau et al. 2015
14	El Antojo	Charcoal	8380 ± 90	7237–7187	INTEGRAL 1997
15	El Jazmín	Charcoal	10,120 ± 70	10,078–9447	Aceituno and Loaiza 2007
		Charcoal	9020 ± 60	8322–7970	INTEGRAL 1997
16	La Pochola	Charcoal	8095 ± 55	7299–7587	Aceituno and Loaiza 2007
		Charcoal	9312 ± 55	8719–8420	Aceituno pers. corr.
		Charcoal	9047 ± 45	8320–8210	Dickau et al. 2015
17	San Germán II	Charcoal	8136 ± 65	7348–6628	Aceituno and Loaiza 2007
18	La Chillona	Charcoal	8200 ± 40	7328–7078	Restrepo 2013
19	La Montañita	Charcoal	9230 ± 50	8572–8302	Restrepo 2013
20	Nuevo Sol	Charcoal	8740 ± 40	7952–7607	Restrepo 2013
21	66PER001	Charcoal	9730 ± 100	9371–8797	Cano 2004
22	La Trinidad I	Charcoal	9542 ± 50	9147–8750	Restrepo 2013
23	La Trinidad II	Charcoal	9333 ± 65	8759–8421	Restrepo 2013
24	El Guatín	Charcoal	10,130 ± 50	10,074–9526	Restrepo 2013
25	Génova	Charcoal	9230 ± 40	8561–8312	Restrepo 2013
26	Salento 21	Charcoal	8430 ± 100	7603–7186	Rojas and Tabares 2000
27	Salento 24	Charcoal	9680 ± 100	9296–8784	Rojas and Tabares 2000
28	Neusa	Charcoal	8370 ± 90	7580–7184	Rivera 1991
29	Checua	Charcoal	8200 ± 110	7521–6913	Groot 1992

TABLE 5.2. (cont'd.) Radiocarbon dates, northwest South America, Late Pleistocene–Early Holocene.

No.	Site	Dated Material	RCYBP	cal BP	References
30	Gachalá	Charcoal	9360 ± 45	8755–8538	Correal 1979
31	Sueva I	Charcoal	10,060 ± 90	10,020–9322	Correal 1979
32	El Abra II	Charcoal	10,720 ± 400	11,370–9371	Correal and van der Hammen 1977
		Charcoal	12,400 ± 160	13,184–12,050	Hurt et al. 1977
		Charcoal	11,210 ± 90	11,311–10,889	
		Charcoal	9340 ± 40	8730–8532	
		Charcoal	9325 ± 100	8832–8292	
		Charcoal	9050 ± 470	9554–7056	
		Charcoal	9025 ± 90	8476–7938	
		Charcoal	8810 ± 430	9177–7001	
		Charcoal	8760 ± 350	8818–7027	
33	Tibitó	Charcoal	11,740 ± 110	11,826–11,391	Correal 1981
34	Galindo I	Charcoal	8740 ± 60	7972–7597	Pinto 2003
35	Tequendama I	Charcoal	10,920 ± 260	11,358–10,193	Correal and van der Hammen 1977
		Charcoal	10,730 ± 105	10,858–10,564	
		Charcoal	10,590 ± 90	10,771–10,427	
		Charcoal	10,460 ± 130	10,744–10,007	
		Charcoal	10,150 ± 150	10,293–9317	
		Charcoal	10,140 ± 100	10,174–9372	
		Charcoal	10,130 ± 150	10,289–9299	
		Charcoal	10,025 ± 95	10,007–9295	
		Charcoal	9990 ± 100	9880–9272	
		Charcoal	9740 ± 135	9467–8747	
36	Pubenza	Charcoal	16,400 ± 420	18,830–16,869	van der Hammen and Correal 2001
37	El Jordán	Charcoal	12,910 ± 60	13,724–13,255	Salgado 1998
		Charcoal	9760 ± 160	9768–8713	
38	Sauzalito	Charcoal	9670 ± 100	9291–8782	Bray et al. 1988
		Charcoal	9600 ± 100	9258–8720	
		Charcoal	9300 ± 100	8780–8295	
39	El Recreo	Charcoal	8750 ± 160	8253–7548	Herrera et al. 1992
40	San Isidro	Charcoal	10,050 ± 100	10,027–9310	Gnecco 2000
		Seed	10,030 ± 60	9825–9321	
		Charcoal	9530 ± 100	9220–8632	
41	Peña Roja	Charcoal	9250 ± 140	8849–8211	Cavelier et al. 1995; Morcote et al. 1998; Mora 2003
		Charcoal	9160 ± 90	8612–8243	
		Charcoal	8510 ± 110	7826–7292	Llanos 1997
		Charcoal	9125 ± 250	8879–7609	Mora 2003
		Phytoliths	8090 ± 60	7301–6823	

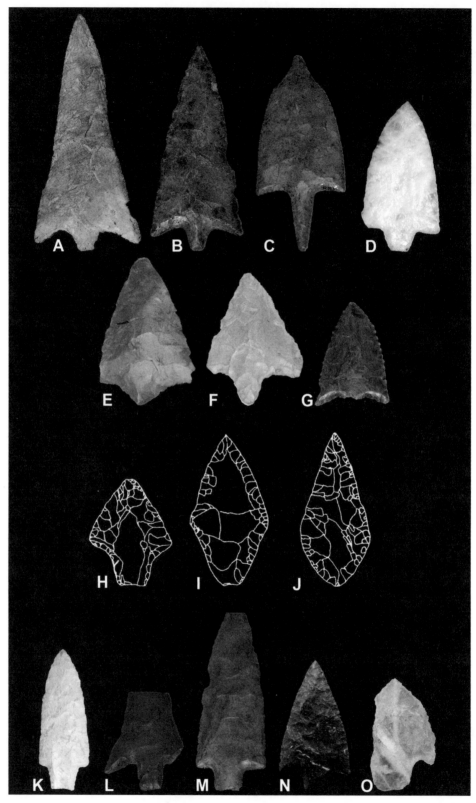

FIGURE 5.2. Projectile Points: (*A–G*) Middle Magdalena (surface collection); (*H–J*) Popayán Plateau (ca. 10,000 BP); (*K*) Middle Porce (10,260 BP); (*L–M*) Medellín River (surface collection); (*N*) Middle Cauca (excavated, no date); (*O*) Middle Cauca (ca. 8,000–8,500 BP).

The Archaeological Record during the Terminal Late Pleistocene and Early Holocene

Between approximately 11,000 and 10,000 RCYBP, there is an increase in archaeological sites and dates in different Andean regions, such as the Sabana de Bogotá, the middle Magdalena River basin (henceforth Middle Magdalena) and the Cordillera Central (Tables 5.1 and 5.2; Figure 5.1). In the Sabana de Bogotá, the Tequendamiense class appears, while megafauna disappears from the archaeological record (Correal 1981, 1990). In the Middle Magdalena, a lithic tradition thrives, characterized by complex artifacts such as plane-convex scrapers and triangular Fishtail projectile points with a long, thin, straight stem made of local chert or quartz, with unifacial flakes (Figure 5.2 A–G). In the Magdalena sites, located at an altitude of about 160 m a.s.l., no plants or zooarchaeological remains were recovered. Some Tequendamiense tools were manufactured from raw material from the Middle Magdalena. This has served to highlight the idea that groups from the Sabana de Bogotá seasonally occupied the Magdalena River lowlands (Correal and van der Hammen 1977:168).

Projectile points similar to the Middle Magdalena have been found in various places of Colombia but mainly in that river basin (Lopez 1995; Reichel-Dolmatoff 1965) and in neighboring regions such as the Porce-Medellín River, the village of Las Piletas (Correal 1993), and Restrepo (Cordillera Occidental), suggesting the expansion of this technological tradition (Figure 5.2 L–M). Fishtail projectile points similar to those found in Panama were also reported. In Gloria Bay, in the Darién region, one surface Fishtail point was found (Correal 1983), along with a lanceolate projectile point, belonging to the Middle Magdalena tradition (Correal 1983). This location, at the gateway to South America, is of particular relevance. An additional Fishtail point was found somewhat farther south, closer to Manizales (Correal 1986).

In the Cordillera Central, there are new sites in three regions: North, Central, and South. In the north of the Cordillera Central, in the Porce-Medellín River basin, sites PIIIOI-52 and PIIIOI-39, located at an approximate altitude of 1000 m a.s.l. (Otero and Santos 2006:59), are worth mentioning, together with La Morena at 2100 m a.s.l. (Santos 2010; Santos et al. 2015). PIIIOI-52 yielded three stone tools manufactured from chert (Otero and Santos 2006:60–62) and associated with the lithic tradition of the Middle Magdalena (Aceituno et al. 2013). In PIIIOI-39, one Middle Magdalena type projectile point was found at the bottom of the site (Figure 5.2, K). At La Morena, the most notable discoveries include grinding stones, milling bases, and hoes, along with unifacial and simple flakes manufactured from local volcanic rocks (Santos 2010).

In the Central part of the Cordillera Central, in the Middle Cauca River Basin (hereafter Middle Cauca), El Jazmín is located at 1650 m a.s.l. It presented artifacts similar to those from La Morena (Aceituno and Loaiza 2007:41). Both lithic traditions are strongly associated with the use of plants, as indicated by starch grains recovered from the stone tools (Aceituno and Loaiza 2014, 2015).

In the south of the Cordillera Central, on the Popayán Plateau, the San Isidro site is at 1600 m a.s.l. (Gnecco 2000:17). Here, thousands of stone tools were discovered, mainly made of chert, with lanceolate bifaces and preforms among the most diagnostic. In addition to the manufactured artifacts, some milling stones and a polished axe have been found (Gnecco 2000: 60–62). As in other Andean regions, thousands of charred seeds and starch grains were recovered alongside lithic artifacts (Gnecco 2003; Piperno and Pearsall 1998:200). This indicates the importance of plants in the adaptation of early groups to the environment of Cordillera Central, in contrast to the sites of the Middle Magdalena and the Sabana de Bogotá (Aceituno and Loaiza 2015). La Elvira, another locality from the Popayán Plateau, lacks early dates. Nonetheless, the projectile points it contains— some made from local obsidian—indicate a probable contemporaneity (Gnecco 2000:74). One El Inga-type projectile point is strikingly similar to Fishtail points (Figure 5.2, H; Ranere and López 2007), while another is akin to what has been found at Chobschi Cave (Ecuador). Comparative dating corresponds to the Terminal Pleistocene and Early Holocene (Gnecco 2000, 88, 90). Other point styles provide diverging chronology, such as the type known as Ayampitín (Ecuador), which has a pentagonal and elongated shape and is typologically dated between 8000 and 6000 RCYBP (Figure 5.2, I–J; Gnecco 2000, 80, 87).

Between 10,000 and 8000 RCYBP, the trend of the previous period continues, with an increase in sites and radiocarbon dates. Sites are concentrated mainly along the Andean region of Colombia (Aceituno and Castillo 2005; Aceituno and Loaiza 2007; Cardona 2012; Castillo and Aceituno 2006; Cardale et al. 1989; Dickau et al. 2015; Herrera et al. 1992; Salgado 1988–1990; Otero and Santos 2006, 2012; Rojas and Tabares 2000). However, for the first time there is a site within the Colombian Amazon (Peña Roja, on the Caquetá River; Cavelier et al. 1995; Mora 2003), increasing the number of regions involved in the expansion and adaptability of early groups.

In the Cordillera Central, along the Porce River and the Middle Cauca, the number of sites increases considerably (Aceituno and Loaiza 2007; Cardona 2012; Dickau et al.2015; Otero and Santos 2012; Santos et al. 2015). Stone tools related to plant use are very common in the archaeological records of both regions, highlighting the increased use of axes and hoes. Both tools become one of the most diagnostic artifacts among groups inhabiting valleys within the Cordillera Central. However, there are some differences between the two regions. On the middle course of the Porce River, there is a quartz lithic industry, attested through debitage and thousands of tools, including several stemmed projectile points (Castillo and Aceituno 2006). In Cauca, on the other hand, the amount of debitage and tools recovered from sites is much lower and, except for the quartz assemblage found at El Antojo (Aceituno and Loaiza 2007), recovered tools are manufactured from local volcanic rocks. Meanwhile, in the Middle Cauca, two projectile points were re-covered, one in quartz and another one in chert (Figure 5.2 N–O; Herrera et al. 2011).

Discovery of these points with technological and stylistic similarities supported a hypothesized inmigration to the Cordillera Central from the lowlands of the Middle Magdalena (Aceituno 2007; Aceituno et al. 2013). The chronological range may include the San Isidro site, with more than 100 bifaces recovered (Gnecco 2000:61), some of which clearly possess attributes of projectile points, with a predominance of lanceolate point type. The Holocene projectile points of the Middle Porce and Middle Cauca share certain traits with the Middle Magdalena points and the two points found on the surface on the Medellín River (Aburrá Valley).

The other region with data within this chronological range is the Calima River basin (Cordillera Occidental), where the Sauzalito and El Recreo sites are located at about 1750 m a.s.l. (Cardale et al. 1989; Salgado 1988–1990). The lithic technology here is similar to that from the Middle Cauca and the Medellín/Porce River, again highlighting artifacts related to plant use (milling stones, handstones, and hoes; Herrera et al. 1992; Salgado 1988–1990). These contexts provided charred palm seeds of palms and *Persea* sp. (avocado), as well as palm, bamboo, and *Maranta* sp. phytoliths (Piperno 1985; Piperno and Pearsall 1998:202).

The Peña Roja site is situated outside the Colombian Andes, in the lowlands of the Caquetá River basin (Cavelier et al. 1995; Gnecco and Mora 1997; Mora 2003:102; Mora and Gnecco 2003). The site's lithic assemblage consists of debitage tools (unifacial flakes, choppers, drills) manufactured from local raw materials such as chert, quartz, and igneous rocks, alongside other grinding artifacts such as handstones, milling bases, hammers, and anvils (Cavelier et al. 1995: 31–32). We can highlight this site for the recovery of thousands of charred seeds, mainly of palms and other trees, which again indicates the importance of plants in the archaeological record of the Early Holocene (Cavelier et al. 1995:36–41; Morcote et al. 1998). This interpretation is reinforced by the identification of phytoliths of *Lagenaria* sp., *Calathea allouia*, and *Cucurbita* sp. (Gnecco and Mora 1997), exogenous plants carried to the Caquetá River to be cultivated (Piperno and Pearsall 1998:204–205).

On a larger scale, data from Medellín/Porce River, Middle Cauca, Calima River, Popayán Plateau, and Peña Roja can join those from Panama, with lithic technology associated with the Tropical Forest Archaic (Ranere 1980:35). Those technological traditions clearly indicate the importance of plant processing during the Early Holocene, notwithstanding the exploitation of faunal resources.

Based on the archaeological record, flaked stone technology, and the archaeobotanical data distribution, a dispersion model of multidirectional displacement by small groups with broad-spectrum economies can be hypothesized. These groups simultaneously inhabited different points of the tropical forests of the sub-Andean valleys that traverse and connect the east and west Andean slopes and the respective primary river basins of the Cauca and Magdalena Rivers (Aceituno 2007; Aceituno et al. 2013). This model of settlement is more common in groups with broad-spectrum economies, which depend on resources distributed more evenly, as in the case of tropical rainforests (Anthony 1990).

Methodology

Exploring mobility and regional interaction has been addressed through GIS analysis,[1] specifically *cost surface analysis.* (See an overview of archaeological applications in Wheatley and Gillings 2002:151–159; Conolly and Lake 2006:252–256; and more specific works in Fábrega-Álvarez 2006; Fábrega-Álvarez and Parcero-Oubiña 2007; Howey 2007; Mayoral and Celestino 2011: chapter 4; Murrieta-Flores 2012; White and Barber 2012; Verhagen 2013; Güimil-Fariña and Parcero-Oubiña 2015.) Cost surface analysis elaborates models about mobility by considering the influence of landscape characteristics. We must stress that the present analysis does not aim specifically at an effective reconstruction of ancient routes but is exploratory and comparative in character, focusing on sketching plausible scenarios of past human movement. The basic geographical dataset is

the *cost surface*, a raster layer[2] representing the spatial distribution of the *cost variable*, which quantifies the differing resistance to movement across a landscape and is usually expressed in time or velocity units. The cost surface generated for the present study stores inverse speed values (i.e. slowness) and is based on the algorithm by Gorenflo and Gale (1990:244), which calculates walking speed using terrain slope[3]: $v = 6e^{-3.5|s+0.05|}$ where v is speed, s is the terrain slope (in so much per one, or tangent) and e is the base for natural logarithms.

Cost surface analysis is performed from a set of locations that serve as origin and destination points. In this case, it involves the archaeological sites referred to in Table 5.1. It is important to add that they represent a small and scarce sample, centered in the Colombian Andean region, where most research has been carried out in the last 30 years. This initial analysis must be considered exploratory, and results will change in accordance with data from new archaeological sites, for example in regions such as the Caribbean or Pacific coasts.

Modeling Routes from the Isthmus

MADO[4] is a movement modeling method that establishes least-cost routes from a certain origin, across a given area, and without a specific destination. (See its full formulation in Fábrega-Álvarez 2006 and an archaeological application in Fábrega-Álvarez and Parcero-Oubiña 2007.) It combines both cost surface and hydrological modeling tools, in order to generate a dendritic route network, departing from the origin point and branching across the region of analysis. MADO elaboration has the following steps:

a) creation of a cost distance layer from the origin location.[5] This layer shows how far, in cost units (e.g., time), each point in the analysis area lies from the given origin. For this work, the selected spreading region is the Colombian territory itself. Although arbitrary, due to its current political-administrative delineation, this region covers all potential entry areas (Caribbean, Pacific, Andes);

b) generation of a flow direction layer based on the above-mentioned cost distance layer;[6]

c) generation of the MADO layer through the flow accumulation tool.[7] The result is a raster layer in which each cell has an accumulation value that, interpreted in MADO terms, expresses the degree of accessibility;

d) Boolean reclassification of the MADO layer into the MADO network.[8] The selected threshold is a conventional one, based on standard deviation. Those cells with an accumulation value of more than 1.5 standard deviations from the mean are considered routes;

e) conversion of the MADO network to vector format.[9]

Here, MADO is applied for modeling likely penetration routes (or natural corridors) from the Isthmus of Panama into South America across its northwestern region. Two MADO networks have been elaborated, each from a different origin point in the Isthmus: one in the Caribbean and the other on the Pacific coast.[10] For the Caribbean one, there is an archaeological reference, the Cueva de los Murciélagos site, where typological criteria stand for a Late Pleistocene chronology.

Once both MADO networks were created, we explored their possible relationship with archaeological sites. We calculated linear distances from each site to its nearest route,[11] in order to perform the following comparisons using statistical methods (see a similar comparative approach in Murrieta-Flores 2012): (a) between the whole set of Andean archaeological sites (n = 39) and a random sample (n = 100) generated[12] inside a 100-km buffer defined around the 39 sites[13]; and (b) between sites with Late Pleistocene (n = 11) and Early Holocene chronologies (n = 31).

Exploring Interaction

Next, we explored the spatial links between sites, pair by pair, through two main types of data derived from cost surface analysis: cost distance[14] and least-cost path[15] (or optimal path).

Cost distance is defined as the distance, in cost units, from a given origin to a given destination. Expressed in time, it means the minimum travel duration required to walk that route. For analytical purposes, cost distances have been tabulated in a symmetrical matrix. Time is expressed in hours, which can be easily converted into 10-hour stages, a simple but expressive module for representing regional travel.

Least-cost path (also named optimal path) is defined as the shortest route, in terms of cost distance, that links two locations. Its cartographic representation is an irregular line, simulating a track or a path. Combining several least-cost paths in a same map results in a plausible communication network in the study region.

Work was performed on two scales, local and interregional. On a local scale, microregional clusters were defined by linking those pairs of sites whose cost distance was below a given threshold that fit short-distance displacements; a 10-hour threshold was selected, consistent with a two-day, there-and-back trip.

On an interregional scale, cost distance and least-cost paths between microregional clusters were examined in combination with chronological information and lithic traditions, with the aim of sketching the most likely routes between sites through the Colombian Andes. A synthetic network map has been elaborated through the following procedure:

a) generation of the least-cost paths from each cluster to the rest.[16] After a Boolean reclassification,[17] the result for each origin cluster is a raster layer with two possible values: zero, where there is no path, and a specific value where there is one. This specific value is the number of sites that make up the cluster, in order to give a higher weight to those routes that depart from a denser cluster;

b) generation of the least-cost path network by means of combining all the least-cost path layers created in the previous step.[18] The result is a raster layer with zero value where there is no path and an integer value where there is a path, in correlation with the weight of the route;

c) conversion of the least-cost path network to vector format;[19]

d) conversion of this vector layer to a density map in order to give a smoother appearance to the network, showing vague transit areas rather than sharp, linear routes.[20]

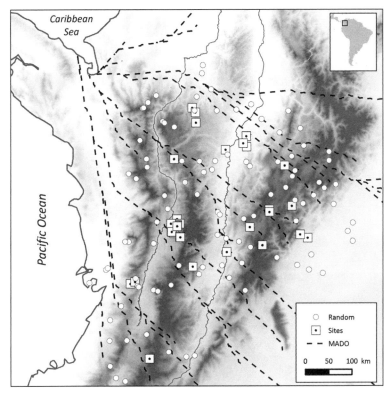

FIGURE 5.3. Archaeological sites (n = 39) and random points (n = 100) mapped in relation to MADO routes traced from the *Caribbean* coast of the Isthmus of Panama.

Results

Observing the Caribbean and Pacific MADO routes, one observes several transverse branches crossing the Andean Cordilleras and main valleys (Cauca and Magdalena) from northwest to southeast (Figures 5.3, 5.4). Sites appear quite close to them, reinforced by statistical comparison with the random sample using a box plot (Figures 5.5 and 5.6) and, above all, the Mann-Whitney U test, which gives a significant difference for both MADO networks (p = 0.011 for the Caribbean MADO; p = 0.008 for the Pacific). On the other hand, testing through the Wilcoxon test (p = 0.557), we do not find significant differences in site placement closer to Caribbean or Pacific MADO routes (Figure 5.7).

Moreover, the Mann-Whitney U test comparing Pleistocene and Holocene contexts offers no significant difference between the MADO from the Caribbean (p = 0.756) and the Pacific (p = 0.933), suggesting a similar relationship be-

tween sites and natural corridors in both periods (Figures 5.8–9).

Regarding cost distances between sites, if we observe the frequency distribution (Figure 5.10), we can distinguish two groups: one around a single stage, with little internal variability and most values even less, and the other with higher values and a much higher internal variability, ranging from 2 to 15 or 16 stages, with a maximum of about 6.

Site pairs linked below the 10-hour threshold (i.e., one stage) were mapped in order to identify 15 microregional clusters (Figure 5.11). Given that clusters are based on site proximity, we assume they represent a small-scale spatial pattern of settlement and exploitation. Six of these clusters include more than one site and are located in the Middle Porce, Middle Magdalena, Middle Cauca, Cundiboyacan high plateau (two cases), and Calima River. Meanwhile, clusters with just one site lie in the Isthmus of Panama, Medellín

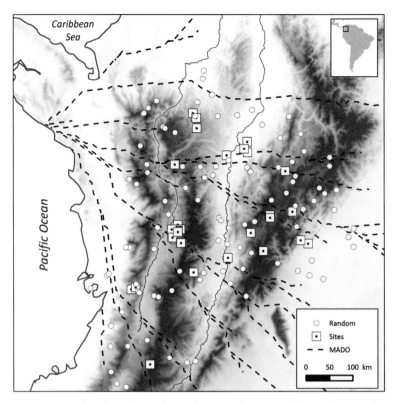

FIGURE 5.4. Archaeological sites (n = 39) and random points (n = 100) mapped in relation to MADO routes traced from the *Pacific* coast of the Isthmus of Panama.

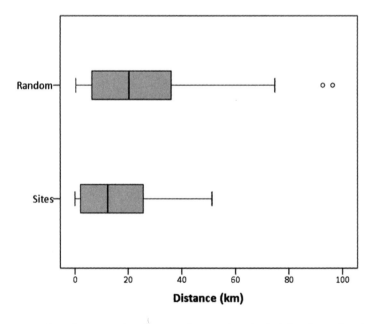

Distance (km)

FIGURE 5.5. Box plot comparing distances from archaeological sites (n = 39) and random points (n = 100) to MADO routes traced from the Caribbean coast of the Isthmus of Panama.

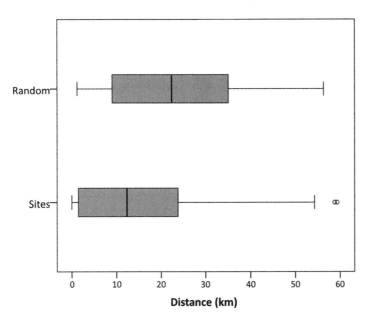

FIGURE 5.6. Box plot comparing distances from archaeological sites (n = 39) and random points (n = 100) to MADO routes traced from the Pacific coast of the Isthmus of Panama.

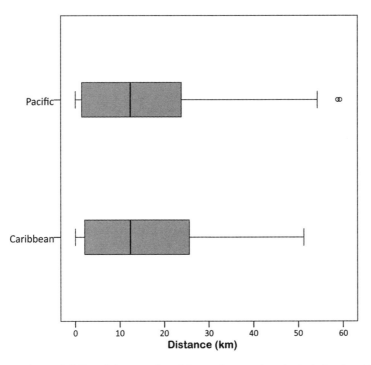

FIGURE 5.7. Box plot comparing distances from archaeological sites (n = 39) to MADO routes traced from the Caribbean and the Pacific coast of the Isthmus of Panama.

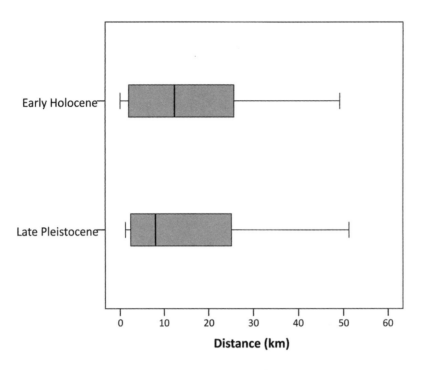

FIGURE 5.8. Box plot comparing distances from sites with Late Pleistocene contexts (n = 11) and sites with Early Holocene contexts (n = 31) to MADO routes traced from the Caribbean coast of the Isthmus of Panama.

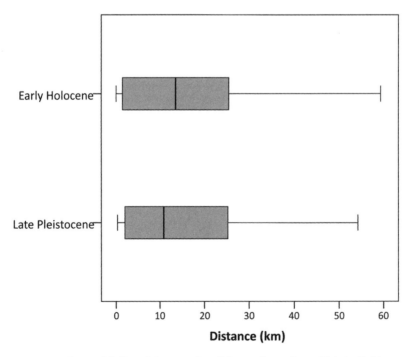

FIGURE 5.9. Box plot comparing distances from sites with Late Pleistocene contexts (n = 11) and sites with Early Holocene contexts (n = 31) to MADO routes traced from the Pacific coast of the Isthmus of Panama.

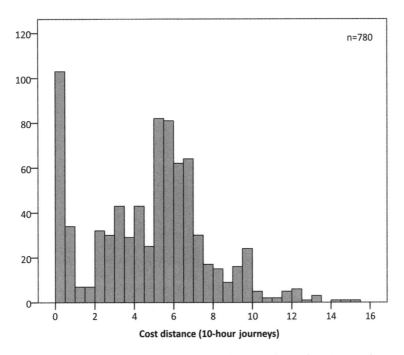

FIGURE 5.10. Histogram showing cost distances (expressed in 10-hour journeys) between all site pairs.

River, Cundiboyacan Plateau (four cases), Magdalena River, Cordillera Central (Tolima), and Popayán Plateau.

It is important to clarify that all the sites from the Cundiboyacan Plateau belong to the same cultural tradition and are located in the same biome. Moreover, the clusters in the Sabana de Bogotá are quite close, with values between 1 and 3 stages from any site to its nearest neighbor, and around 4 between the most distant sites (Tequendama I and Neusa). The same idea can be applied to La Morena (Medellín River), which can be grouped culturally with the Middle Porce sites.

In addition to the spatial relation between sites, the clusters fit well within lithic traditions.

- Cluster 4 (Middle Magdalena): Middle Magdalena lithic tradition, with both Late Pleistocene and Early Holocene chronologies.
- Cluster 5 (Middle Cauca): all lithic industries belong to the Tropical Forest Archaic tradition, primarily with an Early Holocene chronology.
- Cluster 14 (Calima River): the two sites show

Tropical Forest Archaic tradition industries and belong to the Early Holocene period.

- Cluster 2 (Medellín River): two lithic traditions, with intersecting geographical distributions. This seems to indicate a chronological substitution, with the Middle Magdalena tradition in the Late Pleistocene and the Tropical Forest Archaic during the Early Holocene.
- Clusters 6–11 (Sabana de Bogotá): all sites share the Abriense lithic tradition, with Late Pleistocene and Early Holocene dates. We must also mention the presence of the Tequendamiense tradition in cluster 11, corresponding to the Tequendama I site.

Regarding the interregional scale, the highest cost distance is that between Cueva de los Murciélagos, in the Isthmus of Panama, and Gachalá, in the lowlands beyond the eastern Cordillera (around 15 stages or work days). This can be interpreted as the minimum time to cross the Andes and reach the lowlands of Llanos Orientales. We can also mention the cost distance between Cueva de los Murciélagos and the San

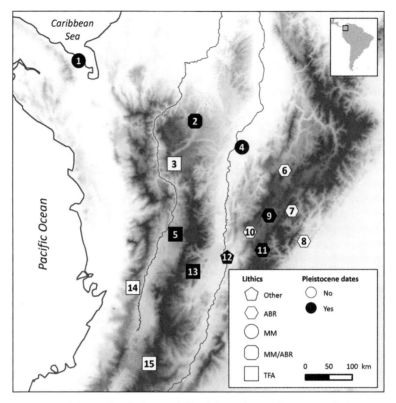

FIGURE 5.11. Microregional clusters defined through cost distance analysis:
(1) Isthmus of Panama, (2) Middle Porce; (3) Medellín River; (4) Middle
Magdalena; (5) Middle Cauca; (6–11) Sabana de Bogotá; (12) Cundinamarca;
(13) Cordillera Central; (14) Calima River; (15) Popayán Plateau. Lithic traditions:
Abriense (ABR); Middle Magdalena (MM); Tropical Forest Archaic (TFA).

Isidro site (in the Popayán Plateau farther south, approximately 14 stages).

There are shorter distances between intermediate sites, marking phases and advance routes followed in the settlement of the Colombian Andes and also linking ecologically different areas in a few stages. Close clusters are separated by cost distances between 2 and 5 stages, while longer distances between distant clusters do not exceed 13 (i.e., between clusters 2 and 15).

The density map showing transit areas (Figure 5.12), in combination with chronological and lithic tradition information, can be interpreted as follows:

(i) two penetration routes from the Isthmus of Panama (cluster 1, Cueva de los Murciélagos), presumably during the Late Pleistocene;

(ii) a northern route, toward the Middle Porce and the Middle Magdalena (clusters 2 and 4

respectively), coinciding with the distribution of the Middle Magdalena lithic tradition. This corridor can be extended to the Cundiboyacan Plateau through the Neusa site (cluster 6), although there are as yet no Pleistocene dates to support this hypothesis;

(iii) a more southerly route through the Middle Cauca, the Cordillera Central, and the Magdalena valley (clusters 5, 12, and 13 respectively), reaching the Cundiboyacan Plateau (in particular, clusters 11 and 9);

(iv) two penetration routes from the Isthmus with later chronologies during the Pleistocene–Holocene transition and the Early Holocene;

(v) an intermediate route toward the Medellín River (cluster 3), apparently subsidiary to the two Late Pleistocene corridors mentioned above, for it does not seem to proceed farther;

(vi) a southern route across the Pacific lowlands

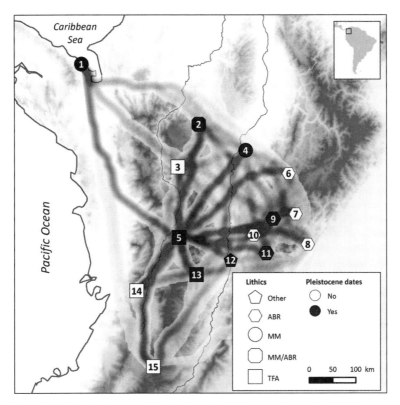

FIGURE 5.12. Synthetic map of optimal routes between microregional clusters, elaborated through least-cost path analysis and smoothed with a kernel density function. Lithic traditions: Abriense (ABR); Middle Magdalena (MM); Tropical Forest Archaic (TFA).

down to the Calima River and Popayán Plateau regions (clusters 14 and 15). This route is strongly associated to the Middle Cauca cluster.

(vii) finally, a north–south oriented route, linked to the Cauca and Medellín/Porce valleys (clusters 2, 3, 5, 14, and 15), with probable digressions to the eastern side of the Cordillera Central (cluster 13). This fits the Tropical Forest Archaic lithic tradition, with Early Holocene chronology.

Discussion

The resulting least-cost paths derived from GIS analysis indicate natural corridors that communicate different areas involved in the settlement of northwestern South America. The results we present here provide new cartographic information for a process that inaugurated the settlement of the South American continent. We hope these results are considered in future studies addressing this topic. They reveal the relation-

ship between the natural corridors and archaeological sites and indicate that the network of proposed optimal paths faithfully represents potential routes used by human groups in the settlement of the Colombian Andes between the Late Pleistocene and Early Holocene.

The first route links the Isthmus of Panama with the Porce River, which is highly interconnected with the Magdalena River lowlands and thus the Sabana de Bogotá highlands. It crosses the Andean region from northwest to southeast until reaching the Sabana de Bogotá, where there are several of the oldest archaeological dates for the Colombian Andes. The route starts in the lowlands of the Gulf of Urabá on the Caribbean coast, crosses the Serranía de Abibe, continues through the lowlands of the upper basin of the Sinú River, crosses the lower basin of the Cauca River, and climbs toward the Cordillera Central, through secondary rivers, eventually reaching the Middle Porce (ca. 900 m a.s.l.). From there, it follows various secondary rivers toward the lowlands (reaching approximately 150 m a.s.l.) of the Middle Magdalena. From the Magdalena River valley, it rises toward the Cundiboyacan Plateau (2,600 m a.s.l.) along tributaries of the Magdalena River up the western slope of the Cordillera Oriental. This route also connects with Aburrá Valley (ca. 1475 m a.s.l.), upstream of the Porce River, where the Medellín River runs. It also links with the controversial Pubenza 3 site, located south of Middle Magdalena.

The route described above would explain the Terminal Late Pleistocene of the Sabana de Bogotá and the Middle Magdalena occupations. The oldest settlements belong to the Abriense class (El Abra II and Tibitó), corresponding to the period before 11,000 RCYBP. For this period, no Abriense tools have been found outside the Sabana de Bogotá. For more recent occupations around 11,000 RCYBP, the archaeological record suggests spatial relationships between clusters in different regions. For example, raw materials from the Middle Magdalena were used in the manufacture of Tequendamiense tools (Correal 1986; Correal and van der Hammen 1977:34; López 1999). Projectile points belonging to Middle Magdalena tradition have been found scattered in the Gulf of Urabá, the Medellín/ Porce valley, and also in the upper basin of the Magdalena River, the Cordillera Occidental (Aceituno et al. 2013; López 1995, 1999; Reichel Dolmatoff 1965), and the Cordillera Oriental (Correal 1993).

The problem of Pubenza 3 is its old chronology, which is difficult to relate with the other sites and the lithic traditions mentioned here. For the time being, Pubenza 3 represents an isolated exception in the discussion of the settlement of South America, the closest reference being the Jobo tradition on the Venezuelan coast, with dates ranging from about 16,400 until approximately 13,000 RCYBP (Bryan et al. 1978; Cruxent and Ochesenius 1979:9–13; Gruhn 1979: 31–33; Ranere and López 2007). Of the routes mentioned above, the Andean route through the Aburrá Valley represents the optimal path to reach Pubenza 3 in the Magdalena Valley. However, we believe that the route taken by the earliest human settlers would be linked to the location of resources, such as megafauna. Remains of *Stegomastodon* sp. and Gomphotheriidae have been reported in the valleys of the Cauca and Magdalena Rivers and at Medellín, among other spots (Rodríguez et al. 2009), suggesting that these valleys probably played an important role in the arrival of pre-Clovis populations.

A second Andean route also departs from the Gulf of Urabá and ascends the western mountains to Cañasgordas (ca. 1300 m a.s.l.). From there, it begins to descend toward the Cauca valley (500 m a.s.l.), rising again through the Cordillera Central to reach the Aburrá Valley. From the Aburrá Valley, the route descends secondary rivers toward the Middle Magdalena lowlands, representing another access route to the Magdalena Valley from the Cordillera Central. As we will see, this route is more related to sites along the Cordillera Central.

Another main corridor to the Andean region goes north-south through the Pacific lowlands. This route takes advantage of the valleys of the Atrato and San Juan Rivers and other secondary courses on the Pacific slope. It includes two entry points to the Andean region, with archaeological sites in the Cordillera Central. The first entry point links to the Middle Cauca sites. Its route coincides with the present-day road connecting the city of Pereira on the Middle Cauca with the city of Quibdó on the Pacific slope. This road rises through the Cordillera Occidental (1700 m a.s.l.) and the Tatamá Natural Park, reaching the Cauca River valley (ca. 900 m a.s.l.) near Virginia. This route connects with El Jordán on the eastern slope of Cordillera Central and Pubenza 3 in the lowlands of the Magdalena River valley. The second route reaches the Calima river sites (ca. 1750 m a.s.l.) and also the Popayán Plateau (ca. 1700 m a.s.l.), crossing the Cordillera Occidental near the natural paths of the Serranía del Pazé and the Sigí and the upper basin of the Cauca River.

This route was long considered a path of rapid penetration to regions farther south, taking advantage of the resources provided by coastal ecosystems along the western slopes of the Andes (Bryan 1986; Dillehay 1999, 2000; Dixon 2001; Anderson and Gillam 2000; Goebel et al. 2008; Lanata et al. 2008; Surovell 2003; Waguespack 2007). Nonetheless, in chronological terms for the Colombian case, dates of the sites connected by this route are not as old as would be expected in order to explain occupations before 11,000 RCYBP.

At the same time, these three clusters (5, 14, 15) are very well interconnected by the valley of the Cauca River, one of the great natural corridors of the Colombian Andes. These sites have strong similarities in lithic technology, particularly the Calima River and the Middle Cauca contexts. The Cauca River also brings these three clusters together with the Medellín/Porce River sites in the north of the Central Cordillera. The Porce River is a natural corridor connecting the valleys of the Cauca and Magdalena Rivers, through the valleys of the Nus and San Bartolomé. It also connects to the lowlands of the Caribbean coast, down the Cauca River. Therefore, the Porce River must have been one of the main natural routes used for crossing the Cordillera Central and connecting the Cauca with the Magdalena. The archaeological contexts from north to south correspond to the same lithic tradition, focused on gathering (Aceituno and Loaiza 2015; Aceituno et al. 2013).

The Middle Cauca, Calima River, and Popayán Plateau clusters are connected with the eastern slope of the Cordillera Central and the Magdalena valley, where there are routes leading to the Cundiboyacan Plateau. For example, the natural connection between sites of the Middle Cauca and Magdalena River valley lies through the Esperanza depression that descends to it through the villages of Letra, Papua, and Fresno. Moreover, the El Jordán site is located in the Cucuana valley, a natural depression that commonly allowed passage toward the western slope of the Cordillera Central (Salgado 1998: 18), connecting the Magdalena River with the Cauca River. From the Magdalena valley, one can access the Sabana de Bogotá using the routes of Puerto Triunfo/Honda, Puerto Berrio/Cimitarra, and El Espinal/Girardot.

Figure 5.12 shows a network of optimal paths connecting different clusters. This structure can map the early settlement of the Colombian Andes, especially between ca. 10,000 and 9000

RCYBP, in the Pleistocene–Holocene transition. The archaeological record during this period presents a significant increase in activity that is indicative of major population movements. The complex network of routes that emerges connects a great diversity of ecosystems and landscapes across the different Colombian mountain ranges. Over relatively short distances, one can go from the lowlands of the Magdalena and Cauca Rivers to the high and intermediate lands of the three mountain ranges that delimit the Colombian Andes. Another feature of the network is the use of natural paths across the challenging Andes at different points, taking advantage of intra-Andean valleys that cross the three ranges (Occidental, Central, and Oriental). This network of trails coincides with the increase in sites from the end of the Late Pleistocene to the Early Holocene, which has been interpreted as a momentum of human dispersal into new ecosystems at a time of climatic change that potentially affect resource availability (Aceituno et al. 2013). According to radiocarbon dates, this dispersal would be represented by sites linked to the Tropical Forest Archaic tradition, which, as we have noted, is closely related to the use and exploitation of plants.

Conclusions

The optimal paths represent potential routes that maintain close spatial relationships with archaeological site clusters. This means human groups took advantage of natural corridors that facilitated transit during settlement of the Colombian Andes.

If we combine radiocarbon dates, site location, and the optimal paths network, some conclusions arise. The first conclusion concerns the arrival of the first human groups, an issue that is still an open question. The oldest date of Pubenza 3 is about 16,000 RCYBP, a date that is not wholeheartedly embraced (Dillehay 2000; Lahaye et al. 2013; Politis 1999; Politis et al. 2008; Scheisohn 2003). The other oldest dates belong to El Abra II and Tibitó (Sabana de Bogotá). Either way, these dates would indicate pre-Clovis settlement prior to 11,500 RCYBP in the north of South America (Cooke et al. 2013; Ranere and López 2007).

The second conclusion is the existence of a route during the Late Pleistocene connecting the Isthmus of Panama to the Sabana de Bogotá, which is linked to the Middle Magdalena and Tequendamiense lithic traditions, mainly characterized by the presence of debitage tools. The projectile point from Gloria Bay (close to Cueva de los Murciélagos) is a Fishtail type, similar to other points that have appeared in several sites in Panama, dated around 11,000 RCYBP and probably linked to Clovis technology (Cooke et al. 2013; Ranere 2008; Ranere and López 2007). Points belonging to the fluted point tradition have been recovered in Venezuela, seen as representing the southernmost expansion of the Clovis tradition (Ranere and López 2007). One can thus infer a relationship between the Middle Magdalena tradition and the Fishtail tradition from Panama (Ranere and López 2007). This corridor appears to have been used around 11,000 RCYBP.

The third conclusion refers to early occupation of sites in the Cordillera Central (Middle Porce, Medellín River, Middle Cauca, Popayán Plateau) and Cordillera Occidental (Calima River) that represent the Archaic Tropical Forest tradition. The lithic assemblages in these sites are not directly associated with the known archaeological record of other sites in Panama and Colombia. For instance, the stone technology meant for plant processing (handstones, milling stones, hoes, axes, etc.) is a later feature in Panama (Cooke et al. 2013), as well as in other Colombian regions such as the Middle Magdalena or Sabana de Bogotá.

To explain the visibility of these sites we suggest two hypotheses, one exogenous and another endogenous. The first requires population movements from Panama that would have taken place after the Terminal Late Pleistocene from sites on the Pacific coast (e.g, Cueva de los Vampiros, Carabalí, Aguadulce, and Corona; Cooke et al. 2013) following the Pacific corridor. It is important to point out that Ranere and López (2007) and others (Faught 2006: 181; Jackson 2006:119) have related the lithic assemblages of Popayán—particularly some points from La Elvira—to the Fishtail tradition. The problem here is the lack of archaeological sites between the Isthmus of Panama and the Cordillera Central and Occidental along the coastal route.

The second hypothesis concerns local adaptations to the sub-Andean valleys by small groups linked to the Middle Magdalena tradition. The dispersion of projectile points in regions such as the Aburrá Valley or Porce River suggests exploratory incursions around 10,500 RCYBP (Aceituno et al. 2013). It can also be evidence of a third scenario that would combine the previous two, with demographic movements from the Isthmus of Panama and the Middle Magdalena river valley, converging in the highlands of the Cordillera Central and Occidental. Despite these proposals and reasoning, however, we are aware that none of the three hypotheses are conclusive in any way.

The extensive network of routes suggests potential relationships between contexts located in different regions of the Colombian Andes, where the valleys of the Cauca and Magdalena Rivers played a crucial role in facilitating the mobility and communication of early human groups. The dispersion of Middle Magdalena projectile points in different parts of the Andean region, for example, suggests displacement that could be linked to the expansion of human groups during the Late Pleistocene (ca. 11,000–10,300 RCYBP). Similarly, contexts belonging to the Archaic Tropical Forest tradition show population movements along the Cordillera Central and Occidental between 10,200 and 9,500 RCYBP.

In conclusion, the GIS analysis detailed above seeks to contribute to the understanding of natural corridors involved in the process of early peopling of the Andean region of Colombia, and hence of South America. Comparing the achieved results with the characteristics of the archaeological record, we managed to develop hypotheses regarding various population movements that may have been involved in this process. Nonetheless, this analysis is only a first step toward a better understanding of the cartography of the settlement of this South American region. The obtained results will hopefully be complemented or corrected in the near future by discovery of new sites in regions previously invisible due to the absence of data: the Caribbean coast, Colombian Amazonia, or the Pacific coast.

Acknowledgments

Our gratitude to Enrique Capdevila (Instituto de Historia, CCHS-CSIC) for his invaluable suggestions during the implementation of GIS analysis.

Notes

1. GIS analysis has been performed using ArcGIS software (v. 10.2.1), and IBM SPSS Statistics (v. 22). The coordinate system selected for the GIS project is UTM 18 North, Datum WGS84. GIS tools used, taken from the ArcGIS-ArcToolbox set, are mentioned in endnotes.
2. There are two main types of spatial data models for organizing geographical information layers: *raster*, a regular grid formed by square cells (pixels), and *vector*, consisting in basic geometrical entities defined by pairs of coordinates (points, lines, and polygons; Burrough and McDonnell 1998:21–27).
3. The slope layer has been derived from Digital Elevation Model (DEM) ArcGIS-ArcToolbox-Surface-Slope. The DEM used is GTOPO30, with a cell size of 30 arc seconds (around 1 km). GTOPO30 is available from the U.S. Geological Survey.
4. MADO (*Modelo de Acumulación del Desplazamiento Óptimo desde un Origen*), "optimal accumulation model of movement from a given origin."
5. ArcGIS-ArcToolbox-Spatial Analysis Tools-Distance-Cost Distance.
6. ArcGIS-ArcToolbox-Spatial Analysis Tools-Hydrology-Flow Direction.
7. ArcGIS-ArcToolbox-Spatial Analysis Tools-Hydrology-Flow Accumulation.
8. ArcGIS-ArcToolbox-Spatial Analysis Tools-Reclass-Reclassify
9. ArcGIS-ArcToolbox-Spatial Analysis Tools-Hydrology-Stream to Feature.
10. UTM coordinates (zone 18 North, Datum WGS84): (1) Caribbean location (Cueva de los Murciélagos), X=272.365 Y=916.265; (2) Pacific location, X=191.058 Y=794.582.
11. ArcGIS-ArcToolbox-Analysis Tools-Proximity-Near.
12. ArcGIS-ArcToolbox-Data Management Tools-Feature Class-Create Random Points. In order to test the randomness of the control sample, we performed a nearest neighbor analysis (ArcGIS–ArcToolbox–Spatial Statistics Tools–Analyzing Patterns–Average Nearest Neighbor) with positive results: nearest neighbor ratio = 0.997; z score = -0.050; p value = 0.960.

13. ArcGIS-ArcToolbox-Analysis Tools-Proximity-Buffer.
14. ArcGIS-ArcToolbox-Spatial Analysis Tools-Distance-Cost Distance.
15. ArcGIS-ArcToolbox-Spatial Analysis Tools-Distance-Cost Path.
16. ArcGIS-ArcToolbox-Spatial Analysis Tools-Distance-Cost Path.
17. ArcGIS-ArcToolbox-Spatial Analysis Tools-Reclass-Reclassify.
18. ArcGIS-ArcToolbox-Spatial Analysis Tools-Map Algebra-Raster Calculator.
19. ArcGIS-ArcToolbox-Conversion Tools-From Raster-Raster to Polyline.
20. ArcGIS-ArcToolbox-Spatial Analysis Tools-Density-Kernel Density.

References

Aceituno Francisco J.

2007 Poblamiento y variaciones culturales en la región andina del noroccidente de Suramérica en la transición Pleistoceno Holoceno. In *Arqueología en las Pampas*, Vol. 1. Edited by Cristina Bayón Alejandra Pupio, Maria I. González, Nora Flegenheimer, and Magdalena Frére, pp. 15–38. Sociedad Argentina de Antropología, Buenos Aires.

Aceituno, Francisco J., and Neyla Castillo

2005 Strategies of Mobility in Colombia's Middle Mountain Range between the Early and Middle Holocene. *Before Farming: The Archaeology and Anthropology of Hunter-Gatherers* 2005(2):1–17.

Aceituno, Francisco J., and Nicolás Loaiza

2007 *Domesticación del bosque en el Cauca medio colombiano entre el Pleistoceno final y el Holoceno medio*. British Archaeological Reports, International Series 1654. Archaeopress, Oxford.

2014 Early and Middle Holocene Evidence for Use of Plants and Cultivation in the Middle Cauca River Basin, Cordillera Central (Colombia). *Quaternary Science Reviews* 86:49–62.

2015 The Role of Plants in the Early Settlement of Northwest South America. *Quaternary International* 363:20–27.

Aceituno, Francisco J., Nicolás Loaiza, Miguel E. Delgado, and Gustavo Barrientos

2013 The Initial Human Settlement of Northwest South America during the Pleistocene/Holocene Transition: Synthesis and Perspectives. *Quaternary International* 301:23–33.

Anderson, David G., and J. Christopher Gillam

2000   Paleoindian Colonization of the Americas: Implications from an Examination of Physiography, Demography, and Artifact Distribution. *American Antiquity* 65(1):43–66.

Anthony, David W.

1990   Migration in Archaeology: The Baby and the Bathwater. *American Anthropologist* 92(4):895–914.

Bray, Warwick, Leonor Herrera, and Marianne C. Schrimpff

1988   Report on the 1984 Field Season. *Pro-Calima. Archäologisch-ethnologisches Projekt im westlichen Kolumbien/Südamerika* 5:2–42.

Bryan, Alan L.

1986   Paleoamerican Prehistory as Seen from South America. In *New Evidence for the Pleistocene Peopling of the Americas*, edited by Alan L. Bryan, pp. 1–14. Center for the Study of Early Man, University of Maine, Orono.

Bryan, Alan L., Rodolfo Casamiquela, Jose M. Cruxent, Ruth Gruhn, and Claudio Oschsenius

1978   An El Jobo Mastodon Kill at Taima-Taima, Venezuela. *Science* 200(4347):1275–1277.

Burrough, Peter A., and Rachael A. McDonnell

1998   *Principles of Geographical Information Systems*. Oxford University Press, New York.

Cano, Martha

2004   Los primeros habitantes de las cuencas medias de los ríos Otún y Consota. In *Cambios ambientales en perspectiva histórica. Ecorregión del Eje Cafetero*, Vol. 1, edited by Carlos López and Martha Cano, pp.68–91. Universidad Tecnológica de Pereira, Programa Ambiental GTZ, Pereira, CO.

Cardale, Marianne, Warwick Bray, and Leonor Herrera

1989   Reconstruyendo el pasado en calima resultados recientes. *Boletín del Museo del Oro* 24:3–33.

Cardona, Luis C.

2012   *Porce III proyecto hidroeléctrico estudios de arqueología preventiva. Del arcaico a la colonia. Construcción del paisaje y cambio social en el Porce Medio.* Empresas Públicas de Medellín, Medellín, CO.

Cardona, Luis C., Luis E. Nieto, and Jorge I. Pino

2007   *Del Arcaico a la Colonia. Construcción del paisaje y cambio social en el Porce Medio. Informe final.* Medellín: Universidad de Antioquia-Empresas de Medellín.

Castillo, Neyla, and Francisco J. Aceituno

2006   El bosque domesticado, el bosque cultivado: un proceso milenario en el valle medio del río Porce en el noroccidente Colombiano. *Latin American Antiquity* 17(4):561–578.

Cavelier, Inés, Camilo Rodríguez, Leonor Herrera, Gaspar Morcote, and Santiago Mora

1995   No solo de la caza vive el hombre: ocupación del bosque Amazónico, Holoceno temprano. In *Ámbito y ocupaciones tempranas de la América tropical*, edited by Inés Cavelier and Santiago Mora, pp. 27–44. Fundación Erigaie, Instituto Colombiano de Antropología, Bogotá.

Cooke, Richard, Anthony J. Ranere, George Pearson, and Ruth Dickau

2013   Radiocarbon Chronology of Early Human Settlement on the Isthmus of Panama (13,000–7000 BP) with Comments on Cultural Affinities, Environments, Subsistence, and Technological Change. *Quaternary International* 301:3–22.

Conolly, James, and Mark Lake

2006   *Geographical Information Systems in Archaeology*. Cambridge University Press, New York.

Correal, Gonzalo

1979   *Investigaciones arqueológicas en los abrigos rocosos de Nemocón y Sueva*. Fundación de Investigaciones Arqueológicas Nacionales, Bogotá.

1981   *Evidencias culturales y megafauna Pleistocénica en Colombia*. Fundación de Investigaciones Arqueológicas Nacionales, Bogotá.

1982   Restos de megafauna en la Sabana de Bogotá. *Caldasia* 13(64):487–547.

1983   Evidencias de cazadores especializados en el sitio de la Gloria, golfo de Urabá. *Academia de Ciencias Exactas Físicas y Naturales* 15(58):77–82.

1986   Apuntes sobre el medio ambiente Pleistocénico y el hombre prehistórico en Colombia. In *New Evidence for the Pleistocene Peopling of the Americas*, edited by Alan L. Bryan. pp. 115–131. Center for the Study of Early Man, University of Maine, Orono.

1990   Evidencias culturales durante el Pleistoceno y Holoceno de Colombia. *Revista de Arqueología Americana* 1:69–89.

1993   Nuevas evidencias culturales Pleistocénicas y megafauna en Colombia. *Boletín de Arqueología* 8(1):3–12.

Correal, Gonzalo, and Thomas van der Hammen
1977   *Investigaciones arqueológicas en los abrigos rocosos del Tequendama.* Biblioteca Banco Popular, Bogotá.

Cruxent, Jose M., and Claudio Ochsenius
1979   Paleo-Indian Studies in Northern Venezuela. In *Taima-Taima: A Late Paleo-Indian Kill Site in Northernmost South America. Final Reports of the 1976 Excavations,* edited by C. Ochsenius and R. Gruhn, 9–13. CIPICS/South American Quaternary Documentation Program, Berlin.

Delgado, Manuel E., Francisco J. Aceituno, and Gustavo Barrientos
2015 ^{14}C Data and the Early Colonization of Northwest South America: A Critical Assessment. *Quaternary International* 363:55–64.

Dickau, Ruth, Francisco J. Aceituno, Nicolás Loaiza, Carlos López, Martha Cano, Leonor Herrera, Carlos Restrepo, and Anthony J. Ranere
2015   Radiocarbon Chronology of Terminal Pleistocene to Middle Holocene Human Occupation in the Middle Cauca Valley, Colombia. *Quaternary International* 363:43–54.

Dillehay, Tom
1999   The Late Pleistocene Cultures of South America. *Evolutionary Anthropology* 7(6): 206–216.
2000   *The Settlement of the Americas.* Basic Books, New York.
2009   Probing Deeper into First American Studies. *PNAS* 106(4):971–978.

Dillehay, Tom D., Carlos Ocampo, José Saavedra, Andre Oliveira, Rodrigo M. Vega, María Pino, Michael B. Collins, et al.
2015   New Archaeological Evidence for an Early Human Presence at Monte Verde, Chile. *PLoS One.* doi:10.1371/journal.pone 0141923.

Dixon, E. James
2001   Human Colonization of the Americas: Timing, Technology, and Process. *Quaternary Science Reviews* 20:277–299.

Fábrega-Álvarez, Pastor
2006   Moving without Destination: A Theoretical GIS-Based Determination of Movement from a Giving Origin. *Archaeological Computing Newsletter* 64:7–11.

Fábrega-Álvarez, Pastor, and César Parcero-Oubiña
2007   Proposals for an Archaeological Analysis of Pathways and Movement. *Archeologia e Calcolatori* 18:121–140.

Faught, Michael K.
2006   Paleoindian Archaeology in Florida and Panama: Two Circumgulf Regions Exhibiting Waisted Lanceolate Projectile Points. In *Paleoindian Occupation in the Americas: A Hemisphere Perspective,* edited by Juliet Morrow and Cristóbal Gnecco, pp. 164–184. University Press of Florida, Gainesville.

Gnecco, Cristóbal
2000   *Ocupación temprana de bosques tropicales de montaña.* Editorial Universidad del Cauca.
2003   Against Ecological Reductionism: Late Pleistocene Hunter-Gatherers in the Tropical Forests of Northern South America. *Quaternary International* 109–110:13–21.

Gnecco, Cristóbal, and Santiago Mora
1997   Late Pleistocene/Early Holocene Tropical Forest Occupations at San Isidro and Peña Roja, Colombia. *Antiquity* 71(273):683–690.

Goebel, Ted, Michael R. Waters, and Dennis H. O'Rourke
2008   The Late Pleistocene Dispersal of Modern Humans in the Americas. *Science* 319(5869): 1497–1502

Gorenflo, J. L., and Nathan Gale
1990   Mapping Regional Settlement in Information Space. *Journal of Anthropological Archaeology* 9(3):240–274.

Groot, Ana M.
1992   *Checua: una secuencia cultural entre 8500 y 3000 años antes del presente.* Fundación de Investigaciones Arqueológicas Nacionales, Banco de la República, Bogotá.

Gruhn, Ruth
1979   Description of the 1976 Excavations in Taima-Taima. In *Taima-Taima: A Late Paleo-Indian Kill Site in Northernmost South America. Final Reports of the 1976 Excavations,* edited by C. Ochsenius and R. Gruhn, 31–33. CIPICS/South American Quaternary Documentation Program. Berlin.

Güimil-Fariña, Alejandro, and César Parcero-Oubiña
2015   "Dotting the Joins": A Non-Reconstructive Use of Least Cost Paths to Approach Ancient Roads. The Case of the Roman Roads in the NW Iberian Peninsula. *Journal of Archaeological Science* 54:31–44.

Herrera, Leonor, Warwick Bray, Marianne Cardale, and Pedro Botero
1992   Nuevas fechas de radiocarbono para el precerámico de la Cordillera Occidental de

Colombia. In *Archaeology and Environment in Latin America*, edited by Omar Ortiz-Troncoso and Thomas van der Hammen, pp.145–163. Institut voor Pre- en Protohistorische Acheologie Albert Egges van Giffen, University of Amsterdam, NL.

Herrera, Leonor, Cristina Moreno, and Omar Peña

2011   *La historia muy antigua del municipio de Palestina (Caldas). Proyecto de rescate y monitoreo arqueológico del aeropuerto del café.* Centro de Museos-Universidad de Caldas, Asociación Aeropuerto del Café (2005–2011), Manizales, CO.

Howey, Meghan C. L.

2007   Using Multi-Criteria Cost Surface Analysis to Explore Past Regional Landscapes: A Case Study of Ritual Activity and Social Interaction in Michigan, AD 1200–1600. *Journal of Archaeological Science* 34(11): 1830–1846.

Hurt, Wesley, Thomas van der Hammen, and Gonzalo Correal

1977   The El Abra Rockshelters, Sabana de Bogotá, Colombia, South America. *Occasional Papers and Monographs* 2. Indiana University Museum, Bloomington.

INTEGRAL

1997   *Arqueología de Rescate. Vía alterna de la troncal de occidente. Río Campoalegre-Estadio Santa Rosa de Cabal.* Informe final al Instituto Nacional de Vías. Report on file. INTEGRAL, Medellín, CO.

Jackson, Lawrence

2006   Fluted and Fishtail Points from Southern Coastal Chile. In *Paleoindian Occupation in the Americas: A Hemisphere Perspective*, edited by Juliet Morrow and Cristóbal Gnecco, pp. 105–122. University Press of Florida, Gainesville.

Lahaye, Christelle, Marion Hernández, Eric Boeda, Gisele D. Felice, Niède Guidon, Sirlei Hoeltz, Antoine Lourdeau, et al.

2013   Human Occupation in South America by 20,000 BC: The Toca Da Tira Peia Site, Piauí, Brazil. *Journal of Archaeological Science* 40:2840–2847.

Lanata, Jose L., Luis Martino, Ana Osella, and Arleen García-Herbst

2008   Ambiente y demografía durante la dispersión humana inicial en Sudamérica. In *Ecología histórica. Interacciones sociedad-ambiente a distintas escalas socio-temporales,*

edited by Carlos E. López and Guillermo Ospina, pp. 19–38. Universidad Tecnológica de Pereira-Sociedad Colombiana de Arqueología-Universidad del Cauca, Pereira.

Llanos, Juan M.

1997   Artefactos de molienda en la región de medio río Caquetá–Amazonía colombiana. *Boletín de Arqueología* 12(2):3–95.

López, Carlos E.

1989   Evidencias paleoindias en el valle medio del río Magdalena (municipios de Puerto Berrío, Yondó y Remedios, Antioquia). *Boletín de Arqueología* 4(2):3–23.

1995   Dispersión de puntas de proyectil bifaciales en la cuenca media del río Magdalena. In *Ámbito y ocupaciones tempranas de la América tropical*, edited by Inés Cavelier and Santiago Mora, pp. 73–82. Fundación Erigaie, Instituto Colombiano de Antropología, Bogotá.

1999   *Ocupaciones tempranas en las tierras bajas tropicales del valle medio del río Magdalena: sitio 05-Yon-002 Yondó-Antioquia.* Fundación de Investigaciones Arqueológicas Nacionales, Banco de la República, Bogotá.

2008   *Landscape Development and the Evidence for Early Human Occupation in the Inter-Andean Tropical Lowlands of the Magdalena River, Colombia.* SyllabaPress, Miami, FL.

Mayoral, Victorino, and Sebastián Celestino (editors)

2011   *Tecnologías de información geográfica y análisis arqueológico del territorio.* CSIC, Madrid.

Mora, Santiago

2003   *Early Inhabitants of the Amazonian Tropical Rain Forest: A Study of Humans and Environmental Dynamics.* University of Pittsburgh Latin American Archaeology Reports 3. Pittsburgh, PA.

Mora, Santiago, and Cristóbal Gnecco

2003   Archaeological Hunter-Gatherers in Tropical Rainforests: A View from Colombia. In *Under the Canopy: The Archaeology of Tropical Rain Forests*, edited by Julio Mercader, pp. 271–290. Rutgers University Press, New Brunswick, NJ.

Morcote, Gaspar, R., Carlos Cabrera, Dany Mahecha, Carlos Franky, and Inés Cavelier

1998   Las palmas entre los grupos cazadores recolectores de la Amazonia colombiana. *Caldasia* 20:57–74.

Murrieta-Flores, Patricia
2012   Understanding Human Movement through
        Spatial Technologies: The Role of Natural
        Areas of Transit in the Late Prehistory of
        South-western Iberia. *Trabajos de Prehisto-
        ria* 69(1):103–122.
Otero, Helda, and Gustavo Santos
2006   *Las ocupaciones prehispánicas del cañón del
        río Porce. Prospección, rescate y monitoreo
        arqueológico. Proyecto hidroeléctrico Porce
        III. Obras de infraestructura. Informe final.*
        Universidad de Antioquia, Empresas de
        Medellín, Medellín, CO.
2012   *Porce III proyecto hidroeléctrico estudios
        de arqueología preventiva. Dinámica de
        cambio en las sociedades prehispánicas de la
        cuenca baja del Porce.* Empresas Públicas de
        Medellín, Pereira, CO.
Pinto, María
2003   *Galindo, un sitio a cielo abierto de cazadores-
        recolectores en la Sabana de Bogotá.*
        Fundación de Investigaciones Arqueológicas
        Nacionales, Banco de la República, Bogotá.
Piperno, Dolores
1985   Phytolithic Analysis of Geological Sediments
        from Panama. *Antiquity* 59(225):13–19.
Piperno, Dolores, and Deborah M. Pearsall
1998   *The Origins of Agriculture in the Lowland
        Neotropics.* Academic Press, San Diego, CA.
Politis, Gustavo
1999   La estructura del debate sobre el pobla-
        miento de América. *Boletín de Arqueología*
        14(2):25–51.
Politis, Gustavo, Luciano Prates, and S. Iván Pérez
2008   *El poblamiento de América. Arqueología y
        bio-antropología de los primeros america-
        nos.* Eudeba, Universidad de Buenos Aires,
        Buenos Aires.
Ranere, Anthony J.
1980   *Adaptive Radiations in Prehistoric Panama.*
        Peabody Museum Monographs 5. Harvard
        University Press, Cambridge, MA.
2008   Lower Central America. In *Encyclopedia
        of Archaeology*, edited by Deborah Pears-
        all, pp. 192–209. Elsevier/Academic Press,
        New York.
Ranere, Anthony, and Carlos E. López
2007   Cultural Diversity in Late Pleistocene/Early
        Holocene Populations in Northwest South
        America and Lower Central America. *Inter-
        national Journal South American Archaeol-
        ogy* 1:25–31.

Reichel-Dolmatoff, G.
1965   *Colombia: Ancient Peoples and Places.*
        Praeger, New York.
Restrepo, Carlos A.
2013   *Monitoreo arqueológico 760 finca Miramar,
        Vereda el Gigante, municipio de Montene-
        gro. Quindío.* Informe Final. Ms. Mi Pollo
        S.A., CO.
Rivera, Sergio
1991   *Neusa 9000 años de presencia humana en
        el páramo.* Fundación de Investigaciones
        Arqueológicas Nacionales, Banco de la
        República, Bogotá.
Rodríguez, Carlos A.
2002   *El valle del Cauca prehispánico: procesos
        socioculturales antiguos en las regiones geo-
        históricas del alto y medio Cauca y la costa
        Pacífica Colombo-Ecuatoriana.* Departa-
        mento de Historia, Facultad de Humani-
        dades, Universidad del Valle, Santiago de
        Cali, CO.
Rodríguez, Carlos D., Ernesto L. Rodríguez, and
Carlos A. Rodríguez
2009   Revisión de la fauna Pleistocénica Gom-
        photheriidae en Colombia y reporte de un
        caso para el valle del Cauca. *Boletín Científ-
        ico Centro de Museos Museo de Historia
        Natural* 13(2):78–85.
Rojas, Sneider, and Dionalver Tabares
2000   *Aportes para una historia en construcción:
        arqueología de rescate en la doble calzada
        Manizales-Pereira-Armenia.* Report on file,
        INVIAS-CISAN, Bogotá, CO.
Salgado, Héctor
1988–1990 Asentamientos precerámicos en el alto-
        medio río Calima, Cordillera Occidental,
        Colombia. *Cespedesia* 57–58:139–162.
1998   *Exploraciones arqueológicas en la Cordillera
        Central Roncesvalles-Tolima.* Fundación de
        Investigaciones Arqueológicas Nacionales,
        Banco de la República, Bogotá.
Santos, Gustavo
2010   *Diez mil años de ocupaciones humanas en
        Envigado (Antioquia). El sitio la Morena.* Al-
        caldía de Envigado, Secretaría de Educación
        para la Cultura, Envigado, CO.
Santos, Gustavo, Carlos A. Monsalve, and Luz
Victoria Correa
2015   Alteration of Tropical Forest Vegetation
        from the Pleistocene–Holocene Transition
        and Plant Cultivation from the End of
        Early Holocene though Middle Holocene in

Northwest Colombia. *Quaternary International* 363:28–42.

Scheisohn, Vivian
2003   Hunter-Gatherer Archaeology in South America. *Annual Review of Anthropology* 32:339–361.

Surovell, Todd A.
2003   Simulating Coastal Migration in New World Colonization. *Current Anthropology* 44(4): 589–591.

van der Hammen, Thomas, and Gonzalo Correal
2001   Mastodontes en un humedal Pleistocénico en el valle del Magdalena (Colombia) con evidencias de la presencia del hombre en el Pleniglacial. *Boletín de Arqueología* 16(1):4–36.

Verhagen, Philip
2013   On the Road to Nowhere? Least Cost Paths Accessibility and the Predictive Modelling Perspective. In *CAA2010, Fusion of Cultures.*

Proceedings of the 38th Annual Conference on Computer Applications and Quantitative Methods in Archaeology, Granada, Spain, April 2010, edited by Francisco Contreras, Mercedes Farjas, and Francisco J. Melero, pp. 383–389. Archaeopress, Oxford.

Waguespack, Nicole M.
2007   Why We're Still Arguing about the Pleistocene Occupation of the Americas. *Evolutionary Anthropology* 16(2):63–74.

Wheatley, David, and Mark Gillings
2002   *Spatial Technology and Archaeology. The Archaeological Applications of GIS.* Taylor and Francis, New York.

White, Devin A., and Sarah B. Barber
2012   Geospatial Modeling of Pedestrian Transportation Networks: A Case Study from Precolumbian Oaxaca, Mexico. *Journal of Archaeological Science* 39(8):2684–2696.

CHAPTER 6

The Clovis-Like and Fishtail Occupations of Southern Mexico and Central America

A Reappraisal

Guillermo Acosta-Ochoa, Patricia Pérez-Martínez,
and Ximena Ulloa-Montemayor

Hypotheses on the peopling of Middle (Central) America are not foreign to the general debate about the peopling of the New World (MacNeish and Nelken-Terner 1983; Pearson 2004; Acosta 2012). These hypotheses have been dominated by the idea that the first settlers were bearers of the fluted point technology that has been suggested as the oldest in the archaeological record for North America (mainly Canada and the U.S.). Some researchers have lately asserted a slight variation that while the Clovis culture is not necessarily the oldest in the New World it is the first "clearly distinguishable" technology in the archaeological record (Sánchez et al. 2014). However, in other regions, such as South America, it is commonly accepted that the Late Pleistocene "distinguishable culture" mosaic is more diverse and complex (Bate 1983; Dillehay et al. 1992). This same complexity is first recorded in Mexico's southeast, albeit with only a few stratified sites for this period (Acosta 2010b). Specific population routes from North to South America have also been proposed based on geographical analyses, artifact typology distribution, and even linguistic data (Morrow and Morrow 1999; Lanata 2011; Acosta et al. 2013; Gruhn 1988).

We consider that some of these approaches do not contribute to a better understanding of the peopling of the Americas, since they still are "aquatic models" that do not account for hunter-gatherer internal structure; while cost-analysis models are mainly useful in a heuristic sense (Acosta et al. 2013). In addition, the characteristics of hunter-gatherer site structure have not been fully addressed in studies of early settlement, despite the age of the Bordes-Binford debate and other proposals on hunters' settlement systems (Binford 1980). We also consider that the characterization of activities between different types of archaeological sites is key to understanding the variety of located artifacts and better defining whether different regional "cultural complexes" cause artifact typology differences, or if they are the result of the differences between various site types. In this sense, surface findings add very little to our understanding of the cycle of activities of these early settlers, while kill sites show only a partial and incomplete view of the total cycle of activities of a hunter-gatherer society and generate an overvaluation of projectile points above other cultural materials.

Thus, this chapter does not present a new synthesis of sites and projectile points typology in the south of Mexico and the rest of Central America, since there are sufficient studies of this subject (i.e., Ranere 2006; Pearson 2004; Perrot-Minot 2013). Instead, we attempt a critical synthesis about these data, assessing them in relation to other aspects that have barely been approached, such as the subsistence patterns and human ecology of groups associated with fluted points in Middle America.

The Geographical and Environmental Setting of Middle America at the End of the Pleistocene

Pleistocene conditions in North America were very different from what we know today. In Mexico, paleoenvironmental research on this period is still scarce, except for the center of the country. There, information seems to show alternation between wet and dry episodes, with the predominance of drier and colder conditions than the present (L. González 1986; Lozano and Ortega 1994). The north of Mexico, however, seems to have been more humid than it is today, with many pine communities and mixed forests in the lower areas (Meyer 1973). In contrast, data from southern Mexico indicate a drier period in the Yucatan Peninsula. In Chiapas, studies suggest a colder but wetter period during the Younger Dryas, probably alternating with dry periods (Hernández 2010; Acosta 2008; Rivera-González 2013).

This climate—an average of 7°C colder and predominantly drier than at present—also favored development of very specific ecosystems, which supported a wide range of now-extinct species. In the north of the continent (including the Pacific slope and the central highlands of Mexico), Nearctic fauna was dominant, including megafauna such as mammoth and extinct species of horse, camel, and Pleistocene wolf (Martin 1967). These animals covered large grassland areas that looked similar to the African Serengeti, dominated by large herds of grazing animals and their predators. In areas with closed vegetation, there were temperate forests and browsing animals such as mastodon, *Megatherium* sloth, and deer.

The South American continent was dominated by diverse tropical ecosystems, home for proboscideans such as gomphotheres, giant armadillos, and various genera of giant sloths (Arroyo-Cabrales et al. 2007). In Middle America, both types of fauna cohabited, which is why it can be considered a transitional zone (Johnson et al. 2006). At the Los Grifos rockshelter, in Chiapas, remains of Pleistocene horse (*Equus* sp.) have been found, along with lithic artifacts in levels between 9000–10,000 BC, which confirms the coexistence of human beings and extinct fauna at the end of this period (Acosta 2010a), though there is no direct evidence of an association between fluted points and megafauna.[1]

Paleoenvironmental reconstructions from central Mexico to Panama suggest that temperate pine-oak forest prevailed in the high areas, with mesophyll rainforest in the wetter regions of the Gulf of Mexico slope. The driest regions of the Pacific slope and the Yucatan Peninsula would have been dominated by deciduous forests, bushes, and grasslands (Piperno and Pearsall 1998).

It should be emphasized that the first settlers of the continent came from temperate-to-tropical ecosystems precisely when entering southern Mexico, which must have involved modification of survival strategies and knowledge of plants and species in environments that were new to them. Modification of hunting-and-gathering strategies implies not only new knowledge about the distribution of resource patches and their seasonality but also the development of new technologies for efficient exploitation of tropical environments. Darts, sling weapons, leather, and wood huts are efficient in temperate and open areas, but in the closed environments of the tropical forest traps, blowpipes, and hammocks are more useful. Of course, this change was not immediate or abrupt. In Santa Marta Cave, in Mexico's southeast, there is evidence of the use of bone needles for the Late Pleistocene (10,500 RCYBP), a technology that accompanied the first settlers of the continent who needed warm clothing with waterproof seams (Dixon 1999). This technology disappears from the Santa Maria record at the end of the Pleistocene when the fog forest is replaced by evergreen and deciduous rainforests. Something similar occurs with the Los Grifos projectile points (Clovis and Fishtail), since they disappear after 9000 RCYBP, until the introduction of the bow and arrow in the region, likely by the year 1000 of our era.

The Lithic "Traditions": Technological and Geographical Aspects

In Middle America, a great number of fluted spearheads has been reported, most on the surface, extending from the Sierra Gorda (State

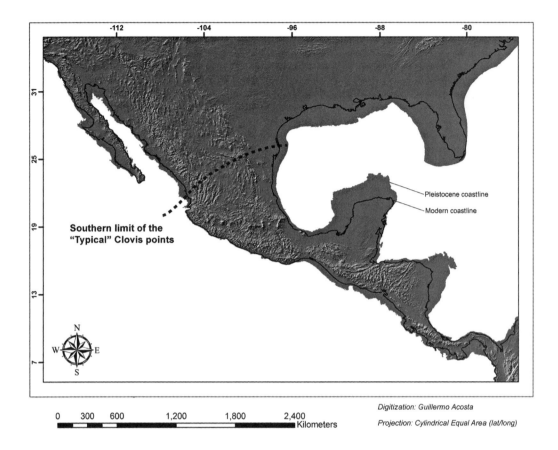

FIGURE 6.1. Southern Mexico and Central America at the end of the Pleistocene and limit of the "typical Clovis" distribution (based on GEBCO Bathymetric Chart: http://www.gebco.net/).

of Querétaro, Mexico) to Panama (Figure 6.2; Acosta 2012). It should be clarified here that the fluted spearheads from the south of Mexico and Central America are not "typical" Clovis points but ones of small size with concave edges, sometimes with real fluting, but often only with simple basal thinning. For that reason, although the literature still labels them as true Clovis points, their morphology has a greater resemblance to those of the North American Late Paleoindian traditions such as the Midland points (Wormington 1957). Hereafter, we will refer to them as "Clovis-like." The production of these points follows the typical pattern of fluted points from the U.S. (Clovis-Folsom): bifacial manufacture using the overshot flake technique with fluting before final touch up, as may be seen at the Turrialba (Costa Rica) workshop site (Snarskis 1979, Pearson 2004).

Other artifacts associated with the classic Clovis industry, such as macro-cores and large blades, are absent from the archaeological record of southern Mexico and Central America. However, materials such as burins and spurred scrapers are clearly associated with the stratified sites of Los Grifos and Los Tapiales (Gruhn et al. 1977; Santamaría and García-Bárcena 1989). These artifacts, which have been linked to "Clovis" groups, also appear in later industries including Folsom sites, which was noted by Gruhn and colleagues (1977:256). This coincides with Joaquín García-Bárcena's position (1980), comparing the Los Grifos spearhead with Folsom points. It is also noteworthy that other Clovis-like spearheads from Oaxaca (Finsten et al. 1989) and Guatemala (Coe 1960), have a groove that resembles those of Folsom spearheads (Figure 6.3: b, h, m, s).

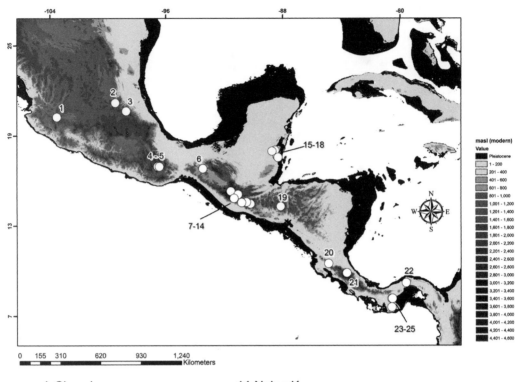

FIGURE 6.2. Fluted point sites ("Clovis" and Fishtail) of Central America.

1. Chapala
2. Jalpan de Serra
3. Oyapa
4. San Juan Guelavía
5. Sitio Orlandini
6. Los Grifos, Chiapas
7. Los Tapiales
8. San Rafael
9. Chajbal
10. Piedra Parada
11. Chivacabé
12. Chujuyub
13. Las Verapaces
14. Nahualá
15. Lowe Ranch
16. Orange Walk
17. Ladyville
18. August Pine Ridge
19. La Esperanza
20. Guardiría (Turrialba)
21. Lago Arenal
22. Lago Alajuela
23. La Mula West
24. Nieto Quarry
25. Cueva los Vampiros

In Central America, Clovis-like projectile points may be associated with Fishtail projectile points, as it occurs at Los Grifos rockshelter (Figure 6.4), although currently it is difficult to establish whether this association occurs because two different groups visited the site, or because the settlers themselves manufactured different point types (Santamaría 1981; Acosta 2010b). The large variation of intermediate forms between Clovis-like and Fishtail classic points seems to indicate at least certain degree of interaction between two groups whose technology seems to have different geographic origins, if we consider the Fishtail point reduction sequence.

The Central American Fishtail points have similar dimensions to their South American homologues, but with a straight-based stem instead an eared one (Cooke 1998). While some authors

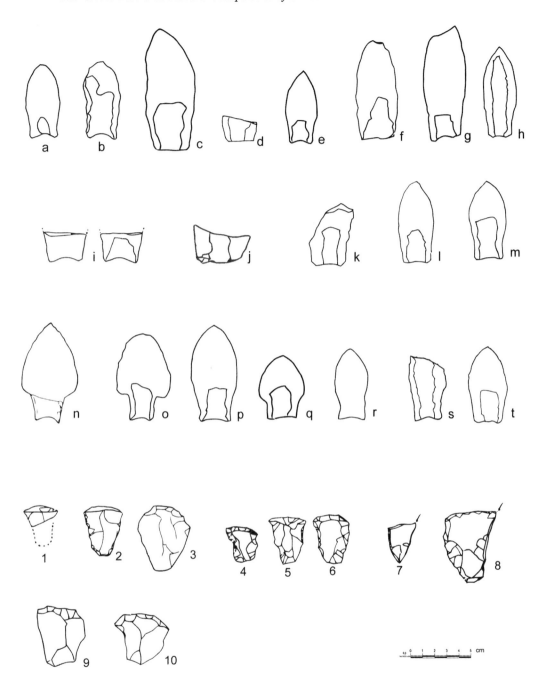

FIGURE 6.3. Clovis and Fishtail artifacts: (*a–t*) fluted points; (*1–10*) endscrapers.

consider the similarities between Clovis and Fishtail points to be diagnostic of a genetic link (Morrow and Morrow 1999), a detailed analysis of these artifacts on a technological level shows important differences that indicate independent development instead of a common origin (Bird 1969; Politis 1991; Pearson 2004). For example, Clovis points are manufactured from large blades or big flakes, which are reduced through percussion and later retouched by pressure

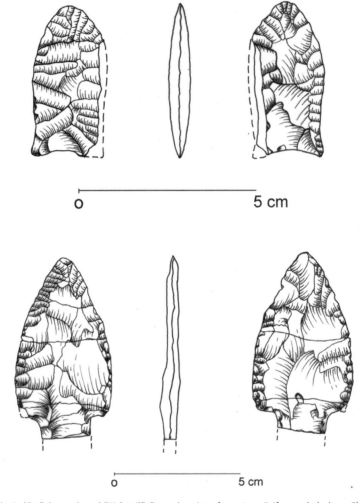

0   5 cm

0   5 cm

FIGURE 6.4. "Clovis-like" (upper) and "Fishtail" (lower) points from Los Grifos rockshelter, Chiapas, Mexico.

and scars usually occur from edge to edge by overshot technique (Bradley 1993; Ranere and Cooke 1991). On the other hand, Fishtail points are manufactured on macro-flakes whose thickness is not greater than the finished spear points (Bird 1969). Fishtails tend to be wider in their distal end, overlapped at the center, and usually retouched on the margins (Ranere and Cooke 1991:239). This causes some researchers to see southeastern Mexico as the area where the technological traditions would have met—Clovis from North America and Fishtail from South America—but in a later period than that of their places of origin (Santamaría and García-Bárcena 1989:101). We will return to this view later.

The Chronological Framework

As mentioned, most Clovis-like and Fishtail points from Mexico to Panama represent surface finds and have only been dated for three sites in Middle America (Table 6.1): Los Grifos (Chiapas, Mexico), Los Tapiales (Guatemala), and Cueva de los Vampiros (Panama). However, it is worth discussing the chronological characteristics of these three sites.

At Los Tapiales, an open campsite located in the highlands of Guatemala, Gruhn and colleagues (1977) reported 10 radiocarbon dates between 11,110 ± 200 and 4730 ± 100 RCYBP, an average occupation hiatus of 8055 years. Charcoal samples came from fireplaces and scattered fragments on occupation surfaces. The dates of the hearths are more spaced, and the authors considered them contaminated, while dates of scattered charcoals are older, and the authors considered the 10,710 ± 170 date correct for the site. However, they accepted that older charcoal could have resulted from natural causes (Gruhn et al. 1977:241). As may be noticed, the early dates at Los Tapiales are problematic because the site presents various dates from the early Holocene, some of them (9800–8800 RCYBP) contemporary with those of Los Grifos rockshelter.

Los Grifos is one of the few sites with fluted points and radiometric dates excavated in Mexico. Joaquín García-Bárcena explored it in 1976 (García-Bárcena 1980; Santamaría and García-Bárcena 1984a, 1984b, 1989). The dates of the Clovis–Fishtail levels range between 8,930 ± 150 and 9,540 ± 150 RCYBP (Table 6.1; Santamaría 1981). Subsequently, the site was reexcavated between 2007 and 2009 in order to obtain new radiometric dates and data on subsistence patterns (Acosta 2008, 2010a, 2011, 2012, 2014). New radiocarbon and paleomagnetic dates were obtained, ranging between 8800 ± 100 and 9440 ± 40 RCYBP (Acosta 2011; Fregoso 2010). The relationships between the dates in both studies seem to support the appearance of fluted points in southeastern Mexico during the Early Holocene (ca. 9500–8900 RCYBP).

Lastly, at Los Vampiros cave, in Panama, a distal fragment of a Fishtail point was found, with preliminary radiocarbon dates placing it between 11,500 and 9000 RCYBP (Pearson and Cooke 2002:932). Even though the authors did not provide further data on the dating of this occupation, previous excavations at the site showed that the level associated with bifacial retouch flakes correspond to 8560 ± 160 RCYBP. As shown, the dates of occupations associated with fluted spear points seem to be related mainly to the Early Holocene.

Nevertheless, some authors still think that these "Paleoindian" groups with fluted points represent an initial human peopling of Central America, or at least that the evidence of older-than-Clovis groups—or different-from-Clovis groups—is practically nonexistent (Pearson 2002; Ranere and Cooke 2003). It has been argued, for example, that other sites in Middle America with early dates either lacked "diagnostic artifacts," such as Piedra del Coyote (Gruhn et al. 1977), or were associated with a fluted point settlement, due to the proximity of Clovis surface sites such as the one in Alvina de Parita (Crusoe and Felton 1974; Pearson 2002:100). However, others have suggested that the groups that manufactured fluted points correspond to only one of the New World Pleistocene cultures. Some of those groups might precede "Clovis," or at least are contemporary to it, such as users of marginal retouch flake technology in South America ("Abriense," "Flake Industry," etc.; Correal 1981; Bate and Acosta 2014), triangular points (Roosevelt et al. 1996), or El Jobo points (Bryan et. al 1978).

What evidence is there of other groups or technologies different from the fluted point technology at the end of the Pleistocene in Central America? For example, the presence of the Paiján "tradition" in Mexico's southeast has also been proposed (García-Bárcena 1989), although the preceramic stemmed points in the Maya area are actually very late (Kelly 1982; Lohse et al. 2006). Another component is represented by the Lerma points, dated between the Late Pleistocene and the Early Holocene, from Mexico's northeast to Oaxaca in the south (Acosta 2010b) and including those associated with megafauna kill sites in central Mexico (Aveleyra and Maldonado 1953; Aveleyra 1956). Lerma points have been identified in Chiapas and the Honduran highlands but only as surface finds (García-Bárcena 1982; Bullen and Plowden 1968).

The only Late Pleistocene dated site that differs from characteristics of subsistence and the technology of fluted point groups is Santa Marta in the Chiapas central depression, a rockshelter just 500 meters from the Los Grifos locality (Figure 6.5; Acosta 2008, 2011). The Santa Marta lithic material is defined by a minimum preparation of edges, trimmed flakes, polyhedral cores, and the absence of bifacial tools, including projectile points (Acosta 2010a). The paleobotanical studies, chemical analysis of occupation surfaces, micro residues, and use-wear analysis of lithic artifacts all indicate a subsistence mode based on the processing of plants, collecting river snails,

TABLE 6.1. Late Pleistocene and Early Holocene dates available for Chiapas, Mexico, and Central America.

Site	Lab. no.	RCYBP	cal BP (2σ)	Dated material	References
Santa Marta, MX	UNAM-1232	11,040 ± 100	12,671–13130	charcoal	Acosta et al. 2013
Santa Marta, MX	UNAM-1237	10,880 ± 90	12,586–12,971	charcoal	Acosta et al. 2013
Santa Marta, MX	UNAM-1236	10,640 ± 90	12,380–12,756	charcoal	Acosta et al. 2013
Santa Marta, MX	UNAM-1228	10,560 ± 90	12,363–12,655	charcoal	Acosta et al. 2013
Santa Marta, MX	Beta-233470 AMS	10,460 ± 50	12,680–12,110	charcoal	Acosta et al. 2013
Santa Marta, MX	UNAM-1235	10,430 ± 90	12,044–12,577	charcoal	Acosta et al. 2013
Santa Marta, MX	UNAM-1233	10,350 ± 90	11,953–12,538	charcoal	Acosta et al. 2013
Santa Marta, MX	UNAM-1234	10,230 ± 90	11,605–12,391	charcoal	Acosta et al. 2013
Santa Marta, MX	UNAM-07-22	10,055 ± 90	11,268–11,848	charcoal	Acosta 2008
Santa Marta, MX	UNAM-1231	9970 ± 90	11,218–11,777	charcoal	Acosta et al. 2013
Santa Marta, MX	Beta-233476 AMS	9950 ± 60	11,690–11,230	charcoal	Acosta et al. 2013
Santa Marta, MX	Beta-233475 AMS	9800 ± 50	11,260–11,170	charcoal	Acosta et al. 2013
Santa Marta, MX	UNAM-1230	9670 ± 90	10,750–11,231	charcoal	Acosta et al. 2013
Santa Marta, MX	I-9260	9330 ± 290	9687–11,293	charcoal	Santamaría and García-Bárcena 1989
Santa Marta, MX	I-9259	9280 ± 290	9673–11,241	charcoal	Santamaría and García-Bárcena 1989
Los Grifos, MX	I-10762	9540 ± 150	10,485–11,233	charcoal	Santamaría 1981
Los Grifos, MX	I-10762	9460 ± 150	10,373–11,182	charcoal	Santamaría 1981
Los Grifos, MX	Beta-305563 AMS	8,950 ± 50	10,220 –9910	charcoal	Acosta et al. 2013
Los Grifos, MX	I-10760	8930 ± 150	9555–10,300	charcoal	Santamaría 1981
Los Tapiales, GT	GaK-4887	7150 ± 130	7687–8204	charcoal	Gruhn et al. 1977
Los Tapiales, GT	GaK-2769	7550 ± 150	8019–8632	charcoal	Gruhn et al. 1977
Los Tapiales, GT	GaK-4888	7820 ± 140	8387–9006	charcoal	Gruhn et al. 1977
Los Tapiales, GT	Birm-703	7960 ± 160	8434–9255	charcoal	Gruhn et al. 1977
Los Tapiales, GT	Tx-1630	8810 ± 110	9580–10,174	charcoal	Gruhn et al. 1977
Los Tapiales, GT	GaK-4890	9860 ± 185	10,736–11,988	charcoal	Gruhn et al. 1977
Los Tapiales, GT	Tx-1631	10,710 ± 170	12,12,3–12982	charcoal	Gruhn et al. 1977
Los Tapiales, GT	GaK-4889	11,170 ± 200	12,718–13320	charcoal	Gruhn et al. 1977
Piedra del Coyote, GT	Tx-1635	9430 ± 120	10,374–11,128	charcoal	Gruhn et al. 1977
Piedra del Coyote, GT	Tx-1634	10,020 ± 260	11,051–12,427	charcoal	Gruhn et al. 1977
Piedra del Coyote, GT	Tx-1632	10,650 ± 1350	8971–16042	charcoal	Gruhn et al. 1977
LaYeguada, PA	multiple samples	11,050		charcoal	Piperno et al. 1991
Corona Rockshelter, PA	Beta-19105	10,440 ± 650	10,280–13488	charcoal	Cooke and Ranere 1992
Alvina de Parita, PA	FSU-300	11,350 ± 250	12,725–13626	charcoal, hearth	Crusoe and Felton, 1974
Aguadulce Rockshelter, PA	NZA-9262	10,529 ± 184	11,801–12,747	phytoliths	Piperno et al. 2000
Aguadulce Rockshelter, PA	NZA-10930	10,725 ± 80	12,537–12,755	phytoliths	Piperno et al. 2000
Cueva de los Vampiros, PA	Beta-5101	8560 ± 650	8030–11,245	charcoal	Cooke and Ranere, 1984

FIGURE 6.5. Los Grifos (*left*) and Santa Marta (*right*) excavations.

and hunting of minor fauna (Acosta 2008, 2010a, 2014; Eudave 2008; Pérez-Martínez 2010). The radiocarbon results include 10 Pleistocene dates, ranging from 11,040 ± 100 to 10,055 ± 90 RCYBP, making it the site with the broadest chronological sequence in the area (Acosta et al. 2013).

Considering the Santa Marta characteristics and dates, it seems feasible that groups or technologies associated with fluted points entered Middle America during the Early Holocene following earlier populations, as other researchers have stated (e.g., Pearson 2004). This would explain the rapid expansion of fluted point technology in the area. However, more research is necessary in order to better define the initial occupation.

Subsistence and Lifeways

As noted, the study of sites with Clovis-like and Fishtail points in Middle America has been dominated by the technological approach. While this approach is still predominant in other regions, the panorama is gradually changing. For in-

stance, it is now recognized that the Clovis materials in the U.S. are not solely associated with megafauna but with a wider and more diverse subsistence mode that includes minor fauna and even turtles and rodents (Haynes 2002).

In our area of interest, Gruhn and colleagues (1977:239) mention that it was not possible to recover faunal remains in Los Tapiales due to soil characteristics, whereas for Los Vampiros cave no data on subsistence is mentioned (Pearson and Cooke 2002:932). Only at Los Grifos, Chiapas, has zooarchaeological data been reported for the Clovis-like and Fishtail occupations, indicating medium-size prey such as white-tailed deer (*Odocoileus* sp.), peccary (*Tayassu* sp.), and Pleistocene horse (*Equus* sp.), in addition to the remains of Sapotaceae and hackberry seeds (*Celtis* sp.). Analyses of micro-residues (Pérez-Martínez 2013) indicate a strong orientation toward fauna processing (Figure 6.6). Nonetheless, starch grains were recovered from some artifacts, and analysis of a premolar associated with an approximate 9500 RCYBP date indicates

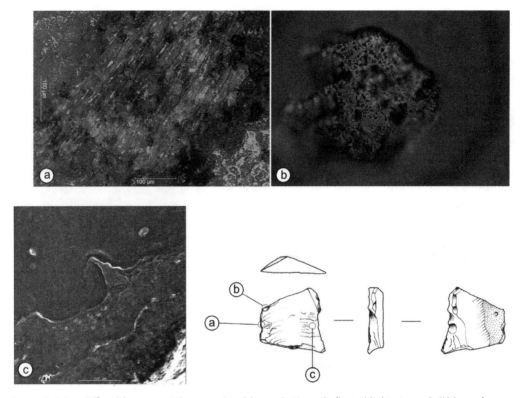

FIGURE 6.6. Los Grifos sidescraper. Micro remains: (*a*) muscle tissue (reflected light at 100x); (*b*) bone fragment (cross-polarized light at 40x). Traceology: (*c*) micro-polish (scanning electron microscope at 600x).

that vegetable intake was also important (Rodríguez and Acosta 2015).

This data contrasts with the "diagnostic artifacts" of lithic tools associated with fluted points, which suggest a subsistence highly dependent on hunting, with specialized instruments for fleshing prey and preparing fur and bone artifacts such as limace-type scrapers and endscrapers with lateral spurs, and shows the relevance of extending subsistence studies for these groups to multidisciplinary approaches.

Summary and Perspectives

Some authors suggest that although the Clovis culture is not necessarily the oldest in the New World, it is indeed the first "clearly distinguishable" technology in the archaeological record (Sánchez et al. 2014). Unfortunately, the urge to "distinguish" human societies in the archaeology of the Late Pleistocene overcomes the simple typological criterion to look for "guide fossils," em-

ploying other methodological and conceptual tools. Such a criterion is the only way to accept that the mosaic of archaeological cultures in the New World during the Late Pleistocene is more diverse than currently recognized for Mexico and Central America, just as has been accepted for decades in South America (Dillehay et al. 1992; Dillehay 2000).

The need to define the different human groups that colonized the most diverse regions of the continent must go beyond simply defining lithic "technologies" or "traditions." Although important, typological analysis of artifacts must surpass the morphological criterion in order to include a complex technological analysis that integrates the *chaîne-opératoire* analysis—the systematic study of traces of use and the recovery of micro-residues. The same should be said about the analysis of the archaeological contexts of sites associated with Clovis-like and Fishtail points, because current archaeological requirements force us to maintain not only a rigorous control of the excavation of sites but also to aim for a systemic recovery of samples for the study of micro-residues (pollen, phytoliths, starch grains) and chemical analyses of occupation floors. This will enable us to reconstruct daily activities and assess specific dependence on plants or animals and also establish the environmental context of occupations.

Finally, it is true that our knowledge of the Late Pleistocene in Central America's tropical area is still fragmentary. Yet, we can also say that this situation is rapidly changing. Recent studies—not only in Chiapas (Acosta 2008, 2010, 2014) but also in Tulum (González et al. 2008), Belize (Lohse et al. 2006), and Honduras (Scheffler 2008)—indicate a growing interest in this period in an area that has heretofore been marginal when compared to other New World regions. These studies also seem to be gradually changing the stereotypical image of the megafauna hunter that prevailed a few decades ago, as data linking human settlement (not only in Chiapas, but on the continent) to the systematic capture of extinct fauna has been almost absent. We do not intend to deny that the first settlers of Middle America interacted with extinct Pleistocene fauna, but we reject a systematic megafaunal hunt.

Los Grifos rockshelter in Chiapas, is a good example because remains of *Equus* sp. have been found there. However, a Pleistocene horse cannot be considered "megafauna" but medium-size fauna, equal to the size of a deer. Therefore, it is more important to assess the ecology of the prey and the particular conditions of its capture. In this case, the horse would have been linked to open areas. Thus, it is likely that when Clovis groups arrived in Central America they did so

through patches of open vegetation in the highlands and on the Pacific slope, where Rancholabrean faunal remains are constantly found. At the beginning of the Holocene, these hunters simply kept occupying similar ecological areas, capturing the available fauna until later points replaced fluted points.

On the other hand, when the Clovis people arrived, the region was already populated by groups with a wide range of subsistence and expedite technology such as Santa Marta. Thus, it is necessary to explain why the latter show no evidence of hunting Pleistocene fauna, although they must have coexisted with it. A reasonable explanation is that they mainly occupied areas inside the tropical rainforest. Hence, it is unlikely that the Rancholabrean fauna would be found in those groups' exploitation areas. Another reason is that they had a deeper engagement in gathering than in hunting and could have focused on small and medium-size prey (Eudave 2008). The possibility that these generalist early settlers, such as those at Santa Marta, had entered the New World by a coastal route, is a suggestion that is still difficult to confirm.

The map of the Pleistocene coastline in Figure 6.1 gives an idea of the great coastal expanses submerged when the sea level rose at the end of the last Ice Age. It also shows that the coastal sites of the Pleistocene, from the south of Mexico to Panama, would actually be several kilometers distant from the current coastline and over 100 m below the sea (Richardson 1981). Consequently, it is necessary to evaluate other regions of the Pacific coast that may have experienced less drastic coastal modifications such as Mexico's southern Pacific coast (from Nayarit to Oaxaca) and the eastern coast of the Yucatan peninsula.

Notes

1. The only direct evidence of Clovis points associated with megafauna in Mexico comes from El Fin del Mundo, a site in Sonora (Sánchez et al. 2014), not Middle America. The only *Mammuthus columbi* association with projectile points in the study region is the Santa

Isabel Iztapan site in the central highlands (Aveleyra 1956), but the projectile points are Lerma, Angostura, and Scottsbluff types, associated with the Late Paleoindian and dated to about 9300 RCYBP.

References

Acosta, Guillermo

2008   *La cueva de Santa Marta y los cazadores-
        recolectores del Pleistoceno final–Holoceno
        temprano en las regiones tropicales de
        México.* PhD dissertation, Department of
        Anthropology, UNAM, México, D.F.

2010a   Late-Pleistocene/Early-Holocene Tropical
        Foragers of Chiapas, Mexico: Recent Studies.
        Current Research in the Pleistocene 27:3–5.

2010b   Nómadas y paleopaisajes en el poblamiento
        de México. In *VI° coloquio Pedro Bosch
        Gimpera. Lugar, espacio y paisaje en arque-
        ología: Mesoamérica y otras áreas culturales,*
        edited by Edith Ortiz, pp. 101–128. UNAM,
        México, D.F.

2011   El poblamiento de las regiones tropicales de
        México hace 12500 años. *Anales de Antro-
        pología* 45:227–235.

2012   Ice Age Hunter-Gatherers and the Coloniza-
        tion of Mesoamerica. In *The Oxford Hand-
        book of Mesoamerican Archaeology,* edited
        by Deborah L. Nichols and Christopher A.
        Pool, pp. 129–140. Oxford University Press,
        New York.

2014   Nuevos estudios sobre las sociedades pre-
        cerámicas de Chiapas. In *Perspectivas de los
        estudios de prehistoria en México: un hom-
        enaje a la trayectoria del ingeniero Joaquín
        García-Bárcena,* edited by Eduardo Corona
        Martínez and Joaquín Arroyo Cabrales,
        pp. 143–167. INAH, México, D.F.

Acosta, Guillermo, Patricia Pérez, and Irán Irais
Rivera González

2013   Metodología para el estudio del procesa-
        miento de plantas en sociedades cazadoras-
        recolectoras: un estudio de caso. *Boletim
        do Museu Paraense Emílio Goeldi, Ciências
        Humanas* 8(3):535–550.

Arroyo-Cabrales, J., O. J. Polaco, C. Laurito, E. Johnson, M. T. Alberdi, and A. L. Valerio

2007   The Proboscideans (Mammalia) from
        Mesoamerica. *Quaternary International*
        169–170:17–23.

Aveleyra, Luis

1956   The Second Mammoth and Associated
        Artifacts at Santa Isabel Iztapan, Mexico.
        American Antiquity 22(1):12–28.

Aveleyra, Luis, and Manuel Maldonado-Koerdell

1953   Association of Artifacts with Mammoth in
        the Valley of Mexico. *American Antiquity*
        18(4):332–340.

Bate, Luis F.

1983   *Comunidades primitivas de cazadores
        recolectores en Sudamérica. Historia General
        de Sudamérica,* Vol. 2. Ediciones de la Presi-
        dencia de la República, Caracas, VE.

Bate, Luis Felipe, and Guillermo Acosta

2014   Cazadores del Trópico Americano. In *Pro-
        puestas para la Arqueología,* Vol. 2, edited
        by Luis Felipe Bate, pp. 187–210. INAH,
        México, D.F.

Binford, Lewis R.

1980   Willow Smoke and Dogs' Tails: Hunter-
        Gatherer Settlement Systems and Archaeo-
        logical Site Formation, *American Antiquity*
        45(1):4–20

Bird, Junius

1969   A Comparison of South Chilean and Ecua-
        dorian "Fishtail" Projectile Points. *Kroeber
        Society Anthropological Papers* 40:52–71.

Bradley, B. A.

1993   Paleo-Indian Flaked Stone Technology in
        the North American High Plains. In *From
        Kostenki to Clovis,* edited by Olga Soffer and
        Nikolai Dmitrievich Praslov, pp. 251–262.
        Springer, Boston, MA.

Bryan, Alan, Roberto Casamiquela, Juan Cruxent,
Ruth Gruhn, and Claudio Ochsenius

1978   An El Jobo Mastodon Kill at Taima-Taima,
        Venezuela. *Science* 200(4347):1275–1277.

Bullen, Ripley P., and William Plowden Jr.

1968   Preceramic Archaic Sites in the Highlands
        of Honduras. *American Antiquity* 28(3):
        382–385.

Coe, Michael D.

1960   A Fluted Point from Highland Guatemala.
        American Antiquity 25(3):412–413.

Cooke, Richard G.

1998   Human Settlement of Central America and
        Northernmost South America (14,000–
        8,000 BP). *Quaternary International* 49/50:
        177–190.

Cooke, R. G., and A. J. Ranere

1984   The "Proyecto Santa Maria": A Multidisci-
        plinary Analysis of Prehistoric Adaptations
        to a Tropical Watershed in Panama. In
        *Recent Developments in Isthmian Archae-
        ology: Advances in the Prehistory of Lower
        Central America,* edited by F. W. Lange,
        pp. 3–30. British Archaeological Reports,
        International Series 212, Oxford.

Cooke, R. G., and A. J. Ranere

1992   Prehistoric Human Adaptations to the

Seasonally Dry Forests of Panama. *World Archaeology* 24(1):114–133.

Correal, Gerardo.
1981   *Evidencias culturales y megafauna pleisto-cénica en Colombia*. Fundación de Investigaciones Arqueológicas Nacionales/Ediciones del Banco de la República, Bogotá.

Crusoe, Daniel, and James Felton
1974   La Alvina de Parita: A Paleoindian Camp in Panama. *Florida Anthropologist* 27(4): 145–148.

Dillehay, Thomas
2000   *The Settlement of the Americas*. Basic Books, New York.

Dillehay, Thomas, Gustavo Politis, Gerardo Ardila, and Maria Beltrao
1992   Earliest Hunters and Gatherers of South America. *Journal of World Prehistory* 6(2): 145–204.

Dixon, E. James
1999   *Bones, Boats, and Bison: Archaeology and the First Colonization of Western North America*. University of New Mexico Press, Albuquerque.

Eudave, Itzel
2008   Subsistencia de los cazadores recolectores, un estudio de los restos faunísticos de la cueva de Santa Marta, Chiapas. Undergraduate thesis in archaeology, ENAH, México, D.F.

Finsten, Laura, Kent V. Flannery, and Barbara Macnider
1989   Preceramic and Cave Occupations. In *Monte Alban's Hinterland*, Part II: *The Prehispanic Settlement Patterns in Tlacolula, Etla, and Ocotlán, the Valley of Oaxaca, Mexico*, by Stephen A. Kowalewski et al., pp. 39–53 Memoirs of the Museum of Anthropology 23. University of Michigan, Ann Arbor.

Fregoso, Daniela
2010   *Estudio arqueomagnético en el abrigo rocoso los Grifos, Chiapas*. Undergraduate thesis, Faculty of Sciences, UNAM, México, D.F.

García-Bárcena, Joaquín
1980   *Una punta acanalada de la cueva de Los Grifos, Ocozocoautla, Chis*. Cuadernos de Trabajo 17, INAH, México, D.F.
1982   *El Precerámico de Aguacatenango, Chiapas, México*. Colección Científica 110. INAH, Mexico, D.F.
1989   El hombre y los proboscideos de América. *Colección Científica* 188:333–345.

González, Arturo, Carmen Rojas, Alejandro Terrazas, Martha Benavente, Wolfgang Stinnesbeck, Jerónimo Aviles, Magdalena de los Ríos, and Eugenio Acevez
2008   The Arrival of Humans on the Yucatan Peninsula: Evidence from Submerged Caves in the State of Quintana Roo, Mexico. *Current Research in the Pleistocene* 25:1–24.

González, Leticia
1986   Ejercicio de interpretación de actividades en un campamentode cazadores-recolectores en el Bolsón de Mapimí. In *Unidades habitacionales Mesoamericanas y sus áreas de actividad*, edited by Linda Manzanilla, pp. 135–157. UNAM, México, D.F.

Gruhn, Ruth
1988   Linguistic Evidence in Support of the Coastal Route of Earliest Entry into the New World. *Man*, New Series 23(1):77–100.

Gruhn, Ruth, A. Bryan, and J. Nance
1977   Los Tapiales: A Paleo-Indian Campsite in the Guatemala Highlands, *Proceedings of the American Philosophical Society* 121(3): 235–273.

Haynes, G.
2002   *The Early Settlement of North America: The Clovis Era*. Cambridge University Press, Cambridge, UK.

Hernández, Laura Elisa
2010   *Análisis estratigráfico del abrigo rocoso de Santa Marta, Chiapas*. Undergraduate thesis in archaeology, ENAH, México, D.F.

Johnson Eileen, Joaquín Arroyo-Cabrales, and Óscar Polaco
2006   Climate, Environment, and Game Animal Resources of the Late Pleistocene Mexican Grassland. In *El hombre temprano en América y sus implicaciones en el poblamiento de la Cuenca de México*, Primer Simposio Internacional, edited by José Concepción Jiménez, Silvia González, José Antonio Pompa, and Francisco Ortíz Pedraza, pp. 231–245. Colección Cientifica 500. INAH, México, D.F.

Kelly, Charles
1982   Preceramic Projectile-point Typology in Belize. *Ancient Mesoamerica* 4(2):205–227.

Lanata, José Luis
2011   Discutiendo diferentes modelos de la dispersión humana en las Américas. In *IVº simposio internacional el hombre temprano en América*, edited by José Concepción

Jiménez et al., pp. 121–148. UNAM-INAH
    Museo del Desierto, Mexico, D.F.

Lohse, Jon, Jaime Awe, Cameron Griffith, Robert
Rosenswig, and Fred Valdez

2006   Preceramic Occupations in Belize: Updating
        the Paleoindian and Archaic Record. *Latin
        American Antiquity* 17(2):209–226.

Lozano, Margarita, and Beatriz Ortega

1994   Palynological and Magnetic Susceptibility
        Records of Lake Chalco, Central Mexico.
        *Palaeogeography, Palaeoclimatology, Palaeo-
        ecology* 109(2–4):177–191.

MacNeish, Richard, and Antoinette Nelken-Terner

1983   The Preceramic of Mesoamerica. *Journal of
        Field Archaeology* 10(1):71–84.

Martin, Paul S.

1967   Prehistoric Overkill. In *Pleistocene Extinc-
        tions: The Search for a Cause*, edited by Paul
        Martin and Henry Wright, pp. 75–120. Yale
        University Press, New Haven, CT.

Meyer, Edward R.

1973   Late Quaternary Paleoecology of the Cuatro
        Ciénegas Basin, Coahuila, Mexico. *Ecology*
        54(5):982–985.

Morrow, Juliet, and Toby Morrow

1999   Geographic Variation in Fluted Projectile
        Points: A Hemispheric Perspective. *Ameri-
        can Antiquity* 64(2):215–231.

Pearson, Georges A.

2002   Pan-Continental Paleoindian Expansions
        and Interactions as Viewed from the Earliest
        Lithic Industries of Lower Central America.
        PhD dissertation, Department of Anthro-
        pology, University of Kansas, Lawrence.

2004   Pan-American Paleoindian Dispersals and
        the Origins of Fishtail Projectile Points as
        Seen through the Lithic Raw-Material Re-
        duction Strategies and Tool-Manufacturing
        Techniques at the Guardiría Site, Turrialba
        Valley, Costa Rica. In *The Settlement of the
        American Continents: A Multidisciplinary
        Approach to Human Biogeography*, edited
        by Michael Barton, Geoffrey Clark, David.
        Yessner, and Georges Pearson, pp. 85–102.
        University of Arizona Press, Tucson.

Pearson, Georges A., and Richard G. Cooke

2002   The Role of the Panamanian Land Bridge
        During the Initial Colonization of the Amer-
        icas. *Antiquity* 76(294):931–932.

Pérez-Martínez, Patricia

2010   Arqueología experimental, análisis de
        huellas de uso e identificación de micro

residuos en el conjunto lítico de la capa XVI
        del abrigo rocoso de Santa Marta, Chiapas.
        Undergraduate thesis in archaeology,
        ENAH, México, D.F.

2013   Patrones de subsistencia y procesos de
        trabajo en grupos de cazadores recolectores
        en zonas tropicales: inferencias a partir del
        análisis funcional de dos conjuntos líticos.
        Master's thesis, UNAM. México, D.F.

Perrot-Minot, Sébastién

2012   Las tradiciones Clovis y cola de pescado
        en Centroamérica. *Anales de la Academia
        de Geografía e Historia de Guatemala* 87:
        181–212.

Piperno, Dolores, and Deborah M. Pearsall

1998   *The Origins of Agriculture in the Lowland
        Neotropics.* Academic Press, San Diego, CA.

Piperno, D. R., M. B. Bush, and P. A. Colinvaux

1991   Paleoecological Perspectives on Human
        Adaptation in Central Panama. II. The
        Holocene. *Geoarchaeology* 6(3):227–250.

Piperno, D. R., A. J. Ranere, I. Holst, and P. Hansell

2000   Starch Grains Reveal Early Root Crop
        Horticulture in the Panamanian Tropical
        Forest. *Nature* 407(6806):894–897.

Politis, Gustavo G.

1991   Fishtail Projectile Points in the Southern
        Cone of South America: An Overview. In
        Clovis Origins and Adaptations, edited by
        Robson Bonnichsen and Karen L. Turn-
        mire, pp. 287–301. Center for the Study of
        the First Americans, Oregon State Univer-
        sity, Corvallis.

Ranere, Anthony

2006   The Clovis Colonization of Central
        America. In *Paleoindian Archaeology: A
        Hemispheric Perspective*, edited by Juliet E.
        Morrow and Cristóbal Gnecco, pp. 69–85.
        University Press of Florida, Gainesville.

Ranere, Anthony, and Richard Cooke

1991   Paleoindian Occupation in the Central
        American Tropics. In *Clovis: Origins and
        Adaptations*, edited by Robson Bonnichsen
        and Karen L. Turnmire, pp. 237–253.
        Center for the Study of the First Americans,
        Corvallis, OR.

2003   Late Glacial and Early Holocene Occupa-
        tion of Central American Tropical Forests.
        In *Under the Canopy: The Archaeology of
        Tropical Rain Forests*, edited by J. Mercader,
        pp. 219–248. Rutgers University Press, New
        Brunswick, NJ.

Richardson, James B., III
1981   Modeling the Development of Sedentary
        Maritime Economies on the Coast of Peru:
        A Preliminary Statement. *Annals of the
        Carnegie Museum* 50:139–150.

Rivera-González, Iran Irais
2013   Modo de vida en el bosque tropical del
        sureste mexicano: un acercamiento al uso
        de vegetación por sociedades cazadoras-
        recolectoras. Master's thesis in anthropol-
        ogy, UNAM, México, D.F.

Rodríguez Floréz C. D., and Guillermo Acosta
Ochoa
2015   Un diente humano de 9500 años AP prove-
        niente de la cueva de los Grifos (Chiapas,
        México). *Revista Española de Antropología
        Física* 35:50–58

Roosevelt, Anna C., M. Lima da Costa, C. Lopes
Machado, M. Michab, N. Mertier, H. Valladas,
J. Feathers, et al.
1996   Paleoindian Cave Dwellers in the Amazon:
        The Peopling of the Americas. *Science*
        272(5260):373–384.

Sánchez, Guadalupe, Vance T. Holliday, Edmund P.
Gaines, Joaquín Arroyo Cabrales, Natalia Martínez-
Tagüeña, Andrew Kowler, Todd Lange, et al.
2014   Human (Clovis)–Gomphothere (Cuviero-
        nius sp.) Association ~13,390 Calibrated
        yBP in Sonora, Mexico. PNAS 111 (30):
        10972–10977.

Santamaría, Diana
1981   Preceramic Occupations at Los Grifos
        Rockshelter, Chiapas. In *Memorias X°
        Congreso UISPP*, edited by Joaquín García-
        Bárcena and Francisco Sánchez, pp. 63–83.
        INAH, México, D.F.

Santamaría, Diana, and Joaquín García-Bárcena
1984a   *Raspadores verticales de la Cueva de los
        Grifos, Ocozocoautla, Chiapas.* Cuaderno
        de Trabajo 22. INAH, México, D.F.

1984b   *Raederas y raspadores de Los Grifos.* Cuad-
        erno de Trabajo 28. INAH, México, D.F.

1989   *Puntas de proyectil, cuchillos y otras her-
        ramientas sencillas de los Grifos.* INAH,
        México, D.F.

Scheffler, Timothy E.
2008   *The El Gigante Rock Shelter, Honduras.* PhD
        dissertation, Department of Anthropology,
        Pennsylvania State University, State College,
        PA. UMI 3325975.

Snarskis, Michael
1979   Turrialba: A Paleoindian Quarry and Work-
        shop Site in Eastern Costa Rica. *American
        Antiquity* 44(1):125–138.

Wormington, H. M.
1957   *Ancient Man in North America*, 4th ed.
        Denver Museum of Natural History Popular
        Series 4. Denver, CO.

CHAPTER 7

Mexican Prehistory and Chiquihuite Cave (Northern Zacatecas)

Studying Pleistocene Human Occupation as an Exercise of Skepticism

Ciprian F. Ardelean, Joaquin Arroyo-Cabrales, Jean-Luc Schwenninger, Juan I. Macías-Quintero, Jennifer Watling, and Mónica G. Ponce-González

Although the current panorama of studies on the earliest human presence in the Americas has shifted, and the existence of older-than-Clovis cultures is better accepted than only a few years ago, the subject must still be considered from a position of carefulness and self-criticism. Within this epistemological order, doing research on early prehistory and the first human occupations in Mexico has become synonymous with a sustained and necessary exercise of skepticism and caution.

Official Mexican paradigms have established, among scientists and the public alike, the habit of accepting fairly easily any early date or arguments in favor of an extremely old human presence in the present country. Tens of thousands of years of cultural manifestations have been traditionally handled with ease in the Mexican specialized literature and displayed in the nation's museums. Hopefully, archaeology in the Americas will one day present undeniable empirical evidence of really old, pristine peopling of the continent, and Mexico certainly will not be the exception. But, until then, scientific argumentation and dogmatic speculation are two different coins altogether.

The charisma of prestigious personalities in Mexican archaeology seems to have always carried more weight than strong argumentation

built upon solid scientific discoveries, replicated results, and thorough analyses (see critique in Ardelean 2013; Ardelean and Macías-Quintero 2016). The popular image has generally been the same for the last five decades or so: humans arrived in Mexico more than 30,000 years ago, after a migration from Asia that must have occurred even earlier. Iconic sites, strongly embedded in the local archaeological vocabulary, were meant to offer undeniable evidence for something that, anywhere else in the Americas, continues to be an academic bloodbath: the when, the where, the who, and the how of the earliest human arrivals. In the archaeology of the United States, for example, the topic of the "early peopling of the Americas" has been a primordial theme and discoveries have been continuously subject to criticism, scrutiny, and constant revision. In Mexico the situation has been different. Whereas north of the Rio Grande purported ancient sites struggled for decades for recognition as valid "pre-Clovis" occupations, the Mexican early sites gained acceptance quickly among local archaeologists and the general public (Figure 7.1). Often, a couple of unreplicated radiocarbon dates obtained decades earlier, plus the name of the person in charge of the discovery, used to be the equivalent of compelling evidence for a very old human presence.

FIGURE 7.1. Political map of Mexico showing the location of presumably ancient sites commonly found in the specialized literature, as well as the location of the study area and cave discussed in this chapter. Not every site in the map is mentioned in the text. They are included to demonstrate how prolific the Late Pleistocene–Early Holocene human occupation is thought to be in traditional views in Mexico.

Although today the situation is changing at an accelerated pace and a wave of Mexican prehistoric investigations conducted by a new generation of scholars seeks to join the continental debates (see Chapter 6, this volume), half a century of paradigmatic domination has caused lingering damage. Criticism was virtually absent for a long time, criteria weakened, skepticism was rarely practiced, and even now the extremely old dates still gain easy general acceptance. So, how did we get to this situation, and how is that we still struggle with it?

There are several primary factors. First, early prehistory (meaning here Late Pleistocene human presence) has never been a privileged topic in Mexican archaeology. Study of the earliest human presence during the Ice Age received much less attention than the later, "greater civilizations" with monumental architecture. The topic remains underdeveloped—empirically and epistemologically—and is underrepresented in publications and the number of specialists or institutions committed to the subject. Whether humans reached Mexico 10,000 or 50,000 years ago does not seem to merit general concern nor is it considered worth approaching critically.

Second, the national egos and historic rivalry between Mexico and the United States have long suffocated academic dialogue between the two countries and contributed to the paradigmatic divergences.

Third, the force of influential personalities weighed heavily on academia, scholars accepting their writings without much—if any—criticism and skepticism. Such a tendency is reversing now, but dissolving cemented paradigms is a work in progress.

As a fourth identifiable factor, the field of prehistoric archaeology in Mexico seems much too comfortable with shallow data. If, elsewhere, one observes an exaggerated inclination toward rejecting any archaeological context that looks too old for still-rigid paradigms, in Mexico the case seems to be just the opposite. If one discovers a new site that yields even a single date, let's say, older than 20,000 radiocarbon years, no matter how suspect the context of provenance, one may well find it greeted enthusiastically by colleagues and the public.

Back in 1967, José Luis Lorenzo (former patriarch of Mexican prehistory) published a small brochure titled *La etapa lítica en México* (*The Lithic Stage in Mexico*), which soon became the keystone of the official paradigm. Lorenzo proposed the first chronological model for the Mexican prehistory. Strangely, this particularistic, anachronistic, and outdated work remains in use among many scholars, despite its evident lack of empirical support—a sort of textbook that was worshiped and rarely—if ever—criticized (Ardelean and Macías-Quintero 2016). Lorenzo established the basic fundamentals of the national dogma: the first people arrived in Mexico many thousands of years ago, a statement to be taken as fact ("Lorenzo said it all" is a popular mantra), no matter the absence of strong, reliable indicators in the archaeological record or whether it noted or ignored global and continental debates.

In the middle of this delicate panorama, what would happen if you discovered a new site that yielded some old-looking artifacts or a couple of really old-looking dates? Three scenarios might apply: (a) many colleagues in Mexico, prehistorians or not, encourage you to present your site as new evidence for really old human occupation, as the discovery would fit gently within the local paradigm; (b) most foreign colleagues (especially from the United States) attack your arguments, question your methodology, criticize your context, and request infinite replications of dates and thorough analyses of every possible detail in your data; (c) you choose the middle path of self-criticism, confronting the discovery yourself, adopting a fallibilistic epistemology, and embracing skepticism (but not a priori denial) before enthusiasm and caution before premature belief. In this third scenario, intriguing finds and controversial radiocarbon or OSL (optically stimulated luminescence) dates should not be dismissed by default, nor should they turn into dogmas at once. They rather serve

for proposing working hypotheses, for attracting attention to *potentially ancient* sites, for stimulating further testing, further digging, and more detailed exploration.

This chapter does not have enough space for a comprehensive assessment of the current archaeological data and currents in Mexican prehistory. However, a brief review of Lorenzo's model and the available archaeological evidence is merited. This review, forming the first half of the chapter, expresses the opinion of the first author and is based on critiques developed elsewhere (Ardelean 2013, 2014, 2016; Ardelean and Macías-Quintero 2016). The second half of the chapter brings into discussion the preliminary results of recent archaeological explorations in the central-northern state of Zacatecas, where at least one archaeological site yielded data that makes it a good candidate for an exercise in academic skepticism and precaution.

Lorenzo's Model

Mexican prehistory has long been predicated on the basis of an assumed chronological scheme that has turned indestructible. The traditional cultural-historical model launched by Lorenzo (1967) specifically for Mexico is both simple and surprising. First, it includes a long period known as the *Arqueolítico* (*Archaeolithic*), starting with the earliest inhabitants, perhaps 40,000 years ago, and ending with the appearance of the first projectile points. It is followed by a period characterized by finer flaked-stone technologies, named the *Cenolitico* (*Cenolithic*), divided in two phases, Upper and Lower. It presumably ends at the beginning of the Holocene and is followed by the so-called "Proto-Neolithic," posited at the dawn of the sedentary life. Together, the three periods form the *Lithic Stage* (*La Etapa Lítica*), the Mexican particularistic and isolationist chronology that displays its own terminology and chronological spans without sustainable correspondence elsewhere.

The name of the model was justified by the fact that flaked stone represents the dominant surviving artifact from those periods and the main available data. Lithic technologies and the distinct employment of artifacts over time form the differential criteria used to separate the horizons that integrate the model (Lorenzo 1967:27). The most striking attribute of this cultural chronology is its extremely ancient starting point and also the oscillating date for its end. With the Archaeolithic in particular, it is intriguing how it addresses astonishing dates ranging far beyond anything accepted scientifically in the Americas without providing reliable archaeological data to support the claims—especially if one remembers that the model was proposed *before* any true older-than-Clovis site was excavated. The supposed date for the earliest occupation was originally set at "only" 25,000 years ago (Lorenzo 1967:28), but it soon reached 30,000–40,000 years in Lorenzo's and his supporters' subsequent publications. The shifts between these multiple options seem random to the reader and are never accompanied by justifications (see Mirambell 2000:224). More recent publications continue to perpetuate Lorenzo's unsustained paradigm, long after his death, without contributing new arguments to the model (Mirambell 2000, 2001; García-Bárcena 2001; Lorenzo and Mirambell 2005; González-González et al. 2006).

Lorenzo wrote that he had taken the term Archaeolithic from Jacques de Morgan (1947:79–80) in reference to the "archaeolithic industries of Europe" and the Upper Paleolithic. The term did not find much acceptance in the Old World but was considered appropriate for a first phase of cultural presence in Mexico (Lorenzo 1967:27). According to the author, the Archaeolithic was characterized by crude and simple stone artifacts, direct percussion flaking, exclusively employing stone hammers. Large items displaying incipient bifacial techniques exist, and large flakes were common together with a variety of scrapers, choppers, chopping tools, and retouched denticulate tools, but specialization was minimal. Lithic typology was extremely reduced, the once-valid "Clactonian" technique could be recognized in various artifacts (*sic*!) and stone projectile points were missing, along with grinding stone implements. The main subsistence practice was hunting, and no direct indicators of gathering can be found in the archaeological record, although these may have perished. The same occurred with spear points and other artifacts of organic materials (Lorenzo 1967:28; Lorenzo and Mirambell 2005:483; Mirambell 1988:315, 2001:47).

How such an attribute list came to life never became clear, as it is clearly unfair to the diverse inventory of Paleolithic life (cf. Adovasio 2015). However, it is understandable that the proposal somehow integrated the tendency of its time when other models insisted on a supposed pre-projectile point phase (cf. Rice 2015). Lorena Mirambell, who coauthored Lorenzo's publications for many years, *assumes* that those first colonizers came from Asia and affirms that "it is sure" that their material culture resembled lithic industries from—surprisingly—places such as northeastern Pakistan, Japan (35,000-year-old materials), and Superior Cave at Zhoukoudian (Mirambell 1988:316).

When he first defined the Archaeolithic, Lorenzo based it on a brief list of allegedly ancient sites: the Diablo Complex in the Tamaulipas caves excavated by Richard MacNeish (1958), elongated bifaces on the shores of the Chapala Lake, the Teopisca industry in Chihuahua, and Chimalacatlán Cave in the state of Morelos. These confusing examples did not supply reliable radiocarbon dating or technological studies and cannot (either then or now) be considered viable examples. Nevertheless, Lorenzo showed much more skepticism than his followers, refusing to involve controversial examples such as Tequixquiac and Valsequillo (Lorenzo 1967:30; cf. Ardelean 2013). Later, Mirambell (2000:236) included new finds from other sites, but again the actual evidence or dates were never discussed. García-Bárcena (2001:29) added even more examples to this phase, as the list seemed to be open to anyone willing to contribute new "pre-Clovis" sites—literally out of thin air. Accepting the supposed human-made hearths and other finds at Tlapacoya and Cedral as having Archaeolithic antiquity (Figure 7.1), García-Bárcena included the male skulls from Chimalhuacán and Balderas Subway, giving them ages of 33,000 and 17,000 years, respectively. Bryan and Gruhn (1989:91) agreed with the chronological scheme, considering that the Archaeolithic "was divisible into a lower substage without bifaces and an upper substage after the innovation of bifacial flaking". Others (Serrano and Nuñez 2011:186) perpetuated the paradigm, without critique, assuming the existence of sufficient "evidence" to support the validity of the Archaeolithic phase: open camps, caves, human remains, lithic materials. The certainty is intriguing, considering that the entire archaeological community in the Americas is continuously searching for a minimum of secure evidence for an older-than-Clovis occupation (Stanford et al. 2015).

After the Archaeolithic comes the Cenolithic. The time range comprised in this chronological period is between 14,000 and 7,000 years ago (Faulhaber 2000; Serrano and Nuñez 2011; Mirambell 2000), although Lorenzo had established its commencement at only 12,000 BP (1967:30–31). As was the custom for decades, the authors never specified whether "BP" referred to calendar (calibrated) or radiocarbon years, nor the criteria for delimiting the period's beginning and end.

For our discussion, only the Lower Cenolithic is relevant. Its chronology is confusing and arbitrary, as expected. This phase is said to last from 14/12,000 BP until 9,000 BP (Mirambell 1988; Lorenzo and Mirambell 2005). The creator of this cultural chronology pushed it up to 7,000 BP, leaving no space for an Upper Cenolithic (Lorenzo 1967:30). No genetic relationship is assumed between the two phases. As a matter of fact, one can take this last assumption into account as a valid working hypothesis that Lorenzo might have anticipated correctly, especially if we look at how different the already known older-than-Clovis industries are from Clovis and later ones.

Supposedly, the characteristic traits of the Lower Cenolithic interval are the following: the appearance of flaked stone projectile points; fluted and lanceolate points; bifaces with pressure retouch; flaking techniques using soft hammers; blade technology and prismatic pressure blades became more common; indirect percussion started to be used; grinding present on bases and corners of bifaces; stemmed points appear, without barbs and the stem may be fluted (such as "Fishtails"); and no clear evidence of grinding stones yet available (Lorenzo 1967; Mirambell 1988:316; Lorenzo and Mirambell 2005:483–484). Clovis and Folsom technologies are implicitly combined in this phase. For subsistence, people relied heavily on hunting, but Lorenzo completely rejected any sort of exclusive preference for big mammals, such as mammoths, which is another aspect that he may have understood earlier than others.

While one might be concerned about a scarcity of well-supported sites showing very early human presence in North America, Lorenzo and his followers did not seem to have that problem. The list of sites used as examples for the Lower Cenolithic is shockingly long. The 14 enumerated sites include San Joaquín (State of Baja California Sur), Guaymas (Sonora), La Mota Samalayucan (Chihuahua), La Chuparrosa (Coahuila), Puntita Negra (Nuevo León), Weicker Ranch (Durango), Cueva del Diablo (Tamaulipas), and Hueyatlaco-Valsequillo (Puebla; some shown in Figure 7.1). Some sites did indeed produce fluted points but only as surface finds. But since the publication of *Etapa Lítica* half a century ago, those localities were not secured as old sites and cannot stand today as arguments for early occupations.

Lorenzo's list could be considered appropriate for his intentions to justify the existence of a phase contemporary with Clovis, Folsom, and Plainview traditions. Nevertheless, three decades later, Mirambell exaggerated the controversy and amplified the list to 33 Lower Cenolithic sites (Mirambell 2000:244). Only 10 coincide with Lorenzo's list, the rest being included unexplainably without a minimal discussion of arguments or dates and without any specification of the evidence available for these newly added sites. Many never appear in the literature again. Why were they assumed to be that old, then? Their deployment as examples to define a chronological period is speculative and unjustified, but their effect on the perpetuation of the paradigm has been immense. As Suárez (2015) has recently written, the premature and speculative claim of ancient human presence in the Americas is harmful to academic practice in American prehistory.

Given this brief review, there is still no reliable chronological model for the prehistory of Mexico. The traditional scheme created by Lorenzo—blindly and uncritically promoted for decades by generations of archaeologists—can no longer be considered of utility. When *Etapa Lítica* was published in 1967, very little data existed about Pleistocene cultural and environmental realities. Even the most important sites, invoked as prime candidates for very old ages (Tlapacoya and El Cedral), were excavated years later. So, any possible candidates to justify an Archaeolithic stage (with its profound time depth) played no role in the initial definition of the scheme, as they were unknown at that time. When these sites finally entered the corpus of data and more and more information came from other investigations, the chronological scheme never adapted to the development of the archaeological knowledge. It simply turned dogmatic.

The long list of sites used as a backup for the legitimacy of the "Lorenzian" model does not represent a realistic image. Their inclusion is merely speculative, especially in the case of the Archaeolithic phase. The historical "guilt" of a 50-year-old publication would have been expiated had there been any significant revisions of its content in the intervening period. Yet, there are still no specialized studies published on most of the above-mentioned sites. Instead, the majority appear primarily in the general literature, mostly for surface finds with no reliable radiocarbon dates to justify claims of extreme antiquity. The separation between the distinct chronological subdivisions remains arbitrary, more guessed than scientifically founded. There is still not a single word explaining why the Archaeolithic ends at 12,000 or 14,000 BP and what that border means in terms of cultural manifestation, geo-environmental data, or absolute dating. Further, the criterion declared in the mentioned publications (differences in lithic technologies) is unsustained by the existing evidence. First, there is absolutely no scientific proof for the alleged age of the artifacts considered representative of the Archaeolithic.

Second, the Lower Cenolithic phase mixes all Paleoamerican lithic traditions in the same box. The transition between the Pleistocene and Holocene is completely effaced, leaving no place for discussions about the relevance of climate changes, subsistence adaptations, and cultural responses for the construction of cultural historical chronologies.

At the moment, there is still no clearly confirmed and solid evidence for a truly older-than-Clovis human presence on Mexican territory. Such a pristine occupation must surely exist. The evidence from the Western Hemisphere entitles us to hope that Mexico is not the exception, but mistakes made by previous archaeological praxis render any evaluation skeptical.

Confronting the Model

The Valsequillo complex in Puebla—once a good candidate for ancient cultural indicators—was the scene of difficult academic and even political confrontation (Armenta 1959, 1978; Irwin-Williams 1967, 1981; Irwin-Williams et al. 1969; Steen-McIntyre 2006; Steen-McIntyre et al. 1981; González et al. 2006a, 2006c; Renne et al. 2005; Morse et al. 2010). Today, with its archaeological localities submerged by the waters behind a dam, the old questions can hardly expect new answers. Tlapacoya, an ancient paleo-beach surrounding a volcanic hill south of Mexico City, was and still is promoted by the official paradigm as a main example of Archaeolithic occupation (Lorenzo and Mirambell 1986, 2005; Mirambell 1973, 1986, 2000, 2001; Caballero 1997). The overview of available data and growing critiques of the 1970s results removed the site from its pole position in the pre-Clovis race (Sánchez 2001; Huddart and González 2006; Acosta 2012). Nor have Tlapacoya finds been critically reassessed since.

Two iconic localities, Santa Isabel Iztapan I and II (Aveleyra and Maldonado-Koerdell 1952, 1953, 1956), now covered by the Mexican capital's urban development, raise doubts on the authenticity of the finds and the cultural and chronological relationship between the flaked-stone artifacts supposedly found with two mammoths (Ardelean 2013; Sánchez 2010).

The artifacts there seem to belong to the Cody complex, but the true cultural affiliation of the finds and the relationship with the proboscidean remains have not been reanalyzed in the past four decades. So, any claims regarding human presence there, or any consideration of its older-than-Clovis age (see Rice 2015), cannot be taken lightly.

El Cedral is a Pleistocene hot spring context in the northwest of the state of San Luis Potosí, close to Zacatecas. It is Lorenzo's and Mirambell's flagship but there has never been a proper presentation of the finds (Lorenzo and Mirambell 1981, 1984, 2005; Mirambell 2001). Nor have the El Cedral stone artifacts and supposed hearths lined with mammoth leg bones ever been reassessed or redated since their alleged discovery in the 1970s. Available radiocarbon dates there have huge standard deviations. Moreover, the finds are not available for independent evaluation. The long-expected publication of the site (Mirambell 2012) left many doubts about the excavated contexts, the actual cultural origin of the hearths, and the relevance of the conventional radiocarbon dates obtained decades ago and unreplicated since.

The few secure Pleistocene occupation sites in Mexico come from Clovis sites with Clovis artifacts, mainly in northwestern Sonora at El Bajío (Robles and Manzano 1972; Montané 1988; Sánchez and Carpenter 2003; Sánchez 2007; Sánchez et al. 2007; Gaines et al. 2009) and El Fin del Mundo sites (Sánchez et al. 2009a, 2009b, 2015; Gaines and Sánchez 2009; Sánchez et al. 2014). There is alleged Clovis presence at Oyapa, in Hidalgo (Cassiano 1992, 1998, 2005; Cassiano and Vázquez 1990), but the surface stone artifacts recovered there await additional evaluations before they can be accepted as conclusive. Acosta and colleagues provide further data on Clovis-like occupations in southern Mexico, as well (see Chapter 6 in this book).

Human skeletal remains in the Basin of Mexico (González et al. 2003, 2006b; Jiménez et al. 2006, 2010), together with recent results from caves in Chiapas (Acosta 2010, 2012; Acosta and Pérez 2012), show a contemporary or slightly younger cultural presence (Figure 7.1). As research on the recent discoveries of human remains on the Caribbean coast of Yucatan advances (González-González et al. 2006, 2008, 2014; Terrazas et al. 2006; Chatters et al. 2014), the archaeological record may well amplify chronological extension beyond the "magical" threshold of 13,500 cal BP. But until the new investigations announce their final conclusions, there is yet little evidence from Mexican prehistory to confirm Lorenzo's model.

Chiquihuite Cave: Old Human Presence or Archaeological Illusion?

Chiquihuite Cave ("Cueva del Chiquihuite", in Spanish), situated on the northeastern border of the state of Zacatecas (Figures 7.1, 7.2), is a newly discovered archaeological site that was explored briefly during two field seasons (2011, 2012), during the doctoral dissertation research of this chapter's first author (Ardelean 2013).[1] Three authors of this chapter (Ardelean, Macías-Quintero, and Ponce-González) participated in the actual exploration of the cave, while the other three (Arroyo, Schwenninger, and Watling) were involved in specialized laboratory analyses. For the two initial campaigns mentioned in this chapter, insufficient funding, time constraints, the small crew, and challenging logistics limited field research in this high-altitude cave to surface exploration, topographic survey, and excavation of only one test pit.

The cave is situated high in the Astillero Mountains, at an altitude of 2740 m a.s.l., near Chiquihuite peak (almost 3,200 m a.s.l. at its highest, one of the highest elevations in the northern half of the country), Concepción del Oro municipality, on the border with the state of Coahuila, along the northeastern edge of an elongated endorheic basin, and in the vicinity of a small village named Guadalupe Garzarón (Figure 7.2). This locality was not considered a promising archaeological site during the initial stages of exploration, and its scientific potential was thought to be primarily for paleoenvironmental reconstruction. Its position at the base of a naked cliff, the steep and unstable rocky slopes, and its altitude at more than one km above the basin's bottom made it seem unsuitable for human habitation. Today, the setting of the cave represents a particular ecological niche repre-

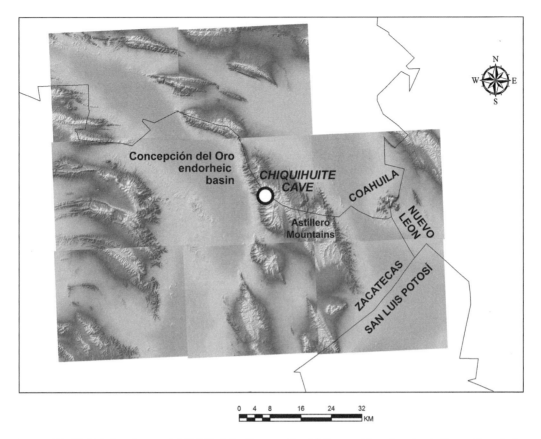

FIGURE 7.2. Digital elevation model (DEM) of the Concepción del Oro semidesert region in the northeast of the state of Zacatecas, with the Concepción del Oro endorheic basin enclosed between several orographic features. Chiquihuite Cave is on the western escarpments of the Astillero Mountains (DEM elaborated by Juan I. Macías-Quintero; modified from Ardelean 2013:172, Fig. 40).

sented by pine, oak, and juniper, with intrusions of cacti and *Yucca* (Joshua trees), surrounded by a vast semidesert ecosystem (Figure 7.3).

Chiquihuite is a relatively large cave, with at least two ample chambers, heavily modified by continuous natural transformations, including thick deposits of alluvial and colluvial clastic material and massive ceiling collapses (Figures 7.5, 7.6). Being the only cave found in the study area, it was a good candidate for paleoenvironmental studies. However, discovery of an interesting projectile point on the surface near the cave mouth, as well as a small anthropic fireplace exposed underneath large blocks of ceiling debris in the second gallery, suddenly transformed Chiquihuite into a potential archaeological site.

The limestones and intrusions forming Chiquihuite Peak are upright cliffs. They are subject to continuous erosion, showing fractures, brittleness, and cleavages. The cave entrance faces west-southwest, with light entering the front gallery during the afternoon and more abundantly in winter (Figure 7.5). The access path is on a steep and long slope surrounded by vertical stone walls. That slope is completely covered by large, angular, loose boulders and cobbles fallen from the ongoing cliff erosion. Cave access requires at least one to two hours of difficult climbing from the dry creek below.

This continuing transformation of the landscape suggests that at the end of the Pleistocene the area may have looked completely different. The mouth of the cave is now small, reduced to two separate openings (Figures 7.4, 7.5). Originally, the entrance could have been large and wide, possibly about 10 m tall and 25 m wide,

FIGURE 7.3. The central section of the Astillero Mountains, viewed from the southwest and the basin floor. At 3,200 m a.s.l., Chiquihuite Peak (rocky cliffs in the center of the image) is one of the highest elevations in the Mexican northern highlands. It holds the cave of the same name. To preserve the cave, its exact location is not indicated (photo by C. F. Ardelean, November 2013).

FIGURE 7.4. The main entrance to Chiquihuite Cave, northeastern Zacatecas. The current access was artificially enlarged in recent, historic times (probably for mining exploration during the Colonial period) piercing cemented sediments that completely obscured the original and much larger entrance (photo by C. F. Ardelean, January 2011; from Ardelean 2013:353, Fig. 212a).

FIGURE 7.5. View from inside Chiquihuite Cave front gallery toward the current double entry, which faces west. Light enters the dark cave during the afternoon, while Josué Guzmán, Alejandro Arteaga, and Javier Ponce (then undergraduate students at the University of Zacatecas) take a break during excavations. One can appreciate the massive amount of debris filling in the gallery, especially from roof collapses. This picture was taken from the location of the test pit X-11 (photo by C. F. Ardelean, January 2012).

with the cave floor several meters lower than today. Huge amounts of clastic material, originating from the surrounding cliffs, moved into the cave through gravity or were carried in by alluvial events. Thus, the entrance and the front gallery were affected by millennia of debris deposition. In the distant past, the cave may have had a larger, more horizontal platform in front of it, with smoother slopes leading to active creeks and springs below. Their dry remains are visible at the base of the slope.

Current vegetation is mixed. The local, endemic ecosystem is a pine-oak forest. Possibly this was the case by the end of the Pleistocene, as well, although detailed paleoenvironmental data for the site is not yet available. Increasing aridity, episodes of drought in recent centuries,

mining activity, deforestation, and goat herding all contributed to the shrinkage of the original biota. Now, desert vegetation is rapidly invading the mountains. Joshua trees, *Larrea* bushes, *agave lechuguilla*, and cacti are found at altitude, even near the entrance of the cave among pinyon pines.

Chiquihuite Cave is situated close to the top of a karst massif of vadose circulation (or of vertical transference). The karst formation was created by differential water erosion at the union between limestones and volcanic intrusive rocks, defining it as an interstratal karst. The cave shows an important speleothem development, with large stalactites and stalagmites, especially in the second, deeper gallery, where exterior elements were less invasive. This large,

FIGURE 7.6. General view of Chiquihuite Cave main gallery, as seen from the entrance. Arrow against the northern wall indicates test pit location (photo by C. F. Ardelean, January 2012).

second gallery—difficult to explore archaeologically because of the total lack of light and abundance of toxic bat guano—presents a truly impressive and complex scene: stalagmites, fistulous stalactites, flag-shaped stalactites, eccentric stalactites, straws, draperies, flowstone, columns, as well as carbonate crystal aggregates known as "moon milk" (Figure 7.13).

The main, frontal gallery contains fewer and smaller speleothems, but the cave is still active and young speleothems are being formed along the northern wall and somewhat to the east and center. There is considerable seeping from the ceiling (mainly during the summer rainy season through capillaries), and the growth of speleothems continues at a relatively accelerated rate. This is definitely not the typical dry cave common to the arid deserts of northern Mexico. Such caves would normally shelter funerary contexts of mummified bodies, as with the

more famous Candelaria Cave in Coahuila to the northwest. However, the seeping is localized on specific spots, and speleothem buildup has more recently slowed. Layers of fine dust on the floor and the seasonal presence of a migratory bat colony (likely an insectivorous or pollenivorous species, which inhabits the dark second gallery during spring and summer months) indicate present drier conditions.

The front gallery is a large dome, with roughly circular floor, measuring about 50 × 50 m horizontally and 10–14 m in height between the lowest points and the ceiling (Figures 7.6, 7.7). The eastern part of the ceiling presents a chimney (karst conduit) that seems to connect to upper conducts, as yet unexplored. The thickness of the invasive clastic sediments is suggested by the 14 m of difference in height between the level of the current entrance and the lowest points at the back (east) of the gallery. At several points in the eastern sector, there are shallow signs of modern anthropic disturbance, such as old looting pits, ephemeral hearths, and garbage. The second, totally dark gallery opens through a vault along the entire southern wall of the first chamber. Our exploration here was cursory. The floor inclines eastward, covered with even larger blocks from roof collapses. Most are very old events, as shown by massive stalagmites formed on top of the debris (Figure 7.13).

Two surface finds provided the first archaeological indicators: a projectile point outside the cave and a human-made combustion feature on the floor of the second gallery.

The elongated biface. While climbing the steep slope in order to explore and map the cave in 2011, we found a biface among the boulders covering the improvised path, about 150 m from the entrance, downslope and westward. The biface is seemingly a projectile point, with its tip missing from an impact fracture (Figure 7.8). A square-angled break on the proximal end suggests bending in the shaft. The color of the piece is opaque white, with dark mineral intrusions. The class of raw material seems to be white-patina silicified limestone or milky chert, possibly the latter. The foliate point was made on a thick flake blank, retaining some high points along the longitudinal ridge on both faces. Consistent, diving flake scars form a central ridge on both sides. Symmetrical and relatively well made, with percussion flaking and pressure retouch (more visible on the distal half), the artifact was probably used, as indicated by the breaks. Additional impact damage, visible on one edge, could have been caused by postdepositional events.

The type and chronology of this artifact are difficult to assess. When compared to point shapes in the Americas, an intriguing possibility appears: its outline is roughly similar to both the "Lermoid" forms of North America and the supposedly older-than-Clovis El Jobo points from South America. Both Lerma and El Jobo are confusing and poorly established types. Rather, they are intuitive taxa based on similarity of shapes, which tend to be related, in some texts, to early occupations of Late Pleistocene–

Early Holocene age (Painter and Hranicky 1990; Cruxent and Rouse 1956). Lerma, in fact, is not even a proper type but a fictitious taxon promoted in the literature following MacNeish's work in northeastern Mexico (see discussion about Lerma in Ardelean 2013:100–104, Ardelean and Macías-Quintero 2016:100–101).

Nevertheless, there is another, even more interesting morphological and technological analogy in North American archaeology: the Nebo Hill points from Western Missouri and Kansas (Shippee 1948). Ardelean personally compared the Chiquihuite artifact with such points curated in the Paleoindian collection of the Smithsonian Institution in 2015. The similarities are striking, in both shape and flaking patterns. The chronology of the Nebo Hill points is not clearly established but tends to be placed during the Late Holocene–Late Archaic, toward 3500 RCYBP. Additionally, our surface specimen will always lack a direct dating, so any temporal/cultural implications of the mentioned analogy must remain sterile.

Now, if one were comfortably situated in an uncritical academic environment, one might be tempted to postulate that the Chiquihuite cave biface could be a local variety of Lerma-like or El Jobo-like forms and that it could be a *hypothetical* indicator of early human occupation. But in fact, beyond any cross-cultural comparisons, the only thing the biface shows is that somebody in the past—perhaps an ancient hunter—passed by the cave, possibly entered, and left cultural traces for us to find. That reasoning stimulated efforts to explore the interior.

The fireplace. This feature was crushed under the massive ceiling collapses of the second gallery, exposed on an artificial profile apparently made by people extracting an iron oxide-rich red, silty material, abundant there (Figure 7.9). The position inside the gallery and the well-defined shape of the feature seemingly excluded any possibility that a burning log from an external wildfire could have rolled naturally into the second chamber.

In profile, the possible fireplace has a lenticular, concave shape, suggesting the fire was made within a small, shallow pit. The feature is not

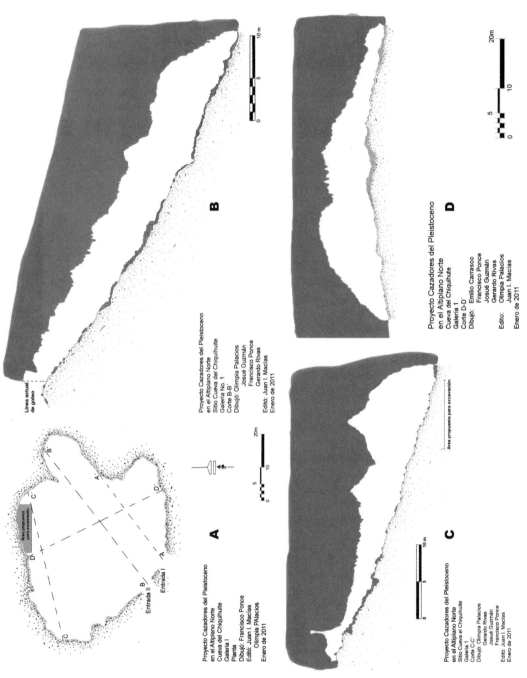

FIGURE 7.7. Chiquihuite Cave floor plan and section drawings of the front, main gallery: (A) main chamber floor plan showing location of the excavations next to the northern wall; (B) cross-section following the B–B′ trajectory shown on the floor plan; (C) cross-section C–C′; (D) cross-section D–D′ (modified from Ardelean 2013:357–358, Fig. 215–216).

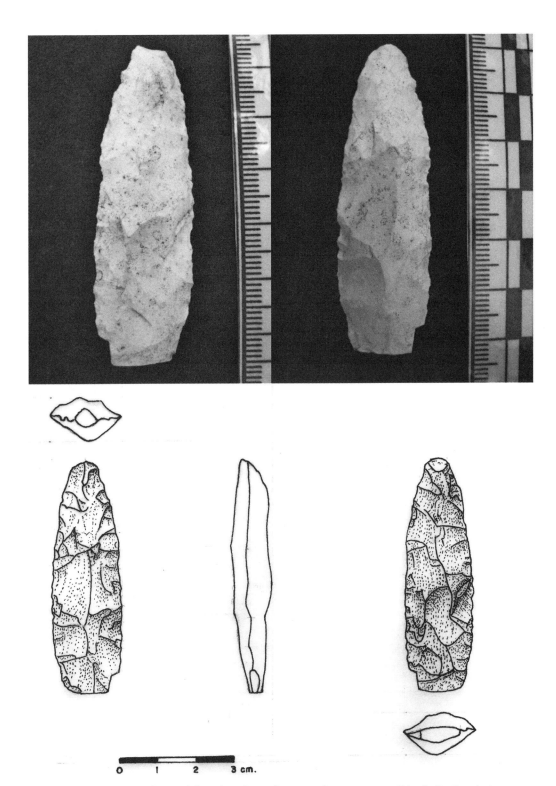

FIGURE 7.8. Biface (projectile point) found on the surface near the entrance to Chiquihuite Cave in January 2011, prior to the initial site exploration. The artifact is 57.9 mm long, 18.0 mm wide, and 18.2 mm thick, weighing 10.0 g (modified from Ardelean 2013:361, Fig. 219–220; photos by C. F. Ardelean; line drawing by Jaime Castrellón).

FIGURE 7.9. Close-up of the human-made fireplace observed beneath large blocks fallen from the ceiling, discovered during the surface exploration of the second gallery in September 2011. The position of the feature deep inside the dark chamber, well removed from the entrance, as well as microscopic and radio-carbon analyses, indicated it was not the result of a natural event but most likely an intentional fire made by humans over 6,000 years ago (photo by C. F. Ardelean, 2011; after Ardelean 2013:363, Fig. 221).

wider than 20 cm. Fine ash and charcoal present several hues of grey, brown, and black, indicating distinct materials burned at different temperatures. Samples were extracted for micromorphology and radiocarbon dating. Micromorphology analysis, performed at the National Autonomous University of Mexico (UNAM), evidenced the feature was created by a sustained and intense fire that burned the sediments beneath, confirming it as a combustion feature, presumably a fireplace or the place where a torch burned. Cremated remains of insects were also found inside the samples.

AMS dating was performed on a sample from the "hearth" (Oxford no. OxA-27073). The charcoal yielded an age of 5934 ± 32 RCYBP. When calibrated (OxCal 4.2, curve IntCal13), it gives a date around 6700 cal BP. Surprisingly, the small

hearth was of Middle Holocene age, which meant that the thick sediments and debris on the floor perhaps were burying even older occupations. The "hearth" was not excavated and did not show any visible artifactual remains. Regardless of the age of the foliate projectile point from outside the cave, humans seem to have used the cave for at least one brief episode about 7,000 years ago. This was an encouraging argument in favor of even earlier cultural presence in the Astillero mountains.

The test pit. The single trench from season 2012 was placed in the only available, boulder-free sector of the first gallery, attached to the north wall, in order to see the stratigraphic relationships between sediments and rock (Figures 7.6, 7.10). The aim was to evaluate the archaeological potential of the cave, possible human

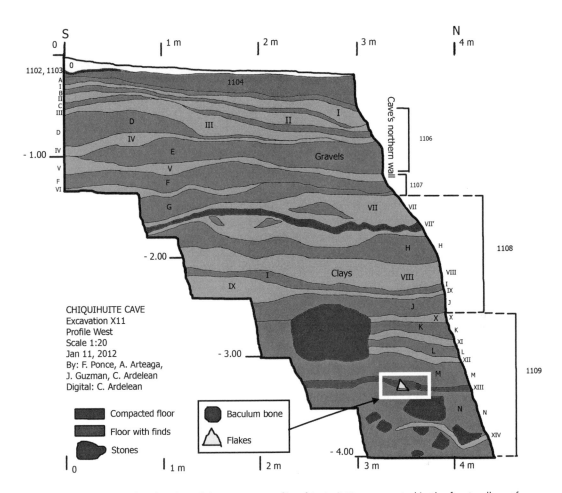

FIGURE 7.10. Stratigraphic drawing of the western profile of test pit X-11, excavated in the front gallery of Chiquihuite Cave, January 2012. The white rectangle marks the layer where the three flakes, the bear penis bone, and the burned phytoliths were found (modified from Ardelean 2013:369, Fig. 226).

presence, and depth of the deposits. The extent of the excavation was 3 × 2 m, with the longest axis oriented north–south. Deposits proved to be unconsolidated, although well settled, mainly sands and gravels, usually with brittle consistence. This required the walls of the trench to be properly inclined in order to avoid collapse. Steps were kept in the southern half, as the dig went deeper, providing access and additional support to the unstable profiles though it progressively reduced the excavated surface. At the end of two weeks of excavation, the unit reached 4 m in depth, with only 1 m² exposed at the very bottom.

The entire stratigraphy, from top to bottom,

represents a long sequence of cycles of alluvial deposition (Figure 7.10). Almost all strata were of sands and gravels, suggesting variable levels of energy, probably produced by floods invading through the cave's mouth, alternating with a few more stable periods marked by layers of clay. The clayey floors could have been formed by particle size sorting during some humid events. The environment in the cave was unstable for the time period reflected in the 4 m of depth. Each identifiable layer of sand, gravels, and clay marks one cave floor. Strata were mostly unconsolidated. Only the upper few centimeters were dry and dusty. Moisture increased gradually with depth, with the sandy sediments turning soggy at the bottom of the trench. Ceiling collapses are almost absent from the excavated surface, and the stratigraphy, in general, seems to be the effect of the sorting of clastic material by colluvial and alluvial processes, with lower-sized clasts moving toward the cave walls. Under these circumstances, any interpretation of paleo-environmental and archaeological data must be proposed cautiously, at a hypothetical level, and with a certain skepticism.

Nine stratigraphic units (1101–1109) were defined for the test pit X-11 (Figure 7.10). They refer to multilayered strata presenting visible differences in color and composition. The nine major units are subdivided into 29 strata or stratigraphic layers. Fourteen strata of clay and silt (I–XIV) alternate with 15 others of sands and gravels (A–O). Apparently, the excavation exposed 15 successive cave floors.

The lowest stratigraphic block is 1109, starting at 2.4 m of depth. Its interface is clearly marked by an erosion horizon above a gravel layer. The unit is dark colored and rich in tiny black dots adhering to gravels and stones. It was thought to be charcoal first, but the test for radiocarbon dating did not confirm it, indicating it rather was of mineral origin (Oxford no. P-32546). Large boulders and slabs were also present, probably from collapse events. This unit was high in moisture. The controlled micro-excavation was difficult, as the matrix was muddy.

No archaeological object, macroscopic plant, or faunal remains appeared anywhere in the excavation before reaching unit 1109, although the sediments were sieved, and the procedure was careful. The situation changed at about 3.3 m deep, starting with the clay floor no. XIII. Several objects appeared together, concentrated in quadrants A4–B4, next to the cave's wall.

Animal bones. In unit 1109, about 30 small animal bone fragments, from a variety of body parts, were found clustered at 3.60–3.80 m of depth. They were identified as bat and rodent bones by Arroyo's team, and some show indications of having been partially digested, probably as owl pellets or from another predator. This could be indirect evidence that these levels were once exposed as a cave floor. However, rodent burrowing is not excluded as a contributing cause.

Most bone materials identified in the excavation are either complete or fragmented long bones. Several mammal mandibles with teeth were also found, allowing more secure identification. It must be remembered that Mexican biodiversity is enormous, both present and past (Ceballos et al. 2010), making some identifications difficult, but most of the site materials had diagnostic attributes that helped at their taxonomic classification. The animals found at the cave include both birds and mammals. The Class Aves is represented by the acorn woodpecker (*Piciformes, Picidae, Melanerpes formicivorus*), and bushfinches and sparrows (*Passeriformes, Emberizidae*). The Class Mammalia shows specimens from 5 orders and 6 families, with bats (*Chiroptera*), rabbits (*Lagomorpha*), gophers, mice, and rats (*Rodentia*), bear (*Carnivora*), and deer (*Artiodactyla*).

Most of the identified mammals are known from grasslands and xerophytic scrub, which is currently the vegetation around the mountain where the cave is located. However, a few are known from temperate forests, which may have been the dominant landscape during the Late Pleistocene, such as black bear and flat-headed *Myotis* bat (the latter requiring a mixed vegetation composed of yucca trees and pinyon pines). As for the birds, sparrows are widespread, while the acorn woodpecker is known mostly from oak or pine woodland.

Burned palm phytoliths. Two 100 ml sediment samples extracted from the lowest layers contained 182 phytoliths analyzed by J. Watling in Exeter. The assemblage constitutes 9 percent grasses (rondel and saddle phytoliths), 50 percent wood phytoliths (globular granulates), and 41 percent palms (globular echinates). Grasses and wood are also present in upper unit 1108, but palms are far less abundant there (5 percent). The genus or species of palms could not be specified. Therefore, it is unknown whether the phytoliths originated from foreign taxa. Furthermore, as these morphotypes are produced by all parts of the plant (stem, leaves, and fruits), their anatomical origin cannot be ascertained.

Intriguingly, one quarter of the palm phytoliths from 1109 exhibit discoloration from burning, which implies direct contact with fire, presumably a hearth. It seems likely therefore, as a hypothesis, that palm products were brought directly to the cave by people, perhaps as fruits for consumption, artifacts made of fiber, or leaves or wood for fuel or construction. Without knowledge of the paleoenvironmental setting of the cave, it remains unknown whether this material originated locally or was brought in from a more distant ecosystem.

Bear baculum (penis bone). At 3.30 m deep, in the same reduced space as the rest of the finds, there was a long, needle-like bone with pointed ends and a smooth, longitudinal ridge on one side (Figure 7.11-A). Arroyo's zooarchaeology team from the National Institute of Anthropology and History (INAH) in Mexico City identified it as a bear *baculum* (penis bone). The genus and species are still debatable, but it almost surely belongs to an American black bear (*Ursus americanus*), an animal long extinct in northeastern Zacatecas.[2] However, it could also belong to Ice Age extinct short-faced bears such as *Arctodus simus* (although bacula of this animal are yet unknown; Schubert and Kaufmann 2003) or *Tremarctos* sp. (cf. Mondolfi 1983). The bone was relatively well preserved, with some erosion marks and a broken end, but lacked any visible anthropic intervention.

A mysterious bone. Next to the bear baculum, there was another bone, closely resembling a rib (Figure 7.11-B). Zooarchaeologists do not agree on its identification yet. However, it can be argued that its shape, morphology, and size make it look either like the proximal fragment of a baculum, perhaps a "floating" rib from an unidentified species, or even a fragment of a large hyoid bone. The stratigraphic association of this bone with the bear's *os penis* is interesting and its taxonomic pertinence is crucial if we argued for a potential human agency in their deposition.

Limestone flakes. Three gray-greenish, presumably human-made, silicified limestone flakes were found by sieving, in the same bucket of sediment excavated from the limit between quadrants A4 and B4, at 3.30–3.40 m deep (Fig-

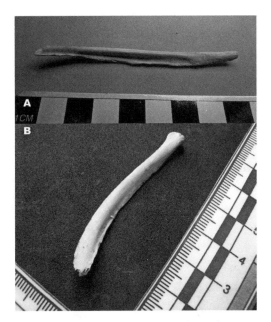

FIGURE 7.11. The two bones recovered together at the bottom of the test pit in the Chiquihuite Cave. The upper one (*A*) was identified as a *baculum* (penis bone) belonging to a bear, possibly *Ursus americanus* (American black bear). It was destroyed during the radiocarbon dating process, yielding a pre-LGM age. The other bone (*B*) may be another penis bone or perhaps a fragment of a large hyoid bone, but its taxonomic identification is still uncertain (photos by C. F. Ardelean).

ure 7.12). They come from the same stratigraphic unit as the penis bone and the burned phytoliths. Flake *A* seems to be a fragmented thinning flake, with parallel edges, platform missing, and a feather termination. It displays two small narrow scars on its dorsal face, probably from the preparation of the striking platform. Flake *B* has a dihedral platform, an impact bulb, and flake scars on its dorsal side. Flake *C* seems to display a "nippled" ground platform. They are made of a variety of the same raw material as the limestone artifacts found at nearby sites, such as Dunas de Milpa Grande and San José de las Grutas (Ardelean 2013; Ardelean and Macías-Quintero 2016). All three show chemical (postdepositional) erosion. While doubts may persist about the artificial origin of flakes *A* and *C*, specimen *B* is definitely a human-made product. The fact that they were discovered together, and no such

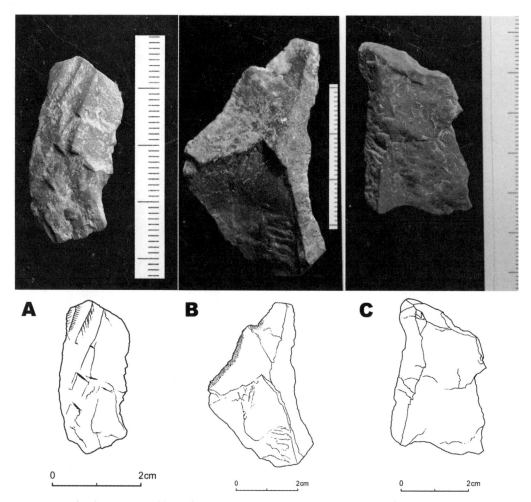

A   **B**   **C**

0   2cm

0   2cm

0   2cm

FIGURE 7.12. The three presumably artificially produced limestone flakes recovered in the sieve from the same layer as the bear penis bone in unit 1109. Their original color was grey. Flake A measures 33 × 15.3 × 4 mm; flake B is 49.6 × 31 × 8.2 mm; and flake C is 48 × 28 × 6.3 mm. They show platforms indicating intentional flaking (photos and line drawings by Mike Rouillard, Exeter).

material was found in any other excavated layer in the cave, may argue in favor of these objects as real artifacts.

Two samples were sent for dating, all from unit 1109 where the flakes, the penis bones, and the burned phytoliths were found. One OSL sample was extracted at 3.30 m of depth, from the eastern profile, close to its juncture with the cave wall. The analysis, performed at the University of Oxford's Research Laboratory for Archaeology and History of Art (RLAHA; sample no. X-4135) by Jean-Luc Schwenninger, offered an interesting result. The laboratory announced

an initial date of 25,870 ± 2120 BP (or 25.87 ± 2.1 ka). A further calculation was made subsequently, taking into account the hypothetical thickness of the cave's roof set at 40 m, based on exterior measurements, which implies a higher protection from cosmic rays. The new luminescence result (based on a total dose rate of 1.69 ± 0.12 Gy/ka) was 29,180 ± 2,570 years of age.

Facing the challenges and doubts raised by these dating attempts, it was decided to sacrifice the bear *baculum* for AMS dating after making a cast. The collagen from the bone (sample no. Beta-345055) yielded an astonishing age of

FIGURE 7.13. Spectacular speleothems, more than 4 m tall (the "Ancestors"), in the western corner of the second chamber at the Chiquihuite Cave, growing on top of ancient, massive ceiling collapses (photo by C. F. Ardelean, 2014).

27,830 ± 150 RCYBP, calibrating (2σ) at about 32,000 cal BP. The two dating results from different methods seemed to match.

Discussion and Conclusions

The discoveries reported above may provoke tempting assumptions, but any interpretation must be made with extreme caution and only on a hypothetical level at this incipient stage of the research. So, were there people living in a cave in Zacatecas more than 30,000 years ago, which Lorenzo's model and the few findings would entitle one to conclude?

The scientific, self-critical posture requires consideration of a few important aspects. The investigation described in this chapter was at a preliminary level, and only a short amount of time was involved in exploration of the cave. No conclusions at all can be reached after only one test pit. Two dates are insufficient, even if using two different procedures, nor are a few archaeological items. The flakes were recovered in the sieve and their potential relationship to the rest of the context could not be documented within the dig.

Nevertheless, skepticism should not mean outright rejection, and there are facts that cannot be denied. In this case, all the archaeological finds appeared at the same level. No indicators of "intrusions" existed before reaching 3.3 m of depth, when the finds started to appear—all clustered in the northern quadrants. No disturbances are visible anywhere on profiles, the layers being continuous and consistent over the entire pit's surface. Nor is there evidence of burrowing, holes, or cleavages. Even the presence of microfauna bones, probably left by predators, suggest that the clay floor XIII was once exposed and receptive to natural and anthropic depositions. Burned phytoliths appear in that level and are of palms, perhaps from exogenous taxa, possibly brought in by humans, in the same stratum that yielded at least one baculum bone associated with three limestone flakes. In addition, the radiocarbon dating of the bone and the OSL dating of the stratum match, with sufficient precision.

Anticipating necessary and imminent critiques, a few questions come to the mind: how could a bear's penis bone reach the cave's ancient floors in the apparent absence of any other bear skeletal fragment? If the materials were intrusive, penetrating from above or beneath, how could they all stop *exactly* at the same level and within the same floor unit? If that happened, what made several anthropic indicators converge in the same reduced place?

Based on these facts, one could propose a working hypothesis that there are potential indicators of an older-than-Clovis human occupation at Chiquihuite Cave, dating to about 30,000 years ago. The cave serves as a case study here, meant to support a discussion about how to manage data that can be mistreated. Here, an early occupation is only a hypothesis, not a conclusion, which it would be according to the national paradigm. Still, there is an exciting and striking possibility suggested by a handful of data that must be handled with care and skepticism but not simply denied for being uncomfortable. Ancient human presence in Chiquihuite still remains a possibility that we must not fear simply because academic dogmas cultivated on one side of a river or the other tell us to feel that way. It is a valid epistemological protocol around an incipient corpus of data that must be further tested by extensive excavations in the cave.

This is the middle path that should be followed in the American prehistory: any discovery and dating results should be taken into account as arguments for the construction of working hypotheses meant to be fully tested by subsequent fieldwork. This is the only mechanism we have to separate the objective reality of the human past from prejudice and speculation.

Endnote

At the time this volume went into publication, Chiquihuite Cave had already witnessed two subsequent intensive and fairly long excavation seasons, in 2016 and 2017. Many of the assumptions and hypotheses stated here have been further tested by detailed explorations. The reader is kindly invited to consult the new publications about the staggering results that we hope are already available by the time you read this. Nevertheless, despite the expansion of knowledge at Chiquihuite during this interval, the first author and project director decided not to modify the format and content of this chapter as it was prepared for the 2014 symposium in Austin for one important reason: this text reflects our thinking and inquiries at the time, soon after the initial studies at the cave. They are a crucial part of the development and growth of the knowledge we acquired of the earliest humans in Mexico. Although we know much more today, this chapter needs to conserve the preliminary form our science had a few years ago.

Acknowledgments

The radiocarbon dating performed under the supervision of Dr. Tom Higham at the Oxford Radiocarbon Accelerator Unit (OXRAU) was possible thanks to a grant from the Natural Environment Research Council (NERC Grant NF/2012/1/18). The PhD research conducted by the first author and the other radiocarbon dating results mentioned here were sponsored through a doctoral scholarship from the Mexican federal funding scheme Programa para el Mejoramiento del Profesorado (PROMEP). Mr. José Roque Ortega-Escalera and Mr. José Antonio Alonso provided substantial sponsorship for the supplies and materials used during the 2012 test excavation. The OSL dating was part of an academic collaboration with the Luminescence Laboratory at the University of Oxford's RLAHA. The authors are deeply grateful to the organizations and people who helped in these tasks, especially the undergraduate students who took part in the surveys and excavations and the local workers from Guadalupe Garzaron village who constantly helped with project logistics.

Notes

1. Chiquihuite Cave has been listed in Mexico's National Register of Sites, G14C6332001, ID 44499.
2. We also performed an extensive comparison of the specimen with bear and carnivore bacula from collections at the Smithsonian Institution in Washington, D.C., thanks to invaluable help provided by our colleagues Dennis Stanford, Stephanie Cannington, and Joseph Villari,

to whom we are deeply grateful. After the derived observations, the American black bear seems to be the most suitable option for this specimen.

References

Acosta, Guillermo
2010   Late-Pleistocene/Early-Holocene Tropical Foragers of Chiapas, Mexico: Recent Studies. *Current Research in the Pleistocene* 27:1–4.
2012   Ice Age Hunter-Gatherers and the Colonization of Mesoamerica. In *The Oxford Handbook of Mesoamerican Archaeology*, edited by Deborah L. Nichols and Christopher A. Pool, pp. 129–140. Oxford University Press, New York.

Acosta, Guillermo, and Patricia Pérez Martínez.
2012   El poblamiento de Chiapas a fines del Pleistoceno. In *Arqueología reciente de Chiapas: contribuciones del encuentro celebrado en el 60° aniversario de la Fundación Arqueológica Nuevo Mundo*, edited by Lynneth S. Lowe and Mary E. Pye, pp. 21–29. New World Archaeological Foundation, Brigham Young University, Provo, UT.

Adovasio, James M.
2015   Plant Fiber Technologies and the Initial Colonization of the New World. In *Pre-Clovis in the Americas. International Science Conference Proceedings*, edited by Dennis J. Stanford and Alison T. Stenger, pp. 192–207. CreateSpace Independent Publishing Platform, Smithsonian Institution edition, Washington, D.C.

Ardelean, Ciprian F.
2013   Archaeology of Early Human Occupations and the Pleistocene–Holocene Transition in the Zacatecas Desert, Northern Mexico. PhD dissertation in archaeology, University of Exeter, Exeter.
2014   The Early Prehistory of the Americas and the Human Peopling of the Western Hemisphere. An Overview of Archaeological Data, Hypotheses, and Models. *Studii de Preistorie* 11:33–95.
2016   The Transitional Period: A Short Terminological Debate around the Pleistocene–Holocene Transition in North American Prehistory. *Studii de Preistorie* 13:43–62.

Ardelean, Ciprian F., and Juan Ignacio Macías-Quintero
2016   ¿Qué tan temprano es lo "temprano"? Consideraciones sobre la prehistoria mexicana y el sitio arqueológico de dunas de Milpa Grande, Zacatecas. In *El poblamiento temprano en América 7*, edited by José-Concepción Jiménez, Felisa Aguilar, Carlos Serrano, and Arturo González González, pp. 97–131. Museo del Desierto and Dirección de Antropología Física–INAH, Saltillo and México, D.F.

Armenta Camacho, Juan
1959   *Hallazgo de un artefacto asociado con mamut, en el valle de Puebla*. Instituto Poblano de Antropología e Historia, INAH Publicación 7. México, D.F.
1978   *Vestigios de labor humana en huesos de animales extintos de Valsequillo, Puebla, México*. Consejo Editorial del Gobierno del Estado de Puebla, Puebla.

Aveleyra Arroyo de Anda, Luis, and Manuel Maldonado-Koerdell
1952   Asociación de artefactos con mamut en el Pleistoceno superior de la cuenca de México. *Revista Mexicana de Estudios Antropológicos* 13(1):3–29.
1953   Association of Artifacts with Mammoth in the Valley of Mexico. *American Antiquity* 18(4):332–340.
1956   The Second Mammoth and Associated Artifacts at Santa Isabel Iztapan, Mexico. *American Antiquity* 22(1):12–28.

Bryan, Alan L., and Ruth Gruhn
1989   The Evolutionary Significance of the American Lower Paleolithic. In *Homenaje a José Luis Lorenzo*, edited by Lorena Mirambell, pp. 81–102. Colección Científica no. 188. INAH, México, D.F.

Caballero Miranda, Margarita E.
1997   The Last Glacial Maximum in the Basin of Mexico: The Diatom Record between 34,000 and 15,000 years BP from Lake Chalco. *Quaternary International* 43/44:125–136.

Cassiano, Gianfranco
1992   El poblamiento de México a fines del Pleistoceno. *Cuicuilco* 29/30:105–124.
1998   Evidencias del poblamiento prehistórico en el área de Metzquititlán, Hidalgo. *Arqueología* 19:25–43.
2005   Cambios en la tecnología lítica entre el Pleistoceno tardío y el Holoceno temprano en el área de Metztitlán-Mezquititlán, Hidalgo. In *Reflexiones sobre la industria lítica*, edited by Leticia González and Lorena Mirambell, pp. 49–81. Colección Científica 475. INAH, México, D.F.

Cassiano, Gianfranco, and A. Vázquez
1990   Oyapa: evidencias de poblamiento
        temprano. Área de Metztitlán, Hidalgo.
        Arqueología, 2nd epoch, 4:25–40.
Ceballos, Gerardo, Joaquin Arroyo-Cabrales, and
Eduardo Ponce
2010   Effects of Pleistocene Environmental
        Changes on the Distribution and Commu-
        nity Structure of the Mammalian Fauna of
        Mexico. *Quaternary Research* 73(3):464–473.
Chatters, James C., Douglas J. Kennett, Yemane
Asmerom, Brian M. Kemp, Victor Polyak, Alberto
Nava Blank, Patricia A. Beddows, et al.
2014   Late Pleistocene Human Skeleton and
        mtDNA Link Paleoamericans and Mod-
        ern Native Americans. *Science* 344(6185):
        750–754.
Cruxent, J. M. and Irving Rouse
1956   A Lithic Industry of Paleo-Indian Type
        in Venezuela. *American Antiquity* 22(2):
        172–179.
de Morgan, Jacques
1947   *La Humanidad Prehistórica*. Traducción de
        la 2ª edición francesa. Editorial Cervantes,
        Barcelona.
Faulhaber, Johanna
2000   Antropología biológica de las sociedades
        prehispánicas. In *Historia antigua de Méx-
        ico*, edited by Linda Manzanilla and Leon-
        ardo López Luján, vol. 1, pp. 23–52. UNAM,
        México, D.F.
Gaines, Edmund P., and Guadalupe Sánchez
2009   Current Paleoindian Research in Sonora,
        Mexico. *Archaeology Southwest* 23(3):4–5.
Gaines, Edmund P., Guadalupe Sánchez, and
Vance T. Holliday
2009   Paleoindian Archaeology of Northern and
        Central Sonora: A Review and Update. *Kiva*
        74(3):305–335.
García-Bárcena, Joaquín
2001   Primeros pobladores. La etapa lítica en
        México. *Arqueología Mexicana* 9(52):28–29.
González, Silvia, José Concepción Jiménez, Robert
Hedges, David Huddart, James O. Ohman, Alan
Turner, and José Antonio Pompa y Padilla
2003   Earliest Humans in the Americas: New
        Evidence from Mexico. *Journal of Human
        Evolution* 44(3):379–387.
González, Silvia, David Huddart, and Matthew
Bennett
2006a   Valsequillo Pleistocene Archaeology and
        Dating: Ongoing Controversy in Central
        Mexico. *World Archaeology* 38(4):611–627.

González, Silvia, David Huddart, Matthew R.
Bennett, and Alberto González Huesca
2006b   Human footprints in Central Mexico, Older
        than 40,000 years. *Quaternary Science
        Reviews* 25:201–222.
González, Silvia, José Concepción Jiménez López,
Robert Hedges, José Antonio Pompa y Padilla, and
David Huddart
2006c   Early Humans in Mexico: New Chronologi-
        cal Data. In *El hombre temprano en América
        y sus implicaciones en el poblamiento de la
        cuenca de México. Primer simposio interna-
        cional*, edited by José Concepción Jiménez
        López, Silvia González, José Antonio Pompa
        y Padilla, and Francisco Ortíz Pedraza,
        pp. 67–76. Colección Cientifica 500. INAH,
        México, D.F.
González-González, Arturo H., Carmen Rojas San-
doval, Alejandro Terrazas Mata, Martha Benavente
Sanvicente, and Wolfgang Stinnesbeck
2006   Poblamiento temprano en la península de
        Yucatán: evidencias localizadas en cuevas
        sumergidas de Quintana Roo, México. In *2º
        Simposio internacional el hombre temprano
        en América*, edited by José Concepción
        Jiménez López, Oscar J. Polaco, Gloria
        Martínez Sosa, and Rocío Hernández
        Flores, pp. 73–90. INAH, México, D.F.
González-González, Arturo H., Carmen Rojas San-
doval, Alejandro Terrazas Mata, Martha Benavente
Sanvicente, Wolfgang Stinnesbeck, Jerónimo Aviles,
Magdalena de los Ríos Paredes, and Eugenio Acévez
2008   The Arrival of Humans on the Yucatan Pen-
        insula: Evidence from Submerged Caves in
        the State of Quintana Roo, Mexico. *Current
        Research in the Pleistocene* 25:1–24.
González-González, Arturo H., Alejandro Terrazas,
Wolfgang Stinnesbeck, Martha E. Benavente,
Jerónimo Avilés, Carmen Rojas, José Manuel
Padilla, Adriana Velásquez, Eugenio Acevez,
and Eberhard Frey
2014   The First Human Settlers on the Yucatan
        Peninsula: Evidence from Drowned Caves
        in the State of Quintana Roo (South
        Mexico). In *Paleoamerican Odyssey*, edited
        by Kelly E. Graf, Caroline V. Ketron, and
        Michael R. Waters, pp. 323–337. Center for
        the Study of the First Americans and Texas
        A&M University Press, College Station, TX.
Huddart, David, and Silvia González
2006   A Review of Environmental Change in the
        Basin of Mexico (40,000–10,000 BP): Im-
        plications for Early Humans. In *El hombre*

temprano en América y sus implicaciones en el poblamiento de la cuenca de México. Primer simposio internacional, edited by José Concepción Jiménez López, Silvia González, José Antonio Pompa y Padilla, and Francisco Ortíz Pedraza, pp. 77–105. Colección Científica 500. INAH, México, D.F.

Irwin-Williams, Cynthia
1967   Association of Early Man with Horse, Camel, and Mastodon at Hueyatlaco, Valsequillo (Puebla, Mexico). In *Pleistocene Extinctions: The Search for a Cause,* edited by P. S. Martin and H. E. Wright Jr., pp. 337–347. Yale University Press, New Haven, CT.

1981   Commentary on "Geologic Evidence for Age of Deposits at Hueyatlaco Archaeological Site, Valsequillo, Mexico." *Quaternary Research* 16(2):258.

Irwin-Williams, Cynthia, Richard S. MacNeish, F. A. Petersen, and H. M. Wormington
1969   Comments on the Associations of Archaeological Materials and Extinct Fauna in the Valsequillo Region, Puebla, Mexico. *American Antiquity* 34(1):82–83.

Jiménez López, José Concepción, Rocío Hernández Flores, Gloria Martínez Sosa, and Gabriel Saucedo Arteaga
2006   La Mujer del Peñón III. In *El hombre temprano en América y sus implicaciones en el poblamiento de la cuenca de México. Primer simposio internacional,* edited by José Concepción Jiménez López, Silvia González, José Antonio Pompa y Padilla, and Francisco Ortíz Pedraza, pp. 49–66. Colección Cientifica 500. INAH, México, D.F.

Jiménez López, José Concepción, Rocío Hernández Flores, and Gloria Martínez Sosa
2010   Catálogo de los esqueletos precerámicos de México. In *El hombre temprano en América. 3º Simposio Internacional,* edited by José Concepción Jiménez López, Carlos Serrano Sánchez, Arturo González González, and Felisa J. Aguilar Arellano, pp. 131–145. UNAM and Museo del Desierto, México, D.F., and Saltillo.

Lorenzo, José Luis
1967   *La etapa lítica en Mexico.* Departamento de Prehistoria, Publicación 20. INAH, México, D.F.

Lorenzo, José Luis, and Lorena Mirambell
1981   El Cedral, San Luis Potosí, México: un sitio con presencia humana de más de 30,000 aP. In *El poblamiento de América: evidencia ar-*

queológica de ocupación humana en América anterior a 11,500 aP, edited by Alan L. Bryan and Lorena Mirambell, pp. 112–125. Unión Internacional de Ciencias Prehistóricas y Protohistóricas, 10th Congress, México, D.F.

1984   Proyecto el Cedral. *Boletín del Consejo de Arqueología,* pp. 39–49. INAH, México, D.F.

1986   *Tlapacoya: 35,000 años de historia del Lago de Chalco.* INAH, México, D.F.

2005   The Inhabitants of Mexico during the Upper Pleistocene. In *Ice Age Peoples of North America: Environments, Origins, and Adaptations,* edited by Robson Bonnichsen and Karen L. Turnmire, pp. 482–496. Center for the Study of the First Americans, Texas A&M University, College Station.

MacNeish, Richard S.
1958   *Preliminary Archaeological Investigations in the Sierra de Tamaulipas, Mexico.* Transactions of the American Philosophical Society 48(6):1–210.

Mirambell, Lorena
1973   El hombre en Tlapacoya desde hace unos 20 mil años. *Boletín del INAH,* 2nd epoch, January–March:3–8.

1986   Las excavaciones. In *Tlapacoya: 35,000 años de historia del lago de Chalco,* edited by José Luis Lorenzo and Lorena Mirambell, pp. 13–56. INAH, México, D.F.

1988   La investigación prehistórica en el INAH. In *Orígenes del hombre Americano. Seminario, 1987,* edited by Alba González Jácome, pp. 307–318. Secretaría de Educación Pública, México, D.F.

2000   Los primeros pobladores del actual territorio mexicano. In *Historia antigua de México,* vol. 1, edited by Linda Manzanilla and Leonardo López Luján, pp. 223–254. UNAM, México, D.F.

2001   Arqueolítico y Cenolítico inferior (30,000–7,000 aC). *Arqueología Mexicana* 9(52): 46–51.

2012   (editor) *Rancho "La Amapola", Cedral. Un sitio Arqueológico–paleontológico pleistocénico–holocénico con restos de actividad humana.* INAH, México, D.F.

Mondolfi, Edgardo
1983   The Feet and Baculum of the Spectacled Bear, with Comments on Ursid Phylogeny. *Journal of Mammalogy* 64(2):307–310.

Montané, Julio
1988   El poblamiento temprano de Sonora. In *Orígenes del Hombre Americano. Seminario,*

1987, edited by Alba González Jácome, pp. 83–116. Secretaría de Educación Pública, México, D.F.

Morse, Sarita A., Matthew Bennett, Silvia Gonzalez, and David Huddart

2010 Techniques for Verifying Human Footprints: Reappraisal of Pre-Clovis Footprints in Central Mexico. *Quaternary Science Reviews* 29(19–20):2571–2578.

Painter, Floyd, and W. J. Hranicky

1990 The Lerma Projectile Point Type in the Eastern and Western Hemispheres. *Central States Archaeological Journal* 37(1):40–51.

Renne, Paul R., Joshua Feinberg, Michael R. Waters, Joaquin Arroyo Cabrales, Patricia Ochoa Castillo, Mario Perez Campa, and Kim B. Knight

2005 Age of Mexican Ash with Alleged Footprints. *Nature* 438(7068):E7–8.

Rice, David G.

2015 Origins and Antiquity of a Western North American Stemmed Point Tradition: A Pre-Clovis Perspective. In *Pre-Clovis in the Americas. International Science Conference Proceedings*, edited by Dennis J. Stanford and Alison T. Stenger, pp. 208–220. CreateSpace Independent Publishing Platform, Smithsonian Institution edition, Washington, D.C.

Robles Ortíz, M., and F. Manzano

1972 Clovis Fluted Points from Sonora, Mexico. *Kiva* 37(4):199–206.

Sánchez, Guadalupe

2001 A Synopsis of Paleo-Indian Archaeology in Mexico. *Kiva* 67(2):119–136.

2007 The Paleoindian Occupation of Sonora, Mexico. *Archaeology Southwest* 21(2)3.

2010 *Los Primeros Mexicanos: Late Pleistocene/ Early Holocene Archaeology of Sonora, Mexico.* PhD dissertation, School of Anthropology, University of Arizona, Tucson. http://hdl.handle.net/10150/146069.

Sánchez, Guadalupe, and John P. Carpenter

2003 La ocupación del Pleistoceno terminal/ Holoceno temprano en Sonora, México. In *Noroeste de México. 1973–2003, 30 años de antropología e historia en el noroeste de México*, pp. 27–34. Consejo Nacional para la Cultura y las Artes and INAH, Hermosillo.

Sánchez, Guadalupe, Edmund P. Gaines, and Joaquín Arroyo Cabrales

2009a El fin del mundo. *Archaeology Southwest* 23(3):6–7.

Sánchez, Guadalupe, Edmund P. Gaines, and Vance T. Holliday

2009b El fin del mundo, Sonora: cazadores Clovis de megafauna del Pleistoceno terminal. *Arqueología Mexicana* 27(97):46–49.

Sánchez, Guadalupe, Edmund Gaines, and Alberto Peña

2007 Current Research at Paleoamerican Sites in Sonora, Mexico. *Current Research in the Pleistocene* 24:64–66.

Sánchez, Guadalupe, Vance T. Holliday, John P. Carpenter, and Edmund P. Gaines

2015 Sonoran Clovis Groups: Lithic Technological Organization and Land Use. In *Clovis: On the Edge of a New Understanding*, edited by Ashley M. Smallwood and Thomas A. Jennings, pp. 243–261. Center for the Study of the First Americans and Texas A&M University Press, College Station.

Sánchez, Guadalupe, Vance T. Holliday, Edmund P. Gaines, Joaquín Arroyo Cabrales, Natalia Martínez-Tagüeña, Andrew Kowler, Todd Lange, Gregory W. L. Hodgins, Susan M. Mentzerg, and Ismael Sanchez-Morales

2014 Human (Clovis)–Gomphothere (Cuvieronius sp.) Association ~13,390 Calibrated YBP in Sonora, Mexico. *PNAS* 111(30)10972-10977.

Schubert, Blaine W., and James E. Kaufmann

2003 A Partial Short-Faced Bear Skeleton from an Ozark Cave with Comments on the Paleobiology of Species. *Journal of Cave and Karst Studies* 65(2):101–110.

Serrano Sánchez, Carlos, and Luis Fernando Núñez Enríquez

2011 Sistemas funerarios durante la etapa lítica de México. In *4° simposio internacional el hombre temprano en América*, edited by José Concepción Jiménez López, Carlos Serrano, Arturo H. González González, and Felisa J. Aguilar, pp. 187–210. INAH, Instituto de Investigaciones Antropológicas de la UNAM, and Museo del Desierto, México, D.F., and Saltillo.

Shippee, J. M.

1948 Nebo Hill, a Lithic Complex in Western Missouri. *American Antiquity* 14(1):29–32.

Stanford, Dennis J., and Alison T. Stenger (editors)

2015 *Pre-Clovis in the Americas. International Science Conference Proceedings.* CreateSpace Independent Publishing Platform, Smithsonian Institution edition, Washington, D.C.

Steen-McIntyre, Virginia
2006   Approximate Dating of Tephra Using the
        Microscope: "Seat-of-the-Pants" Methods
        to Roughly Date Quaternary Archaeologi-
        cal and Paleontological Sites by Associated
        Pumice and Volcanic Ash Layers. In *El
        hombre temprano en América y sus impli-
        caciones en el poblamiento de la cuenca
        de México. Primer simposio internacional*,
        edited by José Concepción Jiménez López,
        Silvia González, José Antonio Pompa y
        Padilla, and Francisco Ortíz Pedraza,
        pp. 155–165. Colección Cientifica 500.
        INAH, México, D.F.

Steen-McIntyre, Virginia, Roald Fryxell, and
Harold E. Malde
1981   Geologic Evidence for Age of Deposits at
        Hueyatlaco Archaeological Site, Valsequillo,
        Mexico. *Quaternary Research* 16(1):1–17.

Suárez, Rafael
2015   Pre-Fishtail Settlement in the Southern
        Cone ca. 15,000–13,100 yr. ca. BP: Synthesis,
        Evaluation, and Discussion of the Evidence.
        In *Pre-Clovis in the Americas. International
        Science Conference Proceedings*, edited by
        Dennis J. Stanford and Alison T. Stenger,
        pp. 153–191. CreateSpace Independent Pub-
        lishing Platform, Smithsonian Institution
        edition, Washington, D.C.

Terrazas Mata, Alejandro, and Martha E. Benavente
Sanvicente
2006   Estudio preliminar de tres cráneos tempra-
        nos, procedentes de cuevas sumergidas de
        la costa este de Quintana Roo. In *IIº sim-
        posio internacional el hombre temprano en
        América*, edited by José Concepción Jiménez
        López, Oscar J. Polaco, Gloria Martínez
        Sosa, and Rocío Hernández Flores, pp. 189–
        198. INAH, México, D.F.

CHAPTER 8

Stone Tool Technology at the Gault Site

Exploring Technology, Patterns, and the Early
Human Occupation of North America

Thomas J. Williams, Nancy Velchoff, Michael B. Collins, and Bruce A. Bradley

Archaeological excavations at Area 15 of the Gault Site, central Texas, USA (Figure 8.1), have yielded a flaked stone tool assemblage from deposits located stratigraphically below Clovis.

The name, Gault Assemblage, is here applied to this early cultural component. During excavation, this assemblage was originally referred to as "older-than-Clovis" (also used in Adovasio and Pedler 2016), however this term is inadequate given its implied relationship to Clovis.

The Gault Assemblage reveals technological similarities and differences with Clovis and provides the opportunity to study both intrasite and intersite relationships.

As discussed by Collins and colleagues (2013), only the Debra L. Friedkin site, located 300 m downstream from the Gault Site, exhibits a similar technological repertoire. The archaeological record indicates that humans occupied central Texas prior to the appearance of Clovis technology. As such, this evidence raises a number of important questions: what was the nature of the human occupation of the Americas before Clovis? How diverse was the archaeological record before ca. 13,000 cal BP? What patterns exist across the Americas?

The excavations at Meadowcroft Rockshelter (Adovasio et al. 1978; Haynes 1980; Adovasio and Carlisle 1982; Adovasio 1983; Adovasio et al. 1990; Adovasio et al. 1999), Monte Verde (Dillehay 1989; Dillehay 1997), and Cactus Hill (McAvoy and McAvoy 1997) have provided some of the best early evidence of a human presence in the

New World (Waters and Stafford 2013). These sites now contribute to a growing pattern of occupation in the Americas before Clovis (Collins et al. 2013; Collins 2014).

Despite the growing evidence for occupation between 15,000 and 17,000 cal BP (Goebel et al. 2008; Waters and Stafford 2013; Meltzer 2013; Madsen 2015), Clovis has become the de facto benchmark for assessment of these early sites (Ardelean 2014), which is problematic for interpreting the early record. The thin, unfluted triangular points and the presence of a prismatic blade technology at Meadowcroft and Cactus Hill, among others (see Barker and Broster, 1996; Dunbar, 2006; Stanford et al., 2014), provide plausible technological evidence for a Clovis predecessor. In contrast, the thick, narrow bifacial points found at Monte Verde share few common technological traits with Clovis points (Dillehay 2000).

While the Clovis benchmark is not wholly indefensible, it is deeply intertwined in the historical context of the research, and archaeologists have argued for a less Clovis-centric debate (Dillehay 2000; Collins 2002; Bryan and Gruhn 2003). With increasing archaeological evidence and dates at least 2,000 years older than Clovis (Waters and Stafford 2013; Madsen 2015), researchers are only now beginning to recognize that there are inherent complexities in the earliest occupations (Collins 2014; Collins et al. 2013).

To understand these occupation signatures,

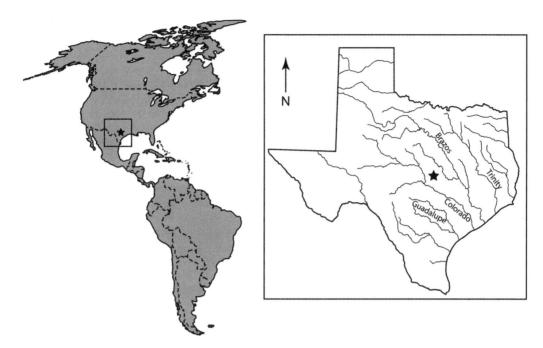

FIGURE 8.1. Location of the Gault Site.

the Clovis origins debate needs to be separated from the earliest human occupations. By keeping these issues detached, all technological patterns can be assessed within the context of both their contemporary and earlier archaeological signatures.

As a means to explore the separation argument, this chapter assesses the evidence recovered from the Gault site. The first section evaluates the manufacturing technologies of Clovis and the Gault Assemblage, including a discussion of the Clovis origins debate. The second section contextualizes the two assemblages, respectively, within the early archaeological record and expands on the need to separate Clovis origins from the early human occupations of the Americas.

The Gault Site

The Gault Site (41BL323) lies at the headwaters of Buttermilk Creek near reliable springs and is situated along the Balcones Escarpment in Bell County, central Texas, USA. This escarpment forms the eastern edge of the Edwards Plateau, a Cretaceous limestone upland that is one of the largest sources of high-quality chert in North

America (Banks 1990). East of the plateau are coastal lowlands known as the Blackland Prairie. These adjoining, prominent regions (Collins 2002) form an ecotone (Diamond et al. 1987) that provided access to sustainable resources for hunting and gathering groups (Collins 2002; Collins et al. 2003).

Intermittent investigations between 1991 and 2013 revealed occupational evidence in the form of diagnostic cultural materials from the Early, Middle, and Late Archaic intervals, as well as the Late Prehistoric period of central Texas (Collins 2002; Collins 2004; Collins 2007). The majority of the site was covered by a dense, 2 m thick, Holocene-age burned rock midden deposit (Collins 2002; Thoms 2009) that dates between about 9,000 and 500 RCYBP (Collins 2004). Clovis-age deposits were encountered in nine of the major excavation areas, with Areas 12 and 15 having cultural evidence that predates 13,000 cal BP.

The midden deposit in Area 15 is approximately 1.8 m thick and overlies a ca. 1.2 m layer of silty clay. The next layer is a 0.20 to 0.50 m thick fluvial gravel layer deposited atop impermeable limestone bedrock known as Comanche

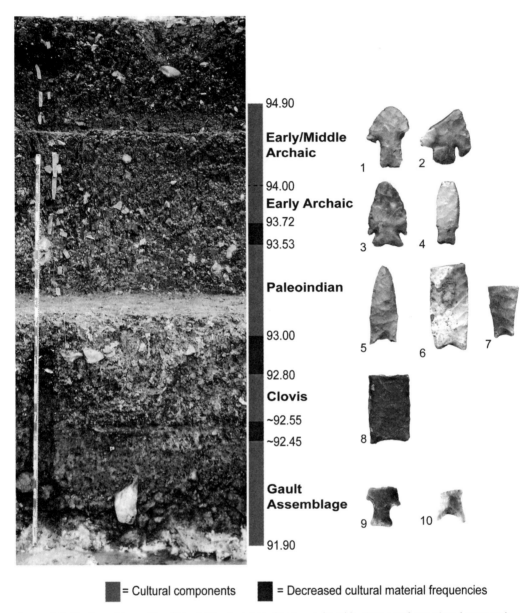

94.90

Early/Middle Archaic

94.00

Early Archaic

93.72

93.53

Paleoindian

93.00

92.80

Clovis

~92.55

~92.45

Gault Assemblage

91.90

■ = Cultural components   ■ = Decreased cultural material frequencies

FIGURE 8.2. Stratigraphic profile of Gault Site Area 15 indicating cultural horizons and associated temporal-diagnostic artifacts; (1) Andice; (2) Bell; (3) Martindale; (4) Hoxie; (5) Dalton; (6) St. Mary's Hall; (7) Angostura; (8) Clovis; (9, 10) Gault. Elevations are based on an arbitrary site datum of 100.00 m. Not to scale.

Peak. The silty clay contained a ~50 cm thick stratified sequence of Late Paleoindian components above a ~25 cm Clovis component. Below this, the Gault component varies from 65 to 80 cm above the bedrock. Excavation records and preliminary data analysis of debitage counts indicate decreased cultural material frequencies between these cultural components. This may correlate with a reduction in site activity or possibly a break in occupation (Figure 8.2).

Optically Stimulated Luminescence (OSL) ages obtained from Area 15 indicate excellent stratigraphic agreement between the temporal-diagnostic artifacts and their associated ages. The OSL ages for the Early–Middle Archaic (about 5.7 ka–5.9 ka), the Early Archaic (approximately 6.7 ka), and the Paleoindian period (8.7 ka–11.6 ka) are all in agreement with the established central Texas chronology and are published elsewhere (Rodrigues et al. 2016).

Clovis deposits in Area 15 indicate an age range of ~13,600 cal BP to 12,600 cal BP (Rodrigues et al. 2016) and conforms with other central Texas Clovis assemblages including the Pavo Real site (OSL dates of 12.69 ± 0.8 ka–12.94 ± 0.8 ka; Collins 2003) and the Wilson-Leonard site (ca. 13,500 cal BP; Collins 1998:140–145, 280–281). OSL dates of 13.22 ± 0.74 ka and 12.92 ± 0.7 ka were obtained from the Clovis deposits in Area 8 at the Gault Site (Waters et al. 2011a). These dates establish a Clovis presence in central Texas between about 13,600 to 12,900 cal BP.

Dates from the early deposits in Area 15 range between 20,000 and 16,000 BP and are in broad agreement with the ages reported from the Debra L. Friedkin site, which reported a range of ca. 17,500 to 14,000 BP (Waters et al. 2011b).

The agreement between the OSL ages and the temporal-diagnostic artifacts above the Gault Assemblage demonstrate that the dating sequence obtained from Area 15 is reliable. Furthermore, the clear stratigraphic boundary between Clovis and Gault Assemblage establishes this material as a separate and older cultural manifestation. While OSL ages are not very precise, making exact ages difficult to determine, the Gault Assemblage present in Area 15 and at the Debra L. Friedkin site indicate a human occupational sequence in central Texas by at least 16,000 cal BP.

The Gault Site Clovis Component

Clovis technology is comprised of three reductive strategies that used biface, blade, and flake production to manufacture flaked stone tools (Bradley et al. 2010:7). Overall, the Clovis component exhibits abundant manufacturing activities evidenced by discarded tools, rejected cores, knapping failures, and related debris.

These deposits contained large Clovis bifaces, preforms, blade cores, macro blades, tools on flakes, discoid-shaped bifaces, as well as various discarded Clovis fluted points.

Clovis Biface Technology

The Clovis assemblage includes projectile points (Figure 8.3, *a–e*), discoidal cores, ovoid-shaped bifaces (Figure 8.3, *f*), and preforms (Figure 8.3, *g*). The discoidal cores are connected to flake production and discussed below. The large ovoid bifaces exhibit distinctive technological traits, including bold flake scars that are rapidly expanding and well spaced, end thinning, and controlled overshot flakes (Figure 8.3, *j*). This assemblage demonstrates the use of proportional bifaces, which include adzes and choppers, as well as thinned bifaces, which include preforms, projectile points, and knives (Bradley et al. 2010:62). These observations are based on width-to-thickness ratios that average ~3:1 in proportional bifaces compared to 6:1 for thinned bifaces (see Bradley et al. 2010:65; Stanford and Bradley 2012:26).

Biface reduction techniques employed direct percussion for shaping and thinning, with relatively minor use of pressure flaking. This is consistent with previous observations where pressure flaking was used primarily to rework damaged points and tools (Bradley et al. 2010:101). Post-fluting retouch used both percussion and pressure techniques that are observed as abrupt, invasive, or marginal scars that rarely occur in a serial fashion and may or may not invade remnant fluting scars (Bradley et al. 2010:64, 96, 101).

Clovis knappers exerted strategic control of flake removals through the careful preparation of striking platforms (Bradley et al. 2010; Morrow 1995) throughout much of the biface reduction process (Velchoff-Littlefield 2015) and were struck marginally. The striking platforms of biface thinning flakes were small and carefully prepared prior to detachment (Bradley et al. 2010:67; Velchoff-Littlefield 2015). Full-face flaking reduced mass relative to the proportion of width loss by passing through the midline of

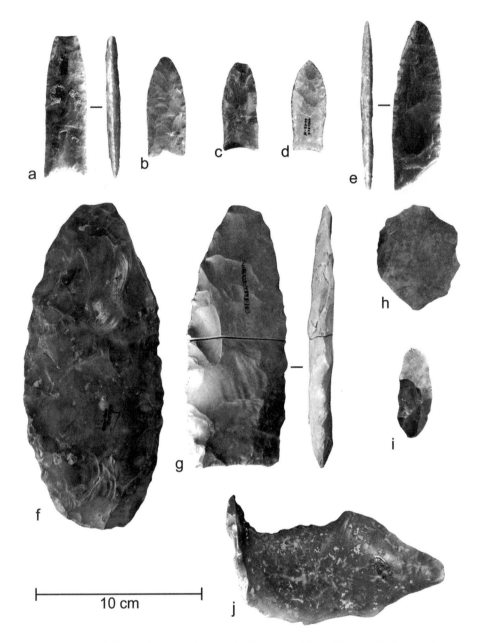

FIGURE 8.3. Clovis biface technology: (*a–e*) projectile points; (*f*) ovoid-shaped biface, early to middle stage point preform; (*g*) preform; (*h*) thinning flake; (*i*) channel flake; (*j*) overshot flake.

the biface without removing the opposite margin. Controlled overshot flaking reduced mass in a similar fashion, but this technique removed a portion of the opposite edge. Channel flakes (Figure 8.3, *i*) were removed longitudinally (Bradley et al. 2010:100), which often resulted in hinge or step scars perpendicular to the long axis. These were frequently corrected by the removal of full-face and/or controlled overshot flaking.

FIGURE 8.4. Clovis blade technology; (*a–f*) blades; (*g, i*) wedge (flat-backed) cores; (*h*) conical core. Photographs by M. Samuel Gardner.

Examination of the Clovis point assemblage reveals most were made from the local Edwards variety chert, with the exception of one Alibates point (agatized dolomite; Collins et al. 1991) and another of optical-quality quartz. The points present minor to severe damage, but rarely exhibit impact damage to the tip. The variation in sizes suggests heavy reworking or maintenance. Most retain the classic Clovis outline with the margins gracefully expanding from the tip and the lateral edges varying between gently curved to excurvate. The lateral edges of the hafted area are generally straight, but some specimens exhibit expanding or contracting bases. Further-

more, the proximal (basal) edges are generally concave, but some specimens exhibiting prominent or slightly flaring basal ears have also been recovered. Heavy grinding is standard on both lateral margins and along the basal edge and generally extends the length of the flute scar.

Clovis Blade Technology

Clovis blade technology from the Gault Site exhibits the use of wedge-shaped (flat-backed) cores and, to a lesser extent, conical cores (Figure 8.4, *g–i*; Collins 1999; Collins and Lohse 2004; Williams 2015). The flat-backed cores exhibit an acute angled prepared platform and a single blade face. The backs of these cores were flattened to allow the lateral edges and base to be flaked from back to front. This technique was crucial in maintaining the longitudinal and transverse curvature of the blade face and continued production (Williams 2015). In contrast, conical cores exhibit a single, prepared, multi-faceted platform where blades were removed from the entire circumference. The blade scars on conical cores are not as curved as the scars on flat-backed cores. The use of an opposed platform is present on the conical and flat-backed cores, but the infrequent occurrence suggests its use was a correctional technique (Collins 1999; Bradley et al. 2010).

Flat-backed core reduction included the production of corner blades, which established the transverse curvature of the core face, along with side and center blades (Bradley et al. 2010; Williams 2015). Evidence from the striking platforms on blades indicates they were prepared individually. This is similar to the preparation of Clovis biface thinning flakes. Core platform maintenance on flat-backed cores entailed the removal of preparation flakes either from the edges of the platform or across the flattened back to remove hinges and reestablish the acute angle. Conical core platforms were rejuvenated by removing core tablet flakes. Clovis blades recovered from the Gault Site range from straight to heavily curved and include numerous snapped blade fragments and modified blade tools, such as serrated knives, endscrapers, and beaked gravers (Figure 8.4, *a–f*).

Clovis Flake Tool Technology

Flake production at the Gault site involved the use of large discoidal cores (Figure 8.5, *a*; Bradley et al 2010). These bifacially flaked cores were manufactured using the same flake removal techniques discussed above, but their size and shape were likely more ideal for producing large, wide flakes of varying shapes and thicknesses. The overall shape and flaking pattern of discoidal cores indicates they were not subsequently reworked into preforms and projectile points. Flakes removed during biface manufacture may also have been used as blanks for tools.

A variety of flake tools recovered from the Clovis deposits include side and endscrapers (Figure 8.5, *d*), gravers (*b, c*), notched flakes (*e*), and punches (*f*).

The Gault Assemblage

The earliest assemblage recovered from the lowest elevations in Area 15 exhibits biface and blade technologies. The assemblage also includes a small discoidal core and a number of utilized and modified flakes that suggest a flake blank technology. Analysis of this assemblage is ongoing, and the synopsis presented here is preliminary.

Gault Biface Technology

The Gault biface assemblage contains large bifaces (Figure 8.6, *b–e*) and stemmed projectile points (Figure 8.7). The technology exhibits the use of proportional bifaces. The large bifaces indicate that flakes were removed using direct percussion with some use of pressure flaking as a retouch technique. In contrast, the much smaller, stemmed projectile points reveal that pressure flaking was a more dominant technique, but there is evidence of pressure scars truncated by relatively larger, deeper scars that suggest direct percussion was used for repair or maintenance. The flaking styles exhibited in the larger bifaces are consistent with the traits observed in proportional bifacial technologies where the scars terminate at, or just past, the midline. The use of this technique is generally confirmed by the width-to-thickness ratios of 3:1 to 4:1. Some thinning scars (full-face) are present but are less frequently applied. Platforms are generally large, relative to the flake size and do show some preparation.

Several projectile points exhibit heavy basal edge grinding and are alternatively beveled in cross section, which may indicate they were heavily retouched or reworked. The projectile point fragments assessed to date exhibit three distinct basal stem morphologies: two exhibit a bifurcated stem with deep basal concavities with rounded ears (Figure 8.7, *a, b*), while a single point has a stem exhibiting a slight flare and a straight basal edge (*c*). Another, nearly intact

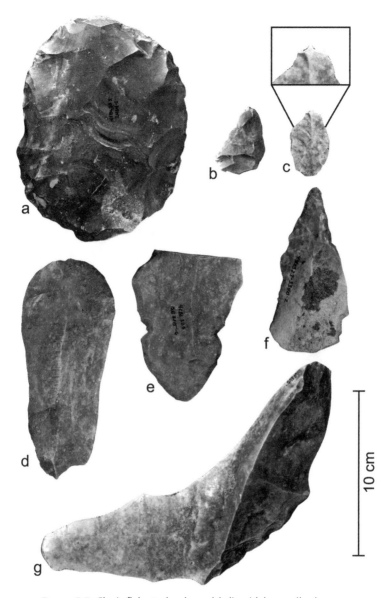

FIGURE 8.5. Clovis flake technology: (*a*) discoidal core; (*b, c*) gravers; (*d*) endscraper; (*e*) notch; (*f*) punch; (*g*) discoidal core flake.

projectile point exhibits rounded shoulders and a contracting stem with a damaged base (Figure 8.7, *d*). The majority of specimens in this assemblage were likely made from the local Edwards chert, with the exception of the contracting stemmed point made of smoky quartz. A probable projectile tip fragment and a cortical-butted knife (Figure 8.6, *a*) were also recovered and exhibit alternate beveling in cross section.

The profile of one point (Figure 8.7, *c*) exhibits longitudinal curvature that suggests it was produced on a flake.

Gault Blade Technology

Gault blade technology reveals a consistent use of unidirectional, flat-backed blade core technology (Figure 8.8, *i–k*) which exhibits blades being removed via direct percussion from

FIGURE 8.6. Gault biface technology: (*a*) cortical-butted knife; (*b–e*) bifaces.

acutely angled core platforms. The blade striking platforms were usually individually prepared (Figure 8.8, *k*) before they were detached. The back and lateral margins of the cores exhibit flake removals to flatten the back, which helped maintain core convexity and aided the reparation of manufacturing errors. While this assemblage is relatively small, the data from the Gault blades (Figure 8.8, *a–e*) and cores indicate the use of corner, side, and central blade removals. Additionally, these blades were curved.

One blade core (Figure 8.8, *k*) exhibits a scar on the platform surface struck from the corner. This may have been intended to rejuvenate the platform, but instead, it reduced the angle between the platform and blade face resulting in

the abandonment of the core. Short, snapped blade segments (Figure 8.8, *f–g*) appear to be an intentional tool blank generated by this technology.

Gault Flake Tool Technology

While the majority of flake tool blanks in this assemblage were likely detached from bifaces, evidence indicates that the flake tool technology may have been produced on blanks from the bifacial cores. A possible discoid biface core was recovered from Area 15 (Figure 8.9, *a*), where the overall morphology and thickness, as well as lack of any micro use-wear, suggest the biface was manufactured for a specific trajectory. Examination of the flake tool assemblage reveals

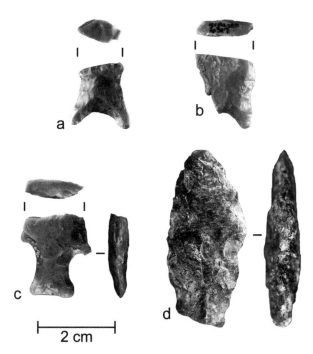

FIGURE 8.7. Gault projectile points.

relatively large, thick flakes that were mostly utilized (Figure 8.9, *d, e*), but includes some modified flakes that are relatively thin and flat. These flakes, for the most part, do not appear to fit with the Gault biface technologies previously discussed. Other recovered flake tools include gravers (Figure 8.9, *b*) and punches (*c*).

Comparing the Clovis and Gault Assemblages

The similarities and differences between the Clovis and Gault assemblages provide evidence concerning the origins of Clovis technology, especially for central Texas. Initial analysis reveals that both used the same technological suite. However, despite this similarity, distinctions in the reduction sequences between Clovis and the Gault Assemblage indicate some technological differences.

The bifacial technologies share some traits, including the use of direct percussion and pressure flaking. However, there were subtle differences in the application of pressure flaking. Clovis technology used pressure flaking as a method of retouch and reworking, while the Gault Assemblage exhibits pressure flaking to finish and shape the points and the stems. The use of proportional bifaces is a commonality, but the additional presence of thinned bifaces and projectile points in Clovis indicates a different reduction strategy. This is emphasized by the flaking styles of full-face and overshot flakes that were systematically used in Clovis to thin bifaces and projectile points, whereas the dominant reduction technique in the Gault biface assemblage was co-medial (midline) flaking. Basal margin grinding is present in both assemblages. Analysis of platform preparation strongly suggests that Clovis platforms were relatively smaller and more heavily prepared than the Gault Assemblage platforms (Gandy 2013; Velchoff-Littlefield 2015).

The small Gault projectile points exhibit distinct basal stem morphologies that represent a different technology not found in Clovis. Furthermore, the technology and morphology of these stemmed points is not present in any later regional manifestations. It is possible that the large bifaces could represent a technology ancestral to Clovis with a significant shift from

FIGURE 8.8. Gault blade technology: (*a–e*) blades; (*f–h*) flat-backed cores.

midline to full-face flaking, but more evidence is needed.

In contrast, the blade technologies are remarkably similar. Both core technologies use one blade face with an acute angled platform. Both the Gault Assemblage and Clovis exhibit similarities in platform preparation of blade cores, as well as individual platform preparation on blades. The only apparent difference between blade technologies is the occasional use of conical cores in Clovis and the presence of snapped blade segments.

While the flake tools present in the Clovis and Gault Assemblage represent similar types, the Gault Assemblage does not appear to be as robust. The small discoidal flake core found in the Gault Assemblage is similar to the larger Clovis discoidal flake cores, but its overall dimensions and flake scars also suggest the production of small flake tools.

This analysis has focused on a small sample of the Gault Assemblage. Findings presented here are tentative, and current interpretations are subject to refinements. The evidence indicates the possibility that blade technology in the Gault Assemblage likely continued into Clovis.

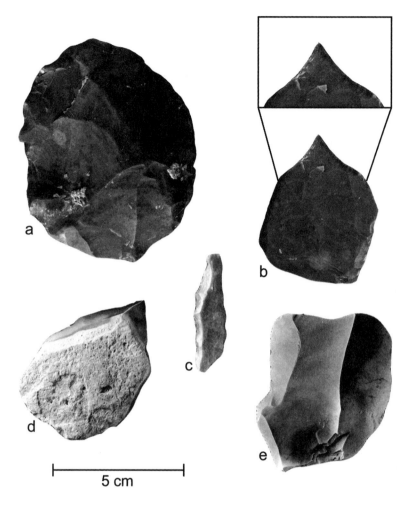

FIGURE 8.9. Gault flake technology: (*a*) possible discoidal core; (*b*) graver; (*c*) punch; (*d, e*) utilized flakes.

Conversely, the biface technologies represent two distinct reduction strategies to biface and projectile point production, whereas flake technologies of Clovis and the Gault Assemblage indicate differences observed in size as well as overall production.

In terms of Clovis origins, this preliminary data can only address Clovis at a regional level. Overall, Clovis biface technology represents a shift away from proportional biface techniques and stemmed points found in the Gault Assemblage toward a dominant reduction strategy of thinning with larger, fluted, lanceolate-shaped projectile points. This shift may be associated with a revitalization movement (Bradley and Collins 2014) that resulted in the spread of Clovis technology into central Texas. The remarkable similarities of the blade technologies of the Gault Assemblage and Clovis suggest some form of continuation or common technological ancestor. As such, it is possible that only Clovis bifacial technologies were introduced into the region.

The Gault Site in a Wider Context
Clovis and Its Contemporaries

Collins and colleagues (2013:531) state that the prehistory of the western hemisphere is longer and more complex than previously thought. Current research indicates a number of different archaeological patterns contemporaneous with Clovis. This complexity indicates that Clovis was not an isolated pattern and should not be considered a benchmark.

Holliday (2000) proposed a range of about 13,500 to 12,900 cal BP for Clovis in the southern Great Plains and a range of about 13,100 to 12,800 cal BP for the northern Great Plains. Waters and Stafford (2007) argued for an estimated maximum range of 13,250 to 12,800 cal BP but constrained this according to a 200-year overlap between dates to 12,900–12,700 cal BP. Meltzer (2009:254) suggested a range of between 13,450 to 12,780 cal BP, which is close to the entire range defined by Holliday (2000). While these age ranges have been heavily debated (Holliday 2000; Waters and Stafford 2007; Haynes et al. 2007; Hamilton and Buchanan 2007; Meltzer 2009), they are not incompatible with each other and indicate that a range of about 13,500 to 12,800 cal BP is reasonable for Clovis. The dating of the Clovis component at the Gault Site, and those of Pavo Real (Collins et al. 2003), Debra L. Friedkin (Waters et al. 2011a), Aubrey (Ferring 2001), and Wilson-Leonard (Collins 1998) in central Texas fit this range.

The Clovis component at the Gault Site exhibits the technological traits associated with Clovis across its geographical range (Hester et al. 1972; Boldurian and Cotter 1999; Huckell 2007; Bradley et al. 2010; Waters, et al. 2011a; Huckell and Kilby 2014), including blade technologies (Green 1963; Stanford et al. 2006; Steffy and Goodyear 2006). Clovis flake tools recovered from the Gault Site, including endscrapers and gravers, have also been widely recognized (Meltzer 1981; Boldurian and Cotter 1999; Huckell 2007; Bradley et al. 2010; Waters et al. 2011a; Eren et al. 2013). However, the Clovis assemblage includes adzes and serrated blades that are not traditionally associated with Clovis (Bradley et al. 2010:62). Bradley and colleagues (2010:59) suggest that the large discoidal and leaf-shaped bifacial cores from the Fenn Cache (Frison and Bradley 1999) and East Wenatchee Cache (Kilby 2008) were cores for the production of Clovis flake tools.

The Western Stemmed tradition (WST) is contemporaneous with Clovis (Beck and Jones 2010). Charcoal recovered from a pit feature (PFA2) at Cooper's Ferry yielded two mean ages 13,262 and 13,316 cal BP and are associated with Western Stemmed points (Davis et al. 2014). Beck and Jones (2010) identify an earlier presence of Western Stemmed points in the Columbia Plateau region (13,300–11,500 cal BP), compared to the Great Basin (13,100–12,500 cal BP). The Western Stemmed point assemblages have been recovered mainly from the Pacific side of the Continental Divide and include a variety of different types (Beck and Jones 2010).

In general, Western Stemmed bifaces are narrow with sloping or rounded shoulders (Jenkins et al. 2012). The contracting stem and blade are usually relatively thick, and the flaking style indicates the use of co-medial (collateral) midline flaking, using percussion flaking before finishing with pressure flaking. The pressure flaking appears to be abrupt or marginal to invasive, and the width-to-thickness ratio of these points appears to be around 2:1, and occasionally 3:1, consistent with proportional to thickened bifacial technology (see Bradley et al. 2010:65; Stanford and Bradley 2012:26). Evidence from Cooper's Ferry indicates that some of these points were beveled as a result of retouching (Davis et al. 2014). Beck and Jones (2010) note the Windust type, which exhibits a concave base, and the Silver Lake type, which has an expanding or bulbous stem. In an analysis of reduction, Davis and colleagues (2014) state that these points were manufactured on both flakes and blades struck from initial cores.

The Western Stemmed toolkit includes crescents, which are usually bifacially flaked but in occasions unifacially retouched (Beck and Jones 2010). These crescents appear to share a similar technological tradition as the stemmed points, with co-medial flaking and abrupt-to-invasive retouch. Blade technology is absent from the WST, but the nonprojectile toolkit includes endscrapers, gravers, beaked (spurred) scrapers, and notches (Beck and Jones 2010).

Erlandson and Braje (2011) argue that there

are technological links between the WST and the Paleocoastal sites around California's Channel Islands. Both collections contain thickened, contracting stemmed points (also known as Amol points) alongside crescents. Additionally, the Paleocoastal assemblages contain Channel Island Barbed points, which have contracted, pointed stems with barbs (Erlandson et al. 2011; Erlandson and Braje 2011). The technology of the Amol points appears remarkably similar to the WST (Jenkins et al. 2012). Furthermore, the Amol points exhibit serrated margins (Erlandson et al. 2011), similar to one of the points from Cooper's Ferry (Davis et al. 2014). The maximum age associated with this technology is 13,000 cal BP but may be more closely associated with an age range of 12,200 to 11,200 cal BP (Erlandson et al. 2011).

Dating from sites in Eastern Beringia indicate that the occupation of this region was contemporaneous with Clovis and WST. Two technological traditions—Nenana (from 13,800 cal BP) and Dyuktai/Denali (from 12,900 cal BP; Vasil'ev 2011)—contain bifacial point technology. The Dyuktai/Denali assemblages contain greater numbers of microblade cores (Flenniken 1987) than the Nenana assemblages, which exhibit a macroblade technology (Goebel et al. 1991). Alongside these is the Northern Paleoindian, which includes bifacial projectile points from Mesa, Tuluaq, Hilltop, Bedwell, and Spein Mountain (Vasil'ev 2011). Rasic (2011) refers to these points as Sluiceway projectile points, while Smith and colleagues (2013) differentiate between the Mesa points and Sluiceway points.

The bifacial technology present in the Nenana assemblages indicates the use of small triangular- or tear-drop-shaped points. Analysis of the Walker Road biface assemblage indicates the use of biface thinning flakes and small retouched chips (Goebel 2011). Retouch on these points ranges from abrupt to invasive. Bifacial points similar to the Nenana points have been recovered from various Denali/Dyuktai sites (Holmes 2001).

The Sluiceway/Mesa Paleoindian points exhibit co-medial (midline) flaking to produce thickened bifaces shaped using collateral pressure flaking. Smith and colleagues (2013:116) argue that the Sluiceway points used a more complex and intensive reduction strategy than the Mesa points.

Nenana macroblade production utilized single and double platforms but represents an informal technology (Goebel et al. 1991; Goebel 2011). The microblade cores recovered from the Swan Point Site are one of the earliest documented assemblages in Alaska (Saleeby 2010). These cores exhibit the same technological features found across Western Beringia (Mobley 1996; West 1996; Holmes 2001), including a bifacial precore and the use of a "ski spall" to prepare the platform (Flenniken 1987). Production utilized the frontal aspect or edge of the biface to detach blades with the use of pressure (Flenniken 1987), similar to the Yubetsu method in Japan and Siberia (Morlan 1970). The flake tools from eastern Beringia include endscrapers, spurred gravers, notches, and denticulates, as well as burins (Rasic 2011; Goebel et al. 1991).

It is worth noting that several contemporaneous technological patterns have been identified in South America. These include the informal Edge-trimmed tradition (Bryan and Gruhn 2003; Dillehay 2013:278) and a bifacial tradition, both of which date to between 14,800 and 11,500 cal BP (Dillehay 2013:278; Collins 2014). The biface tradition includes the manufacture of El Jobo (Cruxent 1979; Bryan and Gruhn 1979), Monte Verde (Collins 1997:423; Collins 2014), and Fishtail points (Bird 1969; Politis 1991; Nami 1997; Nami 2007; Aráoz and Nami 2014; Suárez 2015). The El Jobo/Monte Verde points exhibit controlled flaking oriented perpendicular to the edges converging along the midline with a slight central ridge, a convex cross-section, and exhibit a width-to-thickness ratio of 2:1 (Cruxent 1979:77; Collins 1997:423). The Fishtail points are stemmed, with or without flutes exhibiting expanding stems, concave sides, sharp ears, and a concave base (Bird 1969). Early-stage reduction utilized a flake blank of approximately the desired size that was reduced to the distinctive Fishtail morphology. Fluting was not systematically applied, ranging from unfluted to unifacial or bifacial fluting (Politis 1991; Nami 1997). These points were thinned, and evidence from Uruguay shows the use of overshot flaking (Suárez 2015).

The Earlier Occupational Signatures

Dating of the WST, the thick bifacial traditions (specifically El Jobo-style points) and edge-trimmed traditions from South America indicate that these technologies were contemporaneous with—and older than—the earliest manifestations of Clovis. This is important for understanding the earliest occupations of the Americas and demonstrates Clovis was not first. Significant archaeological patterns are present in the Americas that predate the arrival of Clovis.

The Gault Assemblage exhibits biface, blade, and flake technology. Few other early sites have this range of production other than the Debra L. Friedkin site, which suggests the possibility of a discrete, local cultural assemblage (Collins et al. 2013).

The archaeological record from the eastern seaboard of the continental United States has yielded a number of technologies that may be related, with the best known being those from Meadowcroft and Cactus Hill. The Miller Complex at Meadowcroft includes small triangular points recovered from stratum IIa (Adovasio and Page 2002:156). Stanford and Bradley state that flaking is proportional, but an impact scar and subsequent reworking indicates this is likely not the original configuration (Stanford and Bradley 2012:92; Adovasio and Page 2002). This assemblage dates to approximately 15,402 cal BP and stratigraphic integrity was corroborated by micromorphological analysis (Adovasio et al. 1990; Goldberg and Arpin 1999).

The small, sub-triangular lanceolate bifacial points at Cactus Hill have indented bases and were produced using both percussion and pressure techniques. The points appear to be reworked, are relatively thin, and do not exhibit basal grinding (McAvoy and McAvoy 1997:179; Stanford and Bradley 2012:97). Mean ages for this assemblage range from 18,279 cal BP to 20,054 cal BP (Feathers et al. 2006). The Cactus

Hill assemblage also includes bladelet and flake technologies. The blade cores are small polyhedral cores with plain platforms, manufactured from quartzite, and the flake technology includes edge-worked and edge-used flakes, as well as abrading stones (McAvoy and McAvoy 1997:136).

A number of older patterns have also been identified (Collins at al. 2013), but they are not discussed here due to limited technological data or ongoing archaeological investigations. This includes the large bipointed bifaces from the Chesapeake Bay area (Lowery et al. 2010; Stanford and Bradley 2012:101; Stanford and Bradley 2014; Stanford et al. 2014) and the modified bones of mammoth and other taxa with or without associated flake tools (Anderson 1962, 1975; Wyckoff et al. 2003; Holen 2007; Holen and Holen 2013; Waters et al. 2011c).

Discussion and Conclusion

This study emphasizes the importance of recognizing technological patterns in the earliest archaeological record of the Americas. Clovis is only a part of this larger pattern (Figure 8.10). One of the clearest technological patterns discussed is seen in the thickened, co-medially flaked bifaces along the Pacific coast. The technology used to produce Western Stemmed, Amol, and El Jobo/Monte Verde points appears similar, but differences in the ages show no specific route. This pattern does not appear to cross the continental divide until it passes the Isthmus of Panama and the sites of El Jobo and Taima-Taima in Venezuela. Not accounting for rate of migration, the early dates for this technology at Monte Verde show this pattern was present by 14,500 cal BP.

Synchronous to this early occupational signature is the occurrence of edge-trimmed core and flake technologies, and lithic flakes associated with bone flakes, including human-modified bones. Conservative estimates of these assemblages suggest a date of around 30,000 cal BP. While these traditions are not discussed in detail above, core and flake tools, bone tools, and modified bones have been identified across China and Asia during the Upper Palaeolithic (Zhu

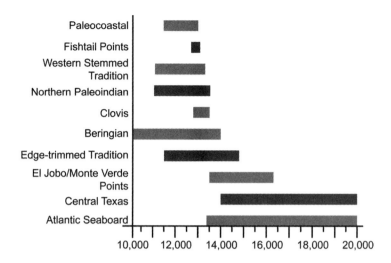

FIGURE 8.10. Chronological sequence of technological patterns discussed in Chapter 8.

et al. 2004; Brantingham et al. 2004; Norton and Gao 2008; Gao 2013).

The evidence from the Atlantic seaboard reveals a very different technological tradition. The well-developed thinned bifaces and small triangular points were made using a markedly different reduction strategy from the one evident in Western Stemmed/El Jobo points. This includes the use of thinning as opposed to thickening, as seen in the flake scars. This technology appears to spread along the Atlantic seaboard into Florida (Collins 2014; Collins et al. 2013). Thus, the early archaeological record of the Americas exhibits a number of patterns that occur around 13,000 cal BP and earlier.

This framework highlights why Clovis technology should not be considered a benchmark for assessing the earliest human occupations of the Americas. While these arguments are subject to further study and debate, they demonstrate the vastly complex nature of the early archeological record.

Excavations at Area 15 of the Gault site and subsequent OSL ages have established a reliable occupational sequence present in good agreement with the known central Texas chronology. Furthermore, decreased cultural material frequencies between the Clovis and Gault components distinguish these two cultural deposits. The evidence indicates that humans were pres-

ent at the Gault Site prior to the spread of Clovis into the region, demonstrating an occupation prior to 16,000 years ago. This regional chronology is supported by evidence from the Friedkin site (Waters et al. 2011b).

Using the assemblages from the Gault Site as an example, the differences in biface manufacture suggest that Clovis technology moved into the region. Analysis of the Gault Assemblage from a Clovis perspective would fail to recognize how this assemblage fits within the wider context. When assessed in relation to its contemporaries, the assemblage appears to represent a regional pattern. Interestingly, the Gault contracting stemmed point fits within the technological and variability range of the WST but is smaller in comparison. However, dating of this sequence does not currently indicate an age range as old as that from the Gault Assemblage.

By carefully assessing the diversity of early humans in the Americas, it is possible to construct a framework to understand the nature of Clovis. Viewed from this perspective, Clovis may represent a colonizing wave that spread across parts of North America and into South America. Equally, it may represent the spread of a technological idea among existing groups. This raises two possibilities for the origins of Clovis: it may represent multiple migrations that eventually brought in a new technology, or that an idea developed into a technology that quickly spread across parts of North America—or perhaps an amalgamation of the two.

By making a clear distinction between the earlier human occupation of the Americas and the origins of Clovis, the possibility of identifying different patterns and dispersals becomes apparent. As evidence of cultures predating Clovis become more acceptable, researchers in North America can learn much from their South American counterparts and consider viewing the earliest human occupations of all the Americas without Clovis-tinted spectacles.

Acknowledgments

The authors would like to thank Ciprian Ardelean and Rafael Suárez for inviting us to contribute to this volume. We also thank Clark Wernecke, David Madsen, and Robert Lassen for their comments on an earlier draft of this chapter. All photographs by Nancy Velchoff unless otherwise stated. Figures compiled by TJW. This research was funded in part by NSF Grant 0920549 to Texas State University, San Marcos, the Gault School of Archaeological Research, and by the generosity of the Way family and other private donors.

References

Adovasio, J. M.
1983   The AENA Compilation of Fluted Points in Eastern North America: A Perspective from Meadowcroft Rockshelter. *Archaeology of Eastern North America* 11:6–11.

Adovasio, J. M., and R. C. Carlisle
1982   Meadowcroft: Collected Papers on the Archaeology of Meadowcroft Rockshelter and the Cross Creek Drainage. In *Papers Prepared for the Symposium "The Meadowcroft Rockshelter Rolling Thunder Review: Last Act,"* 47th Annual Meeting of the Society for American Archaeology, Minneapolis, MN, 1982. University of Pittsburgh, Department of Anthropology, 1984. Pittsburgh, PA.

Adovasio, J. M., and J. Page
2002   *The First Americans: In Pursuit of Archaeology's Greatest Mystery.* Random House, New York.

Adovasio, J. M., and D. R. Pedler
2016   *Strangers in a New Land: What Archaeology Reveals about the First Americans.* Firefly Books, Ontario, Canada.

Adovasio, J. M., J. Donahue, and R. Stuckenrath
1990   The Meadowcroft Rockshelter Chronology 1975–1990. *American Antiquity* 55(2):348–354.

Adovasio, J. M., J. D. Gunn, J. Donahue, R. Stuckenrath, J. Guilday, and K. Lord
1978   Meadowcroft Rockshelter. In *Early Man in America from a Circum-Pacific Perspective,* edited by A. L. Bryan. Occasional Papers 1. Department of Anthropology, University of Alberta, Edmonton, CA.

Adovasio, J. M., D. R. Pedler, J. Donahue, and R. Stuckenrath
1999   No Vestige of a Beginning nor Prospect for an End: Two Decades of Debate on Meadowcroft Rockshelter. In *Ice Age Peoples of North America: Environments, Origins, and Adaptations of the First Americans,* edited by R. Bonnichsen and K. L. Turnmire. Center for the Study of the First Americans and Oregon State University Press, Corvallis OR.

Anderson, A. D.
1962   The Cooperton Mammoth: A Preliminary Report. *Plains Anthropologist* 7(16):110–112.
1975   The Cooperton Mammoth: An Early Man Bone Quarry. *Great Plains Journal* 12(2): 130–173.

Aráoz, Claudio J. Patané, and Hugo G. Nami
2014   The First Paleoindian Fishtail Point Find in Salta Province, Northwestern Argentina. *Archaeological Discovery* 2(2):26–30.

Ardelean, Ciprian F.
2014   The Early Prehistory of the Americas and the Human Peopling of the Western Hemisphere. An Overview of Archaeological Data, Hypotheses, and Models. *Studii de Preistorie* 11:33–95.

Banks, Larry D.
1990   *From Mountain Peaks to Alligator Stomachs: A Review of Lithic Sources in the Trans-Mississippi South, the Southern Plains, and Adjacent Southwest.* Oklahoma Anthropological Society Memoir 4.

Barker, G., and John B. Broster
1996   The Johnson site (40Dv400): A Dated Paleoindian and Early Archaic Occupation in Tennessee's Central Basin. *Journal of Alabama Archaeology* 42(2):97–153.

Beck, Charlotte, and George T. Jones

2010   Clovis and Western Stemmed: Population Migration and the Meeting of Two Technologies in the Intermountain West. *American Antiquity* 75(1):81–116.

Bird, Junius B.

1969   A Comparison of South Chilean and Ecuadorian "Fishtail" Projectile Points. *Kroeber Society Anthropological Papers* 40:52–71.

Boldurian, Anthony T., and J. Cotter

1999   *Clovis Revisited: New perspectives on Paleoindian Adaptations from Blackwater Draw, New Mexico.* Monograph 103. University of Pennsylvania Museum of Archaeology and Anthropology, Philadelphia, PA.

Bradley, Bruce A., and Michael B. Collins

2013   Imagining Clovis as a Cultural Revitalization Movement. In *Paleoamerican Odyssey*, edited by Kelly E. Graf, M. Ketron, and Michael R. Waters. Center for the Study of the First Americans and Texas A&M University Press, College Station, TX.

Bradley, Bruce A., Michael B. Collins, and C.A. Hemmings

2010   *Clovis Technology.* Archaeological Series 17. International Monographs in Prehistory, Ann Arbor, MI.

Brantingham, P. Jeffrey, Xing Gao, David B. Madsen, Robert L. Bettinger, and Robert G. Elston

2004   The Initial Upper Paleolithic at Shuidonggou, Northwestern China. In *The Early Upper Palaeolithic beyond Western Europe*, edited by P. Jeffrey Brantingham, Steven L. Kuhn, and K. W. Kerry. Plenum, Los Angeles, CA.

Bryan, Alan L., and R. Gruhn

1979   The Radiocarbon Dates of Taima-Taima. In *Taima-Taima: A Late Pleistocene Paleo-Indian Kill Site in Northernmost South America—Final Reports of 1976 Excavations*, edited by Claudio Ochsenius and Ruth Gruhn, pp. 53–58. CIPICS/South American Quaternary Documentation Program, Berlin.

2003   Some Difficulties in Modeling the Original Peopling of the Americas. *Quaternary International* 109–110:175–179.

Collins, Michael B.

1997   The Lithics from Monte Verde, A Descriptive-Morphological Analysis. In *Monte Verde: A Late Pleistocene Settlement in Chile*, Vol. 2, *The Archaeological Context and Interpretation*, edited by Tom D. Dille-

hay, pp. 383–506. Smithsonian Institution, Washington, D.C.

1998   Early Paleoindian Components. In *Wilson-Leonard, an 11,000-Year Archeological Record of Hunter-Gatherers in Central Texas*, edited by Michael B. Collins, pp. 123–159. Studies in Archeology 31. Texas Archeological Research Laboratory, University of Texas and Archeology Studies Program Report 10. Texas Department of Transportation, Environmental Affairs Division, Austin, TX.

1999   *Clovis Blade Technology.* University of Texas Press, Austin.

2002   The Gault Site, Texas, and Clovis Research. *Athena Review* 3(2):31–42.

2003   Paleoindian Pavo Real. In *Pavo Real (41BX52): A Paleoindian and Archaic Camp and Workshop on the Balcones Escarpment, South-Central Texas*, edited by Michael B. Collins, D. B. Hudler, and S. L. Black. Studies in Archaeology 41, Texas Archaeological Research Laboratory, University of Texas at Austin. Archaeological Studies Program Report 50, Environmental Affairs Division, Texas Department of Transportation, Austin.

2004   Archaeology in Central Texas. In *The Prehistory of Texas*, edited by T. K. Perttula, pp. 101–126. Texas A&M University Press, College Station, TX.

2007   Discerning Clovis Subsistence from Stone Artifacts and Site Distributions on the Southern Plains Periphery. In *Foragers of the Terminal Pleistocene in North America*, edited by R. B. Walker and B. N. Driskell, pp. 59–87. University of Nebraska Press, Lincoln.

2014   Initial Peopling of the Americas: Context, Findings, and Issues. In *The Cambridge World Prehistory*, edited by C. Renfrew and P. Bahn, pp. 903–922. Cambridge University Press, Cambridge, UK.

Collins, Michael B., and Jon C. Lohse

2004   The Nature of Clovis Blades and Blade Cores. In *Entering America*, edited by D. Madsen, pp. 159–183. University of Utah Press, Salt Lake City.

Collins, Michael B., T. R. Hester, D. Olmstead, and P. J. Headrick

1991   Engraved Cobbles from Early Archaeological Contexts in Central Texas. *Current Research in the Pleistocene* 8:13–15.

Collins, Michael B., D. B. Hudler, and S. L. Black (editors)

2003   *Pavo Real (41BX52): A Paleoindian and Ar-chaic Camp and Workshop on the Balcones Escarpment, South-Central Texas.* Studies in Archaeology 41, Texas Archaeological Research Laboratory, University of Texas at Austin. Texas Department of Transportation, Archeological Studies Program Report 50, Austin.

Collins, Michael B., Dennis J. Stanford, Darrin L. Lowery, and Bruce A. Bradley

2013   North America before Clovis: Variance in Temporal/Spatial Cultural Patterns, 27,000–13,000 cal yr BP. In *Paleoamerican Odyssey*, edited by Kelly E. Graf, C. V. Ketron, and Michael R. Waters, pp. 521–539. Center for the Study of the First Americans and Texas A&M University Press, College Station, TX.

Cruxent, J. M.

1979   Stone and Bone Artifacts from Taima-Taima. In *Taima-Taima: A Late Pleistocene Paleo-Indian Kill Site in Northernmost South America—Final Reports of 1976 Excavations*, edited by Claudio Ochsenius and Ruth Gruhn, pp. 77–89. CIPICS/South American Quaternary Documentation Program, Berlin.

Davis, Loren G., Alex J. Nyers, and Samuel C. Willis

2014   Context, Provenance, and Technology of a Western Stemmed Tradition Artifact Cache from the Cooper's Ferry Site, Idaho. *American Antiquity* 79(4):596–632.

Diamond, D. D., D. H. Riskind, and S. L. Orzell

1987   A Framework for Plant Community Classification and Conservation in Texas. *Texas Journal of Science* 39(3):202–221.

Dillehay, Tom D.

1989   *Monte Verde: A Late Pleistocene Settlement in Chile*, Vol. 1, *The Paleoenvironment and Site Context*. Smithsonian Institution, Washington, D.C.

1997   *Monte Verde: A Late Pleistocene Settlement in Chile*, Vol. 2, *The Archaeological Context*. Smithsonian Institution, Washington, D.C.

2000   *The Settlement of the Americas: A New Prehistory*. Basic Books, New York.

2013   Entangled Knowledge: Old Trends and New Thoughts in First South American Studies. In *Paleoamerican Odyssey*, edited by Kelly E. Graf, C. V. Ketron, and Michael R. Waters, pp. 377–396. Center for the Study of the

First Americans and Texas A&M University Press, College Station, TX.

Dunbar, J. S.

2006   Paleoindian Archaeology. In *First Floridians and Last Mastodons: The Page-Ladson Site in the Aucilla River*, edited by S. D. Webb, pp. 403–435. Springer, Dordrecht, NL.

Eren, Metin I., Thomas A. Jennings, and Ashley M. Smallwood

2013   Paleoindian Unifacial Stone Tool "Spurs": Intended Accessories or Incidental Accidents? *PloS One* 8(11)e78419.

Erlandson, Jon M., and Todd J. Braje

2011   From Asia to the Americas by Boat? Paleogeography, Paleoecology, and Stemmed Points of the Northwest Pacific. *Quaternary International* 239(1–2):28–37.

Erlandson, Jon M., Torben C. Rick, Todd J. Braje, Molly Casperson, Brendan J. Culleton, Brian Fulfrost, Tracy Garcia, et al.

2011   Paleoindian Seafaring, Maritime Technologies, and Coastal Foraging on California's Channel Islands. *Science* 331(6021):1181–1185.

Feathers, J., E. Rhodes, S. Huot, and J. M. McAvoy

2006   Luminescence Dating of Sand Deposits Related to Late Pleistocene Human Occupation at the Cactus Hill Site, Virginia, USA. *Quaternary Geochronology* 1(3):167–187.

Ferring, C. Reid

2001   *The Archaeology and Paleoecology of the Aubry Clovis Site (41DN479) Denton County, Texas*. Center for Environmental Archaeology, Department of Geography, University of North Texas, Denton.

Flenniken, J. Jeffrey

1987   The Paleolithic Dyuktai Pressure Blade Technique of Siberia. *Arctic Anthropology* 24(2):117–132.

Frison, George, and Bruce A. Bradley

1999   *The Fenn Cache: Clovis Weapons and Tools*. One Horse Land and Cattle Co., Santa Fe, NM.

Gandy, J.

2013   Analysis of the Lithic Debitage from the Older-Than-Clovis Stratigraphic Layers of the Gault Site, Texas. Master's thesis, Department of Anthropology, Texas State University, San Marcos.

Gao, Xing

2013   Paleolithic Cultures in China. *Current Anthropology* 54(S8):S358–S370.

Goebel, Ted

2011   What Is the Nenana Complex? Raw Material

Procurement and Technological Organization at Walker Road, Central Alaska. In *From the Yenisei to the Yukon: Interpreting Lithic Assemblage Variability in Late Pleistocene/Early Holocene Beringia*, edited by Ted Goebel and I. Buvit. Texas A&M University Press, College Station, TX.

Goebel, Ted, R. Powers, and N. Bigelow
1991   The Nenana Complex of Alaska and Clovis Origins. In *Clovis: Origins and Adaptations*, edited by R. Bonnichsen and K. Turnmire. Center for the Study of the First Americans and Oregon State University Press, Corvallis, OR.

Goebel, Ted, Michael R. Waters, and Dennis H. O'Rourke
2008   The Late Pleistocene Dispersal of Modern Humans in the Americas. *Science* 319(5869): 1497–1502.

Goldberg, Paul, and Trina L. Arpin
1999   Micromorphological Analysis of Sediments from Meadowcroft Rockshelter, Pennsylvania: Implications for Radiocarbon Dating. *Journal of Field Archaeology* 26(3):325.

Green, F. E.
1963   The Clovis Blades: An Important Addition to the Llano Complex. *American Antiquity* 29(2):145–165.

Hamilton, Marcus J., and Briggs Buchanan
2007   Spatial Gradients in Clovis-Age Radiocarbon Dates across North America Suggest Rapid Colonization from the North. *PNAS* 104(40):15625–30.

Haynes, C. Vance
1980   Paleoindian Charcoal from Meadowcroft Rockshelter: Is Contamination a Problem? *American Antiquity* 45(3):582–587.

Haynes, Gary, David G. Anderson, C. Reid Ferring, Stuart J. Fiedel, Donald K. Grayson, C. Vance Haynes, Vance T. Holliday, et al.
2007   Comment on "Redefining the Age of Clovis: Implications for the Peopling of the Americas." *Science* 317(5836):320; author reply 320.

Hester, J. J., E. L. Lundelius, and R. Fryxell
1972   *Blackwater Locality No.1: A Stratified, Early Man Site in Eastern New Mexico*. Fort Burgwin Research Center 8. Fort Burgwin Research Center, Southern Methodist University, Ranchos de Taos, NM.

Holen, Steven R.
2007   The Age and Taphonomy of Mammoths at Lovewell Reservoir, Jewell County, Kansas, USA. *Quaternary International* 169–170: 51–63.

Holen, Steven R., and Kathleen A. Holen
2013   The Mammoth Steppe Hypothesis: The Middle Wisconsin (Oxygen Isotope Stage 3) Peopling of North America. In *Paleoamerican Odyssey*, edited by Kelly E. Graf, C. V. Ketron, and Michael R. Waters, pp. 429–444. Center for the Study of the First Americans and Texas A&M University Press, College Station, TX.

Holliday, Vance T.
2000   The Evolution of Paleoindian Geochronology and Typology on the Great Plains. *Geoarchaeology* 15(3):227.

Holmes, Charles E.
2001   Tanana River Valley Archaeology circa 14,000 to 9000 BP. *Arctic Anthropology* 38(2):154–170.

Huckell, Bruce B.
2007   Clovis Lithic Technology: A View from the Upper San Pedro Valley. In *Murray Springs: A Clovis Site with Multiple Activity Areas in the San Pedro Valley, Arizona*, edited by C. V. Haynes Jr. and Bruce B. Huckell. University of Arizona Press, Tucson, AZ.

Huckell, Bruce B., and J. David Kilby
2014   Clovis Caches: Discoveries, Identification, Lithic Technology, and Land Use. In *Clovis Caches: Recent Discoveries and New Research*, edited by Bruce B. Huckell and J. David Kilby, pp. 1–10. University of New Mexico Press, Albuquerque.

Jenkins, Dennis L., Loren G. Davis, Thomas W. Stafford, Paula F. Campos, Bryan Hockett, George T. Jones, Linda Scott Cummings, et al.
2012   Clovis Age Western Stemmed Projectile Points and Human Coprolites at the Paisley Caves. *Science* 337(6091):223–8.

Kilby, J. David
2008   An Investigation of Clovis Caches: Content, Function, and Technological Organization. PhD dissertation, Dept. of Anthropology, University of New Mexico, Albuquerque.

Lowery, Darrin L., Michael A. O'Neal, John S. Wah, Daniel P. Wagner, and Dennis J. Stanford
2010   Late Pleistocene Upland Stratigraphy of the Western Delmarva Peninsula, USA. *Quaternary Science Reviews* 29(11–12):1472–1480.

Madsen, David B.
2015   A Framework for the Initial Occupation of the Americas. *PaleoAmerica* 1(3):217–250.

McAvoy, J. M., and L. D. McAvoy
1997   *Archaeological Investigations of Site 44SX202, Cactus Hill, Sussex County, Virginia.* Nottoway River Survey Archaeological Research Report 2. Virginia Department of Historic Resources, Richmond, VA.

Meltzer, David J.
1981   A Study of Style and Function in a Class of Tools. *Journal of Field Archaeology* 8(3): 313–326.

Meltzer, David J.
2009   *First Peoples in a New World.* University of California Press, Berkeley.

Meltzer, David J.
2013   Part I: The Peopling of the World during the Pleistocene. In *The Encyclopedia of Global Human Migration: 8 The Human Colonization of the Americas: Archaeology,* edited by Immanuel Ness, pp. 1–9. Blackwell, New York.

Mobley, C. M.
1996   Campus Site. In *American Beginnings: The Prehistory and Palaeoecology of Beringia,* edited by Allen West. University of Chicago Press, Chicago.

Morlan, Richard E.
1970   Wedge-Shaped Core Technology in Northern North America. *Arctic Anthropology* 7(2):17–37.

Morrow, Juliet E.
1995   Clovis Projectile Point Manufacture: A Perspective from the Ready/Lincoln Hills Site, 11JY46, Jersey County, Illinois. *Midcontinental Journal of Archaeology* 20(2):167–191.

Nami, Hugo G.
1997   Investigaciones actualísticas para discutir aspectos técnicos de los cazadores-recolectores del tardiglacial: el problema Clovis-Cueva Fell. *Anales del Instituto de la Patagonia* 25:152–186.

Nami, Hugo G.
2007   Research in the Middle Negro River Basin (Uruguay) and the Paleoindian Occupation of the Southern Cone. *Current Anthropology* 48(1):164–174.

Norton, Christopher J., and Xing Gao
2008   Hominin-Carnivore Interactions during the Chinese Early Paleolithic: Taphonomic Perspectives from Xujiayao. *Journal of Human Evolution* 55(1):164–178.

Politis, G.
1991   Fishtail Projectile Points in the Southern Cone of South America: An Overview. In *Clovis: Origins and Adaptations,* edited by R. Bonnichsen and K. L. Turnmire, pp. 287–301. Center for the Study of the First Americans and Oregon State University Press, Corvallis, OR.

Rasic, J. T.
2011   Functional Variability in the Late Pleistocene Archaeological Record of Eastern Beringia: A Model of Late Pleistocene Land Use and Technology from Northwest Alaska. In *From the Yenisei to the Yukon: Interpreting Lithic Assemblage Variability in Late Pleistocene/Early Holocene Beringia,* edited by Ted Goebel and Ian Buvit, pp. 128–164. Texas A&M University Press, College Station, TX.

Rodrigues, K., W. J. Rink, Michael B. Collins, T. J. Williams, A. Keen-Zebert, and G. I. Lopez
2016   OSL Ages of the Clovis, Late Paleoindian, and Archaic Components at Area 15 of the Gault Site, Central Texas, U.S.A. *Journal of Archaeological Science Reports* 7:94–103.

Saleeby, Becky M.
2010   Ancient Footsteps in a New Land: Building an Inventory of the Earliest Alaskan Sites. *Arctic Anthropology* 47(2):116–132.

Smith, Heather L., J. T. Rasic, and Ted Goebel
2013   Biface Traditions of Northern Alaska and Their Role in the Peopling of the Americas. In *Paleoamerican Odyssey,* edited by Kelly E. Graf, C. V. Ketron, and Michael R. Waters, pp. 105–126. Center for the Study of the First Americans and Texas A&M University Press, College Station, TX.

Stanford, Dennis J., and Bruce A. Bradley
2012   *Across Atlantic Ice: The Origin of America's Clovis Culture.* University of California Press, Berkeley.

2014   Reply to O'Brien et al. *Antiquity* 88(340): 624.

Stanford, Dennis J., Elmo León Canales, John B. Broster, and Mark R. Norton
2006   Clovis Blade Manufacture: Preliminary Data from the Carson-Conn-Short Site (40Bn190), Tennessee. *Current Research in the Pleistocene* 23:145–147.

Stanford, Dennis J., Margaret Jodry, Darrin L. Lowery, Bruce A Bradley, Marvin Kay, Thomas W. Stafford, and R. J. Speakman
2014   New Evidence for a Possible Paleolithic Occupation of the Eastern North Ameri-

can Continental Shelf at the Last Glacial Maximum. In *Prehistoric Archaeology on the Continental Shelf*, edited by A. M. Evans, J. C. Flatman, and N. C. Flemming, pp. 73–93. Springer, New York.

Steffy, K., and Albert C. Goodyear
2006   Clovis Macro Blades from the Topper Site, 38AL23, Allendale County, South Carolina. *Current Research in the Pleistocene* 23: 147–149.

Suárez, Rafael
2015   The Paleoamerican Occupation of the Plains of Uruguay: Technology, Adaptations, and Mobility. *PaleoAmerica* 1(1):88–104.

Thoms, Alston V.
2009   Rocks of Ages: Propagation of Hot-Rock Cookery in Western North America. *Journal of Archaeological Science* 36(3):573–591.

Vasil'ev, Sergei A.
2011   The Earliest Alaskan Archaeological Record: A View from Siberia. In *From the Yenisei to the Yukon: Interpreting Lithic Assemblage Variability in Late Pleistocene/Early Holocene Beringia*, edited by Ted Goebel and I. Buvit, pp. 119–127. Texas A&M University Press, College Station, TX.

Velchoff-Littlefield, Nancy.
2015   *Exploring the Interpretive Potential of Clovis Waste Flakes.* MPhil dissertation, Archaeology, University of Exeter, http://hdl.handle.net/10871/17564.

Waters, Michael R., and Thomas W. Stafford
2007   Redefining the Age of Clovis: Implications for the Peopling of the Americas. *Science* 315(5815):1122–1126.

2013   The First Americans: A Review of the Evidence for the Late-Pleistocene Peopling of the Americas. In *Paleoamerican Odyssey*, edited by Kelly E. Graf, C. V. Ketron, and Michael R. Waters, pp. 541–560. Center for the Study of the First Americans and Texas A&M University Press College Station, TX.

Waters, Michael R., Charlotte D. Pevny, and D. L. Carlson
2011a   *Clovis Lithic Technology: Investigation of a Stratified Workshop at the Gault Site, Texas.* Texas A&M University Press, College Station, TX.

Waters, Michael R., Steven L. Forman, Thomas A. Jennings, Lee C. Nordt, Steven G. Driese, Joshua M. Feinberg, Joshua L. Keene, et al.
2011b   The Buttermilk Creek Complex and the Origins of Clovis at the Debra L. Friedkin Site, Texas. *Science* 331(6024):1599–603.

Waters, Michael R., Thomas W. Stafford, H. Gregory McDonald, Carl E. Gustafson, Morten Rasmussen, Enrico Cappellini, Jesper V. Olsen, et al.
2011c   Pre-Clovis Mastodon Hunting 13,800 Years Ago at the Manis Site, Washington. *Science* 334(6054):351–3.

West, F. H.
1996   Onion Portage, Kobuk River: Akmak and Kobuk Components. In *American Beginnings: The Prehistory and Palaeoecology of Beringia*, edited by F. H. West. University of Chicago Press, Chicago.

Williams, T. J.
2015   *Testing the Atlantic Ice Hypothesis: The Blade Manufacturing of Clovis, Solutrean and the Broader Technological Aspects of Production in the Upper Palaeolithic.* PhD dissertation, Archaeology, University of Exeter.

Wyckoff, Don G., Jame Theler, Brian J. Carter, G. Robert Brakenridge, Brian J. Carter, J. Czaplewski, Wakefield Dort, et al.
2003   *The Burnham Site in Northwestern Oklahoma: Glimpses beyond Clovis?* Oklahoma Anthropological Society Memoir 9. Sam Noble Oklahoma Museum of Natural History, Norman.

Zhu, R. X., R. Potts, F. Xie, K. A. Hoffman, C. L. Deng, C. D. Shi, Y. X. Pan, et al.
2004   New Evidence on the Earliest Human Presence at High Northern Latitudes in Northeast Asia. *Nature* 431(7008):559–562.

CHAPTER 9

The End of an Era? Early Holocene Paleoindian Caribou Hunting in a Great Lakes Glacial Refugium

Ashley K. Lemke and John M. O'Shea

Models for understanding the colonization of the Americas have always been intimately linked to the advances and retreats of continental ice sheets and the closely correlated changes in global sea level and climates. As such, archaeologists have had to come to terms with the complex and dynamic patterns of sea-level change and their effects on the local environments in which early Paleoindians lived. At the same time, it has made archaeologists keenly aware that vast portions of the Paleoindian landscape are now underwater. Huge expanses of once-habitable land along the continental shelf and large inland lakes are now submerged. These areas would have been prime territory for hunter-gatherers due to abundant littoral and coastal resources and thus contain archaeological records critical for understanding the peopling of the Americas.

Similar to global changes in sea level, water-level changes associated with the withdrawal of the Laurentide ice sheet in the North American Great Lakes exposed and then submerged vast areas of land within the basin. These freshwater lakes are the largest in the world and constitute a unique region with specific climatological and geological attributes, both today and in the past. While it has long been speculated that sites of great antiquity were likely submerged beneath the Great Lakes (e.g., Ellis et al. 1990; Shott 1999), only recently has sustained underwater research located and investigated such sites.

Research on the Alpena-Amberley Ridge (AAR), a submerged landform stretching across the Lake Huron basin that was dryland 9,000 years ago, has identified a series of archaeological sites attributable to the Late Paleoindian period. To date, over 60 stone-constructed caribou hunting features and related facilities have been identified on the lake bottom.

While underwater research provides unique challenges for the archaeologist, the preservation provided on submerged landscapes is often unparalleled. The cold, fresh waters of the Great Lakes preserve organic materials that are rarely recovered from contemporary terrestrial sites (e.g., wood, bone, charcoal), and the rapid but gentle inundation preserved an ancient landscape that has largely escaped subsequent postdepositional disturbances and modern development. Not only can kill sites and intact stone constructions be observed on the AAR, but the spatial arrangement among such sites can also be mapped and analyzed. As such, the underwater archaeological record preserves unique evidence and provides the basis for a detailed picture of Paleoindian lifeways in the Great Lakes basin.

This chapter provides a brief summary of archaeological and paleoenvironmental findings from the AAR and then considers the age, context, and seasonal patterns of caribou exploitation that these results indicate. Taken together, the data suggest that the AAR acted as a cold-climate refugium where Ice Age fauna and hunt-

TABLE 9.1. Generalized ancient Great Lakes water level stages.

Lake Stage	Date cal BP	Date cal BP
Algonquin (high-water stand)	~14,000–12,000	12,000–10,500
Stanley (low-water stand)	~11,200–8300	9900–7500
Nipissing (high-water stand)	~7600–4000	6000–3500

ing strategies persisted well into the Holocene. This unique situation provides important new insights into foraging lifeways in the Great Lakes region and has potentially significant implications for Paleoindian adaptations more generally.

The Study Context

With the grudging withdrawal of the continental ice sheets at the end of the Pleistocene, Great Lakes water levels oscillated before stabilizing at modern elevations (Karrow 2004; Karrow and Warner 1990; Lewis et al. 2005, 2007). These complex lake-level changes can be generalized into three principal stages: (1) glacial Lake Algonquin, where water levels were much higher; (2) periglacial Lake Stanley, a significant lower water stage; and (3) postglacial Lake Nipissing, where water levels rose again before eventually stabilizing (Table 9.1). These changing water levels, in combination with the lingering presence of the Laurentide Ice Sheet, are unique geologic features of the Great Lakes region, and significantly affected paleoenvironments and human habitation.

The most marked of these oscillations is the Lake Stanley low stand in the Lake Huron Basin (Lake Chippewa in the Lake Michigan basin), which lasted from about 11,200 to 8,300 cal BP (calendar yr BP; 9,900–7,500 RCYBP or radiocarbon yr BP). During this time, water levels were more than 100 m lower than today (Lewis and Anderson 2012; Lewis et al. 2005), and the Huron Basin was divided into two distinct lakes separated by a rocky landform, the Alpena-Amberley Ridge (AAR; Figure 9.1). The

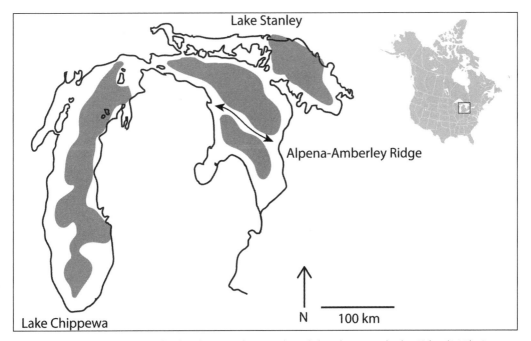

FIGURE 9.1. The Lake Stanley and Lake Chippewa lowstands and the Alpena-Amberley Ridge (AAR). Grey areas indicate ancient water levels, white areas are dry land, solid lines indicate the modern outlines of the state of Michigan, and Lakes Michigan (to the west) and Huron (to the east). Line with two arrows indicates the Alpena-Amberley Ridge.

AAR runs from northern Michigan to southern Ontario and is a narrow (on average 15–20 km) limestone and dolomite formation that resisted glacial erosion. It is currently 12–45 m (~35–150 ft) underwater.

Conventional models of the Paleoindian occupation in the Great Lakes consider the drop from Lake Algonquin as the effective end of the Paleoindian occupation (Lovis et al. 2012; Monaghan and Lovis 2005:19, table 2.1), with the low waters of Lake Stanley ushering in the Early and Middle Archaic periods. This model is based on the apparent absence of Paleoindian sites after Lake Algonquin and the correlation of absolute dates for Archaic sites with dates conventionally assigned to Lake Stanley. Yet most researchers also recognize that the prime areas for human occupation during Lake Stanley, whether Paleoindian or Archaic, were the vast bottomlands now covered by the Great Lakes, resulting in a skewed terrestrial archaeological record. In Lake Huron alone, an estimated 250,000 hectares that were available for occupation during Lake Stanley are now underwater (Lewis and Anderson 2012).

While it has long been axiomatic that archaeological sites were submerged beneath the Great Lakes, it was not until recently that detailed mapping of the lake beds and developments in underwater technology have made submerged prehistoric archaeological research feasible. Detailed bathymetry of Lake Huron has revealed that the AAR was in fact a continuous landform across the Lake Huron basin that would have been a dryland corridor for people and animals during the lower water levels of Lake Stanley. It was then hypothesized that this narrow feature would also channel caribou movement during their biannual migrations and offer an ideal location for strategic intercept hunting. Since 2009, an interdisciplinary study has been conducted on the AAR to evaluate this hypothesis.

Research to date has demonstrated that this landform offered a unique paleoenvironment in the region, and despite an early Holocene chronological age, the environment sustained on the AAR is Pleistocene in character (see Sonnenburg 2015). This is primarily due its periglacial setting, the frigid melt water deriving from the nearby Laurentide Ice Sheet, and the location of the landform itself between two cold bodies of water. Additionally, the AAR likely channeled wind and wave action along its shores and thus experienced cooler temperatures than the mainland, ultimately providing a regional refugium for cold-adapted Pleistocene plants and animals such as caribou (Lemke 2015a; McCarthy et al. 2015).

Caribou are an important component of Great Lakes prehistory—both for environmental reconstructions and Paleoindian lifeways. While long thought to be a primary prey species of Paleoindian hunter-gatherers in the region (Cannon and Meltzer 2004; Gramly 1982; Johnson 1996; Simons 1997), faunal evidence from archaeological sites is limited (Cleland 1965; Robinson et al. 2009; Spiess et al. 1985, 1998; Storck and Spiess 1994). However, paleontological records indicate that caribou were more abundant on the prehistoric landscape than traditionally assumed (Lemke 2015a). In addition, with the evidence of caribou hunting structures on the AAR, it is clear that prehistoric peoples in the region targeted these animals at least on a seasonal basis. The faunal remains of caribou also indicate that archaeological and paleontological records in the region are closely tied to changes in water levels. The absence of caribou remains dating to the Lake Stanley time period suggests that these records have been submerged (Lemke 2015a).

Chronology

Both relative and absolute chronologies date the known human occupation on the AAR. First, relative chronology can be established using lake-level reconstructions for Lake Stanley (Table 9.1). Since the AAR was dryland only for a short period of time, this landform provides tight chronological control for its archaeological sites. Essentially, there is a long enough of period of time for repeated patterns in human behavior but a short enough period that these patterns are fairly free of "noise" from later occupations or postdepositional disturbances—approximately 3000 years between 11,200 and 8,300 cal BP. This

TABLE 9.2. Radiocarbon dates from the Alpena-Amberley Ridge. Sample marked (*) was run at the University of Arizona Accelerator Mass Spectrometry Laboratory. All other dates were run at the National Ocean Sciences AMS facility, Woods Hole, MA.

Dated Material	Lab. no.	RCYBP	cal BP (2σ, IntCal13)
charcoal in stone circle	OS-100526	8080 ± 35	9125–8789
spruce pole	X20851*	8038 ± 46	9073–8723
rooted spruce	OS-99473	7960 ± 55	8995–8641
tamarack pole	OS-100524	7840 ± 40	8765–8542

reconstructed Lake Stanley time frame corresponds to the Late Paleoindian–Early Archaic regional terrestrial records.

In addition to this relative chronology, several absolute dates have been run on organic samples preserved on the lake bottom. Two assays were from pieces of wood (tamarack [*Larix*] and spruce [*Picea*]) recovered near archaeological features. A third wood date was run from a spruce tree that was rooted in situ. Additionally, charcoal recovered from the center of a small stone circle hearth was dated (Table 9.2). The four resulting dates tightly cluster between 9020 and 8640 cal BP. These absolute dates correspond with the Late Paleoindian period generated from the terrestrial regional record, defined as 12,500–8500 cal BP (e.g., Jackson and Hinshelwood 2004).

Paleoenvironment

Paleoenvironmental research on the AAR provides a view of the ancient environment. As the primary research areas occupy a mid-lake location and are a significant distance from shore (50–80 km; O'Shea 2015a), there is no modern sediment covering the landform. Therefore, sediment found on the AAR is ancient and was deposited when it was dryland. Grain size, shape, sorting, and material analyses indicate that movement and transport distance of sediments is limited and point to a variety of depositional regimes (O'Shea et al. 2014, table S1).

In addition to the preserved wood specimens (Table 9.2), macrofossils of pollen and testate amoebae enhance the picture of the AAR paleoenvironment. Spruce pollen, as well as sphagnum moss spores, have been recovered

(Sonnenburg 2015:150, fig. 12.3). Testate amoebae are protist organisms characterized by a test, or hard shell, that preserves after the organism has died. These amoebae survive at the sediment–water interface and are environmentally sensitive. They therefore react more quickly to shifts in water levels and climate than pollen, and different species are indicative of specific local paleoenvironments (McCarthy et al. 1995). Distinct testate amoebae assemblages and pollen recovered from the AAR indicate a mosaic of shallow lakes, small ponds, and sphagnum moss bogs (Sonnenburg 2015).

Overall, the AAR presents a vastly different environment than that observed on surrounding mainland areas. It can generally be characterized as an open subarctic mosaic of intermittent spruce and tamarack trees and sphagnum moss-dominated bogs, with small shallow ponds, wetlands, lakes, and rivers (O'Shea et al. 2014). This reconstruction is consistent with the likelihood that the AAR was cooler than the mainland (Jackson et al. 2004). The cold surrounding waters maintained a subarctic tundra/taiga type of vegetation, and successional reforestation on the AAR appears to have proceeded at a much slower rate than mainland Ontario or Michigan.

Thus, the AAR may have been the preferred habitat and migration route for local caribou populations. The corridor would have been ideal for these animals, with forage, fresh water, and probably fewer insects than the mainland due to significant winds (Lemke 2015a; McCarthy et al. 2015). Likewise, the confined nature of the landform would have provided substantial predictability to herd movement and an ideal ecological niche for hunter-gatherers.

Archaeological Sites and Materials

Underwater archaeological research on the AAR has focused on identifying, mapping, and sampling potential stone hunting structures of the kind known historically and ethnographically from the North American Arctic (O'Shea and Meadows 2009).

Ethnographic (Stewart et al. 2000) and archaeological (Brink 2005) descriptions of caribou hunting structures are consistent in their representation as relatively simple constructions that take full advantage of local landforms and materials. Indeed, some could easily be missed altogether if not actively sought out or identified by an informant (Stewart et al. 2000). The basic shapes and forms observed are also modular, in the sense that they can either be used alone or combined to create more elaborate and complex features. There is a clear economy of effort in the selection and arrangement of materials, and in most cases the structures enhance existing landscape features.

Sought underwater, stone structures of this kind are ideally suited for detection using acoustic sonar surveys, as the hard rocks provide bright reflections. Various sonar techniques (i.e., side-scan, multibeam, scanning) have been utilized to map, measure, and orient these hunting structures on the landscape across the AAR (O'Shea 2015a, b). Once a target of interest is located on the sonar survey, it is then investigated with live video transmitted from a Remote Operated Vehicle (ROV) to confirm its anthropogenic construction. Hunting structures are evaluated and compared to other features on the AAR that result from geological processes such as ice thrusts, glacial moraines, erratics, etc. Archaeologically trained scuba divers then further investigate potential archaeological sites. Samples are collected from these areas in order to recover archaeological materials and environmental indicators (O'Shea 2015a).

Most of the features appear to be hunting-related, although other types of structures have been recorded. These include small rectangular features (which by analogy to Arctic examples may be meat caches or hide processing sites; Stewart 2015); small rings that were used as

TABLE 9.3. Types of stone structures on the Alpena-Amberley Ridge (AAR).

Category	n =
Cluster blind	25
Line	17
Cairn	4
Rectangle	4
Ring	3
Upright Stone	1
V-blind	17
Complex constructions	2
Total	73

hearths (Table 9.2); and cairns and upright standing stones that may have functioned as both territorial markers and components in drive lanes (similar to the Arctic *inuksuit*; Table 9.3).

The majority of the hunting structures are simple hunting blinds situated to take advantage of natural features in the landscape. They occur as both open structures forming a V shape, or as fully enclosed constructions. Two more-complex hunting structures have also been identified on the AAR (O'Shea et al. 2013, 2014). These constructions are modular combinations of simpler elements and include one or more long lines, multiple hunting blinds, cairns, and upright stones. The structures appear to be positioned in natural bottlenecks where the terrain would channel migrating herds, although more people would still be required to drive the animals into the features (Friesen 2013).

To date, 18 lithic artifacts and one faunal remain have been recovered during scuba operations (Lemke 2015a, b). These artifacts were recovered from bulk sediment samples, test pits and screening on the lake bottom, or from 1 × 1 m² excavations using an airlift. The majority of stone artifacts can be classified as flakes and debitage from resharpening, maintaining, or creating lithic tools (n = 17). In addition, one formal artifact was recovered—a thumbnail scraper made on Bayport chert. Thumbnail scrapers similar to this artifact are fairly common in Paleoindian assemblages and use-wear studies suggest they were used for processing hides, wood, antler, and bone (Loebel 2013). Lastly, one cervid tooth fragment was recovered from inside a stone-constructed hunting blind. Although too small to be identified as to species, this tooth may be caribou. All artifacts were recovered in close association in or around hunting structures.

Lithic raw materials include Bayport, a raw material source located south of the AAR on the Michigan "thumb." In addition to this known source, several flakes are made on grey and brown cherts that are common in the local Traverse Formation and may come from outcrops or glacial cobbles on the AAR itself. Two flakes are made on a high-quality black material that remains, as yet, unidentified (see Lemke 2015a, fig. 11.5). Although small, the lithic assemblage on the AAR can be usefully compared to patterns of lithic exploitation known from contemporary terrestrial sites in the region. The Bayport chert quarry is a common material used throughout the Paleoindian period, specifically during the Holcombe phase. While Bayport is found in small amounts during the Early Paleoindian period, it is typically the most common chert source in Late Paleoindian sites by counts and weights (Ellis 1989; Fitting et al. 1966:18–20, 126; Simons 1997; Simons et al. 1984). It appears that hunters on the AAR took advantage of both types of chert but also traveled or traded south to acquire Bayport. Significantly, no fluted points or any indication of large bifacial artifacts common in Paleoindian assemblages have been recovered.

Reconstructing Paleoindian Lifeways on the AAR

The hunting structures and material remains recovered from the AAR reveal a great deal about prehistoric human behavior during Lake Stanley. Similar to caribou hunting structures in other parts of the world, the AAR sites are situated at strategic places on the landscape, such as topographic bottlenecks, river crossings, high ridges, or near migration routes (Lemke 2015c). In addition to this use of local topography, the hunting structures reflect a detailed knowledge of animal behavior and their specific traits. For example, caribou are attracted to linear features, as they are prone to follow other caribou and their trails, ridge lines, and other natural features such as rivers and lakeshores for some time before crossing them (Brink 2005; McCabe et al. 2004:14; Spiess 1979:36). Caribou hunters have long exploited these tendencies by constructing stone drive lanes that funnel caribou into corrals and lakes and toward hunting blinds and waiting hunters (Spiess 1979; Riches 1982:33–39; Gordon 1990). The AAR structures are consistent with this pattern and match the form and function of hunting sites known ethnographically and historically (O'Shea and Meadows 2009). The physical attributes of the hunting structures can also be used to infer weaponry, seasonality, and the size of the group participating in the hunt (Friesen 2013; Morrison 1981; O'Shea et al. 2013, 2014).

Seasonality is one of the most significant factors that can be inferred from the built stone structures, particularly since faunal remains—the typical indicator of seasonality—are rarely preserved in Paleoindian sites in the Great Lakes region. Many of the AAR structures are *directionally dependent*, in that they would only conceal hunters if the animals are moving in a particular direction. This physical property of the structure makes it possible to determine whether it could be employed during caribou migrations and, if so, season of use. Seasonality is inferred using the presumed direction of caribou movement across the AAR during biannual migrations. Running northwest to southeast, the AAR would have provided a natural migration route for caribou herds moving to more southerly rutting grounds in the fall and returning north in the spring to calve. Given this directional association of caribou migration, if a structure is oriented to take animals moving southeast it is presumed to have been used in the fall. If it is oriented to the northwest, it was used in the spring (O'Shea et al. 2013, 2014). Other orientations likely indicate hunting activities that took place other times of the year and not during migrations. These structures are typically situated relative to specific landscape features, such as lake shores or marshes, that would have

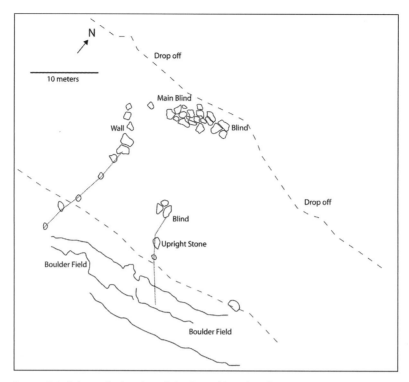

FIGURE 9.2. Schematic drawing of the Funnel hunting site.

naturally attracted animals (similar to ice patch hunting; Hare et al. 2004; Kuzyk et al. 1999).

The majority of the identified AAR structures are oriented to the southeast and would have been used to target caribou during their fall migration. This tendency for autumn hunting is not surprising, as the animals are in their best condition in terms of fat content, quality of hides and sinews, and can be hunted en masse (Blehr 1990:320; Enloe 2003:24; Reimers and Ringberg 1983; Stefansson 1951:337). The majority of structures oriented for autumn hunting are simple blinds—closed, semicircle, or V-shaped. There is one, more-complex hunting site that is oriented for the fall, the Dragon Blind. This site has one long drive lane with a standing stone cairn at one end and at least one associated hunting blind (O'Shea and Meadows 2009, fig. 2; O'Shea et al. 2013, fig. 2).

Striking patterns have emerged on the AAR in terms of spring hunting. The two most complex hunting sites, which are multicomponent in the sense that they are made from several interconnected features such as drive lanes and numerous hunting blinds/walls, are both oriented to the northwest for spring hunting. One of these sites is the Funnel, a site that has some of the most substantial architecture on the AAR, with large stones forming two converging lines and several hunting blinds (Figures 9.2, 9.3). The second complex site is Drop 45, a hunting locality with two lines forming a constricted channel for caribou movement with adjacent hunting blinds (Figure 9.4). The majority of lithic artifacts have been recovered from this site (Lemke 2015b; O'Shea et al. 2014). Both of these complex sites—Funnel and Drop 45—would have required a large number of people to operate them. Mostly likely, small groups of people channeled the caribou toward the funnel or drive lanes, while others waited in the blinds.

These sites strongly suggest seasonal human aggregation for communal hunting during the spring caribou migration. Pregnant caribou females often start the spring migration and are later joined by males (Peers 1986:33). In contrast to the fall migration, the spring migration may slow down or speed up depending on the

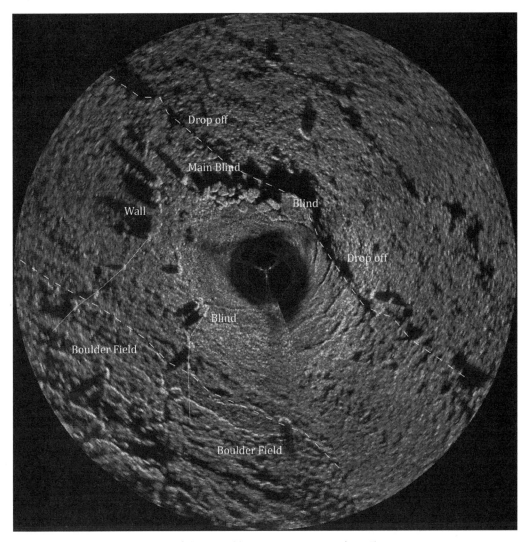

FIGURE 9.3. Scanning sonar image of the Funnel hunting site. Same scale as Figure 9.2.

weather and available forage. Spring migration routes tend to be more direct, and calving grounds are the most consistent (Heuer 2008; Kelsall 1968; Spiess 1979:40). These factors make the spring migration fairly predictable. For hunter-gatherers coming out of winter, the spring hunt would have been a critical subsistence activity, and the aggregation of several families for communal hunting would also provide a predictable meeting time and place for other activities such as information exchange, trade in raw materials, and social interaction.

In addition to the association of complex structures with spring hunting and social aggre-

gation, another emergent pattern is the existence of key locations on the AAR that appear to have been used for both fall and spring migration hunting. The first of these areas includes the Drop 45 site described above. Drop 45 is situated just below the crest of an overlooking high ridge where the AAR narrows significantly. While this site is oriented for spring hunting, several simple structures in the form of V-shaped hunting blinds are located on the crest of this ridge—all of which are oriented for fall hunting (O'Shea et al. 2014, fig. 1B). A similar situation is found in a second locality southwest of Drop 45, termed the Gap area. Here, a set of parallel eskers would

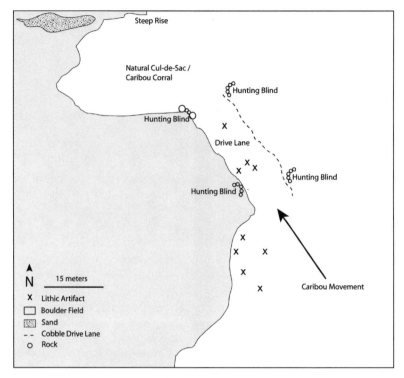

FIGURE 9.4. Schematic drawing of the Drop 45 hunting site.

have served to channel caribou movement through a narrow valley. In this valley, several simple hunting blinds have been located running the length of the landform. These are also V-shaped. Some are oriented for fall and others for spring (O'Shea et al. 2013, fig. 4A).

It is clear from these two localities—as well as from agent-based computer simulations that model the movement of caribou along the AAR—that there are key topographic bottlenecks restricting the movement of migrating herds (Fogarty et al. 2015; Reynolds et al. 2014). These locations would have provided additional predictability for hunters and appear to have been extensively utilized. For example, in addition to the hunting structures near Drop 45, a rectangular structure was identified behind one of the V-shaped blinds. This structure matches ethnographic and archaeological descriptions of meat caches (Stewart 2014, 2015) and may have been used to store meat from the fall hunt for winter.

While the AAR would have been an ideal habitat for caribou and other cold-weather-adapted plants and animals, the same factors may have made it a cold and uncomfortable location for long-term human habitation, particularly during winter. To date, no obvious domestic facilities or large camp sites have been located. A stone-ringed hearth and several smaller constructions that may represent temporary dwellings have been documented (O'Shea 2015b), but these most likely represent small camps occupied briefly during the hunt. Campsites for large social aggregations during the spring may have been temporary and ephemeral, explaining their absence from the AAR thus far.

Modeling the Late Paleoindian Occupation on the AAR

It is clear that caribou were an important resource for Late Paleoindian hunters in the region. Hunting structures demonstrate that these prehistoric populations understood caribou behavior and situated themselves strategically to intercept these animals during migrations using sophisticated hunting techniques and structures. Overall, it appears that relatively small groups of mobile hunters practiced seasonally distinctive subsistence activities but also likely participated in periodic aggregation of larger groups for communal hunting, using complex hunting structures in the spring. These groups utilized local raw materials and also had some connection south to the Bayport quarries directly or through exchange.

From these observations, a model of mobility and seasonal aggregation has emerged. Small groups likely visited the AAR in the fall, in order to target migrating caribou using simple structures such as the V-shaped hunting blinds. Surplus meat from these hunting episodes was stored in rectangular caches located near the hunting sites. In the winter, these groups likely moved inland and spent the season in the more sheltered, forested areas of mainland Michigan and Ontario. Logistical trips to the AAR may have occurred during this season to retrieve frozen meat from caches—a behavior that has long been hypothesized for Paleoindians in the region (Fisher 1987). The ancient lake southwest of the AAR (Figure 9.1) was fairly shallow and likely frozen in winter, enabling a direct path to the central AAR for such retrieval. In spring, large groups appear to have converged on the AAR to operate large, complex hunting structures, such as Drop 45 and Funnel. The structures would have required numerous "beaters" to funnel the caribou into drive lanes, with others stationed in blinds. These social aggregations for communal hunts likely facilitated the exchange of information, material goods, and other social interactions. Finally, in the summer, people likely visited the AAR for fishing and stalking or trapping terrestrial game, although large campsites were again located on the mainland (Lemke and O'Shea 2015).

More broadly, the hunting structures on the AAR support the long-held view from terrestrial Paleoindian sites that caribou were a significant component of the subsistence economy in the Great Lakes and Northeast (Cannon and Meltzer 2004; Gramly 1982; Johnson 1996; Robinson et al. 2009; Simons 1997). Furthermore, communal hunting and social aggregation has been suggested for a number of other Paleoindian sites in the region—including some of the largest Paleoindian campsites in North America, such as Nobles Pond and Bull Brook (Robinson et al. 2009; Seeman 1994). In these respects, the underwater and terrestrial archaeological records are consistent with regional patterns. In other aspects, however, the underwater data significantly supplement the picture of Paleoindian societies drawn solely from the terrestrial record.

Discussion

The underwater archaeological record on the AAR preserves direct evidence of Paleoindian lifeways that have been difficult to reconstruct on land, including aspects of the subsistence economy, social organization, and seasonal strategies. In many ways, the *Late* Paleoindian occupation of the AAR resembles more traditional models of *Early* Paleoindians as Ice Age adapted, terrestrial big-game hunting, mobile, small groups of hunter-gatherers. While these traditional models have been questioned for early Paleoindian hunter-gatherers (e.g., Cannon and Meltzer 2004; Collins 2002, 2007), they may be useful for later occupations.

What makes the pattern of Paleoindian subsistence and settlement on the AAR unique is the fact that it occurs at a time when elsewhere in North America—and even within the Great Lakes region itself—Paleoindian systems are being supplanted by Archaic technologies that were better adapted to the improving Holocene environment. This fact has important implications for understanding the archaeological record in the Great Lakes region, and for Paleoindian studies more generally.

First, it reminds us that all these cultural adaptations are tightly linked to their local and regional environments (e.g., Cannon and Meltzer 2008). Furthermore, these environments are highly variable across North America and rapidly changing, particularly at the beginning of the Holocene. Likewise, we should expect heterogeneity in the archaeological record at even regional scales. For example, we can see the reoccupation of southern and central Michigan by Archaic technologies and adaptations (White 2012) at the *same time* that we see Pleistocene-adapted technologies being used to exploit Pleistocene fauna on the AAR. Furthermore, as local environments change, and plant and animal species effectively shift, we can expect societies accustomed to dealing with specific environments to shift with them, either physically, by following prey species and environments, or technologically, by altering toolkits. In the Michigan case, it is easy to envision the AAR caribou hunters moving northward following the retreating ice front and caribou.

The specific technologies employed by Late Pleistocene hunters were tightly linked to the environment and the prey species being exploited. The mosaic of environments and resources available during the final Pleistocene ensured that, rather than a static tool kit carried from continent to continent and region to region, technologies were exquisitely suited to the tasks and environments at hand. As such, it should be the expectation that, as these foragers dispersed into new environments within North and South America, their technological systems and social lifeways should evolve and adapt. For example, it is now widely recognized that the Paleoindian fluted point tradition was a technological system invented in continental North America, with significant variability represented in contemporary technologies from other regions (e.g., the Channel Islands and the Great Basin; Beck and Jones 2010; Erlandson et al. 2011; Jenkins et al. 2012; Rick et al. 2001).

It is likewise reasonable to assume that, regardless of the particular technological package that was initially carried into North America, this suite would have rapidly evolved as new landscapes and new prey species were encountered and others went extinct. The fluted point tradition developed within a continental context and is well adapted to the hunting of large terrestrial fauna. In contrast, the technology of peoples moving along the Pacific coast, exploiting coastal resources, is characterized by stemmed points and crescents (Erlandson et al. 2011). In effect, we can imagine a multistep process with lifeways and technological systems progressively adapted to new settings. Such new settings would have been encountered by all Paleoindian populations in the Americas due to significant environmental changes during this period. Either people moved into new territories

and thus encountered different environments, or people stayed within a small region and local environments themselves changed. This perhaps accounts for the apparent "late" arrival of fluted point tradition technologies in Alaska and the Arctic (e.g., Dixon 1999; Goebel et al. 2008:1498; Hoffecker and Elias 2007).

We believe that the AAR refugium provides a fleeting glance of a nonfluted point Paleoindian technology that was particularly adapted to subarctic, periglacial conditions and resources (Figure 9.5). This technological system, which relied on small tools (e.g., thumbnail scraper) and likely wood and bone implements (O'Shea et al. 2013), would have a very low visibility profile in terrestrial settings and be very difficult to date, although it is both visible and dated on the AAR. In many ways, the characterization of the AAR technologies is similar to earlier, nonfluted artifact assemblages that were likely near ice front settings, such as the Miller projectile point from Meadowcroft Rockshelter in Pennsylvania (Adovasio and Carlisle 1988; Adovasio et al. 1990; see also Goodyear 2005:104) and the triangular points from Cactus Hill, Virginia (McAvoy 2000). We can envision such an ice-front technology being used by people occupying the periglacial zone south of the Laurentide Ice Sheet as it slowly retreated. Hunters using this adaptation would have drifted progressively northward after the end of the Pleistocene and may ultimately find expression in the later small-tool traditions found in the Arctic (Bielawski 1988). In this regard, the relative invisibility of these sites in terrestrial settings would similarly hold for more northerly regions until such times that Archaic forms began to mix with the earlier technological tradition. Such a technology is only visible and/or datable farther south because it is found in deeply stratified deposits, e.g., Meadowcroft, Cactus Hill, or underwater. Such a technology may be more common along the receding Laurentide ice front as this periglacial subarctic niche was contracting over time and space.

Overall, the Late Paleoindian record on the AAR under Lake Huron is available due to its preservation in an underwater context. Despite methodological challenges, underwater research

FIGURE 9.5. Conceptual schematic of Late Pleistocene technological traditions.

has the potential not only to supplement the terrestrial archaeological record but also to expand our picture of Paleoindian lifeways and provide significant missing links in the prehistory of the Americas. The broader implications drawn from the AAR research further highlight the need for additional submerged prehistoric investigations, particularly on the ocean coasts. These inundated landscapes, such as the unique Holocene glacial refugium on the AAR, can reveal new insights into human adaptability and technological change. In this respect, the end of an era can tell us a great deal about the era itself.

References

Adovasio, James M., and R. C. Carlisle
1988   The Meadowcroft Rockshelter. *Science* 239(4841):713–714.
Adovasio, James M., Donahue, J., and R. Stuckenrath
1990   The Meadowcroft Rockshelter Radiocarbon Chronology 1975–1990. *American Antiquity* 55(2):348–354.
Beck, Charlotte, and George T. Jones
2010   Clovis and Western Stemmed: Population Migration and the Meeting of Two Technologies in the Intermountain West. *American Antiquity* 75(1):81–116.
Bielawski, E.
1988   Paleoeskimo Variability. The Early Arctic Small-Tool Tradition in the Central Canadian Arctic. *American Antiquity* 53(1):52–74.
Blehr, Otto
1990   Communal Hunting as a Prerequisite for Caribou (Wild Reindeer) as a Human Resource. In *Hunters of the Recent Past,*

edited by Leslie Davis and Brian Reeves, pp. 304–326. Unwin Hyman, London.

Brink, Jack W.

2005   Inukshuk: Caribou Drive Lanes on Southern Victoria Island, Nunavut, Canada. *Arctic Anthropology* 42(1):1–28.

Cannon, Michael D., and David J. Meltzer

2004   Early Paleoindian Foraging: Examining the Faunal Evidence for Large Mammal Specialization and Regional Variability in Prey Choice. *Quaternary Science Reviews* 23(18–19):1955–1987.

2008   Explaining Variability in Early Paleoindian Foraging. *Quaternary International* 191(1): 5–17.

Cleland, Charles E.

1965   Barren Ground Caribou (*Rangifer arcticus*) from an Early Man Site in Southeastern Michigan. *American Antiquity* 30(3):350–351.

Collins, Michael B.

2002   The Gault Site, Texas, and Clovis Research. *Athena Review* 3(2):24–36.

2007   Discerning Clovis Subsistence from Stone Artifacts and Site Distributions on the Southern Plains Periphery. In *Foragers of the Terminal Pleistocene in North America*, edited by R. B. Walker and B. N. Driskill, pp. 59–87. University of Nebraska Press, Lincoln.

Dixon, James E.

1999   *Bones, Boats, and Bison: Archaeology and the First Colonization of Western North America*. University of New Mexico Press, Albuquerque.

Ellis, Christopher J.

1989   The Explanation of Northeastern Paleoindian Lithic Procurement Patterns. In *Eastern Paleoindian Lithic Resource Use*, edited by Christopher J. Ellis and Jonathan C. Lothrop, pp. 139–164. Westview Press, Boulder, CO.

Ellis, Christopher J., I. Kenyon, and M. Spence

1990   The Archaic. In *The Archaeology of Southern Ontario to AD 1650*, edited by C. J. Ellis and C. Ferris, pp. 65–124. Ontario Archaeological Society Occasional Publication 5. London, ON.

Enloe, James G.

2003   Acquisition and Processing of Reindeer in the Paris Basin. In *Zooarchaeological Insights into Magdalenian Lifeways: Acts of the 14th UISPP Congress, University of Liege, Belgium, 2–8 September 2001, Colloque/*

Symposium 6.4, edited by S. Costamagno and V. Laroulandie, pp. 23–31. British Archaeological Reports International Series 1144. Archaeopress, Oxford.

Erlandson, Jon M., Torben C. Rick, Todd J. Braje, Molly Casperson, Brendan Culleton, Brian Fulfrost, Tracy Garcia, et al.

2011   Paleoindian Seafaring, Maritime Technologies, and Coastal Foraging on California's Channel Islands. *Science* 311(6021):1181–1185.

Fisher, Daniel C.

1987   Mastodont Procurement by Paleoindians of the Great Lakes Region: Hunting or Scavenging? In *The Evolution of Human Hunting*, edited by Matthew H. Nitecki and Doris V. Nitecki, pp. 309–421. Plenum, New York.

Fitting, James E., Jerry De Visscher, and Edward J. Wahla

1966   *The Paleo-Indian Occupation of the Holcombe Beach*. Museum of Anthropology Anthropological Papers 27. University of Michigan, Ann Arbor.

Fogarty, James, Robert G. Reynolds, Areej Salaymeh, and Thomas Palazzolo

2015   Serious Game Modeling of Caribou Behavior across Lake Huron Using Cultural Algorithms and Influence Maps. In *Caribou Hunting in the Upper Great Lakes: Archaeological, Ethnographic, and Paleoenvironmental Perspectives*, edited by E. Sonnenburg, A. K. Lemke, and J. O'Shea, pp. 31–51. Museum of Anthropology Memoirs 57. University of Michigan, Ann Arbor.

Friesen, T. Max

2013   The Impact of Weapon Technology on Caribou Drive System Variability in the Prehistoric Canadian Arctic. *Quaternary International* 297:13–23.

Goebel, Ted, Michael R. Waters, and Dennis H. O'Rourke

2008   The Late Pleistocene Dispersal of Modern Humans in the Americas. *Science* 319(5869): 1497–1502.

Goodyear, Albert C.

2005   Evidence for Pre-Clovis Sites in the Eastern United States. In *Paleoamerican Origins: Beyond Clovis*, edited by Robson Bonnichsen, Bradley T. Lepper, Dennis Stanford, and Michael R. Waters, pp. 103–112. Center for the Study of the First Americans and Texas A&M University Press, College Station, TX.

Gordon, Bryan

1990   World *Rangifer* Communal Hunting. In

Hunters of the Recent Past, edited by Leslie Davis and Brian Reeves, pp. 277–303. Unwin Hyman, London.

Gramly, Richard M.

1982   *The Vail Site: A Palaeo-Indian Encampment in Mainell*, Vol. 30. Buffalo Society of Natural Science Bulletin, Buffalo, NY.

Hare, P. Gregory, Sheila Greer, Ruth Gotthardt, Richard Farnell, Vandy Bowyer, Charles Schweger, and Diana Strand

2004   Ethnographic and Archaeological Investigations of Alpine Ice Patches in Southwest Yukon, Canada. *Arctic* 57(3):260–272.

Heuer, Karsten

2008   *Being Caribou: Five Months on Foot with an Arctic Herd*. Milkweed Editions, Minneapolis, MN.

Hoffecker, John F., and Scott A. Elias

2007   *Human Ecology of Beringia*. Columbia University Press, New York.

Jackson, Lawrence J., and Andrew Hinshelwood (editors)

2004   *The Late Palaeo-Indian Great Lakes: Geological and Archaeological Investigations of Late Pleistocene and Early Holocene Environments*. Mercury Series, Archaeology Paper 165. Canadian Museum of Civilization, Gatineau, QC.

Jenkins, Dennis L., Loren G. Davis, Thomas W. Stafford Jr., Paula F. Campos, Bryan Hockett, George T. Jones, Linda Scott Cummings, et al.

2012   Clovis Age Western Stemmed Projectile Points and Human Coprolites at the Paisley Caves. *Science* 337(6091):223–228.

Johnson, M. F.

1996   Paleoindians Near the Edge: A Virginia Perspective. In *The Paleoindian and Early Archaic Southeast*, edited by David G. Anderson and Kenneth E. Sassaman, pp. 187–212. University of Alabama Press, Tuscaloosa.

Karrow, Paul F.

2004   Ontario Geological Events and Environmental Change in the Time of Late Paleoindian-Early Archaic Cultures. In *The Late Palaeo-Indian Great Lakes: Geological and Aarchaeological Investigations of Late Pleistocene and Early Holocene Environments*, edited by L. Jackson and A. Hinshelwood, pp. 1–23. Archaeology Papers, Mercury Series 165. Canadian Museum of Civilization, Gatineau, QC.

Karrow, Paul F., and B. Warner

1990   The Geological and Biological Environ-

ment for Human Occupation in Southern Ontario. In *The Archaeology of Southern Ontario to AD 1650*, edited by C. Ellis and N. Ferris, pp. 5–35. Ontario Archaeological Society Occasional Publication 5. London, ON

Kelsall, J. P.

1968   *The Migratory Barren-Ground Caribou of Canada*. Queen's Printer and Controller of Stationery, Ottawa, ON.

Kuzyk, G., D. E. Russell, R. S. Farnell, R. M. Gotthardt, P. G. Hare, and E. Blake

1999   In Pursuit of Prehistoric Caribou on Thandlät, Southern Yukon. *Arctic* 52(2): 214–219.

Lemke, Ashley K.

2015a   Great Lakes *Rangifer* and Paleoindians: Archaeological and Paleontological Caribou Remains from Michigan. *PaleoAmerica* 1(3):276–283.

2015b   Lithic Artifacts from Submerged Archaeological Sites on the Alpena-Amberley Ridge. In *Caribou Hunting in the Upper Great Lakes: Archaeological, Ethnographic, and Paleoenvironmental Perspectives*, edited by E. Sonnenburg, A. K. Lemke, and J. O'Shea, pp. 139–146. Museum of Anthropology Memoirs 57. University of Michigan Ann Arbor.

2015c   Comparing Global Ungulate Hunting Strategies and Structures. In *Caribou Hunting in the Upper Great Lakes: Archaeological, Ethnographic, and Paleoenvironmental Perspectives*, edited by E. Sonnenburg, A. K. Lemke, and J. O'Shea, pp. 73–79. Museum of Anthropology Memoirs 57. University of Michigan, Ann Arbor.

Lemke, Ashley K., and John M. O'Shea

2015   Hunters and Hunting on the Alpena-Amberley Ridge during the Late Paleoindian and Early Archaic Periods. In *Caribou Hunting in the Upper Great Lakes: Archaeological, Ethnographic, and Paleoenvironmental Perspectives*, edited by E. Sonnenburg, A. K. Lemke, and J. O'Shea, pp. 169–176. Museum of Anthropology Memoirs 57. University of Michigan, Ann Arbor.

Lewis, C. F. M., and T. W. Anderson

2012   The Sedimentary and Palynological Records of Serpent River Bog, and Revised Early Holocene Lake-Level Changes in Lake Huron and Georgian Bay Region. *Journal of Paleolimnology* 47(3):391–410.

Lewis, C. F. M., S. M. Blasco, and P. L. Gareau
2005   Glacial Isostatic Adjustment of the Lauren-
       tian Great Lakes Basin: Using the Empirical
       Record of Strandline Deformation of Early
       Holocene Paleo-Lakes and Discovery of a
       Hydrologically Closed Phase. *Géographie
       Physique et Quaternaire* 59(2–3):187–210.
Lewis, C. F. M., C. W. Heil, J. B. Hubney, J. W. King,
T. C. Moore Jr., and D. K. Rea
2007   The Stanley Unconformity in Lake Huron
       Basin: Evidence for a Climate-Driven Closed
       Lowstand about 7900 ^{14}C BP, with Similar
       Implications for the Chippewa Lowstand.
       Journal of Paleolimnology 37(3):435–452.
Loebel, Thomas
2013   Endscrapers, Use-Wear, and Early Paleo-
       indians in Eastern North America. In *The
       Eastern Fluted Point Tradition*, Vol. 1, edited
       by Joe Gingerich, pp. 315–330, University of
       Utah Press, Salt Lake City.
Lovis, William A., Alan F. Arbogast, and G. William
Monaghan
2012   *The Geoarchaeology of Lake Michigan
       Coastal Dunes*. Michigan State University
       Press, East Lansing.
McAvoy, J. M., J. C. Baker, J. K. Feathers,
R. L. Hodges, L. J. McWeeney, and T. R. Whyte
2000   Summary of Research at the Cactus Hill Ar-
       chaeological Site, 44SX202, Sussex County,
       Virginia: Report to the National Geographic
       Society in Compliance with Stipulations of
       Grant 6345–6398. Nottoway River Survey,
       Sandston, VA.
McCabe, R. E., B. O'Gara, W. O'Gara, and
H. M. Reeves
2004   *Prairie Ghost: Pronghorn and Human Inter-
       action in Early America*. University Press of
       Colorado, Boulder.
McCarthy, Francine M. G., E. S. Collins,
John H. McAndrews, H. A. Kerr, D. B. Scott,
and F. S. Medioli
1995   A Comparison of Postglacial Arcellacean
       ("Thecamoebian") and Pollen Succession in
       Atlantic Canada, Illustrating the Potential of
       Arcellaceans for Paleoclimatic Reconstruc-
       tion. *Journal of Paleontology* 69(5):980–993.
McCarthy, Francine M. G., John H. McAndrews,
and Elli Papangelakis
2015   Paleoenvironmental Context for Early
       Holocene Caribou Migration on the
       Alpena-Amberley Ridge. In *Caribou Hunt-
       ing in the Upper Great Lakes: Archaeological,
       Ethnographic, and Paleoenvironmental

Perspectives*, edited by E. Sonnenburg,
       A. K. Lemke, and J. O'Shea, pp. 13–30.
       Museum of Anthropology Memoirs 57.
       University of Michigan, Ann Arbor.
Monaghan, William G., and William A. Lovis
2005   *Modeling Archaeological Site Burial in
       Southern Michigan: A Geoarchaeological
       Synthesis*. Michigan State University Press,
       East Lansing.
Morrison, David
1981   Chipewyan Drift Fences and Shooting-
       Blinds in the Central Barren Grounds. In
       *Megaliths to Medicine Wheels: Boulder Struc-
       tures in Archaeology*, edited by M. Wilson,
       K. L. Road, and K. J. Hardy, 171–187. Proceed-
       ings of the 11th Annual Chacmool Confer-
       ence. University of Calgary, Calgary, AL.
O'Shea, John M.
2015a Strategies and Techniques for the Discovery
       of Submerged Sites on the Alpena-Amberley
       Ridge. In *Caribou Hunting in the Upper
       Great Lakes: Archaeological, Ethnographic,
       and Paleoenvironmental Perspectives*,
       edited by E. Sonnenburg, A. K. Lemke, and
       J. O'Shea, pp. 105–114. Museum of Anthro-
       pology Memoirs 57. University of Michigan,
       Ann Arbor.
2015b Constructed Features on the Alpena-
       Amberley Ridge. In *Caribou Hunting in the
       Upper Great Lakes: Archaeological, Ethno-
       graphic, and Paleoenvironmental Perspec-
       tives*, edited by E. Sonnenburg, A. K. Lemke,
       and J. O'Shea, pp. 115–138. Museum of
       Anthropology Memoirs 57. University of
       Michigan, Ann Arbor.
O'Shea, John M., and Guy A. Meadows
2009   Evidence for Early Hunters beneath the
       Great Lakes. *PNAS* 106(25):10120–10123.
O'Shea, John M., Ashley K. Lemke, and Robert G.
Reynolds
2013   "Nobody Knows the Way of the Caribou":
       Rangifer Hunting at 45° North Latitude.
       Quaternary International 297:36–44.
O'Shea, John M., Ashley K. Lemke, Elisabeth
Sonnenburg, Robert G. Reynolds, and Brian Abbot
2014   A 9000-Year-Old Caribou Hunting Struc-
       ture beneath Lake Huron. *PNAS* 111(19):
       6911–6915.
Peers, Laura
1986   Ontario Paleo-Indians and Caribou Preda-
       tion. *Ontario Archaeology* 43:31–40.
Reimers, E., and T. Ringberg
1983   Seasonal Changes in Body Weight of

Svalbard Reindeer from Birth to Maturity.
Acta Zoologica Fennica 175:69–72.

Reynolds, Robert G., Areej Salaymeh, John M.
O'Shea, and Ashley K. Lemke
2014   Using Agent-Based Modeling and Cul-
       tural Algorithms to Predict the Location
       of Submerged Ancient Occupational Sites.
       AI Matters 1(1):12–14.

Riches, David
1982   *Northern Nomadic Hunter-Gatherers.*
       Academic, New York.

Rick, Torben C., Jon M. Erlandson, and René L.
Vellanoweth
2001   Paleocoastal Marine Fishing on the Pacific
       Coast of the Americas: Perspectives from
       Daisy Cave, California. *American Antiquity*
       66(4):595–613.

Robinson, Brian S., Jennifer C. Ort, William A.
Eldridge, Adrian L. Burke, and Bertrand G. Pelletier
2009   Paleoindian Aggregation and Social Context
       at Bull Brook. *American Antiquity* 74(3):
       423–447.

Seeman, Mark F.
1994   Intercluster Lithic Patterning at Nobles
       Pond: A Case for "Disembedded" Procure-
       ment among Early Paleoindian Societies.
       American Antiquity 59(2):273–288.

Shott, Michael
1999   The Paleoindians: Michigan's First People.
       *Retrieving Michigan's Buried Past: The Ar-
       chaeology of the Great Lakes State*, edited by
       John Halsey, pp. 71–82. Cranbrook Institute
       of Science Bulletin 64. Bloomfield Hills, MI.

Simons, Donald B.
1997   The Gainey and Butler Sites as Focal Points
       for Caribou and People. In *Caribou and
       Reindeer Hunters of the Northern Hemi-
       sphere*, edited by Lawrence J. Jackson and
       Paul T. Thacker, pp. 105–131. Ashgate Pub-
       lishing, Burlington, VT.

Simons, Donald B., Michael J. Shott, and Henry T.
Wright
1984   The Gainey Site: Variability in a Great Lakes
       Paleo-Indian Assemblage. *Archaeology of
       Eastern North America* 12:266–279.

Sonnenburg, Elizabeth
2015   Paleoenvironmental Reconstruction on
       the Alpena-Amberley Ridge Submerged
       Landscape during the Lake Stanley Low-
       stand (ca. 8.5–9ka cal BP), Lake Huron. In
       *Caribou Hunting in the Upper Great Lakes:
       Archaeological, Ethnographic, and Paleo-
       environmental Perspectives*, edited by Eliza-

beth Sonnenburg, Ashley K. Lemke, and
John M. O'Shea. Museum of Anthropology
Memoirs 57. University of Michigan Ann
Arbor.

Spiess, Arthur E.
1979   *Reindeer and Caribou Hunters: An Archaeo-
       logical Study.* Academic, New York.

Spiess, Arthur E., D. Wilson, and J. W. Bradley
1998   Paleoindian Occupation in the New
       England-Maritimes Region: Beyond Cul-
       tural Ecology. *Archaeology of Eastern North
       America* 26:201–264.

Spiess, Arthur E., M. L. Curran, and J. R. Grimes
1985   Caribou (*Rangifer tarandus* L.) Bones from
       New England Paleoindian Sites. *North
       American Archaeologist* 6(2):145–159.

Stefansson, Vilhjalmur
1951   *My Life with the Eskimo.* Macmillan, New
       York.

Stewart, Andrew M.
2014   Viewing Cultural Landscapes in the Long
       and Short Term: Inland Inuit Settlement
       Patterning on the Lower Kazan River, Nun-
       avut, Canada. Paper presented at the 79th
       Annual Meeting of the Society for American
       Archaeology, Austin, TX.
2015   Searching for Archaeological Evidence on
       the Alpena-Amberley Ridge—Is the Arctic
       Record Informative? In *Caribou Hunting in
       the Upper Great Lakes: Archaeological, Eth-
       nographic, and Paleoenvironmental Perspec-
       tives*, edited by E. Sonnenburg, A. K. Lemke,
       and J. O'Shea, pp. 81–103. Museum of
       Anthropology Memoirs 57. University of
       Michigan, Ann Arbor.

Stewart, Andrew M., T. Max Friesen, Darren Keith,
and L. Henderson
2000   Archaeology and Oral History of Inuit
       Land Use on the Kazan River, Nunavut:
       A Feature-Based Approach. *Arctic* 53(3):
       260–78.

Storck, Peter L., and Arthur E. Spiess
1994   The Significance of New Faunal Identifi-
       cations Attributed to an Early Paleoindian
       (Gainey Complex) Occupation at the Udora
       Site, Ontario, Canada. *American Antiquity*
       59(1):121–142.

White, Andrew A.
2012   The Social Networks of Early Hunter-
       Gatherers in Midcontinental North
       America. PhD dissertation, Department
       of Anthropology, University of Michigan,
       Ann Arbor.

CHAPTER 10

Late Pleistocene Occupation(s) in North America

J. M. Adovasio and David R. Pedler

As recently as 20 years ago, or perhaps as few as 10, a chapter like this would have met with extreme skepticism, if not downright scorn. And, why not? The preeminent model for the peopling of the New World had been ascendant for more than half a century. Moreover, despite hundreds of site candidates that ultimately failed to successfully challenge the model, the unshakeable idea endured that, sometime around 12,000 RCYBP, a small but obviously intrepid band of focused big-game hunters crossed the Bering Platform dry-shod, entered the Bering Refugium, and then passed south through the McKenzie Corridor to the interior of the New World. These first migrants arrived at the very tip of South America not in the biblical fullness of time, but rather in an Olympian 500-radiocarbon-year sprint. At some time and some place unknown, these hardy first folk—or their progeny—invented fluted projectiles that they then employed to extirpate 35 genera of Late Pleistocene fauna in North America alone. Called Clovis First after the signature projectile points, this andro-litho-centric model would be the received wisdom of the North American archaeological community—at least until very recently.

As with all such too tidy theories turned gospel writ, Clovis First served to constrain rather than enhance any discussions that addressed the possibility of earlier-than-Clovis migrations, multiple population pulses, diverse non-Clovis technologies, or disparate non-big game–hunting lifestyles. To the grief of only a few straggling mourners, Clovis First finally met its timely end after a lingering illness in October 2013 with the overwhelming consensus reached by attendees of the Paleoamerican Odyssey Conference in Santa Fe, New Mexico. There, it was concluded that humans were definitely in the New World before the efflorescence of Clovis technology. It was also essentially agreed that these older-than-Clovis migrants probably represented multiple movements of genetically, linguistically, technologically, and behaviorally different populations that occurred contemporaneously with at least some portion of the Last Glacial Maximum (LGM, 26,500–19,000 cal BP) and well before the opening of the Ice-Free Corridor that had been presumed to make the Clovis colonization episode possible.

This contribution briefly addresses the evidence for some of these earlier populations in North America, including both the usual suspects and several more recent discoveries (Figure 10.1). It concludes with a brief discussion of the possible relationships between some of these sites and their implications for future archaeological research.

The Sites
Meadowcroft Rockshelter

Meadowcroft Rockshelter is a deeply stratified south-facing rockshelter located on a minor tributary of the Ohio River in southwestern Pennsylvania. The 11 strata at this site have yielded

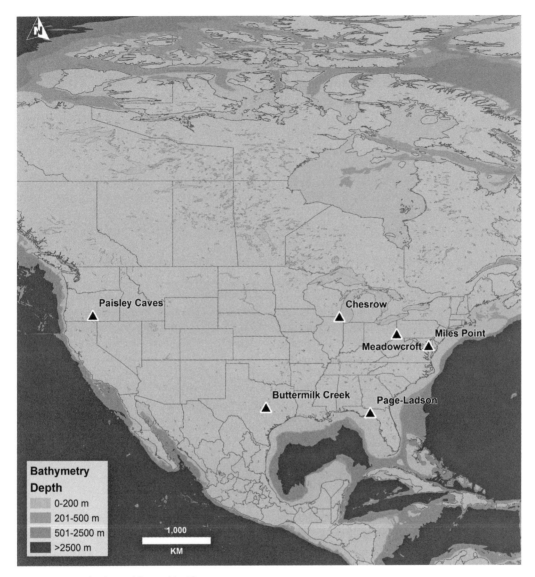

FIGURE 10.1. Main sites addressed in Chapter 10.

the longest occupational sequence from eastern North America and one of the longest in the Americas. The site's upper strata (Upper IIa–XI), whose temporal provenance has never been seriously disputed, span the entire Holocene with a *terminus ad quem* dating to just before the American Revolutionary War (AD 1775–1783). The lower culture-bearing strata (Middle and Lower IIa) and their attendant radiocarbon dates, however, have been the subject of four decades of vigorous debate and controversy.

Continued criticism has pivoted around alleged contamination of only the 11 oldest radiometric determinations from the site, along with the absence of a final report. Despite the fact that the final report has not yet appeared, Meadowcroft is the most intensely studied, the most extensively documented, and—with its 52 radiocarbon assays—one of the most thoroughly dated of all the putative pre-Clovis sites in North America (Adovasio 1993; Adovasio and Pedler 1996, 2000, 2013, 2014; Adovasio et al. 1977a, 1977b,

1979–1980a, 1979–1980b, 1984, 1985, 1988, 1989, 1990, 1992, 2004; Carlisle and Adovasio 1982). Suffice to note, no evidence of any form of contamination has ever been demonstrated in *any* of the Meadowcroft samples, and there appears to be an emerging consensus on the antiquity of the site's deepest levels.

Applying the most conservative interpretation of the available chronometric data, the latest age for the presence of human populations in this portion of the Ohio River basin is in the range of 12,000–10,600 RCYBP. Radiocarbon dates on charcoal from fire pits identified in Meadowcroft's Lower Stratum IIa range from 16,175 ± 975 RCYBP to 12,800 ± 870 RCYBP. The oldest date from this level of the site, run on a carbonized, bilaterally cut fragment of bark-like material (possibly representing basketry), is 19,600 ± 2,400 RCYBP. The configuration of the element is consistent with plaiting strips in later basketry specimens and may also be a fragment of a basket wall. In any case, it is anthropologically altered.

The lithic artifact assemblage associated with the earliest Meadowcroft populations is relatively small (ca. 700 specimens) but sufficient to characterize the industry. The lithic debitage sample reflects secondary and tertiary core reduction and biface thinning from late-stage manufacture, as well as the refurbishing of finished implements. The essentially curated toolkit notably includes an unfluted lanceolate bifacial point (the Miller point) and small prismatic to triangular (in cross section) blades struck from small prepared cores. Additionally, bone, wood, and plant-fiber artifacts were also recovered from the site's earlier-than-Clovis levels. These include plaited basketry, a bone punch, bone awl fragments, and a bipointed wooden tool, all apparently made by generalized foragers who exploited white-tailed deer (*Odocoileus* sp.) and smaller game, along with hickory nuts (*Carya* sp.), walnuts (*Juglans* sp.), and hackberries (*Celtis* sp.) during their predominately short-term fall visits.

The publication of the initial series of radiocarbon dates from Meadowcroft in the mid-to-late 1970s, arguably when the Clovis First paradigm was at its zenith, constituted the first serious challenge to that paradigm and was immediately met with skepticism and withering criticism. The intervening years, however, have witnessed the gradual unraveling of Clovis First in the face of mounting evidence to the contrary, both in the form of newly discovered Clovis contemporaries and earlier-than-Clovis sites (which as of this writing number at least 30) and more subtle strains of evidence marshaled through advances in analytical techniques, multidisciplinary research initiatives, and innovative approaches. Molecular genetics, bioanthropological research, and historical linguistics, for example, have been enlisted in the search for points of departure for the early colonizers of the Americas. Moreover, continued archaeological research and refinements in historical geology, historical glaciology, and geomorphology have permitted a better understanding of earlier population movements through the Russian Arctic and Siberia and an exploration of their implications for human subsistence and adaptability, as well as the timing and route(s) of entry. Freedom from the strictures of received wisdom has also permitted consideration of factors and approaches that might have previously been ruled out, such as coastal (or even maritime) routes of entry to the Americas.

Cactus Hill

The Cactus Hill site in Virginia is a stratified, multicomponent, open site situated in a 1.8 m thick aeolian dune deposit adjacent to the Nottaway River on the interior coastal plain of Virginia. The site was investigated by two independent groups, one directed by J. McAvoy (McAvoy et al. 2000) and the other by M. Johnson (Johnson 1997). The occupational sequence at Cactus Hill is roughly confined to the upper 1 m of the dune deposit but, like Meadowcroft, extends from before Clovis times to the Historic period. In several sections of the site, a Clovis occupation has been identified, beneath which lies a thin but clearly separated earlier-than-Clovis component. The Clovis occupation is dated to ca. 10,920 ± 250 RCYBP on the basis of firepit-derived charcoal. The earlier-than-Clovis component has a series of radiocarbon and complementary Optically Stimulated Luminescence (OSL) determinations. Notable are dates of 15,070 ± 70 RCYBP from a probable hearth and 16,670 ± 730 RCYBP from a charcoal concentration beneath a lithic tool cluster. A second date of 16,940 ± 50 RCYBP appears to confirm the other dates, as do the OSL assays. Collectively, these data suggest one or more earlier-than-Clovis occupations.

Lithic analysis of the approximately 70 flaked stone tools from Cactus Hill's earlier-than-Clovis component(s) indicate a core-and-blade technology with two different kinds of small cores: conical platform cores (with and without faceting) and thick, chopper-like cores. The locally obtained quartzite cores were flaked with soft stone hammers or hardwood billets thought to have been prepared elsewhere then brought to the site for blade or blade-flake production. Also represented are at least two thin, subtriangular to lanceolate unfluted bifaces (McAvoy and McAvoy 1997). The excavators suggest that the blade and biface technology was employed by generalized foragers, not specialized big-game hunters. Additionally, the resemblance of the early Cactus Hill toolkit to its counterpart at Meadowcroft is readily apparent in all but raw material choices.

Chesrow Complex

Sites of the Chesrow complex, defined on the basis of 35 localities on the west side of Lake Michigan in southeastern Wisconsin (Joyce 2013; Overstreet 2005; Overstreet and Kolb 2003; Overstreet and Stafford 1997), include both habitation and mammal kill/processing localities. Two of the sites, Schaefer and Hebior, are reported to contain cultural materials associated with Late Pleistocene megafauna in well-dated contexts. The Chesrow artifact suite, as derived from numerous sites, includes unfluted lanceolate to basally thinned concave-base points, other weakly stemmed points, bifaces, cores, utilized flakes, and hammerstones made largely from locally available quartzite cobbles. Two of the kill/processing sites have produced radiocarbon determinations allegedly associated with

artifacts and extinct fauna. Schaefer yielded eight dates ranging from 12,610 ± 80 RCYBP to 10,960 ± 100 RCYBP, with seven of the eight in the thirteenth millennium BP. Hebior yielded three dates ranging from 12,590 ± 50 to 12,480 ± 60 RCYBP. At both sites, the principal associated fauna is mammoth (*Mammuthus primigenius*). Two additional Chesrow Complex sites, Mud Lake and Fenske, have also yielded apparently butchered mammoths but without artifact associations. Mud Lake yielded two dates of 13,530 ± 50 and 13,440 ± 60 RCYBP. Fenske produced two dates of 13,510 ± 50 and 13,470 ± 50 RCYBP. Notably, the excavators of the dated Chesrow sites see technological resemblances between the Chesrow lanceolate bifaces and those recovered from Cactus Hill and Meadowcroft Rockshelter.

Page-Ladson and Other Florida Localities

Knowledge of the initial human occupation of Florida is currently undergoing intensive refinement, based not only on ongoing terrestrial and underwater research but also on previous excavations. Three sites with particularly informative data sets are Page-Ladson, Sloth Hole, and Wakulla Springs. Page-Ladson and Wakulla Springs have substantive evidence of earlier-than-Clovis utilization, while all three evidence sporadic occupations from Clovis well into the Early Holocene and later. Significantly, all three sites exhibit an extensive Pleistocene faunal assemblage of at least 30 species at each locus.

Page-Ladson is a sinkhole in the submerged bed of the Aucilla River in the Big Bend area of Florida (Dunbar 2006; Webb 2006; Halligan et al. 2016). Excavations in the deepest levels have produced older-than-Clovis evidence that includes an assortment of Late Pleistocene megafauna, notably mammoth (*Mammuthus primigenius*), horse (*Equus* sp.), ground sloth (*Megalonyx* sp.), and Paleollama (*Llama glama glama*). An anthropogenically modified mastodon tusk (*Mammut americanum*) was associated with four radiocarbon dates averaging 12,425 ± 35 RCYBP, and a direct assay on peat removed from within the tusk dated to 12,940 ± 70 RCYBP (Webb 2006:334). Recovered artifacts include unfluted Page-Ladson lanceolate points, a uniface, lithic debitage, and eight ivory tool fragments. Later levels produced Clovis and Suwannee material, and other later Paleoindian material was also recovered from surface exposures across the site.

The relatively nearby Wakulla Springs site, a large first-magnitude spring locus, and the adjacent Wakulla Ledge site collectively constitute an extensive multicomponent Paleoindian locus with plausible earlier-than-Clovis stone tools and associated fauna in dated contexts. Modest amounts of diagnostic Clovis, Suwannee, and Simpson materials have also been recovered, indicating continuing occupancy through the Late Pleistocene. Mastodon bones collected from this locality over the last two centuries include a number of anthropogenically modified pieces and a fragment of a suspected Clovis-age ivory tool, providing further evidence of human utilization of this mastodon by early Floridians.

Sloth Hole is another now-inundated site in the Lower Aucilla River. Though lacking a definitive earlier-than-Clovis component, this locus was intensively occupied/utilized during Clovis times. Investigations at Sloth Hole produced a mastodon kill and/or processing event and camp debris with extensive evidence of both lithic and ivory tool manufacture. In fact, a significant portion of all worked ivory tools from North America derive from Sloth Hole. Six different tool types/forms with an MNI of nearly 100 specimens have been documented. Tool forms include thrusting and casting/launching points, bead platforms, variations of haft and tool handles, and the tip of an ivory needle. An unstained ivory point haft fragment of apparent Clovis ascription, directly dated to 11,050 ± 50 RCYBP, was recovered 68 cm above a land surface that had been inundated around 12,300 RCYBP.

Delmarva Peninsula

Recent research on the western shore of the Delmarva Peninsula in Maryland has revealed multisequel soil horizons attributable to the Late Pleistocene. At Miles Point and several other localities in western Talbot and Dorchester Counties, investigators have defined two episodes of soil formation in either fluvial/estuarine sediments or in coarse aeolian deposits (Lowery et al. 2010). The upper soil yielded artifacts attributable to the Early Archaic, while the deeper paleosol—called the Tilghman soil—is substantially earlier in age. Well dated by multiple radiocarbon assays and OSL analysis to an apparent period of landscape stability ca. 25,000–18,000 RCYBP, the Tilghman soil produced a series of indisputable artifacts that are among the earliest ever recovered in eastern North America. According to Lowery and colleagues (2010:4–5), an in situ artifact scatter was recovered from the Tilghman soil, and several other artifacts were also identified as having eroded from it.

Artifacts encountered from the Tilghman layer included a quartzite anvil, two quartzite hammerstones, an unfluted lanceolate projectile point made of chert, a quartzite bipolar core or wedge, a small chert polyhedral blade core, and two blade flakes. The eroded artifact suite included two more quartzite blade flakes, a retouched chert blade flake, a chert burinated biface fragment, a retouched chert flake, a possible burin spall, a split chert pebble evidencing apparent use-wear, and a retouched basalt flake. It should be stressed that the lanceolate point, polyhedral cores, and blade flakes strongly echo those from Meadowcroft and Cactus Hill.

The AMS dates from this paleosol include assays of 21,490 ± 140 RCYBP, 26,920 ± 230 RCYBP, and 27,240 ± 230 RCYBP. A bulk soil date from the Tilghman soil is 25,670 ± 160 RCYBP. Significantly, this paleosol, or its analogues, are also expressed and directly dated elsewhere on the Atlantic seaboard, although presently without artifact associations. Additional exposures include St. Catherine's Island in Georgia (Frank J. Vento, personal communication 2013) and Vero Beach in Florida (Hemmings et al. 2014).

Continental Shelf Investigations in Florida

Since 2007, an ongoing major underwater investigation has been conducted off the west coast of Florida on the inundated continental shelf. This jointly sponsored National Oceanic and Atmospheric Administration (NOAA)–Mercyhurst Archaeological Institute (MAI) operation has employed side-scan sonar and sub-bottom profilers to map the submerged landscape and the LGM coastline as far as 160 km into the Gulf of Mexico from Florida's current coastline. Using terrestrial analogues of Paleoindian site location in Florida, a series of over 1,500 target localities have been identified, three of which have been preliminarily examined. One of these loci on the Paleo-Suwannee has produced tool stone of now-desilicified chert, though no definitive artifacts have yet been recovered (Adovasio et al. 2010; Hemmings et al. 2014). By June and July 2015, the NOAA–MAI research team would have intensively investigated the chert-bearing locus.

Buttermilk Creek Complex

Separated by only 244 m, the Gault and Debra L. Friedkin loci in Texas are almost certainly artificially circumscribed portions of the same very large site. Both of them have been ascribed by their respective excavators to the same temporal-cultural construct, the Buttermilk Creek complex, named after the stream that runs south of both localities. Gault and Debra L. Friedkin are located in southwestern Bell County, some 65 km north of Austin and 320 km from the Gulf Coast. The sites lie within the Lampasas Cut Plain segment of the Edwards Plateau, which is a transitional zone of mesas and wide valleys between the limestone uplands of central Texas and the Gulf Coast plain. Contiguous to the Live Oak Mesquite Savanna and Blackland Prairies, this resource-rich area contains a diverse array of animals and plant foods and also provides ready access to a major lithic tool source in the form of the Edwards Plateau chert.

Gault (see Chapter 8, this volume), when initially excavated in the late 1920s, yielded extensive Archaic and Late Prehistoric materials spanning the period between 9,000 and 400 years ago, along with a small collection of Clovis-age material. Thereafter, the site was looted by pothunters until 1998, when Michael Collins reinstated professional excavations. Subsequent work has revealed Gault to be one of the largest archaeological sites in Texas and one that has also proven to be the largest Clovis-era locus in the Americas. All of the components at Gault are distributed over an area of some 16 ha, while the Clovis component subsumes a total area of

about 2.8 ha. To date, the Clovis component at Gault has provided well in excess of half a million lithic artifacts, which is by far the largest Clovis-era assemblage in North America (Collins 2002; Collins and Bradley 2008).

Gault's Clovis assemblage contains several varieties of diagnostic Clovis points, end scrapers and gravers on blades, serrated blades, bifacial knives, and bone tools. It is underlain by a much smaller earlier-than-Clovis assemblage. While exhibiting some similarities to Clovis in the form of blade tools and bifaces, the earlier-than-Clovis materials from Gault contain many distinctly unique formal tool types. These include two diminutive, unfluted, expanding stem points and one unfluted lanceolate biface—all of which are non-Clovis in aspect.

Unique to the earlier-than-Clovis horizon at Gault and, for that matter, *any* such locality in North America, is a 3.7 m^2, roughly rectangular, stone apron overlain by discrete concentrations of mammal bone and lithic detritus. This phenomenon has been interpreted as a food processing area.

The Debra L. Friedkin locality has only been under investigation since 2002, when work began under the direction of Michael Waters and colleagues from Texas A&M University. Prior to that time, the site had fortunately escaped the vandalism wrought at Gault. While the Clovis component is much smaller at Debra L. Friedkin than at Gault, the earlier-than-Clovis assemblage is much larger (Waters et al. 2011). Excavations have been conducted at two areas, one of which has produced in excess of 15,000 artifacts, mostly flaking detritus. The formal toolkit is composed of some 56 items, notably including 1 discoidal core, 12 bifaces, 23 edge-altered flakes, 5 blade fragments, 14 bladelets, and a piece of polished hematite. Significantly, many of the bladelets and blades exhibit edge wear indicative of use.

As at Gault, conditions at Debra L. Friedkin are inimical to the preservation of carbon. As a result, two stratigraphic columns of samples were collected for OSL dating, yielding ages that range between 15,5 ka and 13,2 ka (Waters and Stafford 2013:550). This time frame is congruent with the pre-Clovis levels at the nearby Gault site.

The Paisley Five Mile Point Caves

The Paisley Five Mile Point Caves are a complex of eight small (approximately 27–66 m²), closed (i.e., cave and rockshelter) sites located on the extreme northwestern margin of the Great Basin (Jenkins 2007; Jenkins et al. 2013). Situated just north of the town of Paisley, Oregon, the caves are tightly arranged (about 25 m apart) in a more or less lineal fashion on a ridge 200 m above the shallow, alkaline Summer Lake. Summer Lake, along with nearby Lake Albert and the Upper and Lower Chewaucan Marshes, were once part of the Late Pleistocene pluvial Lake Chewaucan. Lake Chewaucan reached its maximum extent of 1,200 km² prior to 18,000 cal BP, after which time its margins and depth generally shrank.

Between 14,500 and 12,500 years ago, however, water levels rose again, and around the apparent time the caves were first visited the lake margin was about 3 km away and less than 50 m below the caves. The Paisley Cave site complex would have been highly attractive to Native Americans not only for the shelter provided by the reentrants but also for the great diversity of plant and animal life available in the perilacustrine environment.

The history of research at the Paisley Five Mile Point Cave sites is not dissimilar to that of Gault. Originally excavated by L. Cressman of the University of Oregon between 1938 and 1940 (Cressman and Williams 1940), the sites were then despoiled by vandals for decades. Professional excavations under Dennis Jenkins of the Museum of Natural and Cultural History, University of Oregon, resumed in 2002 and continue to the present. Cressman originally focused on Caves 1, 2, and 3, which Jenkins also revisited. Like Cressman, Jenkins noted that all three caves contained a distinctive layer of aeolian volcanic ash (or tephra) from an eruption of Mount Mazama dated to around 7700 RCYBP. Cultural materials occurred both above and below the tephra. Unlike Cressman, Jenkins additionally excavated at heavily vandalized Cave 5, which also contained the Mazama ash marker bed.

The earliest evidence of anthropogenic use of the Paisley Five Mile Point Cave complex derives from Caves 2 and 5. The oldest of six radiocarbon assays from a hearth circumscribed by burned bone and lithic debitage discovered in Cave 2 dates to 11,625 ± 35 RCYBP. The oldest feature in Cave 5 is the so-called Bone Pit, which produced 10 radiocarbon assays in association with both extinct (e.g., camel, horse) and recent fauna (e.g., mountain sheep), as well as coprolites, human hair, and lithic debitage. The age of the Bone Pit ranges from 12,400 ± 60 to 11,130 ± 40 RCYBP, rendering its lower reaches almost 1,000 years older than Clovis.

Perhaps the most definitive and surely the most controversial evidence of an early human presence at the Paisley Five Mile Point Caves takes the form of human coprolites, 28 of which have been directly dated. The most recent assays are ascribable to the Late Holocene, dating to 2295 ± 15 RCYBP, while the oldest are as early as 12,400 ± 60 RCYBP. The human ascription of the coprolites has been aggressively challenged (Goldberg et al. 2009; Poinar et al. 2009), but the most parsimonious interpretation of their origin, based on form, composition, and DNA analysis, is that they are in fact human (Jenkins et al. 2013).

The nondebitage lithic artifact suite from the pre-Clovis levels in Caves 2 and 5 is diminutive but does include the two oldest dated examples of Western Stemmed points from western North America. One of them dates to 13,520–13,290 cal BP, while the other is slightly younger at 12,910–13,600 cal BP. In either case, the points are older than the Clovis horizon and clearly indicate the existence of a penecontemporaneous, nondescendant, non-Clovis lithic technology.

Discussion

The site summaries provided above clearly demonstrate that human populations were using the unglaciated landscapes of North America substantially before the appearance and spread of Clovis technology. Moreover, based on certain congruities between the recovered durable artifact suites at several sites, it is possible to identify patterns that appear to characterize some of the older-than-Clovis populations. Perhaps the most striking of these is the co-occurrence of unfluted lanceolate to subtriangular projectile points with small blades or blade flakes and polyhedral or conical blade cores. Such points occur at Meadowcroft (as well as elsewhere in the Cross Creek drainage), Cactus Hill, the Chesrow Complex sites, and on the Delmarva Peninsula. Additionally, the primary author has observed such points from sites as widely separated as Ohio and Florida. The small blade or blade flake component with polyhedral/conical blade cores is also represented at Cactus Hill and the Delmarva sites, to name but a few.

As suggested over 25 years ago (Adovasio et al. 1988), this lithic assemblage may be the substrate within which Clovis ultimately emerges and/or spreads, probably from the American Southeast. The existence of other types of projectile points, notably the Suwannee and Simpson points in Florida, as well as the occurrence of willow leaf or foliate points in both submerged and terrestrial contexts like the Paisley Five Mile Point Caves and other sites in the far west, suggests that the early inhabitants of North America were technologically diverse, again as posited several years ago (Adovasio and Pedler 2004). Such diversity is also supported by the presence of other blade core types at Cactus Hill, side by side with the polyhedral/conical variety.

From a subsistence and behavioral perspective, the floral and faunal assemblages from many of these sites also suggest considerable diversity. The earliest inhabitants of Meadowcroft Rockshelter (like those of the site's later components) were clearly broad-spectrum foragers, as apparently were the groups that frequented Cactus Hill, Gault, and Debra L. Friedkin. Conversely, the Chesrow complex folk and some of the early Floridians may have been more oriented to big-game procurement, as were the occupants of Paisley Five Mile Point Caves—at least occasionally. Parenthetically, we note that, in any case, the lifestyles of either broad-spectrum foragers or more-focused big-game hunters were probably at least as dependent, if not more so, on nondurable technology, as evidenced by the very early occurrence of plaited basketry at Meadowcroft (Stile 1982), twined basketry at Hiscock, New York (Adovasio et al. 2003), and nonlithic projectile points in Florida (Dunbar 2006).

Whether or not these diverse toolkits and subsistence behaviors reflect different genetic and linguistic profiles is presently a moot point. So too are the timing and direction(s) of the various peopling pulses that brought humans into North America. While a northeastern Asian connection is genetically and linguistically irrefutable, other sources of colonizing populations cannot be absolutely ruled out (cf. Stanford and Bradley 2013). Similarly, while it is certain that humans were on various North American landscapes during the LGM, the earliest arrivals may have not yet been found on the submerged landscapes of the continental shelf or in the lower reaches of deep stratigraphic sequences such as those at the Topper site (Goodyear 1999; Waters et al. 2009).

Whatever the ultimate resolution—if indeed there can ever be one—to any of these who-what-where-when questions, it is clear that in North America, like the rest of the hemisphere, our pictures of the first peoples are being dramatically revised. The new images are far from the sepia, monochrome renderings of Clovis First and promise to illuminate far more vividly the lives and lifestyles of the earliest populations. This new full-color reality may still be an affront to a few old-school diehards, but it is certainly no surprise to those whose work appears in this volume.

Acknowledgments

The authors wish to thank C. Andrew Hemmings for providing valuable information on the investigation of Late Pleistocene archaeological localities in Florida, and Jeffery S. Illingworth for his assistance in the production of this contribution. The authors also wish to thank Miguel Garcia-Rubio for his assistance and contributions to a Spanish version of this paper.

References

Adovasio, J. M.
1993   The Ones Who Will Not Go Away: A Biased View of Pre-Clovis Populations in the New World. In *From Kostenki to Clovis: Upper Paleolithic-Paleo-Indian Adaptations*, edited by O. Soffer and N. D. Praslov, pp. 119–218. Plenum, New York.

Adovasio, J. M., and D. R. Pedler

1996   Pioneer Populations in the New World: The
        View from Meadowcroft Rockshelter. Paper
        presented at the 13th International Congress
        of Prehistoric and Protohistoric Sciences,
        Forli, Italy.

2000   A Long View of Deep Time at Meadowcroft
        Rockshelter. Paper Presented at the 65th
        Annual Meeting of the Society for American
        Archaeology, Philadelphia, PA.

2004   Pre-Clovis Sites and Their Implications
        for Human Occupation Before the Last
        Glacial Maximum. In *Entering America:
        Northeast Asia and Beringia before the Last
        Glacial Maximum*, edited by D. B. Madsen,
        pp. 139–158. University of Utah Press, Salt
        Lake City.

2013   The Ones That Still Won't Go Away:
        More Biased Thoughts on the Pre-Clovis
        Peopling of the New World. In *Paleoameri-
        can Odyssey*, edited by K. E. Graf, C. V. Ket-
        ron, and M. R. Waters, pp. 511–520. Center
        for the Study of the First Americans and
        Texas A&M University Press, College
        Station, TX.

2014   Meadowcroft Rockshelter: Retrospect. In
        *Pre-Clovis in the Americas: International
        Science Conference Proceedings Held at the
        Smithsonian Institution, Washington, D.C.*,
        edited by D. J. Stanford and A. T. Stenger,
        pp. 192–207. Smithsonian Institution, Wash-
        ington, D.C.

Adovasio, J. M., A. T. Boldurian, and R. C. Carlisle

1988   Who Are Those Guys? Some Biased
        Thoughts on the Peopling of the New World.
        In *Americans Before Columbus: Ice-Age
        Origins*, edited by R. C. Carlisle, pp. 45–61.
        Ethnology Monographs 12. Department of
        Anthropology, University of Pittsburgh, PA.

Adovasio, J. M., R. C. Carlisle, K. A. Cushman,
J. Donahue, J. E. Guilday, W. C. Johnson, K. Lord,
P. W. Parmalee, R. Stuckenrath, and P. W. Wiegman

1985   Paleoenvironmental Reconstruction at
        Meadowcroft Rockshelter, Washington
        County, Pennsylvania. In *Environments
        and Extinctions: Man in Late Glacial North
        America*, edited by J. I. Mead and D. J. Melt-
        zer, pp. 73–110. Peopling of the Americas
        Series. Center for the Study of Early Man,
        University of Maine, Orono.

Adovasio, J. M., J. Donahue, R. C. Carlisle,
K. Cushman, R. Stuckenrath, and P. Wiegman

1984   Meadowcroft Rockshelter and the
        Pleistocene/Holocene Transition in
        Southwestern Pennsylvania. In *Contribu-
        tions in Quarterly Vertebrate Paleontology:
        A Volume in Memorial to John E. Guilday*,
        edited by H. H. Genoways and M. R. Daw-
        son, pp. 347–369. Special Publication 8.
        Carnegie Museum of Natural History,
        Pittsburgh, PA.

Adovasio, J. M., J. Donahue, and R. Stuckenrath

1990   The Meadowcroft Rockshelter Radiocarbon
        Chronology 1975–1990. *American Antiquity*
        55(2):348–354.

1992   Never Say Never Again: Some Thoughts on
        Could Haves and Might Have Beens. *Ameri-
        can Antiquity* 57(2):327–331.

Adovasio, J. M., J. Donahue, R. Stuckenrath, and
R. C. Carlisle

1989   The Meadowcroft Radiocarbon Chronology
        1975–1989: Some Ruminations. Paper Pre-
        sented at the 1st World Summit Conference
        on the Peopling of the Americas, University
        of Maine, Orono.

Adovasio, J. M., J. D. Gunn, J. Donahue, and
R. Stuckenrath

1977a   Meadowcroft Rockshelter: Retrospect 1976.
        Pennsylvania Archaeologist 47(2–3):1–93.

1977b   Meadowcroft Rockshelter: A 16,000 Year
        Chronicle. In *Amerinds and Their Paleo-
        environments in Northeastern North
        America*, edited by W. S. Newman and
        B. Salwen. Annals of the New York Academy
        of Sciences 288:137–159.

Adovasio, J. M., J. D. Gunn, J. Donahue, R. Stuckenrath, J. E. Guilday, and K. Lord

1979–1980a Meadowcroft Rockshelter-Retrospect
        1977: Part 1. *North American Archaeologist*
        1(2):3–44.

1979–1980b Meadowcroft Rockshelter-Retrospect
        1977: Part 2. *North American Archaeologist*
        1(2):99–137.

Adovasio, J. M., C. A. Hemmings, and J. S. Illingworth

2010   Inundated Superpositioning: Archaeolog-
        ical Investigation of the Submerged Inner
        Continental Shelf on Florida's Gulf Coast. In
        *ACUA Underwater Archaeology Proceedings
        2010*, edited by C. Horrell and M. Damous,
        pp. 192–199. Advisory Council on Under-
        water Archaeology, Pensacola, FL.

Adovasio, J. M., R. S. Laub, J. S. Illingworth,
J. H. McAndrews, and D. C. Hyland

2003   Perishable Technology from the Hiscock
        Site. In *The Hiscock Site: Late Pleistocene
        and Holocene Paleoecology and Archaeology*

of Western New York State, edited by R.S. Laub, pp. 272–280. Bulletin 37. Buffalo Society of Natural Sciences, Buffalo, NY.

Carlisle, R.C., and J.M. Adovasio (editors)
1982   *Meadowcroft: Collected Papers on the Archaeology of Meadowcroft Rockshelter and the Cross Creek Drainage.* Department of Anthropology, University of Pittsburgh, PA.

Collins, M.B.
2002   The Gault Site, Texas, and Clovis Research. *Athena Review* 3(2):31–41.

Collins, M.B., and B.A. Bradley
2008   Evidence for Pre-Clovis Occupation at the Gault Site (41BL323), Central Texas. *Current Research in the Pleistocene* 25:70–72.

Cressman, L.S., and H. Williams
1940   Early Man in Southcentral Oregon: Evidence from Stratified Sites. In *Early Man in Oregon: Archaeological Studies in the Northern Great Basin*, edited by L.S. Cressman, H. Williams, and A.D. Krieger, pp. 53–78. University of Oregon Monographs, Studies in Anthropology 3. University of Oregon, Eugene.

Dunbar, J.S.
2006   Paleoindian Archaeology. In *First Floridians and Last Mastodons: The Page-Ladson Site in the Aucilla River*, edited by S.D. Webb, pp. 403–425. Springer, Dordrecht, NL.

Goldberg, P., F. Berna, and R.I. Macphail
2009   "Comment on DNA from Pre-Clovis Human Coprolites in Oregon, North America." *Science* 325(5937):148.

Goodyear, A.C.
1999   The Early Holocene Occupation of the Southeastern United States: A Geoarchaeology Summary. In *Ice Age Peoples of North America*, edited by R. Bonnichsen and K.L. Turnmire, pp. 432–81. Center for the Study of the First Americans, and Oregon State University Press, Corvallis.

Halligan, J.J., M.R. Waters, Angelina Perrotti, I.J. Owens, J.M. Feinberg, M.D. Bourne, B. Fenerty, et al.
2016   Pre-Clovis Occupation 14,550 Years Ago at the Page-Ladson Site, Florida, and the Peopling of the Americas. *Science Advances* 2(5). doi 10.1126/sciadv.1600375.

Hemmings, C.A., J.M. Adovasio, A.E. Marjenin, F.J. Vento, and A. Vega
2014   The Old Vero Man Site (8IR009): Current Investigations Suggest Pleistocene Human Occupation. Paper Presented at the 71st Annual Southeastern Archaeological Conference, Greenville, SC.

Jenkins, D.L.
2007   Distribution and Dating of Cultural and Paleontological Remains at the Paisley Five Mile Point Caves in the Northern Great Basin. In *Paleoindian or Paleoarchaic: Great Basin Human Ecology at the Pleistocene–Holocene Transition*, edited by K. Graf and D. Schmidt, pp. 57–81. University of Utah Press, Salt Lake.

Jenkins, D.L., L.G. Davis, T.W. Stafford, Jr., P.F. Campos, T.J. Connolly, L.S. Cummings, M. Hofreiter, et al.
2013   Geochronology, Archaeological Context, and DNA at the Paisley Caves. In *Paleoamerican Odyssey*, edited by K.F. Graf, C.V. Ketron, and M.R. Waters, pp. 485–510. Center for the Study of the First Americans and Texas A&M University Press, College Station, TX.

Johnson, M.F.
1997   Excavation of the Cactus Hill Site, 44SX202, Areas A–B, Spring 1996: Summary Report of the Activities and Findings. In *Archaeological Investigations of Site 44SX202, Cactus Hill, Sussex County, Virginia*, Addendum. Research Report Series 8. Virginia Department of Historic Resources, Richmond.

Joyce, D.J.
2013   Pre-Clovis Megafauna Butchery Sites in the Western Great Lakes Region, USA. In *Paleoamerican Odyssey*, edited by K.E. Graf, C.V. Ketron, and M.R. Waters, pp.467–484. Center for the Study of the First Americans and Texas A&M University Press, College Station, TX.

Lowery, D.L., M.A. O'Neal, J.S. Wah, D.P. Wagner, and D.J. Stanford
2010   Late Pleistocene Upland Stratigraphy of the Western Delmarva Peninsula, USA. *Quaternary Science Reviews* 29(11–12):1472–1480.

McAvoy, J.M., and L.D. McAvoy
1997   *Archaeological Investigations of Site 44SX202, Cactus Hill, Sussex County Virginia.* Research Report Series 8. Virginia Department of Historic Resources, Richmond.

McAvoy, J.M., J.C. Baker, J.K. Feathers, R.L. Hodges, L.J. McWeeney, and T.R. Whyte
2000   *Summary of Research at the Cactus Hill Archaeological Site, 44SX202, Sussex County, Virginia: Report to the National Geographic Society in Compliance with Stipulations of*

Grant #6345-98. Nottaway River Survey, Sandston, VA.

Overstreet, D. F.

2005   Late-Glacial Ice-Marginal Adaptation in Southeastern Wisconsin. In *Paleoamerican Origins: Beyond Clovis*, edited by R. Bonnichsen, B. T. Lepper, D. Stanford, and M. R. Waters, pp. 183–195. Center for the Study of the First Americans and Texas A&M University Press, College Station, TX.

Overstreet, D. F., and M. Kolb

2003   Geoarchaeological Contexts for Late Pleistocene Archaeological Sites with Human-Modified Wooly Mammoth Remains in Southeastern Wisconsin, USA. *Geoarchaeology* 18(1):91–114.

Overstreet, D. F., and T. Stafford

1997   Additions to a Revised Chronology for Cultural and Non-Cultural Mammoth and Mastodon Fossils in the Southwestern Lake Michigan Basin. *Current Research in the Pleistocene* 14:70–71.

Poinar, H., S. Fiedel, C. E. King, A. M. Devult, I. Bos, M. Kuch, and R. Debruyne

2009   Comment on "DNA from Pre-Clovis Human Coprolites in Oregon, North America." *Science* 325(5937):148.

Stanford, D. J., and B. A. Bradley

2013   *Across Atlantic Ice: The Origin of America's Clovis Culture.* University of California Press, Berkeley.

Stile, T. E.

1982   Perishable Artifacts from Meadowcroft Rockshelter, Washington County, South-western Pennsylvania. In *Meadowcroft: Collected Papers on the Archaeology of Meadowcroft Rockshelter and the Cross Creek Drainage*, edited by R. C. Carlisle and J. M. Adovasio, pp. 130–141. Prepared for the Symposium "The Meadowcroft Rockshelter Rolling Thunder Review: Last Act" at the 47th Annual Meeting of the Society for American Archaeology, Minneapolis, MN.

Waters, M. R., and T. W. Stafford Jr.

2013   The First Americans: A Review of the Evidence for the Late-Pleistocene Peopling of the Americas. In *Paleoamerican Odyssey*, edited by K. E. Graf, C. V. Ketron, and M. R. Waters, pp. 541–560. Center for the Study of the First Americans and Texas A&M University Press, College Station, TX.

Waters, M. R., S. L. Forman, T. A. Jennings, L. C. Nordt, S. G. Driese, J. M. Feinberg, J. L. Keene, et al.

2011   The Buttermilk Creek Complex and the Origins of Clovis at the Debra L. Friedkin Site, Texas. *Science* 331(6024):1599–1603.

Waters, M. R., S. L. Forman, T. W. Stafford Jr., and J. Foss

2009   Geoarchaeological Investigations at the Topper and Big Pine Tree Sites, Allendale County, South Carolina. *Journal of Archaeological Science* 36(7):1300–1311.

Webb, D. S.

2006   *First Floridians and Mastodons: The Page-Ladson Site on the Aucilla River.* Springer, Dordrecht, NL.

CHAPTER 11

Midwestern Paleoindians, Stone Tools, and Proboscidean Extinctions

Michael J. Shott

Today, North Americans go to zoos when they want to see elephants. That was not always necessary. The poster taxa of Pleistocene North America are proboscideans, the hairy elephants that inhabited the continent when people arrived. In the American Midwest, they included mastodons (*Mammut americanum*) and mammoths (*Mammuthus columbi, M. primigenius*; Agenbroad 2005: Figure 1; Yansa and Adams 2012). Proboscideans were part of the Paleoindians' world, but at length they passed from experience to memory and, ultimately, the fossil record. How and why proboscideans disappeared remains unresolved, exercising both imagination and reason to this day.

Over evolutionary time, life is an existential game. The question never is, "Will you survive?" but, "What will kill you?" Identifying the causes of Pleistocene megafaunal extinctions and disentangling their interactions and effects is difficult in the best of circumstances. The specter of equifinality—the inability to distinguish between competing arguments because evidence is limited and much of it consistent with them equally—is common in archaeology. This specter is aggravated in the Paleoindian case by a "confounding mix of…disparate data interpretations" (Waguespack 2014:312), and unresolved questions about the timing and routes of human colonization and timing and rate of proboscidean decline. Only the brave or foolish venture firm opinions on this subject.

This chapter originated in an earlier study (Shott 2004a) that synthesized then-current data on Paleoindians of the American Midwest (Figure 11.1). It evaluates recent arguments on the human-agency or "overkill" question—difficult if even possible to resolve. Instead of trying, the chapter adopts a narrow focus on one aspect of the much larger question: evidence for human-proboscidean association in stone tools. Those data cannot be understood in isolation, requiring comparison to evidence from elsewhere in North America and the Old World.

The text was completed before a number of relevant sources either appeared or were accessed. These include Agam's and Barkai's (2018) synthesis consistent with this chapter's view; Old World sites that evidently support patterns documented here (Aureli et al. 2015; Huguet et al. 2017; Zutovski and Barkai 2016), or might complicate them (Wright et al. 2014), as well as New World sites that may support patterns documented here (Halligan et al. 2016; C. Haynes et al. 2014). Other, extraordinary, recent claims (Holen et al. 2017) lack "extraordinary evidence" (Braje et al. 2017:200) to support them. Finally, Surovell's and colleagues' latest extended argument also appeared after analysis was completed (Surovell et al. 2016).

Where Ohio rolls his turbid stream
Dig for huge bones, thy glory and thy theme
—William Cullen Bryant, 1808

FIGURE 11.1. The Midwestern United States study area.

Proboscideans in North America

In North America, Europeans found mastodon fossils in the eighteenth century (Greene 1959: 94; Saunders 1996:274; Tankersley et al. 2009). Bad poetry thus inspired good science and wonder about the prospect of living proboscideans in what to Europeans was the unexplored west. In 1803, Thomas Jefferson advised Lewis and Clark to seek mastodons in the course of their expedition (King and Saunders 1984:315). Jefferson's injunction issued from a combination of scientific and political interests, entangling Pleistocene megafauna in nationalist impulses, the desire to demonstrate to European critics the vitality, not derivation, of natural and cultural America (Rigal 1993).

As with Jefferson, proboscideans continue to fascinate Paleoindian archaeologists. Obviously, whether people hunted or scavenged proboscideans bears upon the question of human agency in Late Pleistocene extinction. Yet how it bears on that question is not always clear. For instance, we cannot read diet directly from available remains. Large-animal kill sites are more visible than small-animal ones and hence more likely

to be discovered. Available evidence may be skewed toward the occasional large kill because "very large-bodied prey are greatly overrepresented relative to their actual importance in the diet" (O'Connell et al. 1992). Even if people hunted or scavenged proboscideans, surely they also ate many other foods, some surviving today (Dincauze and Curran 1983; Gingerich 2011; Seeman et al. 2008; Storck and Spiess 1994; cf. G. Haynes 2002a, 2002b, 2013). A recent synthesis concluded that Paleoindian evidence is consistent with big-game specialization at some sites but balanced to generalized diet at most (DeAngelis and Lyman 2016).

Midwestern Proboscidean Habitat and Time-Space Distribution

Proboscidean life-history strategies and habitat preferences are described at length elsewhere (e.g., Agenbroad 2005; Fisher 2009; G. Haynes 1991; Metcalfe et al. 2013; Teale and Miller 2012; Yansa and Adams 2012). Mammoths mostly were grazers, mastodons browsers. Yet possible intestinal contents from Burning Tree (Saunders 1996:275; Lepper et al. 1991:125; Teale and Miller

2012) and elsewhere suggested that mastodons were not strictly browsers.

Proboscidean abundance and distribution varied considerably as Late Pleistocene paleoenvironments changed, at best establishing dynamic equilibrium with environment (Ugan and Byers 2007; Zazula et al. 2014). As biotic communities underwent environmental change, effects upon proboscideans could be magnified (Cooper et al. 2015; Graham and Lundelius 1984). Whether such dynamism means that mammoths and mastodons were contemporaries in the Late Pleistocene Midwest (McAndrews and Jackson 1988:168; Metcalfe et al. 2013) or that mastodons replaced mammoths (Overstreet and Stafford 1997:70) is uncertain, or perhaps itself variable across the Midwest. Some degree of overlap seems likely, and in general mastodons were more abundant in Ohio and Michigan, mammoths more abundant westward (Agenbroad 2005; Holven 2002; Yansa and Adams 2012:180).

There are no constraints on the time-space distribution of proboscidean fossils in the southern Midwest. Northward, however, Late Pleistocene proboscideans cannot predate ice retreat, so their fossil distribution is constrained in time. Yet half or more of dated proboscidean occurrences in Ohio postdate human colonization (McDonald 1994:27–28), one example of the chronological bias in fossil evidence toward the Pleistocene–Holocene transition (Meltzer and Mead 1985), unless we argue that proboscidean numbers spiked as humans arrived. Paleoindian and proboscidean spatial distributions have at least broadly similar distributions (Cleland et al. 1998:Figure 3; Abraczinskas 1993:Figure 1; Yansa and Adams 2012:Figure 2).

Surprisingly late proboscidean dates obtained in the early years of radiocarbon dating (Thomas 1952:5; Williams 1957:366–367) are questionable at face value. Later, Meltzer and Mead (1985:Figure 1) suggested a terminal date near the Pleistocene–Holocene boundary. Recent dating results are noteworthy in several respects. First, Grayson and Meltzer (2015) noted revisions in our understanding of the chronological distribution of proboscideans

from new dates—in both directions. But certitude about the chronology of proboscidean demise is a chimera "shrouded in confidence intervals" (Waguespack 2014:314). Another concerns large-scale compilations, some of which indicate limited human chronological overlap with proboscideans (Boulanger and Lyman 2014; Guthrie 2006; Zazula et al. 2014). A third, contrary, result is the surprisingly late dates of some proboscideans (e.g., Agenbroad 2005; Feranec and Kozlowski 2012; Fisher 2009:Table 4.2; Woodman and Athfield 2009; see Suárez 2017 for persistence into the Holocene of South American megafauna). Clearly, the reasonable practice of dating associated organics may sometimes provide only maximum dates, and direct dates on properly processed proboscidean bone are preferable (Griggs and Kromer 2008:59; Woodman and Athfield 2009:361). So, dating the demise of proboscideans remains uncertain despite the large databases compiled partly with that goal in mind.

It is well known that on the Ohio, and in many parts of America further north, tusks, grinders, and skeletons [of proboscideans] *of unparalleled magnitude, are found in great numbers, some lying on the surface of the earth....*

Thomas Jefferson,
Notes on the State of Virginia
(1954:43–44).

The Fossil Record and Its Representativity

As Jefferson noted more than two centuries ago, the proboscidean fossil record is large but highly variable in salient qualities. By 1807, more than 300 megafauna bones had been excavated at Big Bone Lick, Kentucky (Rigal 1993:21). Before the American Civil War, Albert Koch amassed more than 600 mastodon teeth and 73 mandibles from Missouri (McMillan 1976:83; Morrow 1996:85–87). In the Midwest, proboscideans occur in "singular abundance as fossils," many lost to science (King and Saunders 1984:315).

Therefore, we simply do not know the difference between discoveries made and discoveries reported. Around 1800, Jefferson failed to rescue a fossil elephant whose bones were dispersed among local residents as "common property" (Greene 1959:109). The doomed effort at least demonstrated interest in North American natural history at the highest levels of government. Not so for two centuries since. Yet we Midwestern archaeologists should count our blessings. Even today, the great number of Pleistocene mammoth fossils found in Alaska and Siberia "do not end up in museums, but are kept in… homes and sheds…[or] are scattered across the country, taken home as souvenirs" (Guthrie 1990:239; see also Basilyan et al. 2011).

Thus, relative abundance in the accumulated fossil record may reflect relative abundance in the past, or preservation, or sample bias (O'Connell et al. 1992). Only systematic searching in bogs and elsewhere will yield valid estimates of the abundance and distribution or proboscidean fossils, let alone of Late Pleistocene standing hooves (cf. G. Haynes 2009). Manifest causes of sample loss and bias complicate efforts to estimate living populations and trends from the fossil record (G. Haynes 2009), and proposed proxies are questionable (Robinson et al. 2005; cf. Feranec et al. 2011). Certainly, the fossil proboscidean corpus is respectably large, including hundreds of occurrences in the Midwest (Yansa and Adams 2012; Zazula et al. 2014) and adjacent areas (Agenbroad 2005; Thompson et al. 2008). But in view of the tortured history of fossil collecting, these figures are minima. We cannot know if the corpus of proboscidean remains is a biased record of living animals and preserved fossils but can only reason plausibly to its direction and magnitude.

Arguments for Overkill

Proboscideans' demise coincided, at least broadly, with human arrival in North America. Enter people, exit elephants. This circumstance suggests a causal relationship that has not escaped archaeologists. In Paleoindian studies, overkill is a popular conclusion.

Martin's (1973) blitzkrieg model blamed megafaunal extinctions almost entirely on marauding Paleoindians. It gained fame, whatever its dubious merits (Krech 1999:29). The model is a just-so story based on a set of unlikely as-

sumptions about human population density and growth rates, land use and patterns of expansion, hunting practices and how they change as prey density declines (Webster and Webster 1984), and prey susceptibility. Involving fairly complex interactions between variables, the model's results were not particularly robust (Yule et al. 2014). Thus, changing human population values, advance rate, or prey biomass altered the magnitude and timing of extinction or even whether it occurred at all (Whittington and Dyke 1984). Remarkably, Martin (1973:969) cited the paucity of confirming evidence—kill sites of now-extinct megafauna—to support, not refute, his view. He argued that the Paleoindian hordes advanced so quickly and left so many half-consumed carcasses to spoil on the surface that we should expect few to be preserved, let alone discovered. The great improbability of Martin's argument has given later extinction models a bad reputation, but they deserve serious regard outside its shadow.

Other simulations used questionable assumptions and produced ambiguous results. Alroy's (2001) population densities, high compared to ethnographic data (Binford 2001:Table 5.1), predicted extinction of some extant species and were as indifferent to empirical test as Martin. In Alroy's view, "further 'tests'…are not really necessary" (1999:105) because Martin proved the case. Such indifference to proof reinforces suspicions that some advocates raised overkill from scientific hypothesis to article of faith. In fact, existing "'successful' single-cause models… do not rule out the possibility that Pleistocene extinctions resulted from multiple causes" (Yule et al. 2014:04).

Detailed study of the archaeological and fossil evidence seems more promising. Thus, G. Haynes (2002b, 2013) is a more persuasive advocate of Pleistocene overkill. Haynes's own view has changed over time, irrelevant to the merits of his argument. Once, "The evidence of human hunting and processing of proboscideans" (G. Haynes 1991:205) was less substantial than claimed, and extinctions "were outcomes of environmental stress, resulting from unstable and harsh climatic conditions in the Late Glacial interval" (G. Haynes:315). Later, "Human foragers in Late Pleistocene North America hunted mammoths and mastodons, and this hunting" (G. Haynes 2002a:409) caused over-kill. Acknowledging natural factors, G. Haynes mostly discounted them, arguing the absence of evidence for environmental stress and that pro-boscidean extinction was not synchronized to the Younger Dryas event (2002a:392–393; Fiedel and Haynes 2004:124). He also adduced consid-erable evidence of Paleoindian–proboscidean association, including possibly at Heisler and Pleasant Lake in the Midwest (2002a:Table 3), where human presence is not yet established, partly on the strength of doubts that he himself (1991:251) expressed.

Against the view of Paleoindians as dietary generalists (e.g., Dincauze and Curran 1983; Byers and Ugan 2005), G. Haynes revived the traditional alternative that Paleoindians ate megafauna "more frequently than anything else" (2002a:399). G. Haynes (2002a:396) explicitly excluded stone tools as necessary evidence of association but also noted blood residue—some identified as proboscidean—on what are or may be Paleoindian tools (2002a:Table 5). Martins Creek, a western Iowa "isolated find," and other Midwestern evidence cited by G. Haynes all reported cervid residue. But among them only Martins Creek also reported proboscideans. At face value, this evidence suggests greater Paleoindian preference for extant cervids than extinct elephants. Residue analysis must be in-terpreted with caution, as G. Haynes himself noted (2002b:176; see also Grayson and Meltzer 2015). None of this disproves overkill; but none of it proves it either. It also is significant that, across North America, G. Haynes's evidence for overkill (2002a:Table 3) spanned nearly 1,500 radiocarbon years (calibrated to less than 1,000 calendar years but still a long span). Such a wide span seems at odds with the view that overkill proceeded "swiftly and unexpectedly" (2002a:392).

Otherwise, G. Haynes's argument was plau-sible: optimal hunting patterns would not ex-clude proboscideans when they fell to low densities and their trails would make finding

them easy (2013:93). In places, it was highly orig-inal, suggesting for example "partnerships with other hunters and scavengers, such as ravens and wolves" [2002a:408]). Fiedel and Haynes (2004: 127) cited evidence for Paleoindian "staging areas" and "exploratory stations" in their prog-ress across the Americas, contra Martin's sim-plistic scenario. Staging areas are possible, but the evidence adduced for them (regional fluted biface concentrations, "aggregation" sites with distinct loci) also must consider taphonomic effects of surface geology, the distribution of modern populations (Prasciunas 2011; Shott 2002), and that "loci" at sites can be ambigu-ous inferences (Shott 2004b). The argument is unconvincing, considering the various natu-ral processes that unfolded during the span of proboscidean extinction (climatic change and catastrophic fragmentation of previously diverse biotic communities) that, by G. Haynes's own account (2002a:406), relegated proboscideans to diminishing refugia.

Surovell and colleagues (e.g., Faith and Sur-ovell 2009; Surovell and Grund 2012; Surovell et al. 2016; Surovell and Waguespack 2008; Waguespack 2014) are overkill's most sophis-ticated, if sometimes arguable, advocates. For brevity, only some of their most recent views are addressed. Dismissing Martin's imaginative scenario, Surovell and Grund (2012:673) still argued that "circumstantial evidence"—coarse global correlation of instances of human coloni-zation with large-animal demise and dispropor-tionate extinction of megafauna—proved rapid overkill. Against this, they posed and rejected the "associational critique" (e.g. Grayson and Meltzer 2015), using sophisticated modeling and debatable logic. They devised a taphonomic model estimating that under 7 percent of overkill sites remain today, in conjunction with a sub-stantial but limited radiocarbon database, sug-gest a proportionally brief chronological overlap with proboscideans. Thus, there are many over-kill sites but few remain undiscovered, and all fall in a short time interval that leaves little room for any cause but people.

To Surovell and Grund (2012:675–677), absolute scarcity of Paleoindian overkill sites derives partly from the decline in prey density that Paleoindians caused, a good example of the equifinality that Waguespack (2014) invoked against alternative views. Extinction by natural causes also is consistent with declining proboscidean density. Criticism that their radiocarbon database (2012:678) used only charcoal dates is unfair, since the problems in charcoal-date associations with proboscideans have only recently emerged (e.g., Woodman and Athfield 2009). For their New Zealand comparison, Surovell and Grund (2012:678–679) dismissed sample bias, even though human-megafaunal overlap encompasses 25 percent of local prehistory but 40 percent of radiocarbon dates. The vanishingly low percentage of North American dates in its overlap interval might indicate undersampling or taphonomic ravages, but there is also the unevaluated possibility of radiocarbon oversampling or more organics to date in later sites.

Surovell's and Grund's taphonomic modeling is impressive but explicitly assumes random sampling of the time-ravaged record (2012:677). Across North America, Clovis points have been found in thousands of sites, most of which preserve no fauna. In the Midwest alone, Clovis and/or Gainey points are documented by the hundreds if not thousands (e.g., Morrow 1996; Shott 2004a, 2005), and Midwestern archaeologists reasonably suppose that caribou were common prey. Yet caribou remains are exceedingly rare (e.g., Storck and Spiess 1994). Kimmswick aside (Graham et al. 1981), if other claims of association are taken at face value, then on available evidence Midwestern Paleoindians ate much more elephant than caribou (e.g., Surovell and Grund 2012:681). If no less is true of the western Clovis record, then arguing that 90 percent of well-documented sites have megafaunal associations (e.g., Surovell and Waguespack 2008:90) and that those sites are a representative sample amounts to concluding that megafaunal evidence and consumption was that common when the record formed.

Nothing in our understanding of the structure and composition of their biotic communities suggests that proboscideans were nearly so important to Paleoindians (Byers and Ugan 2005; cf. G. Haynes 2013:96, Surovell and Grund

2012:680, and Waguespack 2014:315). Instead, and again taking at face value the many claims for human association, the evidence seems much more consistent with three explanations. First, remains of abundant smaller game essentially have disappeared. Second, the size and density of proboscidean bones not only make megafauna more resistant to decay, facilitated by their common occurrence in bogs, but much easier to notice by the farmers and drag-line operators who find most of them. Third, in the Midwest and across North America, the undeniable glamor of Pleistocene remains, and possible human association, is a powerful spur to archaeological interest and imagination.

It requires documentation far beyond this chapter's scope, but at face value the probability of serious sample bias deserves consideration. Across North America, archaeologists disproportionately attack the record at its chronological margins. The early extreme is Paleoindian and pre-Clovis everywhere, whose enduring popularity is clear to anyone who knows the literature and conference programs. Available evidence, though coarse, suggests that the Paleoindian and earlier Archaic intervals across North America are overrepresented (Peros et al. 2010: 662). For the Midwest, scholarly publication patterns suggest that the Paleoindian record is oversampled compared to subsequent Archaic periods by a factor of two to five (Jeske et al. 2015:Figure 1; Seeman 2015), and the distribution of fluted points and other Paleoindian evidence is a compound of original distribution and modern sampling bias (Shott 2002, 2013:156 and references therein).

What bias implies about the quality and detail of our knowledge of the vast range between roughly 10,000–2,000 BP also is beyond this chapter's scope but worth contemplation. If only 6.8 percent of possible original megafaunal kill sites remain, they attract what may be several times more attention than that slim figure suggests. Not all sample effects are natural. If Paleoindians responded rationally to food choices, archaeologists are no less rational in their pursuit of stature. There is more glory in hunting Late Pleistocene elephants than mid-Holocene rabbits or acorns. Thus, when

Lovewell was mistakenly identified as Illinoian, archeologists promptly abandoned it "because they thought it was too old for human association" (Holen 2006:55–56), which it still may be. From a sample likely to contain strong bias, we must not rush to the judgment that people ate more elephants than small game and plants.

It is arguable that the kind, amount, and pattern of evidence favor overkill (Surovell and Grund 2012:681) but more conservative to conclude that the representativity of about 15 mostly western Clovis kill sites remains undetermined. Despite their much greater sophistication, Surovell and colleagues in some respects channel Martin, arguing that the comparatively modest body of evidence prima facie constitutes overwhelming evidence for overkill. Rather than ask, "How many kills are X?" we might ask, "How can such argument be falsified?"—assuming as it does that available evidence is representative and therefore more than sufficient to prove overkill.

Midwestern Evidence

Midwestern evidence rarely is central to extinction models or their testing. A notable exception is Fisher's work on dental forensics and proboscidean life-history phenomena, which argued that surprisingly many Great Lakes mastodon sites were kills (1987, 2009). Comparing Fisher's sources suggests some tendency to reinterpret natural deaths as hunted or scavenged remains and generally to increase the proportion of human associations. In several cases, whereas spring death once was evidence of natural causes (1987:Table 1), later it was evidence of scavenging (2009:59–61). In a chain of inference so closely related to analogy with living elephants, when taphonomic data do not match living analogues (e.g., evidence of tusk injury from musth combat) they are explained away (e.g., "different tusk geometry" [2009:62]).

Fisher's scenarios involve extensive use of at least a few casually discarded bone tools but no discard of presumably extensively used stone ones. G. Haynes (1991, 2002b:155) considered this scenario improbable—like using shovels to dig for sharp-edged rocks that then could be used to dig further. The taphonomy of cutmarks is highly contested (Borrero and Martin 2012; Krasinski 2010). It is interesting, if not conclusive, that butchering of modern elephants using modern tools can yield no discernable cutmarks (G. Haynes 1991:185). Patterns of disarticulation are influenced by skeletal anatomy, not just human and natural predation (O'Connell et al. 1992:333; Stopp 1997).

Fisher explained the absence of stone tools at his kill sites by noting that some were not excavated to archaeological standards, particularly sediment screening, and higher "degree of curation and conservation of lithic materials by Paleoindians of the Great Lakes" (1987:316) than, presumably, elsewhere. The first point is legitimate but applies only to some of Fisher's sites. Even those professionally excavated yielded no tools, and even fine-scale recovery elsewhere yielded few or no tools (Kimmswick excepted). The second is unpersuasive without specific theoretical explanation or evidence of highest Paleoindian curation rates in the Midwest. Western Clovis elephant sites greatly surpass the Midwest in tool incidence, yet western Clovis, if anything, should have higher curation rates.

Caching also figures in Fisher's argument (1996; 2009:58), partly to explain the absence of stone tools not needed in such contexts. But his ethnographic analogy is equivocal (Taylor 1969: 145). It clearly describes meat caches on land— not the water-caching inferred—and possible discard inconsistent with Fisher's "passive-solar-ice" scenario followed by desperate retrieval months later when food was short (2009:58). Two passages describe retrieval of what may have been carcasses apparently not cached but discarded (Taylor 1969:154, 163). There is possible but ambiguous ethnographic support for the caching that Fisher inferred. On balance, of his three arguments to explain the scarcity of stone tools at Midwestern proboscidean sites, one is partially supported, one is undemonstrated, and one is equivocal.

Arguments against Overkill

If many archaeologists advocate overkill, others demur. Few archaeologists would deny Paleoindians some role in hastening extinctions. The question is whether proboscideans would have gone extinct, perhaps slightly later, if people were not there to help them along. These archaeologists argue, in effect, that extinction was largely a natural process aided secondarily by people. To them, proboscideans were extinctions waiting to happen.

If extinction was caused chiefly by natural processes that unfolded at Pleistocene's end, it is fair to ask why earlier maxima produced no comparable large-scale events. Before Pleistocene's end, after all, the most recent extinction pulse in proboscideans occurred 4.5 million years ago (Fisher 1996:296–297). It remains to determine the timing and character of environmental change during each glacial cycle in the Pleistocene. Nevertheless, the end-Pleistocene Younger Dryas event, whether global or not, may have differed qualitatively from earlier interglacial changes in pacing and severity (McFarlane 1999:102), although recent research implicates warming, not cooling, trends in Holarctic extinctions (Cooper et al. 2015).

Mammoths had rather narrow ecological tolerances that almost certainly doomed them in the Late Pleistocene's climatic furies even had humans never reached North America. No less was the case in Europe, central Asia, and Siberia (Lorenzen et al. 2011; Owen-Smith 1999:58; Pitulko and Nikolskiy 2012; Soffer 1993:41–44). Broader diet and habitat preferences made mastodons a hardier species but one already experiencing natural stresses that invited extinction before humans arrived (Guthrie 1984; King and Saunders 1984; Teale and Miller 2012). In particular, they may have been declining in size at Pleistocene's end (King and Saunders 1984: 331; again, so too in the Old World [Soffer 1993: 41]), evidence of selective conditions that acted against large animals (cf. Fisher 1996:313). Also, the distribution and abundance of their forage deteriorated markedly (King and Saunders 1984:336).

Global patterns of Pleistocene megafaunal extinctions are complex and vary by taxa (Cooper et al. 2015; Lorenzen et al. 2011; Owen-Smith 1999:58; Wroe and Field 2006). In Eurasia, recent interpretations of the time distribution of end-Pleistocene fossils suggest that "the process of mammoth extinction was complex in time and space" (Stuart et al. 2002:1568; see also Ugan and Byers 2007) and occurred as a single broad range fragmented. Isolated populations in shrinking patches of range went extinct separately, and in cases at surprisingly late times (Fisher 2009:Table 4.2; MacPhee et al. 2002; Stuart et al. 2002:Tables 1, 3; Vartanyan et al. 1995; Woodman and Athfield 2009). By implication, something other than similar environmental changes between North America and Eurasia must explain the difference. Yet differences between Eurasia and North America may be illusory. Extinctions were synchronous on the two continents and there were more megafaunal taxa in North America, hence more candidates for extinction there (McFarlane 1999:102). The time-space complexity of Eurasian extinctions may owe as much to thorough sampling and comparatively fine chronological resolution as to actual differences between the regions.

Around the world, some taxa went extinct well before Pleistocene's end, others circa 12,000–10,000 RCYBP, whatever their association with humans. Although Mithen (1993; see also Soffer 1993:36–38) considered Eurasian mammoths highly susceptible to extinction, their persistence long after the arrival of modern humans suggests that people hunted mammoths very little (although Table 11.1 compiles some relevant data). Even if hunting contributed to mammoth extinction there (Drucker et al. 2015), it followed millennia of coexistence. Megafauna like rhinoceri and mammoths survived in Europe to Pleistocene's end (Lorenzen et al. 2011; Ugan and Byers 2007), nearly 30,000 rc years *after* modern humans—let alone Neanderthals—hunted them there, and the correlation in Australia between human arrival and megafaunal extinction may be more apparent than real (Wroe and Field 2006). There is no clear correspondence between human (biologically modern or otherwise) colonization and megafaunal extinction. The pattern suggests that range fragmentation caused extinction in a series of local events patchily distributed across Eurasia (Lorenzen et al. 2011; Stuart et al. 2002:1567). Calibrating for time-space differences, evidence of human hunting of now-extinct fauna is 27 times greater in France than in North America (Grayson and

Meltzer 2002:341; cf. Surovell and Grund 2012). Yet few archaeologists see a human role in Pleistocene extinctions in France. Dramatic natural reordering of biotic communities and selection regimes attended Late Pleistocene environmental change, change that was bad for large-bodied, slow-reproducing mammals (e.g., Cooper et al. 2015; Graham and Lundelius 1984; Lorenzen et al. 2011).

At Pleistocene's end, North America was populated also by sloths and other megafauna found in the Midwest in apparent human association (Redmond et al. 2012; Redmond and Tankersley 2005). Yet few archaeologists ascribe their demise to Paleoindian hunters (Martin et al. 1985 and possibly Surovell and Grund 2012 are exceptions, at least with respect to sloths; cf. Borrero and Martin 2012; McFarlane 1999:101). Among these taxa, extinction generally occurred earliest in larger ones, suggesting natural causes (Tankersley and Redmond 2000:46). Moreover, Midwestern and nearby Paleoindians hunted caribou and small game (e.g., Storck and Spiess 1994) that survive today. Limited evidence of hunting does not prove overkill.

The noticeable Late Pleistocene spike in dated North American proboscidean and other megafaunal fossils (e.g., Ugan and Byers 2007:Figure 6) does not characterize all proboscidean taxa and may owe less to human agency than to the disproportionate rewards for studying discoveries that might bear on the question of human role in extinctions (Meltzer and Mead 1985) or preservation effects (Ugan and Byers 2007: 3068). Even at face value, the sharp terminal-Pleistocene decline in North America leaves recorded occurrences at high rates relative to the earlier Pleistocene (Ugan and Byers 2007:Figure 6). Late Pleistocene spikes and latest-Pleistocene drops may be sample effects so are not unambiguous population measures (Grayson and Meltzer 2015; cf. G. Haynes 2009).

Some unusual evidence thought to bear upon overkill is ambiguous. Trends in *Sporormiella* dung fungi—an esoteric data source if ever one existed—might reflect proboscidean population trajectories in ways considered consistent (e.g., Fiedel 2009:25; Halligan et al. 2016; Robinson et al. 2005) or inconsistent (Gill et al. 2009)

with overkill. Yet specific fungi are not firmly and uniquely associated with proboscideans, nor is their abundance clearly calibrated to corresponding proboscidean abundance. Neither does the proboscidean radiocarbon record clearly correlate with *Sporormiella* abundance (Feranec et al. 2011). Until this proxy measure is improved, it is not a reliable basis for inference.

Scientific questions such as Pleistocene extinctions are not settled simply by consensus. In this case, natural scientists do not all agree on overkill (cf. Waguespack 2014:312) nor that climatic causes are "vague" (cf. Fiedel 2009:21). To Saunders, for instance, "Environmental insularity explains the extinction of *M. americanum*" (1996:279; see also Barnosky et al. 2004; Brook and Bowman 2004; Cooper et al. 2015; Feranec et al. 2011; Graham 2001:708–709; Guthrie 2006; King and Saunders 1984; Lima-Ribeiro and Diniz-Filho 2013; Lorenzen et al. 2011; Lundelius 1987; Nogués-Bravo et al. 2008; Prescott et al. 2012; Saunders 1996; Teale and Miller 2012; Ugan and Byers 2007; Wolverton et al. 2009; Yansa and Adams 2012; Yule et al. 2009; Zazula et al. 2014). Moreover, the reproductive constraints of large body size may be graver than appreciated (Cardillo et al. 2005) and, at least in places, the chronological overlap of humans and proboscideans may have been short (Boulanger and Lyman 2014; Guthrie 2006), although again some evidence suggests that proboscideans survived to surprisingly late times (e.g., Woodman and Athfield 2009). To some archaeologists and natural scientists, therefore, the fate of North American mastodons and mammoths suggests a natural process of global extent that occurred amid drastic environmental change. Humans may have hastened the end (Cooper et al. 2015: 605–606; Pitulko and Nikolskiy 2012) but not necessarily have caused it.

Evidence of Human Association

Human-proboscidean association must be proven, not assumed merely from common occurrence in geological deposits. Stone-tool evidence is desirable, but not always definitive. The mere presence of stone of any kind in deposits where it cannot occur naturally may be evidence of association, but elephants ingest stones and can pass them up to 50 km from their sources (G. Haynes 1991:139). G. Haynes discovered flakes and possible flake tools in spurious stratigraphic association with bones from a natural site frequented by African elephants (1991:139, Figure 4.16). Stone tools and animal bones also associated spuriously if they accumulated in the same deposits by different natural processes (Stopp 1997:4–6; Villa and Soressi 2000:203). Taphonomy provides many examples of the need first to demonstrate association and then to explain it in behavioral or other terms (e.g., Brain 1981; Stopp 1997). Gamble (1999:146) assayed the problem in European Paleolithic studies. In North America, the Hiscock site may be partly a lag deposit whose human-elephant association owes to geological, not cultural, processes (Laub et al. 1988). Krasinski found no evidence of mastodon butchery there (2010:378). The Moon Mammoth may be associated with "netstones" (Kirkpatrick and Fisher 1993:70). In Kentucky, the Adams site yielded no chipped stone tools but did produce limestone cobbles apparently not of natural occurrence there, possibly used to fracture mastodon bone (Walters 1988:46).

Still, fluted bifaces or other chipped-stone tools of undoubted human origin are strong evidence of association, particularly if found in quantity. They are in western North America (e.g., G. Haynes 1991:Table 7.1; Saunders 1981). On the Plains, association between humans and proboscideans at Clovis sites such as Dent now appears certain (Brunswig 2007; cf. Hofman 1996:51, 53). Hofman doubted association at Lange-Ferguson because Clovis specimens were found some distance from mammoth bones, but at least one flake lay in the bone bed (Hannus 1990:Figure 4). Recent excavations at Page-Ladson yielded an unquestionable biface and several flakes distributed along with elements of at least two mastodons in three depositional units, two of which bear combined chronological spans of >750 years (Halligan et al. 2016:Figures 2, S25, Table S6). Comparable Midwestern evidence is more elusive. Proboscideans may have been associated with stone tools at Koch Springs and Boney Springs in western Missouri, although the associations seem secondary

(McMillan 1976:84, 92). Demonstrably late Holocene artifacts occurred at depth near proboscidean fossils, but McMillan (1976:92) considered the association geological, not archaeological. At least one biface from Koch Springs is stemmed (Wood 1976:Figure 6.8), probably Early Archaic in age. Similar "late introductions" at nearby Trolinger Springs also were associated with mastodon bones (Wood 1976:99).

We can only wonder what Midwestern evidence was unearthed long ago but not properly documented. Koch Springs and Boney Springs (McMillan 1976:83–84; Williams 1957:362–364), Boaz (Palmer and Stoltman 1976), Hardin (Lepper 1983), Ashtabula County (Murphy 1983), and other Ohio sites (McDonald 1994:28) are candidates for tool–proboscidean association that cannot be resolved on current evidence. The 1897 Boaz discovery and much later memory documentation render the association unknowable. Passing reference to "spear heads" found with mastodons at Sedalia, Missouri circa 1880 are intriguing (Mehl 1966:5). Indiana's Richmond mastodon may have been killed by humans, although the corner-notched bifaces found near it probably are not associated (Kevin Smith, personal communication 2001), and Orleton Farms *might* be associated with a stemmed biface (Williams 1957:365–366, Figures 5g–i), although its excavator did not think so (Thomas 1952:5). Koons's (2014) microscopic examination of Orleton bones found no evidence of human association. Nor do mastodon remains found within several km of northeastern Wisconsin Paleoindian sites constitute association (Mason 2007). McDonald reported possible but unauthenticated human-proboscidean associations in Ohio (1994:28). There is a late-nineteenth century reference to association of fluted points and proboscideans at Big Bone Lick, but in modern excavations tools "appear to lie in a secondary context among a palimpsest of mastodon bone" (Tankersley et al. 2009:566). Willard yielded two "flint finishing tools" 20 m from mastodon remains; to judge from the associated site records, one is an Early Archaic stemmed or bifurcate-base point (Falquet and Hanebert 1978). In 1921, an Illinois farmer reported three fluted bifaces "found with a tooth as big as your fist" (Munson and Tankersley 1991:3).

Tantalizing possibilities aside, by conventional standards only Kimmswick provides unequivocal evidence: fluted bifaces found near proboscidean bones, along with lithic debris (Graham et al. 1981). Grayson and Meltzer (2002:337–341) added only Pleasant Lake and, ambiguously, Hebior among Midwestern occurrences to their continental list of accepted associations. An update deleted Hebior (Grayson and Meltzer 2015). Elsewhere, the best associations are at Martins Creek and Schaefer, which yielded proboscidean remains in apparent association with stone tools of various kinds (Brush and Smith 1994; Overstreet 1996, 1998; Overstreet and Kolb 2003; cf. Grayson and Meltzer 2015). At Trolinger Springs, however, chert pieces that were originally claimed as chipped debris are not apparently cultural in origin (Wood 1976:99). Kimmswick's faunal assemblage is diverse (Graham and Kay 1988:Table 1). Stone tools there might be associated with various taxa, but fluted points were found very near mastodon bones (Graham et al. 1981:1115). Earlier, poorly documented excavations suggest that the original Kimmswick assemblage was larger still (McMillan 1976; Morrow 1996:85–88).

There is possible evidence of bone tools elsewhere in North America (e.g., Gustafson et al. 1979:157 [cf. Grayson and Meltzer 2015]; Hannus 1990:Figures 7–20; Laub 2000 [cf. G. Haynes 2002b:127–128]; Norton et al. 1998; Webb 2006). Pleasant Lake and other Midwestern sites have possible expedient tools fashioned from the victim's bones (Fisher 1987; Shipman et al. 1984; Smith and Surface-Evans n.d.), but both direct evidence and the elaborate scenario of procurement and use makes the case uncertain (G. Haynes 1991:251–252). A possible wooden tool was found with the Dansville mastodon (Holman 1986), otherwise interpreted as a natural death (Fisher 1987). A "megamammal" long bone from Sheriden Cave, Ohio, was fashioned into a pointed tool (Tankersley 1999:70), although there is no other evidence of proboscideans there. Such evidence cannot be accepted until it survives the taphonomic scrutiny of incised proboscidean bone (Krasinski 2010; Purdy

et al. 2011) and European equivalents (e.g., Villa and d'Errico 2005).

Midwestern Evidence in Global Context

In the Midwest, most human-proboscidean associations are uncertain. Poor sampling (by circumstance, not design), relatively few well-excavated deposits, and the inherent ambiguity of interpretation all complicate the matter. Boaz, Koch Springs, and others offer no more than tantalizing possibilities. Sheriden Cave contained a fluted point, other stone tools, and possible bone tools (Redmond and Tankersley 2005:518–519) but no evidence for hunting or scavenging of proboscideans. Most Midwestern associations derive from taphonomic study of mastodons. The Rappuhn mastodon (Kapp 1986; Wittry 1965), the Grundel mastodon (Mehl 1966), Fisher's various sites (1987:Table I; 1996:Table 30.1; Kapp et al. 1990; Smith and Surface-Evans n.d.), and perhaps the Orleton Farms mastodon (Thomas 1952) are based on taphonomic evidence suggestive of human agency. Yet Grundel and the Miami mastodon in Missouri have questionably old dates (and equivocal stone tools at Miami; G. Haynes 2002b:53) so are difficult to accommodate to accumulated archaeological knowledge. "Chesrow Complex" sites have few tools, none diagnostic (Overstreet 1998).

Midwestern Paleoindians were merely a small part of the last great episode of prehistoric colonization, the human settlement of the Americas. It is common in western Clovis archaeology to place the American record in broader Pleistocene Eurasian context (e.g., Shott 2013). Accordingly, it is worth comparing Midwestern lithic and related evidence to data elsewhere on human-proboscidean association, whether hunting or scavenging. The comparison might even improve the chances of resolving the question in the Midwest. The question is, are Midwestern sites typical of proboscidean associations in their stone-tool counts? If so, there is no need to belabor the question. If not, then the difference demands explanation, not special pleading.

Table 11.1 crudely summarizes archaeological evidence from a selection of Old and New World

TABLE 11.1. Possible human-proboscidean associations from a selective global sample.

Continent	Midwest?	Site	Age[1]	Area Excavated[2]	MNI elephant	MNI mastodon	MNI mammoth	Chipped Stone[3]	Sources
Africa	no	Mwanganda	LP	96	1			314	Clark & Haynes 1970; cf. Wright et al. 2014
Africa	no	FLK North 1	LP	34	1			123	Clark & Haynes 1970:405; Leakey 1971:64
Africa	no	FLK North	LP					39	Leakey 1971:85
Africa	no	Barogali	LP	35	1			569	Berthelet & Chavaillon 2001
Africa	no	BK4b	LP	46				290	Domínguez-Rodrigo et al. 2014
Asia	no	Holon	LP	120	6			1415	Horwitz et al. n.d.
Asia	no	Revadim B2	LP	92	3			18,956	Rabinovich et al. 2012
Europe	no	Notachirico	LP	24	1			42	Milliken 1999; Mussi 2005; Piperno & Tagliacozzo 2001
Europe	no	Bilzingsleben	LP	355				2486	Gamble 1999:155–61
Europe	no	Ambrona AS3	LP	141	3			18	Villa et al. 2005:355–357
Europe	no	Ambrona AS4	LP	81				51	Villa et al. 2005:363–370
Europe	no	Ambrona	LP	57				2	Freeman 1994:Table 27-2; Howell 1966
Europe	no	Ambrona	LP					12	Freeman 1994:Table 27-2; Howell 1966
Europe	no	Ambrona	LP					3	Freeman 1994:Table 27-2; Howell 1966
Europe	no	Ambrona	LP					12	Freeman 1994:Table 27-2; Howell 1966
Europe	no	Ambrona	LP					13	Freeman 1994:Table 27-2; Howell 1966
Europe	no	Ambrona	LP					16	Freeman 1994:Table 27-2; Howell 1966
Europe	no	Ambrona	LP					3	Freeman 1994:Table 27-2; Howell 1966
Europe	no	Ambrona	LP					4	Freeman 1994:Table 27-2; Howell 1966
Europe	no	Ambrona	LP					32	Freeman 1994:Table 27-2; Howell 1966
Europe	no	Ambrona	LP					18	Freeman 1994:Table 27-2; Howell 1966
Africa	no	Olorgesailie 15	MP	64				2322	Potts et al. 1999
Africa	no	Nadung'a 4	MP	53	1			6797	Delagnes et al. 2006
Asia	no	GBY	MP	15	1			1491	Goren-Inbar et al. 1994
Europe	no	Lynford	MP	~250	11			2720	Schreve 2006; G. Smith 2012
Europe	no	Arenero de Rojas	MP		1			29	Panera et al. 2014; Yravedra et al. 2012
Europe	no	PRERESA	MP	255	1			754	Panera et al. 2014; Yravedra et al. 2012

Table 11.1. (cont'd.) Possible human-proboscidean associations from a selective global sample.

Continent	Midwest?	Site	Age[1]	Area Excavated[2]	MNI elephant	MNI mastodon	MNI mammoth	Chipped Stone[3]	Sources
Europe	no	EDAR Culebro 1	MP	150?	1			243	Panera et al. 2014; Yravedra et al. 2014
Europe	no	Southfleet Rd.	MP	24?	1?			~100	Wenban-Smith et al. 2006
Europe	no	Castel Guido	MP	1100+	11			1110	Boschian & Saccà 2010; Mussi 2005
Europe	no	Rebibbia	MP	~1200				~1500	Boschian & Saccà 2010; Mussi 2005
Europe	no	Isernia	MP?	80	1			~10,000	Gamble 1999:146–147; Milliken 1999
Europe	no	Grobern	MP	35	1			26	Gamble 1999:245; Gaudzinski 2004; Weber 2000
Europe	no	Karlich-Seeufer	MP	417				128	Gaudzinski et al. 1996
Europe	no	Aridos 1	MP	112	1			331	Santonja et al. 2001; cf. Gamble 1999:146
Europe	no	Aridos 2	MP	12	1			34	Gamble 1999:146; Santana et al. 2001
Europe	no	Torralba	MP	558				69	Freeman 1994; Howell 1966
Europe	no	Torralba	MP	558				111	Freeman 1994; Howell 1966
Europe	no	Polledrara	MP	20	1			61	Anzidei et al. 2012; Gamble 1999:147; Palombo et al. 2003
Europe	no	Soleihac	MP	24	2?			~20	Bonifay et al. 1976; Fosse 2000
Europe	no	Salzgitter-Lebenstedt	MP	150	16			2000	Gamble 1999; Staesche 1983
Europe	no	Lehringen	MP					25	Gamble 1999; Gaudzinski 2004; Weber 2000
Europe	no	Asolo	MP		1			5	Mussi 1999; Mussi & Villa 2008
Europe	no	Arriaga 2	MP	56	1			43	Panera et al. 2014; Santonja et al. 2001
Europe	no	La Cotte 3[4]	MP		7			129?	Callow 1986:Table 26.17; K. Scott 1986:Fig. 18.1; B. Scott et al. 2014; G. Smith 2015:Table 8
Europe	no	La Cotte 6[4]	MP		11			8	Callow 1986:305; K. Scott 1986:Fig. 18.1
Europe	no	Ariendorf	MP	~70	1			37	Gaudzinski et al. 2004
Asia	no	Lk. Nojiri	UP	40? 6700?	1				Kondo et al. 2001
Asia	no	Shikaevka 2	UP	740	2			35	Kuzmin 2008
Asia	no	Lugovskoye	UP		27			~300	Maschenko et al. 2003
Europe	no	Fastov	UP	220	11			1888	Soffer 1985
Europe	no	Kurovo	UP	248	1			25	Soffer 1985

Table 11.1. (cont'd.) Possible human-proboscidean associations from a selective global sample.

Continent	Midwest?	Site	Age[1]	Area Excavated[2]	MNI elephant	MNI mastodon	MNI mammoth	Chipped Stone[3]	Sources
Europe	no	Pushkari 2	UP	58	17			85	Soffer 1985
Europe	no	Yudinovo	UP	800	63			80000	Germonpré et al. 2008
Europe	no	Halich	UP	65				105	Wojtal & Cyrek 2001
Europe	no	Krems-Wachtberg 3	UP	15	8			2300	Fladerer 2001
Europe	no	Kraków Spadzista	UP	150	86			7405	Wojtal & Sobczyk 2005; cf. Soffer 1993
Europe	no	Valea Morilor	UP	1264	6			73	Obada et al. 2012
N. Amer.	no	Fin del Mundo	UP	~56		2		31	Sanchez et al. 2014
N. Amer.	no	Guest	UP	54			2	7	Rayl 1974
N. Amer.	no	Domebo	UP	22			1	6	Leonhardy 1966
N. Amer.	no	Miami, TX	UP	75			5	4	Holliday et al. 1994
N. Amer.	no	Naco	UP	34			1	8	Haury 1953
N. Amer.	no	Lehner	UP	63			8	30	Haury et al. 1959
N. Amer.	no	Colby	UP	123			7	36	Frison & Todd 1986
N. Amer.	no	Dent	UP				15	3	Brunswig 2007
N. Amer.	no	Lubbock Lk.	UP	161			3	0	Johnson & Holliday 1987
N. Amer.	no	Lange-Ferguson	UP	34			2	1	Hannus 1990
N. Amer.	no	Coates-Hines	UP	17		1		34	Breitburg et al. 1996; Deter-Wolf et al. 2011
N. Amer.	no	Sloth Hole	UP			1		1	Hemmings 1998
N. Amer.	no	Manis	UP	158		1		1	Gustafson et al. 1979
N. Amer.	no	Blackwater Dr.	UP	47			1	11	Boldurian & Cotter 1999
N. Amer.	no	Moon	UP	60		1		0	Kirkpatrick & Fisher 1993
N. Amer.	no	Adams	UP	16		1		0	Walters 1988
N. Amer.	no	Duewall-Newberry	UP	21			1	0	Steele & Carson 1989
N. Amer.	no	Owl Cave	UP				1	11	Miller 1989; Miller & Dort 1978
N. Amer.	no	Page-Ladson	UP	46				8	Webb 2006; Halligan et al. 2016
N. Amer.	no	Wenas Ck.	UP	46			1	2	Lubinski et al. 2007; Lubinski et al. 2008; Lubinski et al. 2009
N. Amer.	no	Escapule	UP	124			1	2	E. Hemmings & Haynes 1967
N. Amer.	no	Murray Springs	UP	350			1	9481	C. Haynes & Huckell 2007
N. Amer.	no	Lovewell	UP	13			1	0	Holen 2006
N. Amer.	no	Hiscock	UP			8		7	Laub et al. 1988
N. Amer.	yes	Grundel	UP	1580		1		0	Mehl 1966
N. Amer.	yes	Power	UP	52		1		0	Garland & Cogswell 1985
N. Amer.	yes	Kimmswick C1[5]	UP	20		1		~100	Graham 1986; Graham et al. 1981; Graham & Kay 1988
N. Amer.	yes	Kimmswick C3[5]	UP	48		1		~100	Graham 1986; Graham et al. 1981; Graham & Kay 1988

TABLE 11.1. (cont'd.) Possible human-proboscidean associations from a selective global sample.

Continent	Midwest?	Site	Age[1]	Area Excavated[2]	MNI elephant	MNI mastodon	MNI mammoth	Chipped Stone[3]	Sources
N. Amer.	yes	Martins Creek	UP	64			1	10	Brush & Smith 1994; Brush & Yerkes 1996
N. Amer.	yes	Hebior	UP	30			1	3	Overstreet 1998
N. Amer.	yes	Pleasant Lk.	UP	36			1	0	Shipman et al. 1984
N. Amer.	yes	Rappuhn	UP				1	0	Kapp 1986; Wittry 1965
N. Amer.	yes	Richmond	UP	82			1	2	Sanford 1935
N. Amer.	yes	Orleton	UP	15			1	0	Thomas 1952
N. Amer.	yes	Willard	UP				1	2	Falquet & Hanebert 1978
N. Amer.	yes	Schaefer	UP	42			1	2	Joyce 2006, 2014; Overstreet 1998
N. Amer.	yes	Buesching	UP	92			1	0	Smith & Surface-Evans 2003; Surface-Evans 2004
N. Amer.	yes	Burning Tree	UP					0	Fisher et al. 1994
N. Amer.	yes	Dansville	UP				1	0	Holman 1986
N. Amer.	yes	Miami, MO	UP				1	3?	Hamilton 1993
N. Amer.	yes	Andrews	UP				1	0	Kuehn et al. 2010

[1] LP = Lower Paleolithic; MP = Middle Paleolithic; UP = Upper Paleolithic/Paleoindian
[2] in square meters
[3] all chipped stone, including flakes
[4] La Cotte de St. Brelade
[5] Kimmswick is exceptional by Midwestern standards, but its tool-count remains uncertain. The site has a complex excavation history (Morrow 1996:85–88, 114). One fluted point excavated in the early 1900s may derive from the C1 and C3 strata that were the focus of Graham et al.'s (1981) fieldwork. Kimmswick C1 includes at least four undoubted stone tools (Graham and Kay 1981:Fig. 2) and "hundreds" of flakes (Graham 1986:65; Graham and Kay 1981:1115). C3 includes at least two tools and unspecified "chert flakes" (Graham and Kay 1981:1115). Graham and Kay reported no additional tools but a projection from apparently limited sampling to "thousands of microflakes" (1988:238) in both C1 and C3. The site was excavated using ¹⁄₁₆-in (3.2-mm) mesh (Graham and Kay 1988:228; Morrow 1996:110), much finer than the ¼-in (6.3 mm) mesh used in most excavations. Absent detailed reporting, how many of the thousands of flakes estimated for each stratum are ≥6.3 mm—the fraction recovered in most excavations—is unknown. Graham's and Kay's wording implies that only by counting flakes ≤6.3 mm do the C1 and C3 assemblages exceed 1,000, but also that the assemblages include flakes from "resharpening of...tools, and initial tool manufacture" (1988:238), many of which probably are ≥6.3 mm and should be counted among artifacts. In this uncertainty, I assume that "thousands" = 1,000 and that one-tenth of that figure is tools and flakes that measure ≥6.3 mm, thus estimating that each Kimmswick stratum contains ~100 flakes and tools.

Notes:
Discrepancies in area excavated. At Notarchirico, Milliken (1999:22) reported 500+ m² excavated, Gamble (1999: 145–146) only 24 m², a major discrepancy that presumably reflects overall excavated area versus a smaller elephant locus. Assuming that Milliken's higher figure pertains to the entire site, not just the level or area that bears elephant bones, I use Gamble's figure. Gaudzinski (2004:204) reported 20 m² excavated at Grobern, while Gamble (1999:Fig. 5.12) showed elephant bones in an excavation area measuring about 35 m². Excavated areas are difficult to estimate from K. Scott (1980:Figs. 5, 6; 1986:Figs. 18.2, 18.3). As very rough estimates, Layer 3 encompasses at least 13 m², Layer 6 18 m². Scott did not report numbers of stone tools found. Two sources consulted on Owl Cave (Miller 1989; Miller and Dort 1978) reported the faunal and tool assemblages but not area excavated. Nor was such information reported for Manis (Gustafson et al. 1979). Elsewhere, area excavated was not reported but could be estimated from scaled plans (e.g., Johnson 1987:Fig. 10.1; Rayl 1974). Even when reported, figures can be uncertain. Coats-Hines (Breitburg et al. 1996; Deter-Wolf et al. 2011) is one site, but four sections were excavated separated by 20–60 m. Area excavated was estimated from small-scale maps. Area B apparently measured about 35 m² in total (Deter-Wolf et al. 2011:Fig. 1), its "bone bed" only about 14 m² (Deter-Wolf et al. 2011:Fig. 6). To maximize tool density, I use the smaller figure. Some reported artifacts are unconvincing, to judge from illustrations (Deter-Wolf et al. 2011:Fig. 11).

Discrepancies in tool-count. For Martins Creek, Brush and Smith (1994:15) reported six tools, Brush and Yerkes (1996:55) 10 tools. Jones (1980:Table 2) reported different figures for stone tools at Mwanganda, FLK NI Bed 1, and Lehringer than did other sources cited. I use the higher figures on the assumption that Jones did not also count unused flakes. For instance, Clark and Haynes (1970:394) reported 314 stone tools at Mwanganda's Village, Jones (1980:Table 2) only 172. Presumably the higher figure includes unretouched flakes omitted from Jones's table. Goren-Inbar et al. (1994:107) reported apparently partial tool-counts of 1,491 at GBY but also 37,000 artifacts <2 cm. To K. Scott there were "virtually no artefacts" (1980:141) in the mammoth bone beds of Levels 3 and 6 at La Cotte de St. Brelade, but Callow (1986:Table 26.17) reported 129 stone tools from Levels 3, and eight from Layer 6 (1986:305). Moreover, B. Scott et al. (2014:25) reported 786 from Layer 3 and 31,847 from the underlying stratum with which they associated it. If so, then La Cotte Layer 3's stone tool-count is as low as 129 or as high as 786 + 31,847 = 32,633, a difference that exceeds two orders of magnitude and that probably also derives from a much larger area than shown for Layer 3.

Asolo's tool-count may be low. Mussi reported that "only 5" tools were retained from this "incomplete assemblage" (1999:56). Milliken (1999:16) reported "tens of thousands" of stone tools from 80 m² of floor 3a at Isernia La Pineta; Gamble (1999:147), 137 tools from 130 m². Horwitz et al. (n.d.) reported 1,415 stone tools at Holon; Malinsky-Buller (2014:Table 1), 2,941. Five stone tools were found at Miami (Holliday et al. 1994:236–240), but the site was not screened, so small flake debris may have passed unnoticed. At Owl Cave, Miller and Dort (1978:131) reported three Folsom fluted points, one biface, "fragments" of obsidian, basalt flakes, and "miscellaneous" thinning flakes. Miller (1989:Table 1) reported the same four bifaces along with seven flakes. None of the fluted points retained the base (Miller and Dort 1978:Fig. 6). Although flute channels approached the tip, Folsom assignment must be uncertain. Channel erosion may have removed stone tools from Aridos, affecting the tool-count much more than proboscidean MNI (Santoja et al. 2001: 604–605). Stone artifact counts, including flakes, may not be comparable across sites, depending upon collection practices and scale of recovery.

Lacking such information in many cases, I use figures at face value, mindful of the possible error. Most discrepancies in tool-counts were settled by using the smaller figure (e.g., La Cotte). For some analytical purposes, high tool-count sites (e.g., Kimmswick, Murray Springs, and several Eurasian Upper Paleolithic sites) were omitted. Before any analysis, however, even more extreme outliers Yudinovo and Isernia were removed entirely from the dataset. Some counts are approximate (indicated by "~" in Table 11.1).

Other Problems. For Notarchirico, Gamble reported an elephant MNI of 1, but Milliken said that most animal bones found were of elephant, which suggests but does not prove a higher MNI. Many possibly relevant cases do not appear or are incomplete in Table 11.1 because they lack figures for some categories, usually area excavated (e.g., various Ambrona loci [Freeman 1994]) but sometimes proboscidean MNI or stone tool-count. Milliken (1999, 2001) reported elephant bones from several tool-bearing Italian Middle Paleolithic sites, but details of excavation and tool and faunal assemblages were limited. Among them is Asolo, where in 1878 a single mammoth was found with stone tools (Milliken 2001:24; Mussi 1999:56–57). Unfortunately, only five of a larger assemblage of stone tools were retained. Kondo and colleagues reported unspecified "flakes and chips" (2001:286) at Lake Nojiri. Mont-Dol yielded elephant remains and a substantial tool assemblage, but neither the assemblage's size nor excavated area were reported (Monnier et al. 1995). Lower Bed II at Olduvai Gorge's FLK North yielded deinotherium fossils and 39 artifacts, including manuports, but area excavated was not indicated (Leakey 1971:85). From Antoine and colleagues' (2006) Figure 2, relevant excavated area at Caours measures roughly 85 m², and that source reported about 300 tools from two excavation areas (2006:309), and *P. antiquus* MNI of 1. But it does not report from which of the two excavated areas the proboscidean remains derived. Taubach's excavation area measured over 1 *km²*, and Moncel and Rivals (2011) did not report MNI or tool-counts. Mammoth MNI = 21 at Milovice Sector G (Péan and Patou-Mathis 2003:Fig. 5). Sector G's area might be approximated as 420 m² (Brugère et al. 2006:Fig. 3), but the substantial lithic assemblage there was not enumerated in sources consulted. Some sites omitted nevertheless testify to substantial stone-tool assemblages associated with proboscideans. The Zoo Park elephant was associated with "a quartz stone industry" (MacCalman 1967:102) of unspecified size. Foz do Enxarrique's megafaunal remains were associated with a "very rich lithic assemblage" (Sousa and Figueiredo 2001:614).

This table was compiled, and its data analyzed in early 2015. Halligan and colleagues (2016) reported at least two mastodons and other megafauna associated with at least five flakes and one biface from Page-Ladson, all in deposits dated to pre-Clovis age. Most proboscidean elements were reported from Unit 3c, but others were found in a depositional sequence from Unit 3a to 4b. A sequence of equally spaced radiocarbon dates (at approximately 7-cm intervals) taken across this depositional range is not entirely consistent (Halligan et al. 2016:Fig. 2H). The highest position in this sequence gave two dates, 12,335 ± 35 and 12,270 ± 30, the lowest a single date of 12,615±35. Other dates near the sequence's base are probably statistically indistinguishable from those at its top. Between them are several dates >13,000 RCYBP and one at 14,510 ± 40. Halligan and colleagues (2016:Table S6) report that Units 4b and 3c alone span >300 yr each. Page-Ladson deposits may not be primary. If so, the human-proboscidean association is unclear.

sites where people and proboscideans evidently were associated. Proboscideans were found at all listed sites but are not always the most common taxon as measured by MNI (minimum number of individuals) or otherwise. MNI in Table 11.1 are for proboscideans only. Although they are identified as mastodon, mammoth, and other elephant taxa, in analysis all are pooled as unspecified proboscidean. Table 11.1 lists only chipped stone tools, not also cobbles possibly that were used as netstones, etc. Distinctions drawn between deposits—stratigraphically and spatially—are taken as reported.

Elsewhere in North America, only the Southwest has apparently unambiguous evidence of human association. Yet Owl Cave in eastern Idaho also suggests that Paleoindians hunted these animals (Miller 1989). Possible tools fashioned from mastodon bone found at Hiscock in New York State document association there, if not necessarily implicating people in the demise of the animals. Also, there are many possible associations reported from Florida stream channels and sinkholes (e.g., Halligan et al. 2016; Webb 2006). Besides the possible bone tools noted above, a single stone flake of possible human origin was found at Manis in western Washington (Gustafson et al. 1979:Figure 6). Dixon (2001:278) considered this evidence unequivocal (2001:278), but G. Haynes asserts that its pattern and distribution "are not unusual noncultural occurrences for elephant skeletons in the wild" (2002b:71; see also Grayson and Meltzer 2015; C. Haynes and Huckell 2016). The Clovis area at Lubbock Lake, Texas, included mammoths and other megafauna in possible fluvial context (Johnson 1987:121). "Pounding stones and…boulders" but no chipped stone tools were associated with proboscideans, and such cobbles were on a gravel bar "buried by sandy over-bank sediments" (Johnson and Holliday 1987:101). I excluded La Sena in Nebraska (Holen 2006), both because its age is extreme even by the current liberal pre-Clovis standard and because human association was based entirely on skeletal taphonomy that G. Haynes and Krasinski questioned (2010:194–196).

Latin America is vast but poorly investigated by comparison to North America. Despite the confidence of some archaeologists there, claims for antiquity and association are ambiguous and difficult to reconcile with the evidence of human antiquity elsewhere in the Americas. The growing Latin American evidence (e.g., Arroyo-Cabrales et al. 2006; Politis et al. 2014:57–63) deserves careful study not attempted here. I ignore it except for Fin del Mundo (Sanchez et al. 2014), given its proximity to political North America.

Old World evidence is much more abundant, probably a consequence of the history of archaeological research there. Even so, comparison remains problematic in some respects. First, the differences of time and place with North America are further complicated by taxonomy: many sites of possible associations there are with Lower or Middle Paleolithic premodern hominids. Second, the vast European literature was accessed only in Spanish, French, or English and too often via secondary sources. Third, that vast record also is diverse. Sites often contain other megafauna as well as proboscideans, which by minimum number of individuals (MNI) or inferred meat yield sometimes are minor constituents. Some sites lack elephants or include few among the taxa reported (e.g., the Salzgitter-Lebenstedt site; Staesche 1983:176–179). To some degree, it is arbitrary to separate Old World sites with elephants from the larger corpus of megafaunal evidence. Fourth, the same taphonomic doubts that plague New World sites occur in the Old World. Old World scholars pioneered taphonomic studies that repeatedly threw doubt on archaeological associations between people and Pleistocene animals (e.g., Villa et al. 2005; Villa and Soressi 2000; see also Domínguez-Rodrigo 2006:137, who considered Olduvai's FLK North, cited in Table 11.1, mostly a palimpsest with only possible hominid associations). Fifth, extent of sampling was measured by area excavated in m², estimated from scaled plans when not reported, but depth of excavation was not recorded.

Torralba and Ambrona are prime examples of ambiguity. Howell (1966:127–131) reported the number of stone tools for various floors or other contexts, but excavation size only for a few. Recent work and sophisticated taphonomic interpretation cast doubt on earlier interpretations (Villa et al. 2005). Elsewhere in Italy, Isernia included "tens of thousands" of tools, flakes, and elephant bones amid a diverse faunal assemblage (Milliken 1999:16) but may be a secondary deposit (Gamble 1999:146–147). Kärlich-Seeufer in the central Rhineland traditionally is interpreted as an Acheulean *Elephas* kill site, partly on the strength of wooden and bone tools, but may be a secondary association (Gaudzinski et al. 1996). Among eastern European Upper Paleolithic sites, only the few identified as kills or otherwise lacking obvious bone used as building material were included (Soffer 1985:Tables 2.3, 2.5; 1993).

Returning to North America, not all listed Midwestern sites are universally accepted. Grayson and Meltzer (2015) rejected several sites listed here, questioning the distribution of bones and association with possible stone tools, cutmarks, and dating for Hebior, Schaefer, and other southeastern Wisconsin sites. On taphonomic grounds, Mehl (1966:20–21) argued for human agency in the Grundel mastodon's death, but the individual's age and condition (1966: 8–9) are more consistent with Fisher's natural-death scenario. Krasinski (2010:364,376) could not confirm identification of "cutmarks" at Mud Lake, Wisconsin, not considered here.

Table 11.1 surely is not comprehensive. G. Smith (2015:Table 8) reported about 30 western European Middle Paleolithic sites with proboscidean remains not accessed here, although proboscideans were not the most common taxon in many. A number of North American mastodon sites, some possibly with human associations, listed in Fiedel (2009:Table 2.1), Fisher (2009:Table 4.1), and G. Haynes (2002b:Table 5.8; 2009:Table 3.2) either are not published or sources were unavailable. (Table 11.1 includes only Pleasant Lake, Buesching, and Burning Tree among the 29 mastodons reported by Fisher [2009:Table 4.1].) Table 11.1 includes most "reliable" mastodon-association dates listed by Faith and Surovell (2009:Table S2), all of Grayson and

Meltzer's (2015:Table 6), as well as some that neither source listed (e.g., Hebior, which Grayson and Meltzer omit). I did not consult the substantial northeastern North American proboscidean occurrences compiled by Boulanger and Lyman (2014:supplementary data). On balance, Table 11.1 data are necessarily incomplete and unavoidably noisy. Only the most robust patterns should be sought in them.

Interpreting the Evidence

Whatever problems that reside in evidence from world proboscidean sites, Midwestern data can only profit from comparison. Before considering tool-count itself, I seek possible effects of excavated area ("area") and proboscidean MNI on tool-counts. All else being equal, higher tool-count might be expected where larger areas were excavated and/or more proboscideans found. However, data must be filtered, in cases by confining analysis to sites associated with modern humans, and/or by removing outliers. Tool-count distribution has outliers in the Midwest (Kimmswick C1 and C3), elsewhere in North America (Murray Springs; C. Haynes and Huckell 2007), and in the Old World Upper Paleolithic (Kraków Spadzista and others).

There is no correlation between area and tool-count in Midwestern data ($r = -.18$, $p = .62$), in all North American data ($r = .14$, $p = .46$), in all modern-human data ($r = .05$, $p = .77$), nor in all data ($r = .01$, $p = .92$). Sequential omission of two pairs of outliers (extreme ones Murray Springs and Kraków Spadzista, lesser ones Krems-Wachtberg 3 and Fastov) does not alter results. Area and tool-count are uncorrelated.

In the Midwest, all MNI = 1, so correlation with tool-count is impossible, although again Kimmswick is unusual due to its diverse faunal assemblages. In all North American data, MNI and tool-count are ambiguously correlated ($r = -.08$, $p = .64$; $r_s = .35$, $p = .03$). When Murray Springs is omitted, ambiguous correlation persists ($r = -.08$, $p = .62$; $r_s = .40$, $p = .01$), Kimmswick now the outlier. With both outliers removed, correlation improves ($r = .33$, $p = .05$; $r_s = .50$, $p = .00$). However, the resulting scatterplot is diffuse (Figure 11.2a). In all modern-

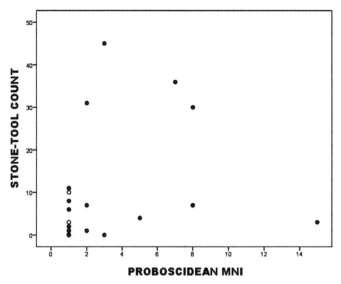

FIGURE 11.2a. Tool-count vs. proboscidean MNI. North American cases only, tool-count <100 (open circles = Midwest, shaded circles = other North American).

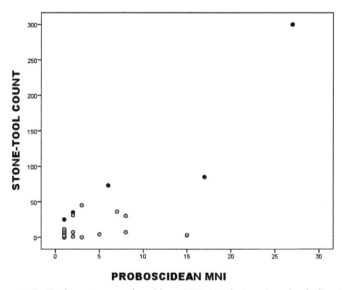

FIGURE 11.2b. Tool-count vs. proboscidean MNI. North American (excluding Midwest) and Old World Upper Paleolithic tool-count <1000 (shaded circles = Other North American, solid circles = Old World).

human data excluding the Midwest, with all four outliers noted above, or with Murray Springs and Kraków Spadzista omitted, or with all four omitted, correlation persists (e.g., without outliers, r = .81, p<.01). Even then, Lugovskoye is an outlier (Figure 11.2b), but the pattern seems as robust and further filtering seems unwise. Pattern persists even in all data (r = .27, p = .02). Tool-count and MNI are correlated. Although the relationship is diffuse, this result justifies comparison of Midwestern data not just to all other sites but also to single-carcass ones.

TABLE 11.2. Mean tool-count at Midwestern and other sites.

	All Cases		MNI = 1		Tool-count <100		MNI = 1 & Tool-count <100	
	n		n		n		n	
Midwest	17	12.9	17	12.9	15	1.3	15	1.3
Other N. America	23	421.5	12	793.6	22	9.7	11	3.8
Old World Upper Pal.	9	1357.3	1	25	4	54.5	1	25.0
All other Upper Pal.[1]	32	684.7	13	734.5	26	16.6	12	5.6
Old World Lower/Middle Pal.	46	969.0	20	685.6	24	24.3	8	34.6
All Old World	55	1032.5	21	654.1	28	28.8	9	33.6

[1] Includes other North American Paleoindian cases.

Tool-Count

Midwestern sites are not conspicuously under-sampled. On the contrary, mean area at Midwestern sites exceeds area elsewhere in North America, in all cases and where MNI = 1. It is lower than Old World values, but not significantly so. There is no statistical basis for concluding that Midwestern tool-count is low as a function of area excavated.

Tool-count at Midwestern sites is extremely nonnormal, Kimmswick swamping all others. Association is not doubted at Kimmswick, so to compare possible Midwestern sites with those elsewhere and to control for extreme outliers, Kimmswick must be distinguished for some analyses. In all analytical permutations, even those that include Kimmswick, mean Midwestern tool-count is less than comparators' (Table 11.2), so the question of difference reduces to statistical significance (Table 11.3). Confining cases to tool-count <100 omits Kimmswick in the Midwest, Murray Springs elsewhere in North America, and Kraków Spadzista and other Eurasian Upper Paleolithic sites. Confining cases to MNI = 1 focuses on single-carcass sites elsewhere (but again, other taxa occur at some sites), like all Midwestern sites except Kimmswick.

Working outward, Midwestern tool-count is significantly less than all other North American cases in U but not t, and other North American sites where tool-count <100 in both t and U. Despite a difference in means of a factor of about 60, Midwestern tool-count is not significantly less than other North American sites when MNI = 1, nor where MNI = 1 and tool-count <100, although in that case U nearly attains conventional significance. Even in these permutations, however, the distribution of values seems very different (Figure 11.3a).

Other North American sites differ in U, not t, from Old World Upper Paleolithic ones in tool-count, despite a mean that is less than one-third the Eurasian value. Likewise, Midwestern site tool-count differs in U, not t, from Eurasian Upper Paleolithic sites, despite a mean that is scarcely one percent of the Eurasian value. Midwestern and Eurasian Upper Paleolithic sites where MNI = 1 do not differ, despite a lower Midwestern mean (but Old World n = 1). Midwestern sites and all other modern-human ones combined differ significantly in U, not t, and again exhibit quite different distributions by region (Figure 3b). Finally, Midwestern sites differ significantly from all Eurasian ones.

Recall that high tool-count sites such as Yudinovo were omitted, and high tool-count values at sites such as La Cotte were not used. Also, many comparisons omitted Kimmswick and its considerable tool-count. That is, comparisons were as favorable as possible to the Midwestern sites that contain few or no tools. Yet in most comparisons, differences were significant, as measured by U (and two other U tests nearly attained significance), some as measured by t. Given the nonnormal distributions in many cases, nonparametric U probably is a more robust test for difference.

To "stubbornly insist" (Garland and Cogswell 1985:36; see also Johnson 2007:79–80) upon stone tools at Midwestern proboscidean

TABLE 11.3. Summary of student's *t* and Mann-Whitney *U* tests of significant differences in mean tool-count. Results significant @ .05 shaded.

	t	p	U	p
Midwest x other N. American				
all	0.85	0.40	113.5	0.02
MNI = 1	0.98	0.34	71	0.15
tool-ct.<100	2.93	0.01	69.5	<.01
MNI = 1 & tool-ct. <100	1.71	0.11	49	0.06
Midwest x Old World Upper Pal.				
all	1.66	0.14	8.0	<.01
MNI = 1	0.36	0.73	2.0	0.17
tool-ct. <100	3.67	0.04	0.0	<.01
MNI = 1 & tool-ct. <100	8.73	<.01	0.0	0.06
Midwest x all other Upper Pal.[1]				
all	1.90	0.08	121.5	<.01
MNI = 1	0.99	0.34	73.0	0.01
tool-ct. <100	3.40	<.01	69.5	<.01
MNI = 1 & tool-ct. <100	1.93	0.08	49.0	0.03
Other N. American x Old World Upper Pal.				
all	1.13	0.27	15.0	<.01
Midwest x all Old World				
all	2.64	0.01	47.5	<.01
MNI = 1	1.93	0.07	21.0	<.01
tool-ct. <100	6.33	<.01	9.5	<.01
MNI = 1 & tool-ct. <100	6.24	<.01	1.0	<.01

[1] Includes other North American Paleoindian cases

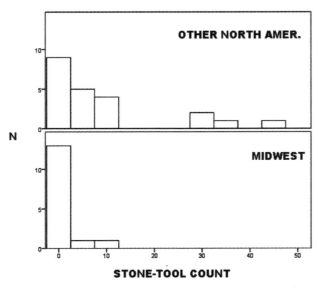

FIGURE 11.3a. Tool-count histogram: North American cases (tool-count <100).

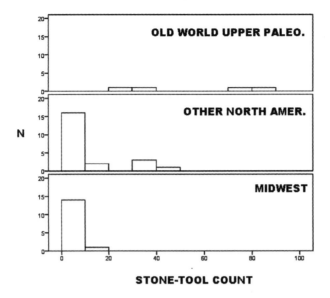

FIGURE 11.3b. Tool-count histogram: Midwestern, other North American, and Old World Upper Paleolithic cases (tool-count <100).

sites may seem churlish. Of course, people who hunted or scavenged proboscideans might leave no tools behind. Yet so many conspicuous absences and, Kimmswick excepted, the overall paucity of stone tools in one relatively small part of proboscideans' Pleistocene range compared to the conspicuous abundance of elephant-associated stone tools elsewhere surely beg the question. The Midwestern record is highly unusual, in ways not satisfactorily explained unless some artifacts and sites claimed as archaeological are instead natural. Moreover, the relative abundance of evidence for cutmarks (itself subject to taphonomic revision in light of recent studies [Krasinski 2010]), in the complete absence of the stone tools that presumably made the marks, demands explanation.

Some Suggestions for Future Research

On a question where ambiguity abounds, even narrow focus on the Midwest and tool-counts at possible proboscidean sites fails to produce unambiguous results. If the balance of evidence and probability fails to support the case for human association at these places, how can we better resolve the question? There is no panacea, but several lines of research are worth considering.

We need compilations of relevant data to incorporate but surpass small databases like Table 11.1 here and others that are much larger but still incomplete (Agenbroad 2005; Boulanger and Lyman 2014; Fisher 2009:Table 4.1; Lorenzen et al. 2011; Faith and Surovell 2009). Such compilations should include radiocarbon dates, detailed excavation plans and records, data on scale of recovery (e.g., screen size), and exportable digital models of at least selected artifacts and proboscidean elements bearing possible cutmarks so that other analysts can evaluate the evidence independently. PIDBA (Anderson et al. 2010) comes to mind, but the wealth of Old World evidence justifies even larger-scale databases.

Of course, more sites should be excavated and reported, but decades of inconclusive debate suggest that neither quantity nor quality of evidence alone will settle the matter. To evaluate the argument for taphonomic degradation of the Paleoindian record, we also need representativity analysis (e.g., Shott 2005) for the complete North American sequence, including the understudied Archaic periods. With reasonable estimates of the record's size, we can determine whether the Paleoindian record truly is oversampled as some of us suspect. Only then can we know whether Paleoindian evidence is under-represented purely as a function of greatest age or possibly overrepresented as a function of popularity and status competition.

Stone tools, mostly flakes, possibly associated with proboscideans should be scanned and their three-dimensional digital models distributed for study. Accurate digital models can be easily produced today (Shott 2014) and their examination by independent analysts can verify and corroborate their identification.

Conclusion

So, did Paleoindians drive proboscideans to extinction? Only strong evidence can support the conclusion. It is natural to seek certainty but, on present evidence, perilous to claim certitude. On balance, Midwestern stone-tool evidence does not seem strong enough. In many cases, human association cannot be demonstrated, and the curious scarcity of stone tools is at odds with

global evidence. Mastodons may have survived the Paleoindian interval, making it as hard for Paleoindians to cause their extinction as it was for Thomas Jefferson to win the 2000 U.S. presidential election.

Vigor in advocacy is commendable. But the question of human agency cannot be settled by strength of feeling or by invoking equivocal consensus. Although it excites our passions, we must address the question dispassionately. Until more relevant discoveries occur, the strange paucity of stone tools at Midwestern proboscidean sites that makes them a glaring anomaly in continental and broader comparison must be explained, not explained away. Along with other archaeological and natural-science reservations merely noted here, dispassionate study of the evidence counsels respectful uncertainty. Midwestern Paleoindians may have been a contributing cause of proboscidean demise, but after decades of vigorous search and advocacy the evidence remains equivocal.

Acknowledgments

I thank Rafael Suárez for his kind invitation to contribute to this volume. Although we disagree, Gary Haynes and Todd Surovell made constructive comments that improved the chapter. Any errors are my responsibility.

Note

Circumstances have not permitted major revisions or the incorporation of more recent research since this chapter was composed into its final version in 2015.

References

Abraczinskas, Laura M.
1993   Pleistocene Proboscidean Sites in Michigan: New Records and an Update on Published Sites. *Michigan Academician* 25(4):443–490.
Agam, Aviad and Ran Barkai
2018   Elephant and Mammoth Hunting during the Paleolithic: A Review of the Relevant Archaeological, Ethnographic and Ethno-Historical Records. *Quaternary* 1(1). doi:10.3390/quat1010003.
Agenbroad, Larry D.
2005   North American Proboscideans: Mam-

moths: The State of Knowledge, 2003. *Quaternary International* 126–128:73–92.
Alroy, John
1999   Putting North America's End-Pleistocene Megafaunal Extinction in Context. In *Extinctions in Near Time: Causes, Contexts, and Consequences*, edited by Ross MacPhee and Hans-Dieter Sues, pp. 105–143. Springer, Dordrecht, NL.
2001   A Multispecies Overkill Simulation of the End-Pleistocene Megafaunal Mass Extinction. *Science* 292(5523):1893–1896.
Anderson, David G., D. Shane Miller, Stephen J. Yerka, J. Christopher Gillam, Erik N. Johanson, Derek T. Anderson, Albert C. Goodyear, and Ashley M. Smallwood
2010   PIDBA (Paleoindian Database of the Americas) 2010: Current Status and Findings. *Archaeology of Eastern North America* 38: 63–90.
Antoine, Pierre, Nicole Limondin-Lozouet, Patrick Auguste, Jean-Luc Locht, Bassam Galheb, Jean-Louis Reyss, Élise Escudé, et al.
2006   Le tuf de Caours (Somme, France): mise en évidence d'une séquence eemienne et

d'nn site paléolithique associé. *Quaternaire* 17(4):281–320.

Anzidei, Anna Paola, Grazia M. Bulgarelli, Paloa Catalano, Eugenio Cerilli, Rosalia Gallotti, Cristina Lemonini, Salvatore Milli, Maria Rita Palombo, Walter Pantano, and Ernesto Santucci

2012   Ongoing Research at the Late Middle Pleistocene Site of La Polledrara di Cecanibbio (Central Italy), with Emphasis on Human-Elephant Relationships. *Quaternary International* 255:171–187.

Arroyo-Cabrales, Joaquín, Oscar J. Polaco, and Eileen Johnson

2006   A Preliminary View of the Coexistence of Mammoth and Early Peoples in Mexico. *Quaternary International* 142–143:79–86.

Aureli, Daniele, Antonio Contardi, Biagio Giaccio, Brian Jicha, Cristina Lemorini, Sergio Madonna, Donatella Magri, et al.

2015   *Palaeoloxodon* and Human Interaction: Depositional Setting, Chronology, and Archaeology at the Middle Pleistocene Ficoncella Site (Tarquinia, Italy). *PLoS One.* doi:10.1371/journal.pone.0124498.

Barnosky, Anthony D., Paul L. Koch, Robert S. Feranec, Scott L. Wing, and Alan B. Shabel

2004   Assessing the Causes of Late Pleistocene Extinctions on the Continents. *Science* 306(5693):70–75.

Basilyan, A. E., M. A. Anisimov, P. A. Nikolskiy, and V. V. Pitulko

2011   Wooly Mammoth Mass Accumulation next to the Paleolithic Yana RHS Site, Arctic Siberia: Its Geology, Age, and Relation to Past Human Activity. *Journal of Archaeological Science* 38(9):2461–2474.

Berthelet, A., and J. Chavaillon

2001   The Early Palaeolithic Butchery Site of Barogali (Republic of Djibouti). In *La terra degli elefanti [Proceedings of the 1st International Congress]*, edited by G. Cavarretta, P. Gioia, M. Mussi, and M. Palombo, pp. 176–179. Consiglio Nazionale delle Recherche, Rome, IT.

Binford, Lewis R.

2001   *Constructing Frames of Reference: An Analytical Method for Archaeological Theory Building Using Ethnographic and Environmental Data Sets.* University of California Press, Berkeley.

Boldurian, Anthony T., and John L. Cotter
        Clovis Revisited: New Perspectives on Paleoindian Adaptations from Blackwater Draw, New Mexico. University Museum Monograph 103. University of Pennsylvania, Philadelphia.

Bonifay, E., M-F. Bonifay, R. Panattoni, and J-J. Tiercelin

1976   Soleihac (Blanzac, Haute-Loire), nouveau site préhistorique du début du Pleistocène moyen. *Bulletin de la Societé Préhistorique Française* 73(1):293–304.

Borrero, Luis A., and Fabiana M. Martin

2012   Ground Sloths and Humans in Southern Fuego-Patagonia: Taphonomy and Archaeology. *World Archaeology* 44(1):102–117.

Boschian, Giovanni, and Daniela Saccà

2010   Ambiguities in Human and Elephant Interactions? Stories of Bones, Sand, and Water from Castel di Guido (Italy). *Quaternary International* 214:3–16.

Boulanger, Matthew T., and R. Lyman

2014   Northeastern North American Pleistocene Megafauna Chronologically Overlapped Minimally with Paleoindians. *Quaternary Science Reviews* 85:35–46.

Brain, C. K.

1981   *The Hunter or the Hunted? An Introduction to African Cave Taphonomy.* University of Chicago Press, Chicago.

Braje, Todd J., Tom D. Dillehay, Jon M. Erlandson, Scott M. Fitzpatrick, Donald K. Grayson, Vance T. Holliday, Robert L. Kelly, Richard G. Klein, David J. Meltzer, and Torben C. Rick

2017   Were Hominins in California ~130,000 Years Ago? *Paleoamerica* 3(3):200–202.

Breitburg, Emanuel, John B. Broster, Arthur L. Reesman, and Richard G. Stearns

1996   The Coats-Hines Site: Tennessee's First Paleoindian-Mastodon Association. *Current Research in the Pleistocene* 13:6–8.

Brook, Barry W., and David M. Bowman

2004   The Uncertain Blitzkrieg of Pleistocene Megafauna. *Journal of Biogeography* 31(4): 517–523.

Brugère, Alexis, Laure Fontana, and Martin Oliva

2006   Mammoth Procurement and Exploitation at Milovice (Czech Republic): New Data for the Moravian Gravettian. In *In Search of Total Animal Exploitation: Case Studies from the Upper Palaeolithic and Mesolithic*, edited by L. Fontana, F.-X. Chauvière, and A. Bridault, pp. 45–69. BAR International Series 2040. Archaeopress, Oxford, UK.

Brunswig, Robert H.

2007   New Interpretations of the Dent Mammoth

Site. In *Frontiers in Colorado Paleoindian Archaeology: From the Dent Site to the Rocky Mountains*, edited by R. Brunswig and B. Pitblado, pp. 87–121. University Press of Colorado, Boulder.

Brush, Nigel, and Forrest Smith
1994   The Martins Creek Mastodon: A Paleoindian Butchery Site in Holmes County, Ohio. *Current Research in the Pleistocene* 11:14–15.

Brush, Nigel, and Richard W. Yerkes
1996   Microwear Analysis of Chipped Stone Tools from the Martins Creek Mastodon Site, Holmes County, Ohio. *Current Research in the Pleistocene* 13:55–57.

Byers, D.A., and A. Ugan
2005   Should We Expect Large Game Specialization in the Late Pleistocene? An Optimal Foraging Perspective on Early Paleoindian Prey Choice. *Journal of Archaeological Science* 32(11):1624–1640.

Callow, Paul
1986   The Flint Tools. In *La Cotte de Saint-Brelade 1961–1978: Excavations by C.B.M. McBurney*, edited by P. Callow and and J.M. Cornford, pp. 251–314. Geo Books, Norwich, UK.

Cardillo, Marcel, Georgina M. Mace, Kate E. Jones, Jon Bielby, Olaf R. Bininda-Emonds, Wes Sechrest, C.David Orme, and Andy Purvis
2005   Multiple Causes of High Extinction Risk in Large Mammal Species. *Science* 309(5738): 1239–1241.

Clark, J. Desmond, and C. Vance Haynes
1970   An Elephant Butchery Site at Mwanganda's Village, Karonga, Malawi, and Its Relevance for Palaeolithic Archaeology. *World Archaeology* 1(3):390–411.

Cleland, Charles E., Margaret B. Holman, and J. Alan Holman
1998   The Mason-Quimby Line Revisited. *Wisconsin Archaeologist* 79:8–27.

Cooper, Alan, Chris Turney, Konrad A. Hughen, Barry W. Brook, H. Gregory McDonald, and Corey J.A. Bradshaw
2105   Abrupt Warming Events Drove Late Pleistocene Holarctic Megafaunal Turnover. *Science* 349(6248):601–606.

DeAngelis, Joseph A., and R. Lee Lyman
2016   Evaluation of the Early Paleo-Indian Zooarchaeological Record as Evidence of Diet Breadth. *Archaeological and Anthropological Sciences*. doi:10.1007/s12520-016-0377-1.

Delagnes, Anne, Arnaud Lenoble, Sonia Harmand, Jean-Philip Brugal, Sandrine Prat, Jean-Jacques Tiercelin, and Hélène Roche
2006   Interpreting Pachyderm Single Carcass Sites in the African Lower and Early Middle Pleistocene Record: A Multidisciplinary Approach to the Site of Nadung'a 4 (Kenya). *Journal of Anthropological Archaeology* 25(4):448–465.

Deter-Wolf, Aaron, Jesse W. Tune, and John B. Broster
2011   Excavations and Dating of Late Pleistocene and Paleoindian Deposits at the Coats-Hines Site, Williamson County, Tennessee. *Tennessee Archaeology* 5(2):142–156.

Dincauze, Dena F., and Mary Lou Curran
1983   Paleoindians as Generalists: An Ecological Perspective. Paper presented at the 48th Annual Meeting of the Society for American Archaeology. Pittsburgh, PA.

Dixon, E. James
2001   Human Colonization of the Americas: Timing, Technology, and Process. *Quaternary Science Reviews* 20(1–3):277–299.

Domínguez-Rodrigo, Manuel
2006   Are All Oldowan Sites Palimpsests? If So, What Can They Tell Us about Hominid Carnivory? In *Interdisciplinary Approaches to the Oldowan*, edited by E. Hovers and D. Braun, pp. 129–147. Springer, Dordrecht, NL.

Domínguez-Rodrigo, Miguel, H.T. Bunn, A.Z. Mabulla, E. Baquedano, D. Uribelarrea, A. Pérez-González, A. Gidna, et al.
2014   On Meat Eating and Human Evolution: A Taphonomic Analysis of BK4b (Upper Bed II, Olduvai Gorge, Tanzania), and Its Bearing on Hominin Megafaunal Consumption. *Quaternary International* 322–323: 129–152.

Drucker, D.G., F. Rivals, S.C. Münzel, and H. Bocherens
2015   Stable Isotope and Microwear Investigation on the Mammoth (*Mammuthus primigenius*) of Kraków Spadzista: Insights into Diet and Environment. In *A Gravettian Site in Southern Poland: Kraków Spadzista*, edited by P. Wojtal, J. Wilczyński, and G. Haynes, pp. 189–202. Institute of Systematics and Evolution of Animals, Polish Academy of Sciences, Krakov.

Faith, J. Tyler, and Todd A. Surovell
2009   Synchronous Extinction of North America's Pleistocene Mammals. *PNAS* 106(49): 20641–20645.

Falquet, R. A., and W. L. Hanebert
1978   The Willard Mastodon: Evidence of Human
        Predation. *Ohio Archaeologist* 28(2):17.
Feranec, Robert S., and Andrew L. Kozlowski
2012   New AMS Radiocarbon Dates from Late
        Pleistocene Mastodons and Mammoths
        in New York State, USA. *Radiocarbon*
        54(2):275–279.
Feranec, Robert S., Norton G. Miller, Jonathan C.
Lothrop, and Russell W. Graham
2011   The *Sporormiella* Proxy and End-Pleistocene
        Megafaunal Extinction: A Perspective. *Qua-
        ternary International* 245(2):333–338.
Fiedel, Stuart
2009   Sudden Deaths: The Chronology of Ter-
        minal Pleistocene Megafaunal Extinction.
        In *American Megafaunal Extinctions at the
        End of the Pleistocene*, edited by G. Haynes,
        pp. 21–37. Springer, Dordrecht, NL.
Fiedel, Stuart J., and Gary Haynes
2004   A Premature Burial: Comments on Grayson
        and Meltzer's "Requiem for Overkill." *Jour-
        nal of Archaeological Science* 31(1):121–131.
Fisher, Daniel C.
1987   Mastodont Procurement by Paleoindians
        of the Great Lakes Region: Hunting or
        Scavenging? In *The Evolution of Human
        Hunting*, edited by M. Nitecki and D. Ni-
        tecki, pp. 309–421. Plenum, New York.
1996   Extinction of Proboscideans in North
        America. In *The Proboscidea: Evolution
        and Palaeoecology of Elephants and Their
        Relatives*, J. Shoshani and P. Tassy eds.,
        pp. 296–315. Oxford University Press,
        Oxford.
2009   Paleobiology and Extinction of Probosci-
        deans in the Great Lakes Region of North
        America. In *American Megafaunal Extinc-
        tions at the End of the Pleistocene*, edited
        by G. Haynes, pp. 55–75. Springer, Dor-
        drecht, NL.
Fisher, Daniel C., Bradley T. Lepper, and Paul E.
Hooge
1994   Evidence for the Butchery of the Burning
        Tree Mastodon. In *The First Discovery of
        America: Archaeological Evidence of the
        Early Inhabitants of the Ohio Area*, edited by
        W. Dancey, pp. 43–57. Ohio Archaeological
        Council, Columbus.
Fladerer, F. A.
2001   The Krems-Wachtberg Camp-Site: Mam-
        moth Carcass Utilization along the Danube

        27,000 Years Ago. In *La Terra degli Ele-
        fanti [Proceedings of the 1st International
        Congress]*, edited by G. Cavarretta, P. Gioia,
        M. Mussi, and M. Palombo, pp. 432–438.
        Consiglio Nazionale delle Recherche,
        Rome, IT.
Fosse, Phillipe
2000   Stratégies d'acquisition des grands mam-
        mifères au très ancien Paléolithique:
        les données fournies par le gisement
        de Soleilhac (Haute-Loire, France).
        Anthropologie et Préhistoire 111:299–307.
Freeman, Leslie G.
1994   Torralba and Ambrona: A Review of Dis-
        coveries. In *Integrative Paths to the Past:
        Paleoanthropological Advances in Honor
        of F. Clark Howell*, edited by R. Corruccini
        and R. Ciochan, pp. 597–637. Prentice-Hall,
        Upper Saddle River, NJ.
Frison, George C., and Lawrence C. Todd
1986   *The Colby Mammoth Site: Taphonomy and
        Archaeology of a Clovis Kill in Northern
        Wyoming*. University of New Mexico Press,
        Albuquerque.
Gamble, Clive
1999   *The Palaeolithic Societies of Europe*.
        Cambridge University Press, Cambridge.
Garland, Elizabeth B., and James W. Cogswell
1985   The Power Mastodon Site. *Michigan Archae-
        ologist* 31:3–39.
Gaudzinski, Sabine
2004   A Matter of High Resolution? The Eemian
        Interglacial (OIS 5e) in North-Central
        Europe and Middle Palaeolithic Subsistence.
        International Journal of Osteoarchaeology
        14(3–4):201–211.
Gaudzinski, Sabine, Felix Bittman, Wolfgang Boe-
nigk, Manfred Frechen, and Thijs van Kolfschoten
1996   Palaeoecology and Archaeology of the
        Kärlich-Seeufer Open-Air Site (Middle
        Pleistocene) in the Central Rhineland, Ger-
        many. *Quaternary Research* 46(3):319–334.
Germonpré, Mietje, Mikhail Sablin, Gennady
Adolfovich, and Galina Vasilievna Grigorieva
2008   Possible Evidence of Mammoth Hunting
        during the Epigravettian at Yudinovo,
        Russian Plain. *Journal of Anthropological
        Archaeology* 27(4):475–492.
Gill, J. L., J. W. Williams, S. T. Jackson, K. B. Lininger,
and G. S. Robinson
2009   Pleistocene Megafaunal Collapse, Novel
        Plant Communities, and Enhanced

Fire Regimes in North America. *Science* 326(5956):1100–1103.

Gingerich, Joseph A.
2011 Down to Seeds and Stones: A New Look at the Subsistence Remains from Shawnee-Minisink. *American Antiquity* 76(1):127–144.

Goren-Inbar, N., A. Lister, E. Werker, and M. Chech
1994 A Butchered Elephant Skull and Associated Artifacts from the Acheulian Site of Gesher Benot Ya'aqov, Israel. *Paléorient* 20/21: 99–112.

Graham, Russell W.
1986 Stratified Cultural and Faunal Horizons at Kimmswick, Missouri. In *Quaternary Records of Southwestern Illinois and Adjacent Missouri*, edited by R. Graham, B. Styles, J. Saunders, M. Wiant, E. McKay, T. Styles, and E. Hajic, pp. 57–68. Illinois State Geological Survey Guidebook 23. Springfield, IL.
2001 Late Quaternary Biogeography and Extinction of Proboscideans in North America. In *La Terra degli elefanti [Proceedings of the 1st International Congress]*, edited by G. Cavarretta, P. Gioia, M. Mussi, and M. Palombo, pp. 707–710. Consiglio Nazionale delle Recherche, Rome, IT.

Graham, Russell W., and Marvin Kay
1988 Taphonomic Comparison of Cultural and Noncultural Faunal Deposits at the Kimmswick and Barnhard Sites, Jefferson County, Missouri. *Bulletin of the Buffalo Society of Natural Sciences* 33:227–240.

Graham, Russell W., and Ernest L. Lundelius Jr.
1984 Coevolutionary Disequilibrium and Pleistocene Extinctions. In *Quaternary Extinctions: A Prehistoric Revolution*, edited by Paul S. Martin and Richard G. Klein, pp. 211–222. University of Arizona Press, Tucson.

Graham, Russell W., C. Vance Haynes, and Marvin Kay
1981 Kimmswick: A Clovis-Mastodon Association in Eastern Missouri. *Science* 213(4512): 1115–1117.

Grayson, Donald K, and David J. Meltzer
2002 Clovis Hunting and Large Mammal Extinction: A Critical Review of the Evidence. *Journal of World Prehistory* 16(4):313–359.
2015 Revisiting Paleoindian Exploitation of Extinct North American Mammals. *Journal of Archaeological Science*, 56:(177)–193.

Greene, John C.
1959 *The Death of Adam: Evolution and Its Impact on Western Thought.* Iowa State University Press, Ames.

Griggs, Carol B., and Bernd Kromer
2008 Wood Macrofossils and Dendrochronology of Three Mastodon Sites in Upstate New York. *Palaeontographica Americana* 61:49–61.

Gustafson, Carl E., Delbert Gilbow, and Richard D. Daugherty
1979 The Manis Mastodon: Early Man on the Olympic Peninsula. *Canadian Journal of Archaeology* 3:157–164.

Guthrie, R. Dale
1984 Ethological Observations from Palaeolithic Art. In *La contribution de la zoologie et de l'ethnologie à l'interpretation de l'art peuples chasseurs préhistoriques*, edited by Hans-Georg Bandi, pp. 35–74. Éditions Universitaires, Fribourg, CH.
1990 *Frozen Fauna of the Mammoth Steppe: The Story of Blue Babe.* University of Chicago Press, Chicago, IL.
2006 New Carbon Dates Link Climatic Change with Human Colonization and Pleistocene Extinctions. *Nature* 441:207–209.

Halligan, J. J., M. R. Waters, A. Perrotti, I. J. Owens, J. M. Feinberg, M. D. Bourne, B. Fenerty, et al.
2016 Pre-Clovis Occupation 14,550 Years Ago at the Page-Ladson Site, Florida, and the Peopling of the Americas. *Science Advances* 2:e1600375.

Hamilton, T. M.
1993 The Miami Mastodon, 23SA212. *Missouri Archaeologist* 54:79–88.

Hannus, L. Adrian
1990 The Lange-Ferguson Site: A Case for Mammoth Bone-Butchering Tools. In *Megafauna and Man: Discovery of America's Heartland*, edited by L. Agenbroad, J. Mead, and L. Nelson, pp. 86–99. Scientific Papers 1. The Mammoth of Hot Springs, South Dakota, Inc., Hot Springs, SD.

Haury, Emil W.
1953 Artifacts with Mammoth Remains, Naco, Arizona. *American Antiquity* 19(1):1–24.

Haury, Emil W., E. B. Sayles, and William W. Wasley
1959 The Lehner Mammoth Site, Southeastern Arizona. *American Antiquity* 25(1):2–30.

Haynes, C. Vance, Jr., and Bruce B. Huckell
2007 *Murray Springs: A Clovis Site with Multiple Activity Areas in the San Pedro Valley, Arizona.* Anthropological Papers of the

University of Arizona 71. University of Arizona Press, Tucson.

2016   The Manis Mastodon: An Alternative Interpretation. *PaleoAmerica* 2(3):189–191.

Haynes, C. Vance, Jr., Todd A. Surovell, and Gregory W. Hodgins

2014   The U. P. Mammoth Site, Carbon County, Wyoming, USA: More Questions than Answers. *Geoarchaeology* 28(2):99–111.

Haynes, Gary

1991   *Mammoths, Mastodonts, and Elephants: Biology, Behavior, and the Fossil Record.* Cambridge University Press, Cambridge.

2002a   The Catastrophic Extinction of North American Mammoths and Mastodonts. *World Archaeology* 33(3):391–416.

2002b   *The Early Settlement of North America: The Clovis Era.* Cambridge University Press, Cambridge.

2009   Estimates of Clovis-Era Megafaunal Populations and Their Extinction Risks. In *American Megafaunal Extinctions at the End of the Pleistocene*, edited by G. Haynes, pp. 39–53. Springer, Dordrecht, NL.

2013   Extinctions in North America's Late Glacial Landscapes. *Quaternary International* 285:89–98.

Haynes, Gary, and Kathryn E. Krasinski

2010   Taphonomic Fieldwork in Southern Africa and Its Application in Studies of the Earliest Peopling of North America. *Journal of Taphonomy* 8(2–3):181–202.

Hemmings, C. Andrew.

1998   Probable Association of Paleoindian Artifacts and Mastodon Remains from Sloth Hole, Aucilla River, North Florida. *Current Research in the Pleistocene* 15:16–18.

Hemmings, E. Thomas, and C. Vance Haynes

1967   The Escapule Mammoth and Associated Projectile Points, San Pedro Valley, Arizona. *Journal of the Arizona Academy of Science* 5(3):184–188.

Hofman, Jack L.

1996   Early Hunter-Gatherers of the Central Great Plains: Paleoindian and Mesoindian (Archaic) Cultures. In *Archeology and Paleoecology of the Central Great Plains*, edited by J. Hofman, pp. 41–100. Arkansas Archeological Survey Research Series 48. Fayetteville, AR.

Holen, Steven R.

2006   Taphonomy of Two Last Glacial Maximum Mammoth Sites in the Central Great Plains of North America: A Preliminary Report on La Sena and Lovewell. *Quaternary International* 142–143:30–43.

Holen, Steven R., Thomas A. Demére, Daniel C. Fisher, Richard Fullagar, James B. Paces, George T. Jefferson, Jared M. Beeton, et al.

2017   A 130,000-Year-Old Archaeological Site in Southern California, USA. *Nature* 544: 479–483.

Holliday, Vance T., C. Vance Haynes, Jack L. Hofman, and David J. Meltzer

1994   Geoarchaeology and Geochronology of the Miami (Clovis) Site, Southern High Plains of Texas. *Quaternary Research* 41(2): 234–244.

Holman, J. Alan

1986   The Dansville Mastodon and Associated Wooden Specimen. *National Geographic Research* 2:416.

Holven, Adam

2002   Mastodon and Mammoth Fossil Remains in Iowa: An Updated Compendium of Fossil Specimens and Their Locations across the State. Bachelor of Science thesis, Department of Earth Sciences, University of Northern Iowa, Cedar Falls.

Horwitz, Liora Kolska, Michael Chazan, Adrian Lister, Hervé Monchot, and Naomi Porat

n.d.   The Late Lower Paleolithic Site of Holon, Israel: Subsistence, Technology, and Chronology. Manuscript on file, Department of Evolution, Systematics, and Ecology, Hebrew University, Jerusalem, IL.

Howell, F. Clark

1966   Observations on the Earlier Phases of the European Lower Paleolithic. *American Anthropologist* 68(2):88–201.

Huguet, R., J. Vallverdú, X. Rodríguez-Álvarez, M. Terradillos-Bernal, A. Bargalló, A. Lombera-Hermida, L. Menéndez, et al.

2017   Level TE9c of Sima del Elefante (Sierra de Atapuerca, Spain): A Comprehensive Approach. *Quaternary International* 433: 278–295.

Jefferson, Thomas

1954   *Notes on the State of Virginia*, edited by W. Peden. Norton, New York.

Jeske, Robert J., David Brose, James A. Brown, William A. Lovis, William Green, and Mark F. Seeman

2015   Sense and Sensibility in Midwestern Archaeology and the *Midcontinental Journal of Archaeology*, Part 1. *Midcontinental Journal of Archaeology* 40(1):4–13.

Johnson, Eileen

1987   Cultural Activities and Interactions. In *Lubbock Lake: Late Quaternary Studies on the Southern High Plains*, edited by Eileen Johnson, pp. 120–158. Texas A&M University Press, College Station, TX.

2007   Along the Ice Margin: The Cultural Taphonomy of Late Pleistocene Mammoth in Southeastern Wisconsin. *Quaternary International* 169–170:64–83.

Johnson, Eileen, and Vance T. Holliday

1987   Lubbock Lake Artifact Assemblages. In *Lubbock Lake: Late Quaternary Studies on the Southern High Plains*, edited by Eileen Johnson, pp. 100–119. Texas A&M University Press, College Station, TX.

Jones, Peter R.

1980   Experimental Butchery with Modern Stone Tools and Its Relevance for Palaeolithic Archaeology. *World Archaeology* 12(2):153–165.

Joyce, Daniel J.

2006   Chronology and New Research on the Schaefer Mammoth (?*Mammuthus primigenius*) Site, Kenosha County, Wisconsin, USA. *Quaternary International* 142/143: 44–57.

2014   Pre-Clovis Megafauna Butchery Sites in the Western Great Lakes Region, USA. In *Paleoamerican Odyssey*, edited by K. Graf, C. Ketron, and M. Waters, pp. 467–484. Texas A&M University Press, College Station, TX.

Kapp, Ronald O.

1986   Late-Glacial Pollen and Macrofossils Associated with the Rappuhn Mastodont (Lapeer Co., Michigan). *American Midland Naturalist* 116:368–377.

Kapp, Ronald O., D. L. Cleary, G. G. Snyder, and D. C. Fisher

1990   Vegetational and Climatic History of the Crystal Lake Area and the Eldridge Mastodont Site, Montcalm County, Michigan. *American Midland Naturalist* 123:47–63.

King, James E., and Jeffrey J. Saunders

1984   Environmental Insularity and the Extinction of the American Mastodont. In *Quaternary Extinctions: A Prehistoric Revolution*, edited by P. Martin and R. Klein, pp. 315–339. University of Arizona Press, Tucson.

Kirkpatrick, M. Jude, and Daniel C. Fisher

1993   Preliminary Research on the Moon Mammoth Site. *Current Research in the Pleistocene* 10:70–71.

Kondo, Y., and N. Mazima

2001   *Palaeoloxodon naumanni* and Its Environment at the Paleolilthic Site of Lake Nojiri, Nagano Prefecture, Central Japan. In *La Terra degli elefanti [Proceedings of the 1st International Congress]*, edited by G. Cavarretta, P. Gioia, M. Mussi, and M. Palombo, pp. 284–288. Consiglio Nazionale delle Recherche, Rome, IT.

Koons, Rachel K.

2014   A Study of Cut Marks on the Orleton Mastodon and the Potential Implications of Anthropogenic Modification. Senior thesis, School of Earth Sciences, Ohio State University, Columbus.

Krasinski, Kathryn E.

2010   Broken Bones and Cutmarks: Taphonomic Analyses and Implications for the Peopling of North America. PhD dissertation, Department of Anthropology, University of Nevada, Reno.

Krech, Shepard

1999   *The Ecological Indian: Myth and History.* Norton, New York.

Kuehn, Steve R., Steven L. Tieken, and David J. Nolan

2010   A Preliminary Report on the Andrew Farm Mastodon, Adams County, Illinois. *Current Research in the Pleistocene* 27: 109–111.

Kuzmin, Yaroslav V.

2008   Siberia at the Last Glacial Maximum: Environment and Archaeology. *Journal of Archaeological Research* 16(2):163–221.

Laub, Richard S.

2000   A Second Dated Mastodon Bone Artifact from Pleistocene Deposits at the Hiscock Site (Western New York State). *Archaeology of Eastern North America* 28:141–154.

Laub, Richard S., M. F. DeRemer, C. A. Dufort, and W. L. Parsons

1988   The Hiscock Site: A Rich Late Quaternary Locality in Western New York State. In *Late Pleistocene and Early Holocene Paleoecology and Archaeology of the Eastern Great Lakes Region*, edited by R. Laub, N. Miller, and D. Steadman. *Bulletin of the Buffalo Society of Natural Sciences* 33:63–81.

Leakey, Mary D.

1971   *Olduvai Gorge.* Vol. 3, *Excavations in Beds I and II, 1960–1963.* Cambridge University Press, Cambridge.

Leonhardy, Frank C.

1966   *Domebo: A Paleo-Indian Mammoth Kill in the Prairie-Plains.* Contributions of the Museum of the Great Plains 1. Lawton, OK.

Lepper, Bradley T.

1983   A Preliminary Report of a Mastodon Tooth Find and a Paleo-Indian Site in Hardin County, Ohio. *Ohio Archaeologist* 33:10–13.

Lepper, Bradley T., Tod A. Frolking, Daniel C. Fisher, Gerald Goldstein, Jon E. Sanger, Dee Anne Wymer, J. Gordon Ogden, and Paul E. Hooge

1991   Intestinal Contents of a Late Pleistocene Mastodont from Midcontinental North America. *Quaternary Research* 36:120–125.

Lima-Ribeiro, Matheus S., and José A. Diniz-Filho

2013   American Megafaunal Extinctions and Human Arrival: Improved Evaluation using a Meta-Analytical Approach. *Quaternary International* 299:38–52.

Lorenzen, Eline D., David Nogués-Bravo, Ludovic Orlando, Jaco Weinstock, Jonas Binladen, Katharine A. Marske, Andrew Ugan, et al.

2011   Species-Specific Responses of Late Quaternary Megafauna to Climate and Humans. *Nature* 479:359–365.

Lubinski, Patrick M., Bax R. Barton, Karl Lillquist, Morris Uebelacker, and Jake T. Shapley

2007   The Late-Glacial Wenas Creek Mammoth Site (45YA1083) in Central Washington. *Current Research in the Pleistocene* 24:178–180.

Lubinski, Patrick M., Bax R. Barton, Karl Lillquist, and Morris Uebelacker

2008   Three Seasons of Excavation at the Wenas Creek Mammoth Site in Central Washington. Poster presented at the 73rd Annual Meeting of the Society for American Archaeology, Vancouver, BC.

Lubinski, Patrick M., Patrick T. McCutcheon, Karl Lillquist, Morris Uebelacker, Bax R. Barton, and Jake T. Shapley

2009   Possible Lithic Artifacts from 2005–07 Excavations at the Wenas Creek Mammoth Site. *Current Research in the Pleistocene* 26: 85–86.

Lundelius, Ernest L.

1987   What Happened to the Mammoth? The Climatic Model. In *Americans Before Columbus: Ice-Age Origins*, edited by R. Carlisle, pp. 75–82. Ethnology Monographs 12. Department of Anthropology, University of Pittsburgh, Pittsburgh, PA.

MacCalman, H. R.

1967   The Zoo Park Elephant Site, Windhoek (1964–1965). *Palaeoecology of Africa* 2: 102–103.

MacPhee, Ross D., Alexei N. Tikhonov, Dick Mol, Christian de Marliave, Hans van der Plicht, Alex D. Greenwood, Clare Flemming, and Larry Agenbroad

2002   Radiocarbon Chronologies and Extinction Dynamics of the Late Quaternary Mammalian Megafauna of the Taimyr Peninsula, Russian Federation. *Journal of Archaeological Science* 29(9):1017–1042

Malinsky-Buller, Ariel

2014   Contextualizing Curational Strategies at the Late Lower Paleolithic Site of Holon, Israel. *PaleoAnthropology* 2014:483–504.

Martin, Paul

1973   The Discovery of America. *Science* 179 (4077):969–974.

Martin, Paul S., Robert S. Thompson, and Austin Long

1985   Shasta Ground Sloth Extinction: A Test of the Blitzkrieg Model. In *Environments and Extinctions: Man in Late Glacial North America*, edited by R. Bonnichsen, pp. 5–14. Center for the Study of Early Man, University of Maine, Orono, ME.

Maschenko, Evgeny N., Alexandr F. Pavlov, Vasiliy N. Zenin, Sergey V. Leshchinskiy, and Luobov A. Orlova

2003   The Lugovskoe Site: Relations between the Mammoth Assemblage and Late Palaeolithic Man. In *Third International Mammoth Conference: Program and Abstracts*, edited by J. Storer, pp. 77–80. Occasional Papers in Earth Sciences 5. Palaeontology Program, Government of Yukon, Whitehorse, NT.

Mason, Richard P.

2007   Mastodons, Fluted Points, and the "Valders Problem" in Northeastern Wisconsin. *Midcontinental Journal of Archaeology* 32(1): 117–138.

McAndrews, J. H., and Lawrence J. Jackson

1988   Age and Environment of Late Pleistocene Mastodont and Mammoth in Southern Ontario. *Bulletin of the Buffalo Society of Natural Sciences* 33:161–172.

McDonald, H. Gregory
1994   The Late Pleistocene Vertebrate Fauna in Ohio: Coinhabitants with Ohio's Paleo-indians. In *The First Discovery of America: Archaeological Evidence of the Early Inhabitants of the Ohio Area*, edited by W. Dancey, pp. 23–39. Ohio Archaeological Council, Columbus.

McFarlane, Donald A.
1999   A Comparison of Methods for the Probabilistic Determination of Vertebrate Extinction Chronologies. In *Extinctions in Near Time*, edited by R. MacPhee, pp. 95–103. Kluwer, New York.

McMillan, R. Bruce
1976   Man and Mastodon: A Review of Koch's 1840 Pomme de Terre Expeditions. In *Prehistoric Man and His Environments: A Case Study in the Ozark Highland*, edited by W. Wood and R. McMillan, pp. 81–96. Academic, New York.

Mehl, Maurice G.
1966   The Grundel Mastodon. *Missouri Geological Survey and Water Resources, Report of Investigation* 35:5–28.

Meltzer, David J., and Jim I. Mead
1985   Dating Late Pleistocene Extinctions: Theoretical Issues, Analytical Bias, and Substantive Results. In *Environments and Extinctions: Man in Late Glacial North America*, edited by J. Mead and D. Meltzer, pp. 145–173. Institute of Quaternary Studies, University of Maine, Orono.

Metcalfe, Jessica Z., Fred J. Longstaffe, and Greg Hodgins
2013   Proboscideans and Paleoenvironments of the Pleistocene Great Lakes: Landscape, Vegetation, and Stable Isotopes. *Quaternary Science Reviews* 76:102–113.

Miller, Suzanne J.
1989   Characteristics of Mammoth Bone Reduction at Owl Cave, the Wasden Site, Idaho. In *Bone Modification*, edited by R. Bonnichsen and M. Sorg, pp. 381–393. Institute for Quaternary Studies, University of Maine, Orono, ME.

Miller, Suzanne J., and Wakefield Dort Jr.
1978   Early Man at Owl Cave: Current Investigations at the Wasden Site, Eastern Snake River Plain, Idaho. In *Early Man in America from a Circum-Pacific Perspective*, edited by

A. Bryan, pp. 129–139. Occasional Papers 1. Department of Anthropology, University of Alberta, AB, Canada.

Milliken, Sarah
1999   The Earliest Occupation of Italy. *ACCORDIA Research Papers* 7:7–36.
2001   Acheulean Handaxe Variability in Middle Pleistocene Italy: A Case Study. In *A Very Remote Period Indeed: Papers on the Palaeolithic Presented to Derek Roe*, edited by S. Milliken and J. Cook, pp. 160–173. Oxbow Books, Oxford, UK.

Mithen, Steven
1993   Simulating Mammoth Hunting and Extinction: Implications for the Late Pleistocene of the Central Russian Plain. In *Hunting and Animal Exploitation in the Later Palaeolithic and Mesolithic of Eurasia*, edited by G. Peterkin, H. Bricker, and P. Mellars, pp. 163–178. Archeological Papers of the American Anthropological Association 4. Washington, D.C.

Moncel, Marie-Hélène, and Florent Rivals
2011   On the Question of Short-Term Neanderthal Site Occupations: Payre, France (MIS 8–7) and Taubach/Weimar, Germany (MIS 5). *Journal of Anthropological Research* 67(1):47–75.

Monnier J.-L., C. Falguères, M. Laurent, J.-J. Bahain, M.-T. Morzadec-Kerfourn, and P. Simonet
1995   Analyse des données anciennes et contributions nouvelles à la connaissance et à la datation du gisement moustérien de Mont-Dol (Ille-et-Vilaine). In *Baie du Mont-Saint-Michel et marais de Dol, milieux naturels et peuplements dans le passé*, edited by L. Langouet and M.-T. Morzadec-Kerfourn, pp. 3–26. Centre Régional d'Archéologie, Saint-Malo, FR.

Morrow, Juliet E.
1996   The Organization of Early Paleoindian Lithic Technology in the Confluence Region of the Mississippi, Illinois, and Missouri Rivers. Ph.D. dissertation, Department of Anthropology, Washington University. St. Louis, MO.

Munson, Patrick J., and Kenneth B. Tankersley
1991   Early Paleoindian Settlement in the Grand Prairie: A Case Study in De Witt County, Illinois. Paper presented at the 56th Annual

Meeting of the Society for American Archaeology, New Orleans, LA.

Murphy, James L.
1983 The Seeley Mastodon: A Paleo-Indian Kill? *Ohio Archaeologist* 33:12–13.

Mussi, Margherita
1999 The Neanderthals in Italy: A Tale of Many Caves. In *The Middle Palaeolithic Occupation of Europe*, edited by W. Roebroeks and C. Gamble, pp. 49–80. University of Leiden Press, Leiden, NL.
2005 Hombres y elefantes en las latitudes medias: una larga convivencia. In *Los yacimientos paleolíticos de Ambrona y Torralba (Soria): un siglo de investigaciónes arqueológicos*, edited by M. Santonja and A. Pérez-González, pp. 396–417. Museo Arqueológico Regional Alcalá de Henares, Madrid.

Mussi, Margherita, and Paola Villa
2008 Single Carcass of *Mammuthus primigenius* with Lithic Artifacts in the Upper Pleistocene of Northern Italy. *Journal of Archaeological Science* 35(9):2606–2613.

Nogués-Bravo, David, Jesús Rodríguez, Joaquín Hortal, Persaram Batra, and Miguel B. Araújo
2008 Climate Change, Humans, and the Extinction of the Woolly Mammoth. *PLoS Biology* 6(4):675–692.

Norton, Mark R., John B. Broster, and Emanuel Breitburg
1998 The Trull Site (40PY276): A Paleoindian Mastodon Association in Tennessee. *Current Research in the Pleistocene* 15:50–51.

Obada, Teodor, Johannes van der Plicht, Anastasia Markova, and Afanasie Prepelitsa
2012 Preliminary Results of Studies of the Valea Morilor Upper Palaeolithic Site (Chişinău, Republic of Moldova): A New Camp of Mammoth Hunters. *Quaternary International* 276–277:227–241.

O'Connell, J. F., K. Hawkes, and N. G. Blurton-Jones
1992 Patterns in the Distribution, Site Structure, and Assemblage Composition of Hadza Kill-Butchering Sites. *Journal of Archaeological Science* 19(3):319–345.

Overstreet, David F.
1996 Still More on Cultural Contexts of Mammoth and Mastodon in the Southwestern Lake Michigan Basin. *Current Research in the Pleistocene* 13:36–38.
1998 Late Pleistocene Geochronology and the Paleoindian Penetration of the Southwestern Lake Michigan Basin. *Wisconsin Archaeologist* 79:28–52.

Overstreet, David F., and Michael F. Kolb
Geoarchaeological Contexts for Late Pleistocene Archaeological Sites with Human-Modified Woolly Mammoth Remains in Southeastern Wisconsin, USA. *Geoarchaeology* 18(1):91–114.

Overstreet, David F., and Thomas W. Stafford
1997 Additions to a Revised Chronology for Cultural and Non-Cultural Mammoth and Mastodon Fossils in the Southwestern Lake Michigan Basin. *Current Research in the Pleistocene* 14:70–71.

Owen-Smith, Norman
1999 The Interaction of Humans, Megaherbivores, and Habitats in the Late Pleistocene Extinction Event. In *Extinctions in Near Time: Causes, Contexts, and Consequences*, edited by Ross D. E. MacPhee, pp. 57–69. Springer, Boston.

Palmer, Harris A., and James B. Stoltman
1976 The Boaz Mastodon: A Possible Association of Man and Mastodon in Wisconsin. *Midcontinental Journal of Archaeology* 1(2):163–177.

Palombo, M. R., A. P. Anzidei, and A. Arnoldus-Huyzendveld
2003 La Polledrara di Cecanibbio (Rome): One of the Richest *Elephas (Palaeoloxodon) antiquus* Sites of the Late Middle Pleistocene in Italy. *Deinsia* 9:317–330.

Panera, Joaquím, Susana Rubio-Jara, José Yravedra, Hugues-Alexandre Blain, Carmen Sesé, and Alfredo Pérez-González
2014 Manzanares Valley (Madrid, Spain): A Good Country for Proboscideans and Neanderthals. *Quaternary International* 326–327:329–343.

Péan, Stéphane, and Marylène Patou-Mathis
Taphonomy of Mammoth Sites. *Deinsea* 9: 331–345.

Peros, Matthew C., Samuel E. Munoz, Konrad Gajewski, and André E. Viau
2010 Prehistoric Demography of North American Inferred from Radiocarbon Data. *Journal of Archaeological Science* 37(3): 656–664.

Piperno, M., and A. Tagliacozzo
The Elephant Butchery Area at the Middle Pleistocene Site of Notarchirico (Venosa, Basilicata, Italy). In *La terra degli elefanti [Proceedings of the 1st International*

Congress], edited by G. Cavarretta, P. Gioia, M. Mussi, and M. Palombo, pp. 230–236. Consiglio Nazionale delle Recherche, Rome, IT.

Pitulko, V. V., and P. A. Nikolskiy
2012   The Extinction of the Woolly Mammoth and the Archaeological Record in Northeastern Asia. *World Archaeology* 44(1):21–42.

Politis, Gustavo G., María A. Gutiérrez, and Clara Scabuzzo
2014   *Estado actual de las investigaciónes en el sitio arqueológico Arroyo Seco 2 (partido de Tres Arroyos, provincia de Buenos Aires, Argentina)*. UNCUAPA-CONICET Serie Monográfica, La Plata, AR.

Potts, Richard, Anna K. Behrensmeyer, and Peter Ditchfield
1999   Paleolandscape Variation and Early Pleistocene Hominid Activities: Members 1 and 7, Olorgesailie Formation, Kenya. *Journal of Human Evolution* 37(5):747–788.

Prasciunas, Mary M.
2001   Mapping Clovis: Projectile Points, Behavior, and Bias. *American Antiquity* 76(1):107–126.

Prescott, Graham W., David R. Williams, Andrew Balmford, Rhys E. Green, and Andrea Manica
2012   Quantitative Global Analysis of the Role of Climate and People in Explaining Late Quaternary Megafaunal Extinctions. *PNAS* 109(12):4527–4531.

Purdy, Barbara A., Kevin S. Jones, John J. Mecholsky, Gerald Bourne, Richard C. Hulbert, Bruce J. MacFadden, Krista L. Church, et al.
2011   Earliest Art in the Americas: Incised Image of a Proboscidean on a Mineralized Extinct Animal Bone from Vero Beach, Florida. *Journal of Archaeological Science* 38(11):2908–2913.

Rabinovich, R., O. Ackermann, E. Aladjem, R. Barkai, R. Biton, I. Milevski, N. Solodenko, and O. Marder
2012   Elephants at the Middle Pleistocene Acheulian Open-Air Site of Revadim Quarry, Israel. *Quaternary International* 276–277:183–197.

Rayl, Sandra Lee
1974   A Paleo-Indian Mammoth Kill Site near Silver Springs, Florida. Master's thesis, Department of Anthropology, Northern Arizona University, Flagstaff, AZ.

Redmond, Brian G., Gregory McDonald, Haskel J. Greenfield, and Matthew L. Burr
2012   New Evidence for Late Pleistocene Human Exploitation of Jefferson's Ground Sloth (*Megalonyx jeffersonii*) from Northern Ohio, USA. *World Archaeology* 44(1):75–101.

Redmond, Brian G., and Kenneth B. Tankersley
2005   Evidence of Early Paleoindian Bone Modification and Use at the Sheriden Cave Site (33wy252), Wyandot County, Ohio. *American Antiquity* 70(3):503–526.

Rigal, Laura
1993   Peale's Mammoth. In *American Iconology: New Approaches to Nineteenth-Century Art and Literature*, edited by David Miller, pp. 18–38. Yale University Press, New Haven, CT.

Robinson, Guy S., Lida Pigott Burney, and David A. Burney
2005   Landscape Paleoecology and Megafaunal Extinction in Southeastern New York State. *Ecological Monographs* 75:295–315.

Sanchez, Guadalupe, Vance T. Holliday, Edmund P. Gaines, Joaquín Arroyo-Cabrales, Natalia Martínez-Tagüeña, Andrew Kowler, Todd Lange, Gregory W. Hodgins, Susan M. Mentzer, and Ismael Sanchez-Morales
2014   Human (Clovis)-Gomphothere (*Cuvieronius* sp.) Association ~13,390 Calibrated yBP in Sonora, Mexico. *PNAS* 111(30):10972–10977.

Sanford, John T.
1935   The Richmond Mastodon. *Proceedings of the Rochester Academy of Science* 7(5). Rochester, NY.

Santonja, Manuel, and Alfredo Pérez-González
2005   Arqueología y elefantes en el pleistoceno medio de la península Ibérica. In *Los yacimientos paleolíticos de Ambrona y Torralba (Soria): un siglo de investigaciónes arqueológicos*, edited by M. Santonja and A. Pérez-González, pp. 382–395. Museo Arqueológico Regional Alcalá de Henares, Madrid.

Santonja, Manuel, Alfredo Pérez-González, G. Vega, and I. Rus
2001   Elephants and Stone Artifacts in the Middle Pleistocene Terraces of the Manzanares River (Madrid, Spain). In *La terra degli elefanti [Proceedings of the 1st International Congress]*, edited by G. Cavarretta, P. Gioia, M. Mussi, and M. Palombo, pp. 597–601. Consiglio Nazionale delle Recherche, Rome, IT.

Santonja, Manuel, Alfredo Pérez-González, Paola Villa, Enrique Soto, and Carmen Sesé
2001   Elephants in the Archaeological Sites of Aridos (Jarama Valley, Madrid, Spain). In

La terra degli elefanti [Proceedings of the 1st International Congress], edited by G. Cavarretta, P. Gioia, M. Mussi, and M. Palombo, pp. 602–606. Consiglio Nazionale delle Recherche, Rome, IT.

Saunders, Jeffrey J.
1996   North American Mammutidae. In *The Proboscidea: Evolution and Palaeoecology of Elephants and Their Relatives*, edited by J. Shoshani and P. Tassy, pp. 271–279. Oxford University Press, Oxford.

Schreve, Danielle C.
2006   The Taphonomy of a Middle Devensian (MIS 3) Vertebrate Assemblage from Lynford, Norfolk, UK, and Its Implications for Middle Palaeolithic Subsistence Strategies. *Journal of Quaternary Science* 21(5):543–556.

Scott, Beccy, Martin Bates, Richard Bates, Chantal Conneller, Matt Pope, Andrew Shaw, and Geoff Smith
2014   A New View from La Cotte de St. Brelade, Jersey. *Antiquity* 88(339):13–29.

Scott, Katherine
1980   Two Hunting Episodes of Middle Palaeolithic Age at La Cotte de Saint-Brelade, Jersey (Channel Islands). *World Archaeology* 12(2):137–152.
1986   The Bone Assemblages of Layers 3 and 6. In *La Cotte de Saint-Brelade 1961–1978: Excavations by C. B. M. McBurney*, edited by P. Callow and J. M. Cornford, pp. 159–184. Geo Books, Norwich, UK.

Seeman, Mark F.
2015   Sense and Sensibility in Midwestern Archaeology and the *Midcontinental Journal of Archaeology*, Part 1. *Midcontinental Journal of Archaeology* 40(1):4–13.

Seeman, Mark F., Nils E. Nilsson, Garry L. Summers, Larry L. Morris, Paul J. Barans, Elaine Dowd, and Margaret E. Newman
2008   Evaluating Protein Residues on Gainey Phase Paleoindian Stone Tools. *Journal of Archaeological Science* 35(10):2742–2750.

Sesé, Carmen, and Enrique Soto
2005   Mamíferos del yacimiento del pleistoceno medio de Ambrona: análisis faunístico e interpretación paleoambiental. In *Los yacimientos paleolíticos de Ambrona y Torralba (Soria): un siglo de investigaciónes arqueológicos*, edited by M. Santonja and A. Pérez-González, pp. 270–280. Museo Arqueológico Regional Alcalá de Henares, Madrid.

Shipman, Pat, Daniel C. Fisher, and Jennie J. Rose
1984   Mastodon Butchery: Microscopic Evidence of Carcass Processing and Bone Tool Use. *Paleobiology* 10(3):358–365.

Shott, Michael J.
2002   Sample Bias in the Distribution and Abundance of Midwestern Fluted Bifaces. *Midcontinental Journal of Archaeology* 27(1):89–123.
2004a   Midwestern Paleoindian Context. In *The Earliest Americans: Paleoindian Sites in the Eastern United States*, edited by E. Seibert, pp. 78–109, 262–297. National Historic Landmarks Survey, U.S. Dept. of the Interior, National Park Service, Washington, D.C. www.cr.nps.gov/aad/design/pubs/nhleam/.
2004b   Hunter-Gatherer Aggregation in Theory and Evidence: The North American Paleoindian Case. In *Hunter-Gatherers in Theory and Archaeology*, edited by G. Crothers, pp. 68–102. Center for Archaeological Investigations, Southern Illinois University, Carbondale.
2005   Representativity of the Midwestern Paleoindian Site Sample. *North American Archaeologist* 25(2):189–212.
2013   Human Colonization and Late Pleistocene Lithic Industries of the Americas. *Quaternary International* 285:150–160.
2014   Digitising Archaeology: A Subtle Revolution in Analysis. *World Archaeology* 46(1):1–9.

Smith, Edward E., and Sarah Surface-Evans
n.d.   Implications for Human-Mastodon Interactions in the Great Lakes Region: A Case Study from the Buesching Mastodon Site in Northeastern Indiana. Manuscript on file, Department of Anthropology, Michigan State University, East Lansing.

Smith, Geoff M.
2012   Middle Palaeolithic Subsistence: The Role of Hominins at Lynford, Norfolk, UK. *Quaternary International* 252:68–81.
2015   Neanderthal Megafaunal Exploitation in Western Europe and Its Dietary Implications: A Contextual Reassessment of La Cotte de St. Brelade (Jersey). *Journal of Human Evolution* 78:181–201.

Soffer, Olga
1985   *The Upper Paleolithic of the Central Russian Plain*. Academic, Orlando, FL.
1993   Upper Paleolithic Adaptations in Central and Eastern Europe and Man-Mammoth

Interactions. In *From Kostenki to Clovis: Upper Paleolithic-Paleo-Indian Adaptations*, edited by O. Soffer and N. Praslov, pp. 31–46. Plenum, New York.

Sousa, M. F., and S. M. Figueiredo
2001   The Pleistocene Elephants of Portugal. In *La terra degli elefanti [Proceedings of the 1st International Congress]*, edited by G. Cavarretta, P. Gioia, M. Mussi, and M. Palombo, pp. 611–616. Consiglio Nazionale delle Recherche, Rome, IT.

Staesche, Ulrich
1983   Aspects of the Life of Middle Palaeolithic Hunters in the N.W. German Lowlands, Based on the Site Salzgitter-Lebenstedt. In *Animals and Archaeology: 1. Hunters and Their Prey*, edited by J. Clutton-Brock and C. Grigson, pp. 173–182. BAR International Series 163. Oxbow, Oxford, UK.

Steele, D. Gentry, and David L. Carlson
1989   Excavation and Taphonomy of Mammoth Remains from the Duewall-Newberry Site, Brazos County, Texas. In *Bone Modification*, edited by R. Bonnichsen and M. Sorg, pp. 413–430. Institute for Quaternary Studies, University of Maine, Orono.

Stopp, Marianne P.
1997   *Early Human Adaptation in the Northern Hemisphere and the Implications of Taphonomy.* BAR International Series 669, Archaeopress, Oxford, UK.

Storck, Peter L., and Arthur E. Spiess
1994   The Significance of New Faunal Identifications Attributed to an Early Paleoindian (Gainey Complex) Occupation at the Udora Site, Ontario, Canada. *American Antiquity* 59(1):121–142.

Stuart, Anthony J., Lepold D. Sulerzhitsky, Lyobov A. Orlova, Yaroslav V. Kuzmin, and Adrian M. Lister
2002   The Latest Woolly Mammoths (*Mammuthus primigenius* Blumenbach) in Europe and Asia: A Review of the Current Evidence. *Quaternary Science Reviews* 21(14–15): 1559–1569.

Suárez, Rafael
2015   The Paleoamerican Occupation of the Plains of Uruguay: Technology, Adaptations, and Mobility. *PaleoAmerica* 1(1):88–104.

Surface-Evans, Sarah
2004   A Case Study for Treating Late Pleistocene Paleontological Finds as Archaeological Sites in the Great Lakes Region. Poster presented at the 69th Annual Meeting of the Society for American Archaeology, Montreal, QC.

Surovell, Todd A., and Bridig S. Grund
2012   The Associational Critique of Quaternary Overkill and Why It Is Largely Irrelevant to the Extinction Debate. *American Antiquity* 77(4):672–688.

Surovell, Todd A., and Nicole M. Waguespack
2008   How Many Elephant Kills Are 14? Clovis Mammoth and Mastodon Kills in Context. *Quaternary International* 191:82–97.

Surovell, Todd A., Spencer R. Pelton, Richard Anderson-Sprecher, and Adam D. Myers
2016   Test of Martin's Overkill Hypothesis Using Radiocarbon Dates on Extinct Megafauna. *PNAS* 113(4):886–891.

Tankersley, Kenneth B.
1999   Sheriden: A Stratified Pleistocene-Holocene Cave Site in the Great Lakes Region of North America. In *Zooarchaeology of the Pleistocene/Holocene Boundary*, edited by Jonathan C. Driver, pp. 67–76. BAR International Series 800. Archaeopress, Oxford, UK.

Tankersley Kenneth B., and Brian G. Redmond
2000   Ice Age Ohio. *Archaeology* 53(6):42–46.

Tankersley, Kenneth B., Michael R. Waters, and Thomas W. Stafford
2009   Clovis and the American Mastodon at Big Bone Lick, Kentucky. *American Antiquity* 74(3):558–567.

Taylor, J. G.
1969   William Turner's Journeys to the Caribou Country with the Labrador Eskimos in 1780. *Ethnohistory* 16(2):141–164.

Teale, Chelsea, and Norton G. Miller
2012   Mastodon Herbivory in Mid-Latitude Late-Pleistocene Boreal Forests of Eastern North America. *Quaternary Research* 78(1):72–81.

Thomas, Edward S.
1952   The Orleton Farms Mastodon. *Ohio Journal of Science* 52(1):1–5.

Thompson, Linda M., George C. McIntosh, and Warren D. Allmon
2008   Discoveries of the American Mastodon (*Mammut americanum*) in New York State. *Palaeontographica Americana* 61:25–41.

Ugan, Andrew, and David Byers
2007   Geographic and Temporal Trends in Proboscidean and Human Radiocarbon Histories during the Late Pleistocene. *Quaternary Science Reviews* 26(25–28):3058–3080.

Vartanyan, S. L., K. A. Arslanov, T. V. Tertychnaya, and S. B. Chernov
1995   Radiocarbon Dating Evidence for Mammoths on Wrangel Island, Arctic Ocean, until 2000 BC. *Radiocarbon* 37(1):1–6.

Veltre, Douglas W., David R. Yesner, Kristine J. Crossen, Russell W. Graham, and Joan B. Coltrain
2008   Patterns of Faunal Extinction and Paleoclimatic Change from Mid-Holocene Mammoth and Polar Bear Remains, Pribilof Islands, Alaska. *Quaternary Research* 70(1): 40–50.

Villa, Paola, and Franceso d'Errico
2005   Las puntas de marfil de Torralba y Ambrona. In *Los yacimientos paleolíticos de Ambrona y Torralba (Soria): un siglo de investigaciónes arqueológicos*, edited by M. Santonja and A. Pérez-González, pp. 288–305. Museo Arqueológico Regional Alcalá de Henares, Madrid.

Villa, Paola, and Marie Soressi
2000   Stone Tools in Carnivore Sites: The Case of Bois Roche. *Journal of Anthropological Research* 56(2):187–215.

Villa, Paola, Enrique Soto, Manuel Santonja, Alfredo Pérez-González, Rafael Mora, Joaquim Parcerisas, and Carmen Sesé
2005   Nuevos datos sobre Ambrona: cerrando el debate Caza versus Carroñeo. In *Los yacimientos paleolíticos de Ambrona y Torralba (Soria): un siglo de investigaciónes arqueológicos*, edited by M. Santonja and A. Pérez-González, pp. 352–381. Museo Arqueológico Regional Alcalá de Henares, Madrid.

Waguespack, Nicole
2014   Pleistocene Extinctions: The State of Evidence and the Structure of Debate. In *Paleoamerican Odyssey*, edited by K. Graf, C. Ketron, and M. Waters, pp. 311–319. Texas A&M University Press, College Station, TX.

Walters, Matthew M.
1988   The Adams Mastodon Site, Harrison County, Kentucky. In *Paleoindian and Archaic Research in Kentucky*, edited by C. Hockensmith, D. Pollack, and T. Sanders, pp. 43–46. Kentucky Heritage Council, Frankfort.

Webb, S. D. (editor)
2006   *First Floridians and Last Mastodons: The Page-Ladson Site in the Aucilla River.* Springer, Dordrecht, NL.

Weber, Thomas
2000   The Eemian *Elephas antiquus* Finds with Artefacts from Lehringen and Gröbern: Are They Really Killing Sites? *Anthropologie et Préhistoire* 111:177–185.

Webster, David, and Gary Webster
1984   Optimal Hunting and Pleistocene Extinction. *Human Ecology* 12(3):275–289.

Wenban-Smith, F. F., P. Allen, M. R. Bates, S. A. Parfitt, R. C. Preece, J. R. Steard, C. Turner, and J. E. Whittaker
2006   The Clactonian Elephant Butchery Site at Southfleet Road, Ebbsfleet, UK. *Journal of Quaternary Science* 21(5):471–483.

Whittington, Stephen L., and Bennett Dyke
1984   Simulating Overkill: Experiments with the Mosimann and Martin Model. In *Quaternary Extinctions: A Prehistoric Revolution*, edited by P. Martin and R. Klein, pp. 451–465. University of Arizona Press, Tucson.

Williams, Stephen
1957   The Island 35 Mastodon: Its Bearing on the Age of Archaic Cultures in the East. *American Antiquity* 22(4):359–372.

Wittry, Warren L.
1965   The Institute Digs a Mastodon. *Cranbrook Institute of Science News Letter* 35:14–19.

Wojtal, Piotr, and K. Cyrek
2001   The Upper Palaeolithic Mammoth Site at Halich (Ukraine). In *La terra degli elefanti [Proceedings of the 1st International Congress]*, edited by G. Cavarretta, P. Gioia, M. Mussi, and M. Palombo, pp. 373–375. Consiglio Nazionale delle Recherche, Rome, IT.

Wojtal, Piotr, and Krzysztof Sobczyk
2005   Man and Woolly Mammoth at the Kraków Spadzista Street (B): Taphonomy of the Site. *Journal of Archaeological Science* 32(2): 193–206.

Wolverton, Steve, R. Lee Lyman, James H. Kennedy, and Thomas W. La Point
2009   The Terminal Pleistocene Extinctions in North America, Hypermorphic Evolution, and the Dynamic Equilibrium Model. *Journal of Ethnobiology* 29(1):28–63.

Wood, W. Raymond
1976   Archaeological Investigations at the Pomme de Terre Springs. In *Prehistoric Man and His Environments: A Case Study in the Ozark Highlands*, edited by W. R. Wood

and R. B. McMillan, pp.97–107. Academic, New York.

Woodman, Neal, and Nancy B. Athfield
2009   Post-Clovis Survival of American Mastodon in the Southern Great Lakes Region of North America. *Quaternary Research* 72(3) 359–363.

Wright, David K., Jessica Thompson, Alex Mackay, Menno Welling, Steven L. Forman, Gilbert Price, Jian-xin Zhao, Andrew S. Cohen, Oris Malijani, and Elizabeth Gomani-Chindebvu
2014   Renewed Geoarchaeological Investigations of Mwanganda's Village (Elephant Butchery Site), Karonga, Malawi. *Geoarchaeology* 29(2):98–120.

Wroe, Stephen, and Judith Field
2006   A Review of the Evidence for a Human Role in the Extinction of Australian Megafauna and an Alternative Interpretation. *Quaternary Science Reviews* 25(21–22): 2692–2703.

Yansa, Catherine H., and Kristin M. Adams
2012   Mastodons and Mammoths in the Great Lakes Region, USA and Canada: New Insights into their Diets as They Neared Extinction. *Geography Compass* 6(4):175–188.

Yravedra, José, Joaquín Panera, Susana Rubio-Jara, Iván Manzano, Alfonso Expósito, Alfredo Pérez-González, Enrique Soto, and Mario López-Recio
2014   Neanderthal and *Mammuthus* Interactions at EDAR Culebro 1 (Madrid, Spain). *Journal of Archaeological Science* 42:500–508.

Yravedra, J., S. Rubio-Jara, J. Panera, D. Uribelarrea, and A. Pérez-González
2012   Elephants and Subsistence: Evidence of the Human Exploitation of Extremely Large Mammal Bones from the Middle Palaeolithic Site of PRERESA (Madrid, Spain). *Journal of Archaeological Science* 39: 1063–1071.

Yule, Jeffrey V., Robert J. Fournier, Christopher X. Jensen, and Jinyan Yang
2014   A Review and Synthesis of Late Pleistocene Extinction Modeling: Progress Delayed by Mismatches between Ecological Realism, Interpretation, and Methodological Transparency. *Quarterly Review of Biology* 89(2): 92–106.

Yule, Jeffrey V., Christopher X. Jensen, Aby Joseph, and Jimmie Goode
2009   The Puzzle of North America's Late Pleistocene Megafaunal Extinction Patterns: Test of New Explanations Yields Unexpected Results. *Ecological Modelling* 220(4):533–544.

Zazula, G., R. MacPhee, J. Metcalfe, A. Reyes, F. Brock, P. Druckenmiller, P. Groves, et al.
2014   American Mastodon Extirpation in the Arctic and Subarctic Predates Human Colonization and Terminal Pleistocene Climate Change. *PNAS* 111(52):18460–18465.

Zenin, Vasiliy N., Evgeny N. Maschenko, Sergey V. Leshchinskiy, Aleksandr F. Pavlov, Pieter M. Grootes, and Marie-Josée Nadeau
2003   The First Direct Evidence of Mammoth Hunting in Asia (Lugovskoye Site, Western Siberia). In *Third International Mammoth Conference, 2003: Program and Abstracts*, edited by J. Storer, pp. 152–155. Occasional Papers in Earth Sciences 5. Palaeontological Program, Government of Yukon. Whitehorse, NT.

Zutovski, Katia, and Ran Barkai
2016   The Use of Elephant Bones for Making Acheulian Handaxes: A Fresh Look at Old Bones. *Quaternary International* 406: 227–238.

CHAPTER 12

Where Tides of Genes Perpetual Ebb and Flow

What DNA Evidence Tells Us about the Peopling of the Americas

Theodore G. Schurr

In this chapter, I present some recent results from our studies of genetic diversity in Northeast Asian and Native American populations.[1] As will be shown, the prehistory of the Altai-Sayan region is crucial to understanding the peopling of the Americas, because it appears to be the area from which human populations began expanding east into the New World some 25,000 years ago.

To begin, I briefly outline some of the questions concerning Native American and Siberian prehistory that we have been trying to address through our genetic studies. Next, I provide a brief overview of mitochondrial DNA and Y-chromosome variation and explain how data generated from these parts of our genome are used for population history studies. I will subsequently elaborate the results of our genetic studies in the Altai-Sayan region and the Americas and situate them in the context of other recent studies of Native American genetic ancestry, particularly those focusing on autosomal variation. Finally, I draw some conclusions from these studies and offer thoughts about future directions for this research.

Research Questions

One of the main questions concerning the prehistory of the Americas is the place of origin of the ancestors of modern Native American populations. For over two decades, it has been thought that the region encompassing Mongo-lia and the Altai-Sayan Mountains represented the areas from which these ancestors may have arisen (Figure 12.1). The four major mitochondrial DNA haplogroups or maternal lineages present in Native Americans are found in populations from this region (Torroni et al. 1993a, b; Kolman et al. 1996; Merriwether et al. 1996; Sukernik et al. 1996; Starikovskaya et al. 2005; Derenko et al. 2010; Dulik et al. 2012a), as are founding Y-chromosome haplogroups or paternal lineages (Santos et al. 1999; Karafet et al. 1997, 1999; Lell et al. 1997, 2002; Bortolini et al. 2003; Zegura et al. 2004; Dulik et al. 2012a). While these observations do not necessarily indicate that the migration or demic expansion that directly led to the colonization of the Americas began in the Altai-Sayan, they do suggest that the genetic lineages most closely similar to those in the Americas arose and have been present in this region for some time.

Regarding the Americas, there has been great effort over the past 25 years to determine the timing and number of migrations that entered the Americas. In particular, researchers have attempted to determine whether all Native American groups—those placed in the Amerind, Eskimo-Aleut, and Na-Dene language stocks by Greenberg and colleagues (1986)—arose from a single wave or multiple independent waves of migration (Bolnick et al. 2004; Schurr 2004a, b; Hunley and Long 2005; Kemp and Schurr 2010; O'Rourke and Raff 2010). There has also been

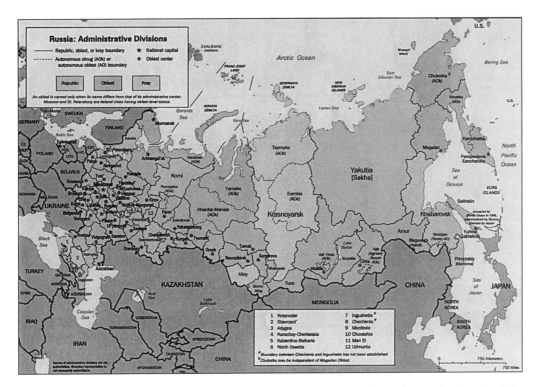

FIGURE 12.1. A map of Russia showing the Altai-Sayan region in southern Siberia, the putative homeland of ancestral Native Americans (http://www.lib.utexas.edu/maps/commonwealth/russia_pol_1994.pdf).

considerable debate over the timing of the initial human entry into the New World, whether the initial colonization followed an interior or coastal route, when an ice-free corridor was available for human passage, and whether the Clovis lithic culture represents the initial colonization populations for the Americas (Figure 12.2; Schurr 2004a, b; Goebel et al. 2008; Meltzer 2009; Kemp and Schurr 2010; O'Rourke and Raff 2010; O'Rourke 2011).

Studies conducted by several research teams (Tamm et al. 2007; Kitchen et al. 2008; Fagundes et al. 2008; Mulligan et al. 2008) have proposed a different scenario—called by some the Beringian Incubator Model—to account for the biological and linguistic diversity of Native American populations (Figure 12.3). In this model, ancient Asian populations expanded eastward from a presumed Altaian or South-Central Siberian homeland into Beringia around 25,000 years ago. In Beringia, which existed as a massive land bridge during the Last Glacial Maximum

(LGM), members of this ancestral population lived in the region for many thousands of years and began to genetically differentiate from their Asian antecedents, becoming "Beringian" in the process. This transformation is evidenced by the evolution of a number of distinctive mtDNA (female) (A2, B2, C1b, C1c, C1d, D1, D4h3, X2a) and Y-chromosome (male) (C3b, Q-M3) haplogroups in ancestral Native American populations (Figure 12.4; Torroni et al. 1993a; Forster et al. 1996; Bonatto et al. 1997; Karafet et al. 1997, 1999; Lell et al. 1997, 2002; Bergen et al. 1999; Tamm et al. 2007; Achilli et al. 2008; Fagundes et al. 2008; Perego et al. 2009, 2010). After this incubation period, ancestral Native American populations expanded southward along the northwest coast of North America some 16–18,000 years ago, reaching the southern reaches of South America by 15,000 cal BP (Dillehay 1999; Goebel et al. 2008; Meltzer 2009).

Somewhat later, populations expanded from Beringia into northern North America and

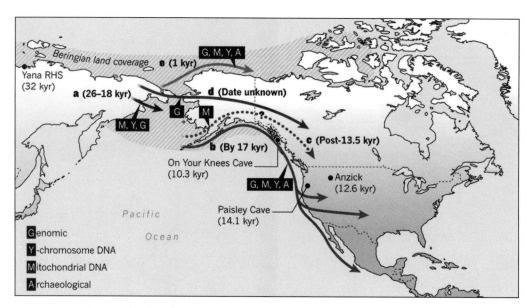

FIGURE 12.2. A diagram showing alternative scenarios for the peopling of the Americas (Raff and Bolnick, 2014, p. 162, reprinted by permission of Macmillan Publishers Ltd.).

settled the deglaciated regions of the continent, establishing themselves there before the eventually submergence of the Bering land mass. In the ancestors of these populations, additional mtDNA (A2a, A2b, C4c, D2, D3, D4a) and Y-chromosome (Q1a5, Q1a6) haplogroups evolved from the original Beringian set, reflecting their divergence from earlier founding lineages (Starikovskaya et al. 1998; Schurr et al. 1999; Saillard et al. 2000; Rubicz et al. 2003, 2010; Helgason et al. 2006; Zlojutro et al. 2006; Dulik et al. 2012b; Schurr et al. 2012). During this period, there also appeared to have been back migration(s) of ancestral Native American groups—including Na-Dene speakers—into interior Siberia, giving rise to the Kettic-speaking populations there (Schurr 2003; Schurr and Wallace 2003; Tamm et al. 2007; Scott and O'Rourke 2010; Vadja 2010).

Various researchers have attempted to synthesize these mtDNA data into a model for the peopling of the Americas. Figure 12.5 shows one such model (Achilli et al. 2013), with the different sets of mtDNA haplogroups that have arisen in the ancestral Native American population(s) and their dispersal patterns. The various colors indicate the timing of these dispersals, hence, the relative ages of the associated maternal lineages. Note the complex pattern that these lineages form within North America over a 15,000-year period. Some researchers have proposed that certain of these lineages represent distinct migratory pulses due to their largely coastal (D4h3) or exclusively North American (X2a) distributions (Figure 12.6; Perego et al. 2009). In fact, unlike the other maternal lineages in the Americas, X2a has sister branches in western Eurasia but none in eastern Eurasia, where all of the other founding lineages originated (Brown et al. 1998; Dornelles et al. 2005; Derenko et al. 2006, 2010; Reidla et al. 2003; Schurr et al. 2010;). However, the debate over whether the founding mtDNA lineages represent a single genetically complex founder population or multiple founder populations continues to this day, beginning with the earliest studies of Native American mtDNA diversity (e.g., Torroni et al. 1992, 1993a; Merriwether et al. 1994) and continuing to this date with genomic studies (e.g., Reich et al. 2012; Rasmussen et al. 2014; Raff and Bolnick 2014).

A related question about the settlement of the Americas is the size of the founding population(s) or colonizing groups, since this demographic feature has important implications for

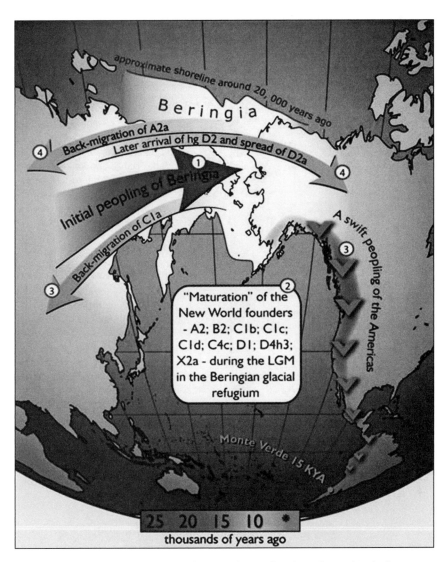

FIGURE 12.3. A schematic illustration of maternal gene flow in and out of Beringia, as proposed in the Beringian Incubator Model. Colors of the arrows correspond to approximate timing of the events and are decoded in the colored time-bar. The initial peopling of Beringia (depicted in light yellow) was followed by a standstill, after which the ancestors of the Native Americans spread swiftly over the New World while some of the Beringian maternal lineages—C1a—spread westwards. More recent genetic exchange (in green) is manifested by back-migration of A2a into Siberia and the spread of D2a into northeastern America that postdated the initial peopling of the New World (from Tamm et al. 2007).

the nature and rate of population dispersal in the Americas. Based on genetic data, some have estimated an effective population size (N_e) for the founder population of between 100 and 1,000 individuals (e.g., Hey 2005; Fagundes et al. 2008), with each estimate implying different census sizes of the population.[2] Given the typical size of nomadic aboriginal populations in Siberia based on ethnographic data (e.g., Levin and Potapov 1964), with some 200–400 persons composing a tribal group, perhaps slightly more, the smaller of these estimates would seem to suggest a rather

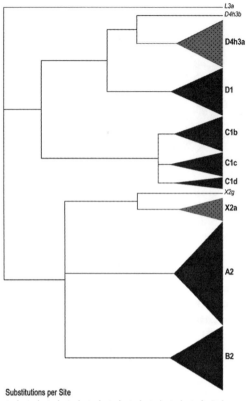

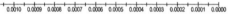

Substitutions per Site

FIGURE 12.4. Evolutionary relationships among 344 complete Native American coding-region sequences. The sequences belong to the pan-American haplogroups (A2, B2, C1b, C1c, C1d, D1) and to the uncommon Native American clades D4h3a and X2a. The evolutionary history was inferred by hand with the maximum-parsimony method, with all the available pan-American coding-region sequences included. The tree is drawn to scale. The evolutionary distances were computed with the maximum-likelihood method and are in the units of number of base substitutions per site. All positions containing gaps and ambiguous data were eliminated from the data set. The triangle width is proportional to the number of sequences, thus representing the internal haplogroup variation (from Perego et al. 2009, reprinted by permission of Elsevier).

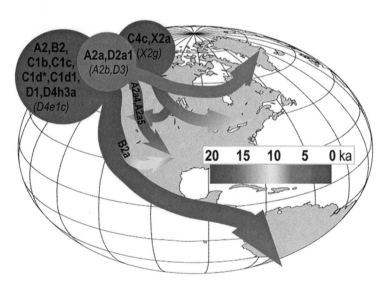

FIGURE 12.5. Model of the colonization of the Americas based on mtDNA mitogenome sequence data. In this schematic overview, the 16 mtDNA founder lineages are associated with three major migratory events. Note that the location of the three spheres is approximate. In parentheses (and in italics) are indicated those founder lineages that are not yet sufficiently analyzed. Two additional events are indicated by stealth arrows. The first arrow corresponds to the recent southward spread of the Athapaskans (marked by A2a4 and A2a5). The second arrow marks the major in situ expansion of B2a (from Achilli et al. 2013, ©2013 National Academy of Sciences).

significant population bottleneck or reduction during the initial peopling of the American continents. Reconstructions of the expansion process using genetic data suggest the founder population(s) underwent some reduction in N_e just before entering the Americas between 23,000–18,000 years ago (Schurr and Sherry 2004; Hey 2005; Tamm et al. 2007; Fagundes et al. 2008), with some estimates suggesting quite a significant reduction (Wall et al. 2011) that then rapidly expanded in size once established in the New World. In this regard, one sees a proliferation of mtDNA lineages/haplotypes at that particular period of time and, based on demographic reconstructions, a slight decrease in N_e around 20,000 cal BP, followed by a rapid expansion in population size (Figure 12.7; Fagundes et al. 2008).

Thus, from this point of view, the genetic bottleneck resulting from the colonization process does not appear to have been extraordinarily strong. While further work is being done to model the founder population sizes, Native American populations did experience significant population reductions due to post-contact disease and warfare (e.g., O'Fallon and Fehren-Schmitz 2011), although these historical effects do not seem to have radically altered the genetic makeup of indigenous populations from a haploid lineage perspective. Yet, previous ancient DNA work has shown that certain mtDNA and Y-chromosome haplotypes are missing from the phylogenies of these lineages, thereby indicating that some loss of haplotypes has occurred within the past 500–1000 years, if not longer (Malhi et al. 2003, 2008; Kemp and Schurr 2010; Schurr 2010; O'Rourke 2011).

The paternal lineages most commonly seen in the Americas (Underhill et al. 1996, 2001; Santos et al. 1999; Lell et al. 1997, 2002; Karafet et al. 1997, 1999) belong to haplogroup Q, an eastern Eurasian lineage with multiple branches in the Old World (Figure 12.8; Karafet et al. 2001, Underhill et al. 2001; Malyarchuk et al. 2011; Dulik et al. 2012a). Another lineage observed exclusively in North America is haplogroup C3b (Bergen et al. 1999; Karafet et al. 1999; Lell et al. 2002; Zegura et al. 2004). It is part of a very old

TABLE 12.1. Ages of Y-chromosome lineages in the Americas.

SNP	Haplogroup	Lineage Age (RCYBP)
L54	Q-L54 (Q1a3a1*)	19,180 ± 2,650
M3	Q-M3 (Q1a3a1a*)	12,890 ± 2,240
NWT01	Q1a6	4,030 ± 970
P89	Q1a5	~5,000
P39	C3b	4,900 ± 1,590

paternal lineage that is distributed across East Asia, Southeast Asia, and Australasia and has differentiated into regional sublineages over the past 40,000 years (e.g., Karafet et al. 2001; Kayser et al. 2001; Hudjashov et al. 2007; Zhong et al. 2010, 2011). All other Y-chromosome haplogroups present in Native American tribes are considered nonindigenous in origin and acquired through historical admixture (e.g., Schurr 2004a).

As seen in Figure 12.9, haplogroup Q in the Americas is represented by two major branches, designated here as Q1a* and Q1a3a.[3] Defined by the M346 mutation (or single nucleotide polymorphism, SNP), Q1a* is the older of the two lineages and gave rise to Q1a3a, which is defined by the M3 SNP (Table 12.1). The M3 SNP is a uniquely American variant, having seemingly arisen as founder populations in Beringia or Northeast Asia were just beginning to expand into the American continents (Underhill et al. 1996; Santos et al. 1996, 1999; Karafet et al. 1997, 1999; Lell et al. 1997, 2002).

Our analysis of Y-chromosome variation in Siberia and the Americas has allowed us to evaluate the ages of these lineages in the two regions (Table 12.1). Q-L54, the ancestral lineage to the unique American Q-M3, has been dated to 25,000 BP in Siberia, and somewhat later date in the Americas (e.g., Dulik et al. 2012a). Q-M3 has a more recent origin, arising in the Americas between 14–16,000 cal BP, and then being widely dispersed in the New World with colonizing populations (Karafet et al. 2001; Lell et al. 2002; Zegura et al. 2004; Dulik et al. 2012b). In both cases, the two major Q lineages arose during the Last Glacial Maximum (LGM), before the

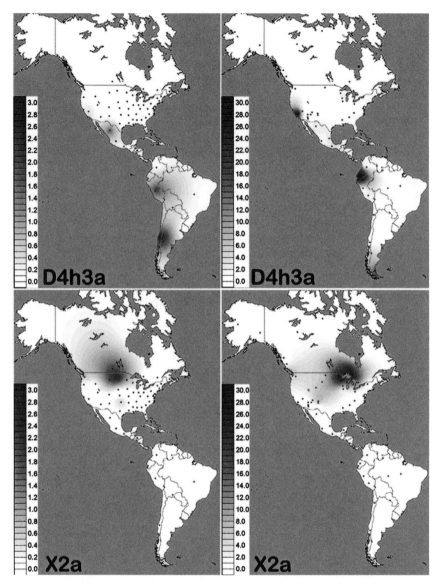

FIGURE 12.6. The spatial-frequency distributions of haplogroups D4h3a and X2a in the Americas. The upper maps show the frequency distributions of haplogroup D4h3a, and the lower maps depict X2a frequencies. On the left are data from general mixed populations of national states, and on the right are those from Native American groups. Note that the frequency scales (%) employed for general mixed populations and Native American groups are different. The dots indicate location of the population samples included in each survey. Frequency maps of haplogroups were obtained as in Olivieri and colleagues (2006; Figure 12.6 from Perego et al. 2009, reprinted by permission of Elsevier).

emergence of the Clovis lithic culture in North America (Goebel et al. 2008; Meltzer 2009).

Along with other researchers (e.g., Derenko et al. 2006; Karafet et al. 2008; Malyarchuk et al. 2011; Zhong et al. 2010, 2011), we have con-tributed data that have further refined the Y-chromosome phylogeny through our work with Asian and indigenous Siberian populations. Based on this work, we observed that there were a number of additional SNPs between the M346

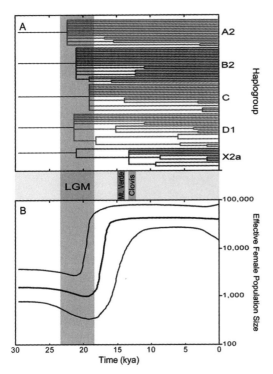

FIGURE 12.7. A phylogenetic tree and Bayesian sky-line plot for Native American mtDNA sequences. (*A*) Maximum-likelihood tree from 80 Native American mtDNA coding region haplotypes. The time axis (in kya) was estimated with a paramet-ric molecular-clock model calibrated with the as-sumption of human versus chimpanzee divergence at 6.5 million yr ago. Branches with bootstrap sup-port <0.5 were collapsed. (*B*) mtDNA Bayesian sky-line plot showing the Native American population size trend with a log-normal relaxed clock with the standard substitution rate of 1.26 3 10_8 sites/yr and a generation time of 25 yr. The *y* axis is the effective number of females. The thick solid line is the median estimate, and the thin lines (blue) show the 95 percent highest posterior density limits es-timated with 60 million chains. Approximate dates for the LGM, Monte Verde, and Clovis sites are shown in the middle panel. The time axis is limited to <30 kya (from Fagundes et al. 2008, reprinted by permission of Elsevier).

and the M3 SNPs that created further structure in the haplogroup Q phylogeny, one being the M54 SNP (Q-M54) that defines the precursor lineage for that defined by the M3 SNP (Q-M3; Figure 12.9).[4] The Q-M54 lineage is present in

both the Altai-Sayan region and the Americas, thereby demonstrating a clear genetic linkage between these regions and affirming south-central Siberia as the homeland of ancestral Na-tive American populations (Dulik et al. 2012a). Using the nomenclature from 2012, the Q-L54 branch is called Q1a3a1 and the Q-M3 branch is called Q1a3a1a. With the discovery of hundreds of new SNPs through Y-chromosome and ge-nomic sequencing work (e.g., The 1000 Ge-nomes Project 2010), numerous new branches in the Americas are being defined, changing the nomenclature for all paternal lineages, including haplogroup Q.

In addition to questions concerning the ini-tial peopling of the Americas, we have been in-vestigating the genetic histories of circumarctic populations, particularly those of Eskimo-Aleut and Athapaskan Indian populations. Over the past few years, we have focused much of our attention on the genetic histories of the Inu-vialuit (Inuit), Gwich'in, and Tlicho (Dene) populations from the Northwest Territories, Canada, where there is considerable linguistic and cultural diversity among Dene First Nations. Some of the questions that we are exploring are the timing of the settlement of northern North America, the genetic relationships between cir-cumarctic groups and Amerindian populations to the south, and the dates at which Eskimo-Aleut and Na-Dene populations emerged. With regard to Eskimo-Aleut speaking populations, we are investigating the peopling of the Arctic through our work with the Inuvialuit, who live in the Mackenzie Delta region and adjacent islands in the Arctic Sea. Data from this area is filling a crucial gap in the sampling of Inuit groups across the Arctic Coast and will help clarify the timing and process of expansion of one or more Eskimoan groups across the region (Starikovskaya et al. 1998; Saillard et al. 2000; Bosch et al. 2003; Helgason et al. 2006; Gilbert et al. 2008; Rasmussen et al. 2010; Rubicz et al. 2010; Dulik et al. 2012b; Vilar et al. 2015).

Through work with circumarctic popula-tions, we have further elaborated the haplo-group Q phylogeny. Our work has revealed two new Q subbranches in Athapaskan (Q1a5)

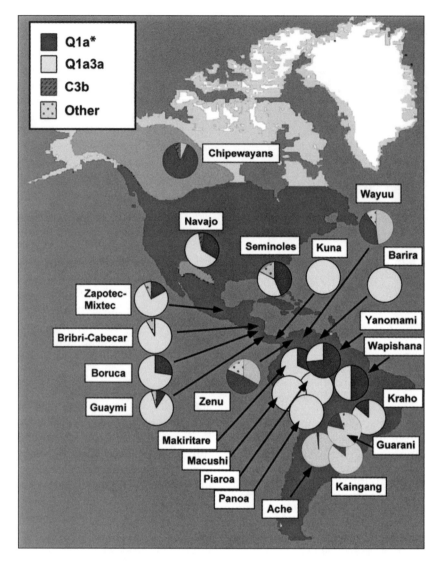

FIGURE 12.8. Frequency distribution of Y-chromosome haplogroups in the Americas (from Schurr 2004a).

and Inuvialuit (Q1a6) populations and suggested C3b to be exclusively Athapaskan in origin (Figure 12.9). All of these sublineages are 4,000–5,000 years old, based on time to most recent common ancestor (TMRCA) estimates and thus appear to have arisen as human populations expanded into the Arctic region of North America (Table 12.1; Dulik et al. 2012b). In fact, Q1a6 appears in many circumarctic populations, based on assessments of Y-STR data from these groups, which include Aleuts,

Yupik, Inuit (Inuvialuit) in North America, and Chukchi and Koryaks in northeastern Siberia, while others, such as Athapaskan groups, may have this lineage through admixture with the other circumarctic groups (Dulik et al. 2012b). Our mtDNA data also support the model of Arctic expansion whereby Paleoeskimo populations initially settled the Arctic coast, differentiated there, and then were later replaced or absorbed by Thule populations expanding from Alaska some 1,000 years ago (Figure 12.10; Gilbert et al.

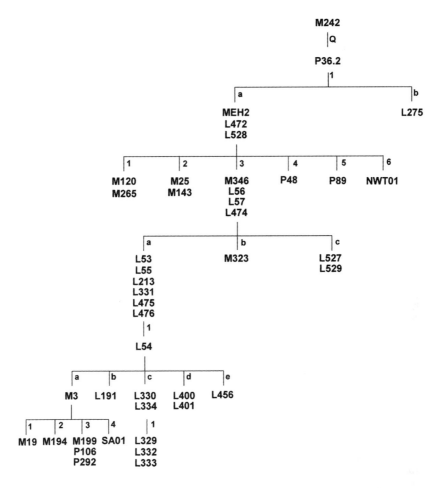

FIGURE 12.9. Y-chromosome haplogroup Q SNP phylogeny. The nomenclature for the branches of haplogroup Q (its lineages) can be read from top to bottom in this diagram, with each step through the tree being marked by a lower-case letter or number. Thus, the branch defined by the M346 SNP is called "Q1a3," and that defined by the M3 SNP is called "Q1a3a1a" (from Dulik et al. 2012a, ©2012 National Academy of Sciences).

2008; Rasumussen et al. 2010; Raghavan et al. 2014; Raff et al. 2015; Vilar et al. 2015).

In addition to these insights into Arctic prehistory, our Y-chromosome research with North American tribal populations has added complexity to the model of the peopling of the Americas. We have observed some of the precursors to the dominant lineages in the Americas (Q-L54 and Q-M3) in North America, these being Q-MEH2 (Q1a) and Q-M346 (Q1a3; Figure 12.9). To date, these lineages have not been observed in Mesoamerica and South America (although more data from populations in those

regions may reveal them), suggesting that they arrived in North America through recurrent and relatively recent gene flow from Beringia or Northeast Asia (Dulik et al. 2012b).

Related work in Mexico and the Caribbean has provided further details about the Y-chromosome Q diversity in the Americas (Figure 12.11). Through high-resolution SNP genotyping, Y-resequencing and Y-STR analysis, and consultation with the published literature, we have identified SNPs that define new branches of haplogroup Q. One of these new subbranches, Q-Z780, splits off from Q-L54,

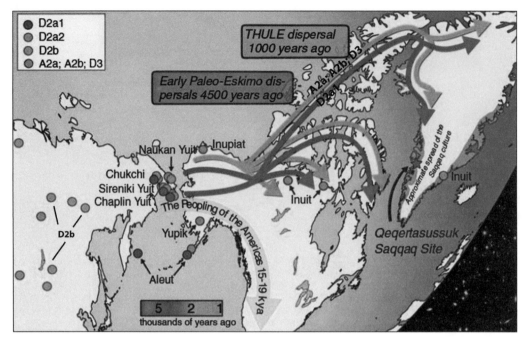

FIGURE 12.10. Sequential waves of human dispersals into the northern extremes of the New World. For clarity, the dispersal that brought the Dorset culture is omitted. Shown are the approximate geographic distribution of contemporary Neo-Eskimo populations, location of the Qeqertasussuk archaeological Paleo-Eskimo (Saqqaq culture) site, and distribution of related extant mtDNA haplogroups. The timing of the initial peopling of the Americas, which did not reach the northern extremes, is shown as estimated by two recent studies (from Gilbert et al. 2008, reprinted by permission of AAAS).

while another likely delineates an intermediate branch between Q-L54 and Q-M3 (perhaps more than one). These new branches appear in both North and Central American populations and probably also appear in South American populations, where additional substructure within haplogroup Q has been shown to occur (e.g., Bisso-Machado et al. 2011; Jota et al. 2011).

While many genetic studies of Native Americans have focused on the haploid portions of the genome (mtDNA, Y-chromosome), researchers are increasingly using autosomal SNP data to assess genetic diversity in the Americas. Such data are more numerous than those available from the mtDNA and Y-chromosome, represent large portions of all of the autosomes (chromosomes 1–22 and the X-chromosome), and also reflect the biparental genetic history of the individuals whose DNA samples are being analyzed.

Reich and colleagues (2012) used autosomal SNP data to assess genetic similarities and differences among Native American groups and between Old and New World populations, as well as model the migration and demographic histories of indigenous American populations. Using these autosomal SNP data, they produced a Neighbor-Joining (NJ) tree representing the genetic distances between all of these populations (Figure 12.12).[5] In this NJ tree, Native Americans were clearly separated from Asians, although Arctic populations were generally closer to them than Amerindians and Athapaskans. In addition, Algonquian/Athapaskan groups clustered together away from tribal populations in the rest of the Americas, implying some shared ancestry, while the larger Amerindian cluster exhibited geographic subdivision between and within continents, with Mexico being distinguishable from lower Mesoamerica. Moreover, there was some concordance in the population branching pattern and the linguistic affiliation of these groups, although this was not absolutely clear cut.

Using these autosomal SNP data, Reich

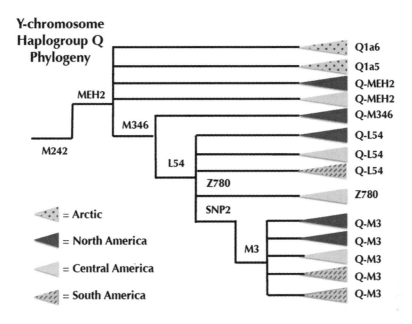

FIGURE 12.11. A revised phylogeny of Y-chromosome haplogroup Q based on published and unpublished data from Siberian and Native American populations.

and colleagues (2012) also tried to model demographic and migration histories of Native American populations. Based on the resulting Treemix diagram (Figure 12.13), they proposed a model involving multiple expansions or streams of founding populations into the Americas. One produced Mesoamerican and South American populations and another produced North American populations. A second, later, stream produced from the same ancestral genetic stock gave rise to Eskimo-Aleuts and a third to Athapaskan Indians (Na-Dene), represented by a single population, Chipewyan. There were also complex interactions between founding population streams in the formation of these ethnolinguistic groups. The northern lineage that gave rise to Athapaskans also substantially influenced the Eskimo-Aleut founder population, while Chipewyans showed significant genetic influences from northern Amerindians (Algonquians).

In some ways, this model of settlement mirrors the older tripartite migration model (Greenberg et al. 1986) while also departing from it in identifying a complex admixture process at the heart of the settlement process. This kind of ad-

mixture was actually implied in the Greenberg and colleagues (1986) model based on classical nuclear markers and dental trait data, as the Na-Dene and Eskimo-Aleut clusters were not clearly distinguished from each other due the probable admixture between them. The multiple stream model also varies in some respects from the Beringian Standstill Model, which purports that a single major expansion gave rise to all founder groups, hence, to all genetic variation observed in the New World. Regardless of these differences, this and related studies are now revealing subtleties in the formation of founder populations that then gave rise to the ancestors of contemporary Native American populations.

Other groundbreaking work focused on characterizing genetic variation in ancient samples from Siberia and the Americas. Such studies provide a view of biological diversity in Eurasia and the Americas that is not entirely evident through the analysis of contemporary populations. The genomic analysis of an ancient individual from the Ma'lta site in southeastern Siberia revealed that admixture had occurred between ancient West and East Eurasian populations prior to the movement of ancestral Native American

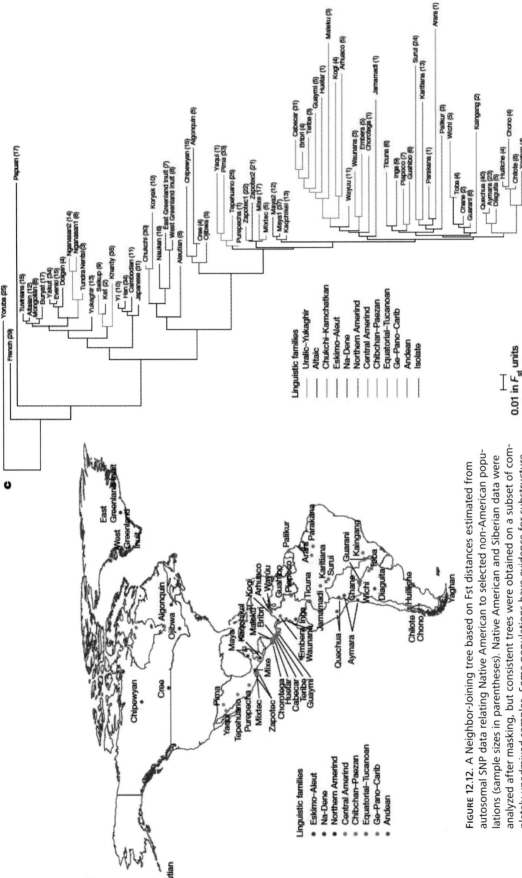

FIGURE 12.12. A Neighbor-Joining tree based on Fst distances estimated from autosomal SNP data relating Native American to selected non-American populations (sample sizes in parentheses). Native American and Siberian data were analyzed after masking, but consistent trees were obtained on a subset of completely unadmixed samples. Some populations have evidence for substructure, and we represent these as two different groups—for example, Maya1 and Maya2 (from Reich et al. 2012, reprinted by permission of Macmillan Publishers Ltd.).

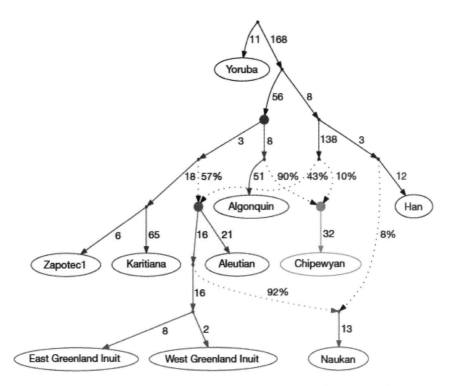

FIGURE 12.13. Distinct streams of gene flow from Asia into Americas. This admixture graph is consistent with three streams of Asian gene flow into America. Solid points indicate inferred ancestral populations, drift on each lineage is given in units proportional to 1,000 x Fst, and mixture events (dotted lines) are denoted by the percentage of ancestry. The Asian lineage leading to First Americans is the most deeply diverged, whereas the Asian lineages leading to Eskimo–Aleut speakers and the Na-Dene-speaking Chipewyan are more closely related and descend from a common Siberian ancestral population that is a sister group to the Han. The inferred ancestral populations are indicated by the filled circles, with the lineages descending from them being colored: First American (blue); ancestors of the Na-Dene-speaking Chipewyan (green); and Eskimo–Aleut (red). The model also infers a migration of people related to Eskimo–Aleut speakers across the Bering Strait, thus bringing First American genes to Asia—the Naukan Yupik are shown, but the Chukchi show a similar pattern (from Reich et al. 2012, reprinted by permission of Macmillan Publishers Ltd.).

populations into Beringia (Figure 12.14; Raghavan et al. 2013). The researchers estimated that approximately one-third of the Ma'lta genome was West Eurasian in origin, whereas the remainder was East Eurasian in ancestry. Interestingly, the Ma'lta sample had a mtDNA lineage (U5) and Y-chromosome lineage (R1a; Rasmussen et al. 2014) that are not present in any ancient Native Americans (e.g., Schurr 2004a; Kemp and Schurr 2010) and not considered indigenous to the Americas, suggesting that this individual, despite being 25,000 years old, was not part of the ancestral Native American population that moved to Americas.

Not long after the Ma'lta study was published, Rasmussen and colleagues (2014) presented a genomic study of a Paleoamerican individual recovered from the Anzick site in Montana. Dating to 10,705 RCYBP, it represents the oldest Clovis skeleton recovered in North America. As with the Ma'lta individual, there was evidence for an ancient West Eurasian influence on the Anzick genome but also new details about the formation and dispersal of the ancestral Native American population in the Americas (Figure 12.14). Somewhat surprisingly, Anzick showed stronger genetic affinities with South and Central American populations as compared to North

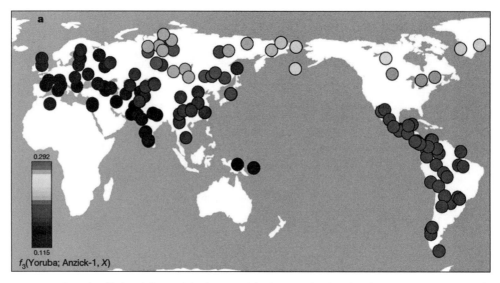

FIGURE 12.14. Genetic affinity of the Anzick-1 boy. Anzick-1 is most closely related to Native Americans. The Heat map represents the estimated outgroup f3 statistics for shared genetic history between the Anzick-1 individual and each of 143 contemporary human populations outside sub-Saharan Africa (from Rasmussen et al. 2014, reprinted by permission of Macmillan Publishers Ltd.).

American groups. In fact, Anzick formed an intermediate branch between NA and SA populations, possibly due to later genetic influences on North American populations by later expansions into the region. These results led the researchers to propose alternative models for the settlement of the Americas, including that a single pulse of migrants, possibly two, expanded into the New World (Figure 12.15).

The Anzick individual also exhibited mtDNA haplogroup D4h3a and Y-chromosome Q-L54. These findings were not entirely surprising, given what is known about the maternal and paternal genetic diversity of Native Americans (see above). The presence of D4h3a was somewhat unexpected, given its general western distribution in the Americas today, with the Anzick haplotype forming a basal branch of this haplogroup. D4h3a has also been identified in the On Your Knees Cave (Alaska) Paleoamerican skeleton, which has been dated to 10,400 years ago (Kemp et al. 2010), confirming the ancientness of this maternal lineage in the Americas. In addition, the Anzick Y-chromosome haplotype formed a distinct branch within Q-L54 relative to those identified in a few comparative populations.

Rasmussen and colleagues (2014) used the autosomal data for an admixture analysis to determine the proportional genetic ancestry of Anzick relative to a global set of data (Figure 12.16). They noted that, regardless of the number of genetic components (K-values) that were used to estimate ancestry proportions, the Anzick-1 sample shared all of the components present in different contemporary Native American tribes. Thus, it clearly derives from the founding population that genetically gave rise to all indigenous populations in the Americas.

We have conducted similar research into genomic diversity in global populations using the GenoChip, a custom microarray designed to interrogate autosomal SNP diversity in human populations (Figure 12.17; Elhaik et al. 2013, 2014). Like Rasmussen and colleagues (2014), we found that Native American populations that were relatively unadmixed (indigenous Mexicans) showed very high levels of indigenous genetic ancestry, while admixed Caribbean populations showed much less. Despite being highly admixed (largely European and African genetic ancestry), Puerto Ricans, who represent ancestral Taino populations, showed 10–20 percent indigenous ancestry based on autosomal data

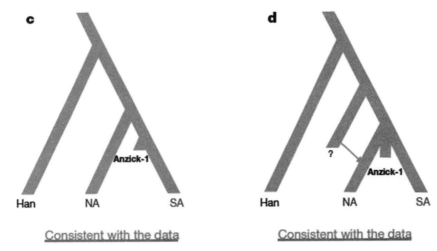

FIGURE 12.15. Alternative models of the population history behind the closer shared ancestry of the Anzick-1 individual to Central and South American (SA) populations than to northern Native American (NA) populations based on genomic data. The data are consistent with a simple tree-like model in which NA populations are historically basal to Anzick-1 and SA, as shown by two D-tests conducted on the Anzick-1 individual, NA and SA. The Han Chinese population was used as an outgroup. When the hypothesis that Anzick-1 is basal to both NA and SA populations was tested using model *c* (Han, Anzick-1; NA, SA), it was rejected. By contrast, a topology with NA populations basal to Anzick-1 and SA populations (model *d*: Han, NA; Anzick-1, SA) was consistent with the data. However, another alternative is that the Anzick-1 individual arose at the time of the last common ancestral population of the Northern and Southern lineages, after which the Northern lineage received gene flow from a more basal lineage (from Rasmussen et al. 2014, reprinted by permission of Macmillan Publishers Ltd.).

(60 percent indigenous mtDNAs and 0 percent indigenous Y-chromosome; Vilar et al. 2014). As can be seen in these several examples, many more fascinating details about Native American history will emerge through autosomal SNP analysis and help to reconstruct the migration history of this part of the world.

Summary

The initial settlement of the Altai-Sayan region (south-central Siberia) occurred between 30,000–40,000 cal BP, as modern humans began colonizing different parts of Eurasia. Analysis of Y-chromosome haplogroup Q shows connections between New World and Old World populations, indicating that southern Altaians and Native Americans shared a common genetic ancestor some 20–25,000 years ago. This connection is also implied by the recent ancient DNA studies of the Mal'ta Boy and Anzick Child, which reveal a significant West Eurasian contribution to the genetic makeup of ancestral Native American populations prior to their expansion

into Beringia (Raghavan et al. 2013; Rasmussen et al. 2014).

On the opposite side of Beringia, the initial expansion into the New World appears to have occurred between 15,000–20,000 years ago. It occurred after "incubation" of the ancestral Native American population, giving rise to a "Beringian" genetic pool from which founders arise. Although there are still some details to resolve, most genetic data generally support single major expansion into the Americas, generating Amerindian populations after the genetic differentiation of their ancestral populations. Following the initial colonization, we observe an increasing complexity of founding lineages in Americas (mtDNA and Y-chromosome), possibly resulting from multiple population "streams" moving into the Americas. Fairly soon after the continental regions were settled, the ancestral Native American population began to differentiate regionally, leading to the patterns of cultural, genetic, and linguistic variation that have largely persisted until today.

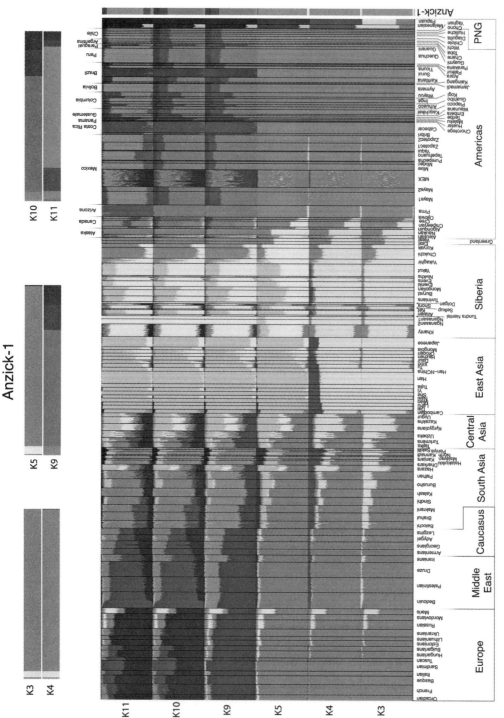

FIGURE 12.16. Ancestry proportions of Anzick-1 as determined by admixture, assuming the number of hypothetical "ancestral" populations or genetic components, K, is 3 to 5 and 9 to 11 for a set of 135 extant Eurasian, Oceanian, and New World populations. Shown are results from one of the converged runs at each K. We note that the model at K511 was found to have the best predictive accuracy, as determined by the lowest cross-validation index values. At each K, each sample is represented by a stacked vertical bar, whereas those of Anzick-1 are magnified and presented horizontally at the top. Note that irrespective of the number of genetic components, K, assumed, the Anzick-1 sample shares all the components present in different contemporary Native American populations (from Rasmussen et al. 2014, reprinted by permission of Macmillan Publishers Ltd.).

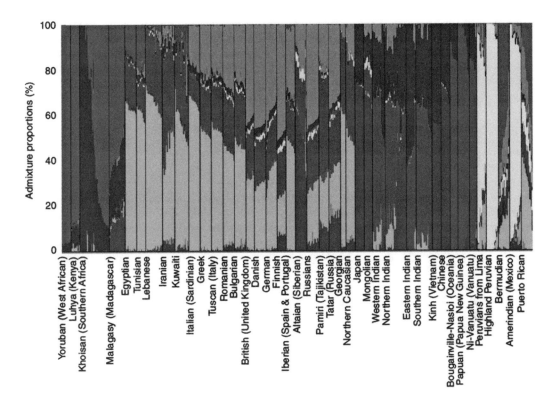

FIGURE 12.17. Admixture analysis of worldwide populations and subpopulations. Admixture analysis was performed for K = 9 ancestry components. For brevity, subpopulations were collapsed. The *x*-axis represents individuals from populations sorted according to their reported ancestries. Each individual is represented by a vertical stacked column of color-coded admixture proportions that reflect genetic contributions from putative ancestral populations (from Elhaik et al. 2014, reprinted by permission of Macmillan Publishers Ltd.).

Secondary expansions into North America by ancestral populations of Eskimo-Aleuts and Athapaskan Indians occurred during the last 10,000 years (see Reich et al. 2012 for a discussion of the autosomal genetic view of this migration history). These circumarctic populations show genetically distinct patterns of mtDNA and Y-chromosome diversity from Amerindian populations to the south, implying a somewhat different evolutionary trajectory for them. New founding NRY lineages (Q1a5 and Q1a6) identified in Inuvialuit and Athapaskan populations, respectively, also reflect the genetic differentiation of these ethnolinguistic groups. Furthermore, new mtDNA and NRY data from populations living around the Americas indicate the existence of more founding maternal and paternal lineages than previously appreciated, suggesting a more complex colonization process than earlier models proposed.

Acknowledgments

I extend my deepest thanks to the members of the indigenous communities from Russia, Canada, Mexico, the U.S., and the Caribbean who have participated in our studies. I am most grateful for the contributions of the following people to the projects described in this paper: Miguel G. Vilar, Jill B. Gaieski, Sergey Zhadanov, Omer Gokcumen, Samara Rubinstein, Amanda C. Owings, Haleigh Zillges, Daniel Brooks,

Ayken Askapuli, Lenore Pipes, and Lydia Gai from the University of Pennsylvania; Alestine Andre, Sharon Snowshoe, and Ruth Wright from the Gwich'in Social and Cultural Institute in Tsiigehtchic, NT, Canada; Crystal Lennie from the Inuvialuit Regional Corporation in Inuvik, NT, Canada; Mary Adele Mackenzie, James Martin and Nancy Gibson from the Tłı̨chǫ Community Services Agency in Behchoko, NT, Canada; Ingrid Kritsch and Tom Andrews from the Prince of Wales Northern Heritage Centre in Yellowknife, NT, Canada; Jada Benn Torres from the University of Notre Dame; Carlalynne Melendez from the Liga Guakia Taina-Ke in Puerto Rico; Ludmila Osipova from the Institute of Cytology and Genetics, Novosibirsk, Russia; and Rocio Gomez, Marco Antonio Meraz Rios, Rafael Camacho-Mejorado, José Antonio Quinto Mora, Gino Noris, and Carla Santana from CINVESTAV-IPN in Mexico. This research was supported by funding from the National Geographic Society; IBM; the Waitt Family Foundation; the National Science Foundation (BCS-0726623); the University of Pennsylvania; the University of Pennsylvania Museum of Archaeology and Anthropology; the Social Sciences and Humanities Research Council (Canada; #412-2005-1004); CONACYT (Mexico); and IFOND (Russia).

Notes

1. Title taken after "Ebb and Flow," a poem by Frances L. Mace, in *Local and National Poets of America: With Biographical Sketches and Choice Selections from Over One Thousand Living American Poets*, edited by Thomas William Herringshaw, 1890. American Publishers Association, Chicago.

2. "N_e and N will play key roles in determining the degree to which populations can avoid extinction from demographically, environmentally, or genetically stochastic events, such as temporary recruitment failures, environmental catastrophes, inbreeding depression, or a loss of genetic diversity at low population size" (Palstra and Fraser 2012:2357).

3. These designations have changed with the availability of hundreds of new SNPs from genomic studies but represent the basic lineages defined by SNP based research as of a few years ago.

4. Current efforts to delineate different branches of the Y-chromosome phylogeny use designations that identify the paternal lineage by the letter-name given to it, based on its major branch status, and then the terminal SNP that is present in the Y-chromosome being studied (Y-Chromosome Consortium 2002; Karafet et al. 2008). Because of the proliferation of SNP data from genomic studies, this naming system is growing increasingly complicated, with multiple new subbranches of Q being observed. For this reason, I will employ a nomenclature that identifies the major branches of the Y-chromosome phylogeny using the major letter designations and the terminal SNPs defining the specific subbranches in which they appear.

5. The branch lengths and positions indicate the relative genetic distances between populations, with those appearing in the same clusters being more genetically similar and those in more distant clusters more distantly related, genetically speaking.

References

Achilli, A., U. A. Perego, C. M. Bravi, M. D. Coble, Q. P. Kong, S. R. Woodward, A. Salas, A. Torroni, and H.-J. Bandelt

2008   The Phylogeny of the Four Pan-American mtDNA Haplogroups: Implications for Evolutionary and Disease Studies. *PloS ONE* 3(3):e1764.

Achilli, A., U. A. Perego, H. Lancioni, A. Olivieri, F. Gandini, H. Kashani B., V. Battaglia, et al.

2013   Reconciling Migration Models to the Americas with the Variation of North American Native Mitogenomes. *PNAS* 110(35):14308–14313.

Bergen, A. W., C. Y. Wang, J. Tsai, K. Jefferson, C. Dey, K. D. Smith, S. C. Park, S. J. Tsai, and D. Goldman

1999   An Asian-Native American Paternal Lineage Identified by RPS4Y Resequencing and by Microsatellite Haplotyping. *Annals of Human Genetics* 63:63–80.

Bisso-Machado, R., M. S. Jota, V. Ramallo, V. R. Paixâo-Côrtes, D. R. Lacerda, F. M. Salzano, S. L. Bonito, F. R. Santos, and M. C. Bortolini

2011   Distribution of Y-chromosome Q Lineages in Native Americans. *American Journal of Human Biology* 23(4):563–566.

Bolnick, D. A., B. A. Shook, L. Campbell, and I. Goddard

2004   Problematic Use of Greenberg's Linguistic Classification of the Americas in Studies of Native American Genetic Variation. *American Journal of Human Genetics* 75(3): 519–522.

Bonatto, Sandro L., and F. M. Salzano
1997   A Single and Early Migration for the
        Peopling of the Americas Supported by
        Mitochondrial DNA Sequence Data. *PNAS*
        94(5):1866–1871.
Bortolini, M. C., F. M. Salzano, M. G. Thomas, S. Stuart, S. P. K. Nasanen, C. H. D. Bau, M. H. Hutz, et al.
2003   Y-Chromosome Evidence for Differing
        Ancient Demographic Histories in the
        Americas. *American Journal of Human
        Genetics* 73(3):524–539.
Bosch, E., F. Calafell, Z. H. Rosser, S. Nørby,
N. Lynnerup, M. E. Hurles, and M. A. Jobling
2003   High Level of Male-Biased Scandinavian
        Admixture in Greenlandic Inuit Shown by
        Y-Chromosomal Analysis. *Human Genetics*
        112(4):353–363.
Brown, M. D., S. H. Hosseini, A. Torroni,
H. J. Bandelt, J. C. Allen, T. G. Schurr, R. Scozzari,
F. Cruciani, and D. C. Wallace
1998   mtDNA Haplogroup X: An Ancient link
        between Europe/Western Asia and North
        America? *American Journal of Human
        Genetics* 63(6):1852–1861.
Derenko, M., B. Malyarchuk, G. A. Denisova,
M. Wozniak, I. Dambueva, C. Dorzhu, F. Luzina,
D. Miscicka-Sliwka, and I. Sakharov
2006   Contrasting Patterns of Y-chromosome Vari-
        ation in South Siberian Populations from
        Baikal and Altai-Sayan Regions. *Human
        Genetics* 118(5):591–604.
Derenko, M., B. Malyarchuk, T. Grzybowski,
G. Denisova, U. Rogalla, M. Perkova, I. Dambueva,
and I. Zakharov
2010   Origin and Post-Glacial Dispersal of Mito-
        chondrial DNA Haplogroups C and D in
        Northern Asia. *PLoS One* 5(12):e15214.
Dillehay, Tom D.
1999   The Late Pleistocene Cultures of South
        America. *Evolutionary Anthropology* 7(6):
        206–216.
Dornelles, C. L., S. L. Bonatto, L. B. de Freitas, and
F. M. Salzano
2005   Is Haplogroup X Present in Extant South
        American Indians? *American Journal of
        Physical Anthropology* 127(4):439–448.
Dulik, M. C., A. C. Owings, J. B. Gaieski, M. G. Vilar,
A. Andre, C. Lennie, M. A. Mackenzie, et al.
2012a   Y-Chromosome Analysis Reveals Genetic
        Divergence and New Founding Native
        Lineages in Athapaskan and Eskimoan-
        Speaking Populations. *PNAS* 109(22):
        8471–8476.

Dulik, M. C., S. I. Zhadanov, L. P. Osipova,
A. Askapuli, L. Gau, O. Gokcumen, S. Rubinstein,
and T. G. Schurr
2012b   Mitochondrial DNA and Y Chromosome
        Variation Provides Evidence for a Recent
        Common Ancestry between Native Ameri-
        cans and Indigenous Altaians. *American
        Journal of Human Genetics* 90(2):229–246.
Elhaik, E., E. Greenspan, S. Staats, T. Krahn,
C. Tyler-Smith, Y. Xue, S. Tofanelli, et al.
2013   The GenoChip: A New Tool for Genetic
        Anthropology. *Genome Biology and Evolu-
        tion* 5(5):1021–1031.
Elhaik, E., T. Tatarinova, D. Chebotarev, I. S. Piras,
C. M. Calò, A. De Montis, M. Atzori, et al., and The
Genographic Consortium
2014   Geographic Population Structure Analysis
        of Worldwide Human Populations Infers
        Their Biogeographical Origin down to
        Home Village. *Nature Communications*
        5:3513. doi:10.1038/ncomms4513.
Fagundes, N. J., R. Kanitz, R. Eckert, A. C. Valls,
M. R. Bogo, F. M. Salzano, D. G. Smith, et al.
2008   Mitochondrial Population Genomics
        Supports a Single Pre-Clovis Origin with a
        Coastal Route for the Peopling of the Amer-
        icas. *American Journal of Human Genetics*
        82(3):583–592.
Forster, P., R. Harding, A. Torroni, and H. J. Bandelt
1996   Origin and Evolution of Native American
        mtDNA Variation: A Reappraisal. *American
        Journal of Human Genetics* 59(4):935–945.
Gilbert, M. T. P., T. Kivisild, B. Grønnow, P. K. An-
dersen, E. Metspalu, M. Reidla, E. Tamm, et al.
2008   Paleo-Eskimo mtDNA Genome Reveals
        Matrilineal Discontinuity in Greenland.
        Science 320(5884):1787–1789.
Goebel, T., M. R. Waters, and D. H. O'Rourke
2008   The Late Pleistocene Dispersal of Modern
        Humans in the Americas. *Science* 319(5869):
        1497–1502.
Greenberg, J. H., C. G. Turner II, and S. L. Zegura
1986   The Settlement of the Americas: A Compar-
        ison of the Linguistic, Dental, and Genetic
        Evidence. *Current Anthropology* 27(5):
        477–497.
Helgason, A., G. Pálsson, H. S. Pedersen,
E. Angulalik, E. D. Gunnarsdóttir, B. Yngvadóttir,
and K. Stefánsson
2006   mtDNA Variation in Inuit Populations of
        Greenland and Canada: Migration History
        and Population Structure. *American Journal
        of Physical Anthropology* 130(1):123–134.

Hey, J.
2005   On the Number of New World Founders: A
        Population Genetic Portrait of the Peopling
        of the Americas. *PLoS Biology* 3:e193.
Hudjashov, G., T. Kivisild, P.A. Underhill, P. Endi-
cott, J.J. Sanchez, A.A. Lin, P. Shen, et al.
2007   Revealing the Prehistoric Settlement of
        Australia by Y Chromosome and mtDNA
        Analysis. *PNAS* 104(21):8726–8730.
Hunley, K. and J.C. Long
2005   Gene Flow across Linguistic Boundaries in
        Native North American Populations. *PNAS*
        102(5):1312–1317.
Jota, M.S., D.R. Lacerda, J.R. Sandoval,
P.P.R. Vieira, S.S. Santos-Lopes, R. Bisso-Machado,
V.R. Paixão-Cortes, et al.
2011   A New Subhaplogroup of Native American
        Y-Chromosomes from the Andes. *American
        Journal of Physical Anthropology* 146(4):
        553–559.
Karafet, T., L. Xu, R. Du, W. Wang, S. Feng,
R.S. Wells, A.J. Redd, S.L. Zegura, and
M.F. Hammer
2001   Paternal Population History of East Asia:
        Sources, Patterns, and Microevolutionary
        Processes. *American Journal of Human
        Genetics* 69(3):615–628.
Karafet, T.M., F.L. Mendez, M.B. Meilerman,
P.A. Underhill, S.L. Zegura, and M.F. Hammer
2008   New Binary Polymorphisms Reshape
        and Increase Resolution of the Human Y
        Chromosomal Haplogroup Tree. *Genome
        Research* 18(5):830–838.
Karafet, T.M., S.L. Zegura, O. Pokush, L. Osipova,
A. Bergen, J. Long, D. Goldman, et al.
1999   Ancestral Asian Source(s) of New World
        Y-Chromosome Founder Haplotypes.
        American Journal of Human Genetics 64(3):
        817–831.
Karafet, T.M., S.L. Zegura, J. Vuturo-Brady,
O. Posukh, L. Osipova, V. Wiebe, F. Romero, et al.
1997   Y Chromosome Markers and Trans-Bering
        Strait Dispersals. *American Journal of Physi-
        cal Anthropology* 102(3):301–314.
Kayser, M., M. Krawczak, L. Excoffier, P. Dieltjes,
D. Corach, V. Pascali, C. Gehrig, et al.
2001   An Extensive Analysis of Y-Chromosomal
        Microsatellite Haplotypes in Globally
        Dispersed Human Populations. *American
        Journal of Human Genetics* 68(4):990–1018.
Kemp, B.M., and T.G. Schurr
2010   Ancient and Modern Genetic Variation
        in the Americas. In *Human Variation in

the Americas: The Integration of Archaeology and Biological Anthropology*, edited
by B.M. Auerbach, pp. 12–50. Center for
Archaeological Investigations, Southern
Illinois University, Carbondale.
Kitchen, A., M.M. Miyamoto, and C.J. Mulligan
2008   A Three-Stage Colonization Model for the
        Peopling of the Americas. *PLoS One* 3(2):
        e1596.
Kolman, C.J., N. Sambuughin, and E. Bermingham
1996.   Mitochondrial DNA Analysis of Mongolian
        Populations and Implications for the Origin
        of New World Founders. *Genetics* 142(4):
        1321–1334.
Lell, J.T., M.D. Brown, T.G. Schurr, R.I. Sukernik,
Y.B. Starikovskaya, A. Torroni, L.G. Moore,
G.M. Troup, and D.C. Wallace
1997   Y-Chromosome Polymorphisms in Native
        American and Siberian Populations: Iden-
        tification of Founding Native American Y-
        Chromosome haplotypes. *Human Genetics*
        100(5–6):536–543.
Lell, J.T., R.I. Sukernik, Y.B. Starikovskaya,
B. Su, L. Jin, T.G. Schurr, P.A. Underhill, and
D.C. Wallace
2002   The Dual Origin and Siberian Affinities of
        Native American Y Chromosomes. *Amer-
        ican Journal of Human Genetics* 70(1):
        192–206.
Levin, M.G., and L.P. Potapov (editors)
1964   *The Peoples of Siberia.* University of Chicago
        Press, Chicago.
Malhi, R.S., A. Gonzalez-Oliver, K.B. Schroeder,
B.M. Kemp, J.A. Greenberg, S.Z. Dobrowski,
D.G. Smith, et al.
2008   Distribution of Y-Chromosomes among
        Native North Americans: A Study of
        Athapaskan Population History. *American
        Journal of Physical Anthropology* 137(4):
        412–424.
Malhi, R.S., H.M. Mortensen, J.A. Eshleman,
B.M. Kemp, J.G. Lorenz, F.A. Kaestle, J.R. Johnson,
C. Gorodezki, and D.G. Smith
2003   Native American mtDNA Prehistory in the
        American Southwest. *American Journal of
        Physical Anthropology* 120(2):108–124.
Malyarchuk, B., M. Derenko, G. Denisova, A. Mak-
simov, M. Wozniak, T. Grzybowski, I. Dambuevaj,
and I. Zakharov
2011   Ancient Links between Siberians and Native
        Americans Revealed by Subtyping the Y
        Chromosome Haplogroup Q1a. *Journal of
        Human Genetics* 56(8):583–588.

Meltzer, David J.

2009   *First Peoples in a New World: Colonizing Ice Age America.* University of California Press, Berkeley.

Merriwether, D. A., W. W. Hall, A. Vahlne, and R. E. Ferrell

1996   mtDNA Variation Indicates Mongolia May Have Been the Source for the Founding Population for the New World. *American Journal of Human Genetics* 59(1):204–212.

Merriwether, D. A., F. Rothhammer, and F. E. Ferrell

1994   Genetic Variation in the New World: Ancient Teeth, Bone, and Tissue as Sources of DNA. *Experientia* 50(6):592–601.

Mulligan, C. J., A. Kitchen, and M. M. Miyamoto

2008   Updated Three-Stage Model for the Peopling of the Americas. *PLoS One* 3(9):e3199.

O'Fallon, B. D., and L. Fehren-Schmitz

2011   Native Americans Experienced a Strong Population Bottleneck Coincident with European Contact. *PNAS* 108(51):20444–20448.

Olivieri A., A. Achilli, M. Pala, V. Battaglia, S. Fornarino, N. Al-Zahery, R. Scozzari, et al.

2006   The mtDNA Legacy of the Levantine Early Upper Palaeolithic in Africa. *Science* 314(5806):1767–1770.

O'Rourke, D. H.

2011   Contradictions and Concordances in American Colonization Models. *Evolution: Education and Outreach* 4(2):244–253.

O'Rourke, D. H., and J. A. Raff

2010   The Human Genetic History of the Americas: The Final Frontier. *Current Biology* 20(4):202–207.

Palstra, F. P., and D. J. Fraser

2012   Effective/Census Population Size Ratio Estimation: A Compendium and Appraisal. *Ecology and Evolution* 2(9):2357–2365.

Perego, U. A., A. Achilli, N. Angerhofer, M. Accetturo, M. Pala, A. Olivieri, B. Hooshiar-Kashani, et al.

2009   Distinctive Paleo-Indian Migration Routes from Beringia Marked by Two Rare mtDNA Haplogroups. *Current Biology* 19(1):1–8.

Perego, U. A., N. Angerhofer, M. Pala, A. Olivieri, H. Lancioni, B. Hooshiar Kashani, V. Carissa, et al.

2010   The Initial Peopling of the Americas: A Growing Number of Founding Mitochondrial Genomes from Beringia. *Genome Research* 20(9):1174–1179.

Raff, J. A., and D. A. Bolnick

2014   Palaeogenomics: Genetic Roots of the First Americans. *Nature* 506(7487):162–163.

Raff, J. A., M. Rzhetskaya, J. Tackney, and M. G. Hayes

2015   Mitochondrial Diversity of Iñupiat People from the Alaskan North Slope Provides Evidence for the Origins of the Paleo- and Neo-Eskimo peoples. *American Journal of Physical Anthropology* 157(4):603–614.

Raghavan, M., M. DeGiorgio, A. Albrechtsen, I. Moltke, P. Skoglund, T. S. Korneliussen, B. Grønnow, et al.

2014   The Genetic Prehistory of the New World Arctic. *Science* 345(6200):1255832.

Raghavan, M., P. Skoglund, K. E. Graf, M. Metspalu, A. Albrechtsen, I. Moltke, S. Rasmussen, et al.

2013   Upper Palaeolithic Siberian Genome Reveals Dual Ancestry of Native Americans. *Nature* 505:87–91.

Rasmussen, M., S. L. Anzick, M. R. Waters, P. Skoglund, M. DeGiorgio, T. W. Stafford Jr., S. Rasmussen, et al.

2014   The Genome of a Late Pleistocene Human from a Clovis Burial Site in Western Montana. *Nature* 506:225–229.

Rasmussen, M., Y. Li, S. Lindgreen, J. S. Pedersen, A. Albrechtsen, I. Moltke, M. Metspalu, et al.

2010   Ancient Human Genome Sequence of an Extinct Palaeo-Eskimo. *Nature* 463:757–762.

Reich, D., N. Patterson, D. Campbell, A. Tandon, S. Mazieres, N. Ray, M. V. Parra, et al.

2012   Reconstructing Native American Population History. *Nature* 488:370–374.

Reidla, M., T. Kivisild, E. Metspalu, K. Kaldma, K. Tambets, H. V. Tolk, J. Parik, et al.

2003   Origin and Diffusion of mtDNA Haplogroup X. *American Journal of Human Genetics* 73(5):1178–1190.

Rubicz, R., P. E. Melton, V. Spitsyn, G. Sun, R. Deka, and M. H. Crawford

2010   Genetic Structure of Native Circumpolar Populations Based on Autosomal, Mitochondrial, and Y Chromosome DNA Markers. *American Journal of Physical Anthropology* 143(1):62–74.

Rubicz, R., T. G. Schurr, P. L. Babb, and M. H. Crawford

2003   Mitochondrial DNA Variation and the Origins of the Aleuts. *Human Biology* 75(6):809–835.

Saillard, J., P. Forster, N. Lynnerup, H. J. Bandelt, and S. Nørby

2000   mtDNA Variation among Greenland Eskimos: The Edge of the Beringian Expansion.

American Journal of Human Genetics 67(3): 718–726.

Santos, F. R., L. Rodriguez-Delfin, S. D. Pena, J. Moore, and K. M. Weiss

1996   North and South Amerindians May Have the Same Major Founder Y Chromosome Haplotype. *American Journal of Human Genetics* 58(6):1369–1370.

Santos, F. R., A. Pandya, C. Tyler-Smith, S. D. Pena, M. Schanfield, W. R. Leonard, L. Osipova, M. H. Crawford, and R. J. Mitchell

1999   The Central Siberian Origin for Native American Y Chromosomes. *American Journal of Human Genetics* 64(2):619–628.

Schurr, T. G.

2003   Molecular Genetic Diversity of Siberian Populations: Implications for Ancient DNA Studies of Archeological Populations from the Cis-Baikal Region. In *Prehistoric Foragers of the Cis-Baikal, Siberia*, edited by A. Weber and M. McKenzie, pp. 155–186. Canadian Circumpolar Institute Press, Edmonton, AL.

2004a   The Peopling of the New World: Perspectives from Molecular Anthropology. *Annual Review of Anthropology* 33:551–583.

2004b   Genetic Diversity in Siberians and Native Americans Suggests an Early Migration to the New World. In *Entering America: Northeast Asia and Beringia before the Last Glacial Maximum*, edited by D. Madsen, pp. 187–238. University of Utah Press, Salt Lake City.

2010   Coastal Waves and Island Hopping: A Genetic View of Caribbean Prehistory in the Context of New World Colonization. In *Island Shores, Distant Pasts: Archaeological and Biological Approaches to the Pre-Columbian Settlement of the Caribbean*, edited by S. M. Fitzpatrick and A. Ross, pp. 177–198. University of Florida Press, Gainesville.

Schurr, T. G., and S. T. Sherry

2004   Mitochondrial DNA and Y Chromosome Diversity and the Peopling of the Americas: Evolutionary and Demographic Evidence. *American Journal of Human Biology* 16(4):420–439.

Schurr, T. G., and D. C. Wallace

2003   Genetic Prehistory of Paleoasiatic-Speaking Peoples of Northeastern Siberia and Their Links to Native American Populations. In *Constructing Cultures Then and Now:*

Celebrating Franz Boas and the Jesup North Pacific Expedition, edited by L. Kendall and I. Krupnik, pp. 239–258. Smithsonian Institution, Washington, D.C.

Schurr, T. G., M. C. Dulik, A. C. Owings, S. I. Zhadanov, J. B. Gaieski, M. G. Vilar, J. Ramos, et al.

2012   Clan, Language, and Migration History Has Shaped Genetic Diversity in Haida and Tlingit Populations from Southeast Alaska. *American Journal of Physical Anthropology* 148(3):422–435.

Schurr, T. G., L. P. Osipova, S. I. Zhadanov, and M. C. Dulik

2010   Genetic Diversity in Native Siberian Populations: Implications for the Prehistoric Settlement of the Cis-Baikal. In *Prehistoric Hunter-Gatherers of the Baikal Region, Siberia: Bioarchaeological Studies of Past Lifeways*, edited by A. Weber, M. A. Katzenberg, and T. G. Schurr, pp. 121–134. University of Pennsylvania Press, Philadelphia.

Schurr, T. G., R. I. Sukernik, E. B. Starikovskaya, and D. C. Wallace

1999   Mitochondrial DNA Diversity in Koryaks and Itel'men: Population Replacement in the Okhotsk Sea-Bering Sea Region during the Neolithic. *American Journal of Physical Anthropology* 108(1):1–40.

Scott, G. R., and D. O'Rourke

2011   Genes across Beringia: A Physical Anthropology Perspective on the Dene-Yeniseian Hypothesis. In *The Dene-Yeniseian Connection*, edited by J. Kari and B. A. Potter, pp. 121–139. Anthropological Papers of the University of Alaska 5(1–2). Fairbanks.

Starikovskaya, E. B., R. I. Sukernik, O. A. Derbeneva, N. V. Volodko, E. Ruiz-Pesini, A. Torroni, M. D. Brown, et al.

2005   Mitochondrial DNA Diversity in Indigenous Populations of the Southern Extent of Siberia, and the Origins of Native American Haplogroups. *Annals of Human Genetics* 69(Pt 1): 67–89.

Starikovskaya, Y. B., R. I. Sukernik, T. G. Schurr, A. M. Kogelnik, D. C. Wallace

1998   mtDNA Diversity in Chukchi and Siberian Eskimos: Implications for the Genetic History of Ancient Beringia and the Peopling of the New World. *American Journal of Human Genetics* 63(5):1473–1491.

Sukernik, R. I., T. G. Schurr, Y. B. Starikovskaya, and D. C. Wallace

1996   Mitochondrial DNA Variation in Native

Inhabitants of Siberia with Reconstructions of the Evolutional History of the American Indians: 1. Restriction Polymorphism. *Genetika* 32(3):432–439.

Tamm, E., T. Kivisild, M. Reidla, M. Metspalu, D. G. Smith, C. J. Mulligan, C. M. Bravi, et al.

2007   Beringian Standstill and Spread of Native American Founders. *PloS One* 2(9):e829.

The 1000 Genomes Project Consortium

2010   A Map of Human Genome Variation from Population-Scale Sequencing. *Nature* 467: 1061–1073.

Torroni, A., T. G. Schurr, M. F. Cabell, M. D. Brown, J. V. Neel, M. Larsen, D. G. Smith, C. M. Fullo, and D. C. Wallace

1993a   Asian Affinities and Continental Radiation of the Four Founding Native American Mitochondrial DNAs. *American Journal of Human Genetics* 53(3):563–590.

Torroni, A., T. G. Schurr, C. C. Yang, E. J. E. Szathmary, R. C. Williams, M. S. Schanfield, G. A. Group, et al.

1992   Native American Mitochondrial DNA Analysis Indicates That the Amerind and the Na-Dené Populations Were Founded by Two Independent Migrations. *Genetics* 130(1):153–162.

Torroni A., Sukernik R. I., T. G. Schurr, Y. B. Starikovskaya, M. F. Cabell, M. H. Crawford, et al.

1993b   mtDNA Variation of Aboriginal Siberians Reveals Distinct Genetic Affinities with Native Americans. *American Journal of Human Genetics* 53(3):591–608.

Underhill, P. A., L. Jin, R. Zemans, P. J. Oefner, and L. L. Cavalli-Sforza

1996   A Pre-Columbian Y Chromosome-Specific Transition and Its Implications for Human Evolutionary History. *PNAS* 93(1):196–200.

Underhill, P. A., G. Passarino, A. A. Lin, P. Shen, M. M. Lahr, R. A. Foley, P. J. Hefner, and L. L. Cavalli-Sforza

2001   The Phylogeography of Y Chromosome Binary Haplotypes and the Origins of Modern Human Populations. *Annals of Human Genetics* 65(1):43–62.

Vadja, E. J.

2010   A Siberian Link with Na-Dene languages. In *The Dene-Yeniseian Connection*, edited by J. Kari and B. A. Potter, pp. 33–99. Anthropological Papers of the University of Alaska 5(1–2). Fairbanks.

Vilar, M. G., M. C. Dulik, A. C. Owings, J. B. Gaieski, C. Lennie, and H. Zillges

2015   Genetic Variation in Inuvialuit Populations from the Northwest Territories: Implications for the Human Colonization of the Arctic. *American Journal of Physical Anthropology* (in review).

Vilar M. G., C. Melendez, A. B. Sanders, A. Walia, J. B. Gaieski, A. C. Owings, T. G. Schurr, and The Genographic Consortium

2014   Genetic Diversity in Puerto Rico and Its Implications for the Peopling of the Island and the West Indies. *American Journal of Physical Anthropology* 155(3):352–368.

Wall, J. D., R. Jiang, C. Gignoux, G. K. Chen, C. Eng, S. Huntsman, and P. Marjoram

2011   Genetic Variation in Native Americans, Inferred from Latino SNP and Resequencing Data. *Molecular Biology and Evolution* 28(8):2231–2237.

Y Chromosome Consortium

2002   A Nomenclature System for the Tree of Human Y-Chromosomal Binary Haplogroups. *Genome Research* 12(2):339–348.

Zegura, S. L., T. M. Karafet, L. A. Zhivotovsky, and M. F. Hammer

2004   High-Resolution SNPs and Microsatellite Haplotypes Point to a Single, Recent Entry of Native American Y Chromosomes into the Americas. *Molecular Biology and Evolution* 21(1):164–175.

Zhong, H., H. Shi, X. B. Qi, Z. Y. Duan, P. P. Tan, L. Jin, B. Su, and R. Z. Ma

2011   Extended Y Chromosome Investigation Suggests Postglacial Migrations of Modern Humans into East Asia via the Northern Route. *Molecular Biology and Evolution* 28(1):717–727.

Zhong, H., H. Shi, Y. Xue, B. Qi, C. J. Xiao, L. Jin L, R. Z. Ma, and B. Su

2010   Global Distribution of Y-Chromosome Haplogroup C Reveals the Prehistoric Migration Routes of African Exodus and Early Settlement in East Asia. *Journal of Human Genetics* 55(7):428–435.

Zlojutro, M., R. Rubicz, E. J. Devor, V. A. Spitsyn, S. V. Makarov, K. Wilson, and M. H. Crawford

2006   Genetic Structure of the Aleuts and Circumpolar Populations Based on Mitochondrial DNA Sequences: A Synthesis. *American Journal of Physical Anthropology* 129(3): 446–464.

CHAPTER 13

Comments and Discussion

Tom D. Dillehay

Over the past quarter century, research on the first Americans has become something of a growth industry in archaeology. Until recently, our reconstruction of the initial peopling of the New World was regarded as unimpeachable—the Clovis First model was firmly in place. Given the demise of this model over the past two decades, our understanding is now a more open and healthier scientific enterprise, with scholars from multiple fields asking new questions and probing new areas of interdisciplinary research. This volume is part of that enterprise. The primary topic in the 12 chapters is actual data, presented in tables, figures, and graphs to support interpretations on a wide range of topics. The chapters are not specifically about methodology. In most cases, this is mentioned only briefly, occasionally with reference to the appropriate literature. Although I do not agree with every interpretation, the evidence that all contributors use in support of their interpretations is usually clear.

This volume is valuable for several reasons. First, most of the studies fill in several local data gaps and chronological sequences and provide new information on technological, settlement, chronological, and economic variation within and across regions. Several chapters present new interregional and subcontinental syntheses of old and new findings. Second, most contributors challenge received ideas and substantiate others.

Third, several chapters are produced by a new group of young scholars, especially from Latin America, researching the peopling theme. Fourth, a significant development is the growing amount of research in Mexico, which had been dormant for decades. Fifth, disappointingly, although the tiresome debate of pre-Clovis and Clovis seems to live on with a few authors, there are some chapters that take new and somewhat refreshing approaches to it. And sixth, in comparing the sample size of the early archaeological record of the New World with that of the Old World, Price (1991) pointed out that when more sites are found, and more data are available in the Americas, then our ideas about the initial peopling will change drastically. This certainly has been happening in recent years.

I welcome this opportunity to deal with a broad spectrum of topics on early Americans. In organizing my comments, two courses seem open to me. One is to group them into broad categories and to deal with various instances of the same general topic together. The second option is to deal with each individual paper topic, although I realize that this leads to overlapping discussion of several topics, such as projectile points, migration, chronology, economy, and so forth. I thus opted for a third choice, to discuss certain themes suggested by the total collection—sampling biases, terms, projectile points, habitats, thematic gaps, and others.

Sampling Issues

Although I find no serious sampling problems in the chapters of this volume, I believe that there are several wider issues in how we test and sample the early archaeological record of the Americas, notably the selective "cherry-picking" of certain databases and radiocarbon dates by some colleagues that is designed to fit specific interpretive agendas. I will elaborate briefly.

Archeologists working with early sites have always been concerned about sample sizes and the representativeness of site types and their cultural materials. Some specific concerns are sampling differences in site type discovery potential, poor preservation of organic ecofacts, relatively few carefully excavated and securely dated site components, complex taphonomic and site formation histories, and the use of radiocarbon dates and other data to support a particular interpretative stance. Site types seem to be an implicit problem alluded to by several authors in the volume (chapters by Franco and Vetrisano, Méndez et al., Martin et al., Acosta et al., Lemke and O'Shea, Shott, and Suárez). In addressing this topic, a convenient point of departure between North and South America is the paucity of megafaunal kill sites in South America. In comparison to North America, very few authentic kill sites have been excavated and adequately reported in South America. Two of the better-known candidates are Tagua-Tagua in Chile and possibly Taima-Taima in Venezuela. We know there must have been others. For instance, it has been interpreted that the remains of a majority of rib and long-bone fragments of several individual gomphotheres at the Monte Verde II site in Chile suggests distant kill or scavenging sites, but these kill localities have not been located.

In discussing early kill sites in North America, Shott's chapter (11) takes a singular approach to faunal bone analyses by considering the wider implications of associated stone tools. Specifically, he focuses on human and proboscidean associations with stone tool industries, methodologically correlating tool-count and MNI, and on sampling biases associated with large

kill sites and what they imply in the archeological record. He notes that in questionable contexts such as some kill sites, the significance of other archaeological signatures, such as lithics and features and their associations with bone assemblages, become even more important as a means to determine agency. He also calls attention to sampling biases in the study of both Paleoindian and Archaic sites, with specific regard to the size of the spatial or site areas excavated and the correlation between MNIs and "tool-counts" in these areas. One message received from his chapter was that some sites are perhaps assigned more significance than others, although they may have a paucity of data, especially stone tools, in proportion to the number of individual animals killed and the size and representativeness of excavation areas. At some point, I was expecting Shott to recommend that some of the classic kill sites in North America be reexcavated, redated, and reanalyzed, especially in terms of the bone taphonomy and sampling procedures, but he seems to stop just short of this. Lastly, he is the only author in this volume to focus on the extinction of large game animals during the Late Pleistocene.

In their chapter on Mexico (6), Acosta and colleagues stress how an excessive focus on kill sites can misrepresent the archaeological record and give perhaps undue emphasis to projectile points. As they note, although there is a strong bias in archaeological field work toward such sites (mainly because they usually are more archaeologically visible), they represent only a part of a continuum of hunter-gatherer activities. There also is the problem of whether the deposition and manipulation of all bones at these kill sites are produced by humans, carnivores, or other agencies, a concern in the Martin and colleagues (1) and Shott (11) chapters too. Agency becomes evident in many sites and the chapters by these authors bring more light to it. The chapter by Martin and colleagues raises an important issue about specific faunal species in the archaeological record. In the Argentine record examined by these authors, the bones of *Lama* and *Lama guanicoe* seem to appear only in archaeological sites, not in geological or other localities. Is this a coincidental occurrence, an interdisciplinary sampling issue, or is it truly related to just human agency?

Another sampling concern is documenting residential base camps (Binford 1980:9) for understanding overall hunter-gatherer adaptive strategies. At present, we are unable to assess whether their structure and function differ fundamentally from other site types, from those occurring later in prehistory, or from those documented ethnographically (Kelly and Todd 1988). Such sites can play a central role in modeling organizational responses to problems of resource acquisition, including notions of planning depth and procurement strategies, which can be seen as structuring residential movements, topics that were of specific concern in the chapters by Acosta and colleagues (6), Suárez (4), and others.

Turning to another point, I am often bewildered by the lack of emphasis on comparative internal site structure and content in many site reports, including not just artifacts but features, stains, and other human- or nature-induced signatures, specifically as it relates to comparing sites and constructing local-to-regional models of economic and spatial behavior. The chapter by Acosta and colleagues pointedly discusses this issue with regard to occupational pattern reconstruction in Mexico. I agree that "characterization of activities between different types of archaeological sites is the key to understanding the variety of artifact assemblages and different regional 'cultural complexes' [caused by] the artifact typology differences, or if they are the result of the differences between various site types." Extending this observation, there also is the issue of small sites or lithic scatters, which often have no site structure, above or below ground. Although generalized, Speth's statement about the ephemerality of North American Paleoindian and early Archaic period sites also seems befitting for many areas of South America: "Most sites are just 'patches' or scatters of artifacts and bones," which makes it difficult to locate, investigate, and explain them (Speth 2006:184). How do we fit these types of archae-

ological records into our understanding of the early peopling process?

Not mentioned by Acosta and colleagues are sampling problems associated with changing site structures and multicomponency in the often-limited spaces excavated at most sites. It seems that few archaeologists take a multiyear approach to excavating wider and deeper areas within sites, regardless of the site type, in order to more fully document the internal site structure and potential for older, deeper cultural deposits. Such efforts require a long-term commitment to the excavation of some archaeological sites. However, when compared to Old World archaeology, New World archaeologists generally seem to be less committed to long-term research at sites, preferring instead to sample (often rather quickly) a wide variety of site types in different contexts. There are exceptions, of course, such as several early cave and rockshelter sites in eastern Brazil, Monte Verde in Chile, Arroyo Seco in Argentina, and several cave sites in southern Patagonia.

There is also the issue of multicomponent sites, as best represented in the chapters by Ardelean and colleagues (7), Méndez and colleagues (3), Franco and Vetrisano (2), Martin and colleagues (1), and Williams and colleagues (8). New questions and methods are required to study these types of sites, particularly those characterized by stratigraphically unclear, ephemeral-use episodes and palimpsest occupations. A specific problem with such sites is related to the standard practices of age-averaging, eliminating apparent dating anomalies, and overreliance on high-profile diagnostic tools and the most visible and recognizable features (e.g., hearths). These practices, along with the expectation for contextual congruence, can potentially mask multicomponent locales and multiepisodic use. Above all, such practices can lead to the rejection of valid single and/or multiple occupational moments because they appear to be too ephemeral, too nondiagnostic, or too stratigraphically mixed.

Lastly, with regard to sampling, there also are serious problems with the genetic modeling of the initial peopling, based on a paucity of early human skeletal material. Far too often, one or two skeletons are used to derive excessively elaborated migration models by geneticists and their archaeological counterparts, the most recent case being the Anzick child dated to Clovis times (Rasmussen et al. 2014).

Caves and Rockshelters

Recent research has sought to redefine models of cave and rockshelter use, bringing renewed attention to the question of how and when early populations incorporated these spaces into persistent hunter-gatherer landscapes. One curiously unresolved issue in North American archaeology is the absence or near absence of diagnostic Clovis artifacts in caves and rockshelters. Why is this so? This does not necessarily imply that Clovis-age or earlier cultural deposits are not present in these places, because there are several instances in North America of pre-Clovis and Clovis-age localities, two of note being Meadowcroft Rockshelter and Paisley Caves. But what is it about these types of sites that present so much regional variation in terms of human chronology and use, with some of them occupied continuously for long periods of time and others often minimally used?

Chapters such as Franco and Vetrisano (2), Ardelean and colleagues (7), Acosta and colleagues (6), and Méndez and colleagues (3) offer some insights into the taphonomy and human-habitable lifespan of these site types. For the La Gruta region of Argentina, Franco and Vetrisano point out that, although rockshelters and caves are scarce, they are more likely to be occupied by humans (due to their physical visibility?) and thus to provide better opportunities for archaeologists seeking early human habitation. In this region, human occupation of rockshelters is highly discontinuous, a fact the authors relate to the existence of erosive episodes during arid periods, when humans may have abandoned the area or exploited it from distant residential sites. Ardelean's and colleagues' research (7) at Chiquihuite Cave in northern Mexico also suggests intermittent human use, some of which also is probably related to different physical and climatic conditions in the cave and to periods of regional climate and humidity. In addition to these case studies, we should keep in mind that some caves and rockshelters may have collapsed or have been buried under colluvial or other deposits and thus are archaeologically invisible (see Collins 1991), as was the case of the Piuquenes Rockshelter in Central Chile (Stehberg 2005) and perhaps at the Anzick site. In short, the taphonomy of caves and rockshelters needs much more geological and archaeological work in order to better understand their chronology and specific role as a site type in the peopling of the Americas.

Expectations
Regarding Older Cultural Deposits

This is not the place to examine the pre-13,000 cal BP materials in archaeological sites, but it appears to me that excavations in the basal layers of many early sites (especially in open-air sites) have been very limited both vertically and horizontally, often with no more than 1 to 2 m² exposed. The scarcity of exposed deeper levels may be related to the excessive depth or difficulty of reaching deeper levels, as was the case with the 30-m-high mound at Huaca Prieta (Dillehay et al. 2012) that covered most of the scattered Late Pleistocene remains, or with roof fall in caves and rockshelters that often prohibit access to basal levels. On the other hand, until recently, the presumption has been if Clovis or Fishtail points were found in deeper stratigraphic contexts, then there likely were no older cultural materials and thus little or no need to probe deeper unless for geological or other reasons. That is, unlike today's more open-minded archaeologists, there once was a paradigmatically imposed stratigraphic and mental barrier to excavating below Clovis and Fishtail deposits. When Adovasio worked at Meadowcroft Shelter in the early 1970s, he excavated the deeper, pre-13,000 cal BP levels for geological reasons, not for archaeological ones that sought pre-Clovis materials (Adovasio, personal communication, 2016).

The same occurred at Huaca Prieta, where we excavated 1–2 m deeper than Bird's 1940s trenches below the large human-made mound at the site. Our intent was to define any erosion and weathering associated with the original surface of the Pleistocene terrace upon which the mound was built. We had no intent of finding early cultural deposits. At the Chiquihuite Cave in Mexico, Ardelean and his colleagues report a 1 m² excavation in the deeper levels that appear to date to ~30,000 cal BP and to be associated with materials possibly related to human activity. The excavators did not anticipate finding these older materials. In a related matter, Méndez and colleagues (3) discuss "a minimal human signal" at a cave in the upper Cisnes River basin in south Chile that dated to ~11,500 cal BP. Only more extensive horizontal excavation in the basal levels of this site and similar sites will resolve chronology issues and provide a wider window of observation as to a truly minimal or more extensive human presence.

Lastly, not only is there a growing presence of older sites in North America but in South America as well. Suárez (4) reports on two archaeological sites (Urupez 2 and K87) located in the grasslands of Uruguay that provide evidence of early human occupations dated between about 14,000 to 13,200 cal BP.

Habitat-Specific and Resource-Specific Adaptations

Chapters by Franco and Vetrisano (2), Lemke and O'Shea (9), Méndez and colleagues (3), and Suárez (4) address habitat-specific adaptations. Do such adaptations lead to longer habitat residence times that might have enabled foragers to more fully exploit their environments? An aspect of this exploitation must have been the domestication of plant and animal species in certain types of habitats, for instance, squash by at least 10,000 cal BP in several different localities throughout the Americas. The domestication of plants required intimate knowledge and some degree of consistency of resource exploitation in similar, if not specific, types of ecological habitats. It would seem that habitat-specific adaptations have different implications and that some require different practices for different resources such as plants and animals.

The skill in consuming animals largely relates to their capture while live. Once killed and

butchered, much of the animal may be consumed without further treatment. The reverse is true with many plants: they are easy to "catch" but they frequently require some preparation, whether grinding, pounding, pasting, detoxing, heating, and so forth before they are digestible. In other words, plants require multistep and perhaps more prolonged processing. As others have pointed out (e.g., Renfrew 2004), multistep food processing has important implications for task-group organization and for cognitive evolution. Also, the kind of transferable "ecological knowledge" that allowed humans to move from the exploitation of one plant type to another (e.g., below-ground tubers to above-ground seed and grain species) is not always directly transferable from one environmental zone to the next, the way hunting animals can be. The transferability of plant ecological knowledge works best when similar and specific types of environments are consistently used, such as humid tropical forests and seasonally dry tropical forests. Such a broad level of transferability of ecological knowledge also would have enabled a significant capacity for plant-food acquisition across resource-rich environments. This transferability also might have allowed more rapid migration through consistently used environments or more permanent colonization.

Previously, I referred to the consistent use of similar types of environments as "niche consistency" (Dillehay 2015). This is the continuous mapping onto, exploitation of, movement through, or settling into familiar environments. One example is coastal habitats—the kelp highway hypothesized by Erlandson and colleagues (2007) for peopling the Pacific coast. Another is the seasonally dry tropical forests that intermittently extend from Central to South America. The appearance and density of early sites in maritime, dry tropical forests, and other niches distributed continuously or discontinuously across the landscape can document the recursive interaction of humans with such niches. Rather than coming into a new setting where strange resources may present a constant challenge, especially new plant species, some people may have continuously moved through rich, varied, but known habitats. Settling into or, where possible, following human-targeted niches and certain niche species (such as marine resources along the coast or bison on the Great Plains) probably were not unique events. As people moved through similar settings, we also would expect continuous, yet changing, technologies and repetitive ways of organizing adaptive strategies.

Habitat consistency has methodological and other implications, such as the types of associated archaeological indicators. One example of a seasonal-habitat focus seems to be in the chapter by Lemke and O'Shea (9). They recovered numerous stone-constructed caribou hunting features and related facilities along a submerged "refugium" shoreline of Lake Huron in North America. Not only are these features well preserved, but they also present new and different methodological and interpretive challenges. Lemke and O'Shea also suggest that the refugium was associated with a nonfluted point technology that was specifically adapted to subarctic, periglacial conditions and resources. This technological system, which relied on small tools and likely wood and bone implements, would have a very low visibility profile in terrestrial settings and be very difficult to date. Another example of habitat consistency is the continued exploitation of paleo-wetlands in the Aysen area of south Chile (see Méndez et al., Chapter 3). He suggests that these habitats may appear as appropriate markers for chrono-stratigraphic recognition of specific environments and site formation processes, but not necessarily as preferred landscapes for late Pleistocene settlement.

Another habitat-specific adaptation relates to the grasslands of the southern cone of South America. Suárez (4) discusses the long-term and sequential development of Paleoamerican stemmed bifacial traditions on the grassland plains of Uruguay. This development is somewhat reminiscent of similar sequences and practices on the Great Plains of North America. Although little is known about the material, economic, and technological cultures of these traditions, the early database from this region of South America suggests an increase in the human population by 13,000 cal BP, which ap-

pears to be associated with the relatively widespread presence of the Fishtail tradition across many areas of the continent. The number of sites also seem to increase around 13,000 cal BP on the Great Plains, as well as other regions of North America, making an interesting case for continent-long comparative analyses.

Diverse and Distinguishable Cultures

Several authors, including Williams and colleagues (8), Acosta and colleagues (6), Suárez (4), and Méndez and colleagues (3), speak to the diversity of subsistence and technological patterns during the Late Pleistocene, especially in Latin America. Archeologists, linguists, and geneticists alike have drawn important inferences from diversity, primarily building on the age-area model, which posits that the area of greater diversity and oldest locale is likely the place of origin (e.g., Kroeber 1931; this is certainly the case with Fishtail points, which are generally considered to originate in the Southern Cone of South America despite serious sampling problems). In light of site sampling problems across time and space, this model probably does not hold much weight in regard to the peopling of the Americas. In this case, variation, can be derived from multiple factors other than places of origin, such as abrupt climatic change, social encounters, and cultural drift, which influenced behavior and other differences. Nonetheless, the concept still deserves some consideration, especially in terms of genetic patterns and possibly technological, subsistence and human anatomical differences.

It has been acknowledged that there is a complex mosaic of diverse technologies and cultures in the Americas by at least 12,500 cal BP (Bryan 1973; Dillehay et al. 1992; see Adovasio and Pedler, Chapter 10). There is beginning to be enough data from some regions of South America, primarily eastern Brazil, the Argentine Pampa, southern Patagonia, and coastal Peru and Chile, to consider this claim more seriously. (Acosta et al. believe that a similar pattern of economic [e.g., broad-spectrum economies] and technological diversity holds true for parts of Mexico, especially in the southeast, but it seems premature to assign this distinction to an area with so few detailed analyses.)

The Clovis culture appears to be the first truly diagnostic or distinguishable subcontinental technology in the archaeological record of North America. However, in South America there does not seem to be a "distinguishable culture" or diagnostic technology that was first and most widespread. The Fishtail point tradition is perhaps the most widespread and best documented to date, but it appears to be at least 1,200 years younger than several other sites in the Andes and in parts of Brazil that are associated with different types of unifacial stone tool industries. As more research is carried out in South America, we also are beginning to see that Paijan-like projectile points may be more widespread than previously anticipated. Thus, Fishtail and Paijan point types may be the first and only times in early South American prehistory where there was anything close to a subcontinent-wide "distinguishable" culture.

Another debate concerning diversity is whether the first mtDNA lineages in the Americas represent a single genetically complex founder population or multiple founder populations, as summarized in Schurr's chapter (12). Some genetic patterns seem rather solid for the Americas, for instance, that Native Americans shared a common genetic ancestor sometime before 15,000 years ago. Schurr also mentions genetic bottlenecks and the Beringian Incubator Model whereby people presumably stayed longer and eventually became "American." Yet, I wonder how many times different ecological, climatic, or other circumstances might have produced bottlenecks, with some groups settling in while others moved on. Less convincing is the idea that after the first human entry from Beringia, there was an "incubation" period within an ancestral Native American population that produced a "Beringian" founders genetic pool. As noted by Schurr, some geneticists believe that multiple expansions or streams of founding populations moved into the Americas, with some producing distinct Mesoamerican and South American populations and others leading to North American populations, with

new discoveries of fluctuations in demographic sizes and expansions, greater regional differentiation, and some genetic markers that are uniquely American (e.g., M3 SNP). Knowing the size of the founding population has implications for the nature and rate of human dispersal patterns. It also has important implications for the number and size of archaeological sites and their visibility across the different landscapes throughout the Americas.

As genetic patterns become better known, they become more complicated, especially with the paternal Y-chromosome line becoming more identifiable. New genetic findings are always exciting, moving in new directions and pointing to greater autosomal variation and discovery of new SNPs. Much like new archaeological models, the genetic postulations are useful for their suggestive value, giving us ideas about the possible ways to reconstruct migration patterns and interregional cultural linkages. Unfortunately, the discipline of early American studies is still far from reconciling hypothetical genetic and archaeological models, specifically the key markers of both, that is, respectively speaking, haplogroup types and diagnostic projectile point types.

The Mighty Projectile Point

Projectile points are the dominant archaeological markers in most chapters of this book. Since projectile points are so diagnostic and dominant in the literature, it is difficult to diminish their role in the interpretation of the initial peopling of the Americas. However, a major problem with projectile points is typological cross-dating that far too often rests on the assumption that diagnostic points found at undated sites are roughly the same age as similar diagnostic points found at radiocarbon-dated sites. In much of the Americas and in most chapters in the book, typological cross-dating is the primary means of assigning ages to nonradiocarbon-dated sites and is especially useful in regions where replicable typologies are based on metric attributes and where there is a lack of well-dated stratified sites.

Cross-dating also is the primary approach used to place most point types chronologically.

But beyond chronology, what is really meant by Clovis, Folsom, Fishtail, Paijan, and other major point types in their technology and adaptations? Despite the utility of cross-dating using point typologies, as the number of radiocarbon dates associated with projectile points has grown in many regions of South America, it has become clear that substantial spatio-temporal variation exists not only among individual point types but among subtypes. That is, defining a type based on sites of a certain age and on points of a certain style is problematic and may be inadvertently undermining efforts to ascertain the range of variation in point types over time and space, their technological derivatives (and antecedents), and site types. This problem is apparent with the "Lermaloid" type of point found on the surface at the Chiquihuite Cave, which led Ardelean and his colleagues (7) to contemplate its chronology in Late Pleistocene times and perhaps affiliate it with El Jobo-type points in Venezuela.

That there are regional differences in morphology and chronology is less evident of what is (or is not) Clovis or Fishtail, and perhaps more a warrant to explore cultural transmission processes in the dispersal of historically related populations. A case in hand is the study by Acosta and colleagues (6), who describe a Late Pleistocene assemblage in Santa Marta, Chiapas, that differs from known fluted point traditions to the north. As the authors note, many projectile points are often not "typical" Clovis spearheads but of small size and concave edges, sometimes with channel flutes, though other times with a simple basal thinning. The lithics from this region are generally based on minimum preparation edge-trimmed flakes, polyhedral cores, and absence of bifacial tools, including projectile points. As the authors note, the few studies in the area indicate a subsistence based on processing plants, collecting of river snails, and hunting of minor fauna. An issue here seems to relate to the cause of typological similarity, which could be due to either migration or cultural drift, or both, in this study area. In either case, the explanation seems to be related to culture transmission in the regions reached late by these point types.

In summary, we must be careful in assigning technological and historical affiliation to similar point styles because slight variation may have a different meaning in a different place and time. This problem has become more accentuated with respect to certain point types, primarily Clovis in North America and Fishtail in South America. The most detailed analysis of these artifacts on a technological level can often show important differences that indicate independent developments instead of a common origin. For example, the Clovis points are manufactured based on large blades or big flakes, which are reduced through percussion and later retouched through pressure, where the scars usually occur from edge to edge by the overshot technique. Meanwhile, the Fishtail points are generally manufactured by macro-flakes, in which thickness was not greater than the finished points themselves. Fishtail points also tend to be wider in their distal end, are overlapped in their center, and usually retouched in the margin.

Some authors have considered that the "fluting" in the Clovis and Fishtail points is a diagnostic feature of their genetic and historical technological linkage (i.e., Morrow and Morrow 1999). However, in the case of Fishtail points, fluting or basal thinning was not systematically applied. They range from unfluted to rare bifacial fluting (e.g., Politis 1991; Nami 1997) and an absence of basal grinding and other features. Within the Fishtail style, Franco and Vetrisano (2) point out the significant diversity of morphology in it. Furthermore, the Central American Fishtail points have similar dimensions to their homonymous examples from South America but with the stem straight instead of having two small "ears" (Cooke 1998), more characteristic of point types to the north. We simply need more data in definable and well-dated archaeological context before we can begin to make continent-long comparisons and historical and genetic linkages between these and other points.

Terms and Nostalgic Biases

As I have discussed previously (Dillehay 2000), there are problems with the continued use of the term "Paleoindian" for all aspects of the peopling

of the Americas, especially South America. Although the term has chronological implications,
it also assumes systematic megafaunal hunting
as the key economic component and places
South American sites within a North America
"Paleoindian" stereotype—the pursuit of megafauna. In South America, this term has little
meaning except as a chronology marker, which
I presume is its use in the chapter by Acosta and
colleagues (6), although it still has meaning in
North America with regard to big-game hunting
(see chapters by Shott [11], Williams et al. [8],
and Lemke and O'Shea [9]). Moreover, there
are late Pleistocene adaptations throughout
many areas of the Americas that reflect more of
a broad-spectrum early Archaic lifeway than a
Paleoindian one. Perhaps a better term is proto-
Archaic, Paleo-Archaic, or as used in several
papers here, Paleoamerican to indicate the type
of broad-spectrum economies that were practiced in many areas during the late Pleistocene.

Along similar lines, although we might quib-
ble with factoids or characterizations of specific
archeological records, there are some areas of
the Americas, particularly areas little affected by
glaciation, whereby the early Archaic or Holocene period is simply the attenuated version of
an older or Late Pleistocene lifeway in a subtly
changing environmental matrix. Important here
is the study of the transition between these two
periods (if such a transition existed). We are beginning to form regional records that are clear
enough for archeologists to agree on the broader
patterns of Pleistocene–Holocene transition,
such that we can now begin to focus on more
detailed patterns, as well as to explain why those
broader or detailed patterns exist.

Méndez and colleagues specifically discuss
the significance of this transition with regard to
landscape and site recognition (3). Pleistocene–
Holocene transition landscapes can be employed as one way to distinguish the surfaces
that the earliest inhabitants used in their open-
air activities. Méndez and colleagues discuss
methods that include recognition of different
ways for dealing with archaeological surface reg-
isters and site-formation processes at different
spatial and temporal scales, either by modeling

glacier-produced features, identifying potential
occupation surfaces where early records are expected, and through a better understanding of
local environments.

There also is a continuous problem with an
over focus on pre-Clovis versus Clovis. Is it not
time to drop this issue, and if not, then begin to
ask new and different questions of it? One way
to sidestep this issue is by applying other terms,
such as the use of OTC or "older-than and contemporaneous with Clovis" used here by Williams and colleagues. These authors employ the
term in order to better understand the different
"occupation signatures" between pre-Clovis and
Clovis cultures. They also suggest that this issue
needs to be separated from the earliest human
occupations that may have different practices
and implications from what we normally consider to be pre-Clovis and Clovis. The similarities and differences between the Clovis and OTC
assemblages may provide evidence concerning
the origins of Clovis technology for the central
Texas region, where the authors base their study
for this volume, but not for other regions.

Lastly, as part of the ongoing debate between
pre-Clovis and Clovis in some areas of the discipline, several colleagues have taken pride in
espousing the idea that harsh criticism and a
high standard of scrutiny of pre-Clovis sites
has been healthy for the discipline. I agree to
a certain extent, but proponents of harsh scrutiny do (and did) not always apply the same high
standards to their own work and criticism (see
Beck and Jones [2012] for a critique of Morrow
and Morrow [1999]), often inventing scenarios
to dismiss pre-Clovis sites and not applying empirical evidence to support their claims against
these sites. Furthermore, it is rarely pointed out
how unhealthy this scrutiny has been for the discipline at large, as discussed by the editorial staff
of Nature a few years ago (see Anonymous 2012;
cf. Dillehay 2015). As Adovasio and Pedler state,
"All such too-tidy theories turned gospel writ,
Clovis First [often] served to constrain rather
than enhance any discussions which addressed
the possibility of earlier-than-Clovis migrations,
multiple population pulses, diverse non-Clovis
technologies, or disparate non-big game hunting

lifestyles." The problem with those scholars who still support the Clovis First theory is that they adhere to an abandoned approach in archeology, one that espouses absolute certainty largely based on self-ascribed authority. Central to their position is speculative imagination, "unsupportable oppositions, ignorance, pure fiction" (Beck and Jones 2012:390–392) to support their criticism, an approach more characteristic of the antiquarian tradition that preceded the modern academic discipline. The writings of these supporters are usually imbued with a nostalgic streak, their archeological imagination being far wider and more creative than the data permit, offering few sustainable and useful insights.

Thematic Gaps

Although it is impossible to cover a wide variety of topics in an edited volume of this nature, there are several themes that are not mentioned here and require slightly more attention. For instance, caching in Clovis (and other) mobility and subsistence behaviors is well known in North America but a topic that is not yet empirically evidenced (and rarely considered) in Central (southern Mexico to Panama) and South America. When considering issues of mobility, technology, and economy, it is important to ask, in Jochim's (1981:65–78) sense, whether caching relates more to "time efficiency" or "labor efficiency," and the conservation of raw materials per se, or to both, depending upon local and other circumstances. Space does not permit a more detailed discussion of this issue here, but it is important, particularly when focusing on hemisphere-long comparative patterns.

Along similar lines, in evaluating the lithic landscape of South America, there is little evidence for routine long-distance transport of raw stone material as there is with materials such as alibates flint, obsidian, and other raw materials in North America, which would suggest that some foragers moved and/or exchanged across wide areas (Sandweiss et al. 1998). There is some evidence for the movement of obsidian for up to 150–200 km in in the Southern Cone of South America (e.g., Stern 2008), but this seems to be associated more with Early-to-Middle Holocene

than Late Pleistocene times. If long-distance mobility or exchange networks were present, we could hypothesize that stone transport may reflect not only the desire for high-quality material but also for its use as a means for population interactions and exchanges aimed at creating or cementing social ties between distant groups.

This brings me to the forgotten or neglected topic of social and exchange networks in this volume. The topic is especially important for understanding the presence of exotic materials in sites, particularly site-specific spatial organization and intersite mobility. These variables need to be factored into stimulation and other models of migration, such as the one presented in the chapter by Aceituno-Bocanegra and Uriarte (5), and perhaps into explaining the distance and time of interregional migration and local mobility in general. Aceituno-Bocanegra and Uriarte discuss "natural corridors" and geographic distances in modeling routes of human entry into Colombia and subsequent dispersion, but they do not consider social distance as a variable possibly affecting the time and place of travel. (I use social distance here to imply possible planned or fortuitous encounters with other groups—presuming a partially inhabited human landscape and not an empty one—that can delay and/or change the direction and purpose of travel.)

There also are forgotten technological and tool systems of the Late Pleistocene. For instance, much less attention is given to the nonprojectile-point component of toolkits, noted here by Acosta and colleagues (6) and Lemke and O'Shea (9). In both North and South America, especially in the Pampa and Patagonia regions of the Southern Cone, slings and slingstones (and *bolas*), for example, were effective in hunting and possibly used in intergroup conflict, but they are rarely discussed in the lithic technology of early Americans. Furthermore, one tool is well represented in parts of South America (e.g., north coast of Peru, eastern Brazil) but rarely discussed: the limace. Limaces are most often unifacially flaked and used as multipurpose tools. They range widely from Colombia to north Chile and from the Pacific to the Atlantic coasts. The limace is one diagnostic unifacial tool that could become another lithic time/space marker in early American archaeology if its variable forms and chronologies were better understood.

An important element of both the Pleistocene and Early Holocene periods, which becomes more archeologically visible in the latter, is the importance of plants in the adaptability of early groups to the environment of these regions. Several early sites reveal this importance, including Peña Roja, San Isidro, and others in Colombia (see Aceituno-Bocanegra and Uriarte, Chapter 5), Huaca Prieta, Quebrada de Jaguay and others in Peru, and Monte Verde in Chile. Peña Roja is situated in the lowlands of the Caquetá River basin in Colombia. The site's lithic assemblage consists of unifacial flakes, choppers, drills, and grinding artifacts (i.e., handstones, milling bases, hammers, and anvils). Thousands of charred seeds, mainly of palms and other trees and *Lagenaria* spp. were recovered. This evidence indicates an early deliberate manipulation of the natural environment, one that Gnecco and Aceituno (2006; c.f., Aceituno et al. 2013) postulated as "*humanized spaces*" (clearing, weeding, planting in the forest) for targeted exploitation of key economic plants at the outset of colonization. This manipulation also appears to be an early form of "niche construction," which also took place in several suitable habitats in Mexico, Panama, Colombia, and Peru where squash (*Cucurbita* spp.) appears as a cultigen by 10,000 cal BP (Piperno and Dillehay 2008; Dillehay 2015).

Briefly, niche construction can be considered a human activity that began to leave conspicuous traces of both intentional and unintentional *lasting* impacts on the environment. It usually requires familiarity and intimate knowledge of resources in order to manipulate a niche to the advantage of a group. Archaeological studies of human niche construction have usually concentrated on either a particular form of environmental modification, such as controlled burning of vegetation, or on human intervention in the life cycle of a particular target species—plants, bison, camelids. But what makes the New World so interesting in this regard is that some of the first pulses of sociocultural complexity—permanently occupied sites, appearance of rustic public architecture, use of domesticated plants and animals—developed only a few millennia after people first arrived, especially in parts of Mesoamerica and the Andes. As a result of more archaeological research, it is becoming clearer that the consistent use of several unique environments (e.g., habitat- and resource-specific adaptations), such as the seasonally dry tropical forests and rich coastlines of parts of the Pacific and Atlantic oceans, played an important role in the appearance of complexity in some areas. Consistent use of certain resources—especially artificial niche construction within them—surely forged continuous and more deeply probing human-landscape relationships, which in turn fostered more complex social patterns, as shown in the central Andes and elsewhere. Although concepts such as niche construction are still rather new in archaeology, the question now is one of identifying and explaining these relationships in the early archaeological record and defining the different types of environments where they began to occur, especially in regard to plant and animal (i.e., camelid) domestication.

The Bigger Picture

While many human migrations in the past may seem extraordinary to us today, they are actually part of a larger, shared history in which humans have, for whatever reason, chosen to move beyond familiar territory in search of something new, different, or better. But not everyone in the Late Pleistocene was likely on the move. Either people moved into new territories and thus encountered different environments, or they stayed within a small region and local environments themselves changed.

The historical processes explicated in these chapters ultimately require drawing variable connections among people, environments, materiality, and landscapes. As interconnections between ancient North and South America continue to be of great interest and are significantly brought into focus, as in the present volume, the historicity and singularity of local sites are likely to further distinguish each region as a place apart from others. In this regard, I wonder whether the hemisphere-long approach adopted in this volume undermines the utility of its focus on local and regional processes. I say this because, in reading the case studies, it seems that the range of variation within the local category was often larger than that between it and other regions. It seems clear that the archaeology of the First Americans still bears the heavy weight of past scholarship that reduced migration and initial entry to a relatively static and uniform model—Clovis First. Many of the chapters in this volume serve as important reminders of the folly of that perspective.

References

Anonymous
2012   Young Americans. *Nature* 485(7396):6. doi:10.1038/485006b.

Aceituno, Francisco J., Nicolás Loaiza, Miguel E. Delgado-Burbano, and Gustavo Barrientos
2013   The Initial Human Settlement of Northwest South America during the Pleistocene/ Holocene Transition: Synthesis and Perspectives. *Quaternary International* 301: 23–33.

Beck, Charlotte, and George T. Jones
2012   Clovis and Western Stemmed Again: Reply to Fidel and Morrow. *American Antiquity* 7(2):386–397.

Binford, Lewis R.
1980   Willow Smoke and Dogs' Tails: Hunter-Gatherer Settlement Systems and Archaeological Site Formation. *American Antiquity* 45(1):4–20.

Bryan, Alan L.
1973   Paleoenvironments and Cultural Diversity in Late Pleistocene South America. *Quaternary Research* 3(2):237–256.

Collins, Michael B.
1991   Observations on Clovis Lithic Technology. *Current Research in the Pleistocene* 7:73–74.

Cooke, R.
1998   Human Settlement of Central America and Northernmost South America (14,000–8,000 BP). *Quaternary International* 49/50: 177–190.

Dillehay, Tom D.
2000   *The Settlement of the Americas: A New Prehistory.* Basic Books, New York.

Dillehay, Tom D.
2015   Entangled Knowledge: Old Trends and New Thoughts in First South American Studies. In *Paleoamerican Odyssey*, edited by K. Graf, C. Ketron, and M. Waters, pp. 377–396. Center for the Study of the First Americans and Texas A&M University Press, College Station, TX.

Dillehay, Tom D., Duccio Bonavia, Steven L. Goodbred, Mario Pino, Victor Vasquez, Teresa Rosales Tham, William Conklin, et al.
2012   Chronology, Mound-Building, and Environment at Huaca Prieta, Coastal Peru, from 13,700 to 4,000 Years Ago. *Antiquity* 86: 48–70.

Dillehay, Tom D., George Ardila Calderón, Gustavo Politis, and Maria C de Moraes Coutinho Beltrão
1992   Earliest Hunters and Gatherers of South America. *Journal of World Prehistory* 6(2): 145–204.

Dillehay, Tom D., Carlos Ocampo, José Saavedra, Andre Oliveira Sawakuchi, Rodrigo M. Vega, Mario Pino, Michael B. Collins, et al.
2015   New Archaeological Evidence for an Early Human Presence at Monte Verde, Chile. *PloS One* 10(11):e0145471.

Erlandson, Jon M., Michael H. Graham, Bruce J. Bourque, Debra Corbett, James A. Estes, and Robert S. Steneck
2007   The Kelp Highway Hypothesis: Marine Ecology, the Coastal Migration Theory, and the Peopling of the Americas. *Journal of Island and Coastal Archaeology* 2(2): 161–174.

Gnecco, Cristóbal, and Javier Aceituno
2006   Early Humanized Landscapes in Northern South America. In *Paleoindian Archaeology: A Hemispheric Perspective*, edited by Juliet Morrow and Cristóbal Gnecco, pp. 86–104. University Press of Florida, Gainesville.

Jochim, M.A.
1981   Review of *Catchment Analysis: Essays on Prehistoric Resource Space*, by Frank J. Findlow and Jonathan E. Ericson. *American Anthropologist.* 83(4):931–933.

Kelly, Robert L., and Lawrence C. Todd
1988   Coming into the Country: Early Paleoindian Hunting and Mobility. *American Antiquity* 53(2):231–244.

Kroeber, Alfred L., and Thomas T. Waterman

1931   *Source Book in Anthropology*. Harcourt, Brace, New York.

Morrow, Juliet E., and Toby A. Morrow

1999   Geographic Variation in Fluted Projectile Points: A Hemispheric Perspective. *American Antiquity* 64(2):215–230.

Nami, Hugo G.

1997   Investigaciones actualísticas para discutir aspectos técnicos de los cazadores-recolectores del tardiglacial: el problema Clovis-Cueva Fell. *Anales del Instituto de la Patagonia* 25:152–186.

Piperno, Dolores R., and Tom D. Dillehay

2008   Starch Grains on Human Teeth Reveal Early Broad Crop Diet in Northern Peru. *PNAS* 105(50):19622–19627.

Politis, Gustavo

1991   Fishtail Projectile Points in the Southern Cone of South America: An Overview. In *Clovis: Origin and Adaptations*, edited by R. Bonnichsen and K. Turnmire, pp. 287–230. Center for the Study of the First Americans and Oregon State University Press, Corvallis, OR.

Price, T. Douglas

1991   The View from Europe: Concepts and Questions about Terminal Pleistocene Societies. In *The First Americans: Search and Research*, edited by Tom D. Dillehay and D. J. Meltzer, pp. 83–103. CRC Press, Boca Raton, FL.

Rasmussen, Morten, Sarah L. Anzick, Michael R. Waters, Pontus Skoglund, Michael DeGiorgio, Thomas W. Stafford Jr., et al.

2014   *The Genome of a Late Pleistocene Human from a Clovis Burial Site in Western Montana*. *Nature* 506:225–229.

Renfrew, Colin

2004   Towards a Theory of Material Engagement. In *Rethinking Materiality: The Engagement of Mind with the Material World*, edited by Elizabeth DeMarrais, Chris Gosden, and Colin Renfrew, pp. 23–31. MacDonald Institute, Cambridge, UK.

Sandweiss, Daniel H., Heather McInnis, Richard L. Burger, Asuncion Cano, Bernardino Ojeda, Rolando Paredes, Maria del Carmen Sandweiss, and Michael D. Glascock

1998   Quebrada Jaguay: Early South American Maritime Adaptations. *Science* 281(5384): 1830–1832.

Speth, John D.

2006   Housekeeping, Neandertal-Style: Hearth Placement and Midden Formation in Kebara Cave (Israel). In *Transitions before the Transition: Evolution and Stability in the Middle Paleolithic and Middle Stone Age*, edited by E. Hovers and S. L. Kuhn, pp. 171–188. Springer, New York.

Stehberg L., Rubén, José Francisco Blanco, and Rafael Labarca E.

2005   Piuquenes Rockshelter, the Earliest Human Pleistocene Settlement in the Andes Mountains of Central Chile. *Current Research in the Pleistocene* 22:35–39.

Contributors

FRANCISCO JAVIER ACEITUNO BOCANEGRA holds a PhD from the Complutense University in Spain and is currently full professor in the Department of Anthropology at the University of Antioquia, Colombia. His professional activity focuses on the study of the origin of the agriculture in the neotropics, archaeobotany, lithic technology, the early peopling of Colombia, and the archaeology of hunter-gatherers.

GUILLERMO ACOSTA OCHOA is associate researcher at the Instituto de Investigaciones Antropológicas of the Universidad Nacional Autónoma de México (UNAM), Mexico City. His research centers on subsistence practices of Paleoindian, Archaic, and Formative peoples of Mexico. He has conducted and collaborated in projects in various regions of Mexico (Chiapas, Veracruz, Tabasco). His current research focuses on early societies in the Basin of Mexico.

JAMES ADOVASIO is widely known for his excavations at Meadowcroft Rockshelter, Pennsylvania, and his contributions to the highly controversial pre-Clovis/Clovis debate. With a PhD in anthropology from the University of Utah in 1970, Adovasio is considered a leading authority on perishable artifacts. He has served as a Postdoctoral Fellow at the Smithsonian Institution (1972–1973) and as Professor and Chairman of the Department of Anthropology at the University of Pittsburgh (1973–1990). For many years, he held the positions of Chairman of the Department of Anthropology/Archaeology and Director of the Mercyhurst Archaeological Institute, where he served until 2015. He is currently Director of Archaeology at the Harbor Branch Oceanographic Institute, Florida Atlantic University.

CIPRIAN F. ARDELEAN is a Romanian-born archaeologist who graduated in ancient history and archaeology from Babes-Bolyai University in Cluj, Romania (1998). He obtained a Master's in Archaeology at the Escuela Nacional de Antropología e Historia (ENAH) in Mexico City. He holds a PhD in archaeology from the University of Exeter, United Kingdom. Since 2001,

he has been working in Mexico, holding a lecturer-researcher position at the University of Zacatecas, where he teaches several assignments at undergraduate level related to world archaeology, prehistory, hunter-gatherers, and archaeological theory. At the beginning of his career, he conducted field investigations on ancient Mayans. In the last decade, he switched interests toward the peopling of the Americas and the earliest prehistory of the continent. He is currently leading research projects and sustained field explorations on the earliest human occupations in arid regions of central-northern Mexico, focusing on the Pleistocene.

JOAQUIN ARROYO-CABRALES is a biologist and Quaternary paleontologist with a PhD from the Texas Tech University in Lubbock (1994). He is a principal researcher at the Zooarchaeology Laboratory of the Subdirección de Servicios Académicos, within the National Institute of Anthropology and History (INAH), Mexico City. He has been involved for decades in the analysis of animal remains from archaeological and paleontological contexts in Mexico and elsewhere across the continent. His main interests are oriented to the study of archaeological and modern bats (*Chiroptera*), as well as extinct Pleistocene megafauna.

LUIS ALBERTO BORRERO is principal researcher at CONICET (Consejo Nacional de Investigaciones Científicas y Técnicas), Argentina, holding a PhD from the University of Buenos Aires. His main interests are the processes of human colonization of South America, archaeology of hunter-gatherers, and taphonomy. He has directed many projects on the archaeology of southern Patagonia and Tierra del Fuego.

BRUCE A. BRADLEY is Emeritus Professor of Prehistory in the archaeology department at the University of Exeter, United Kingdom. He specializes in lithic technology, stone tool replication, Clovis technology, and the peopling of the Americas. He obtained a PhD in experimental archaeology from the University of Cambridge, UK.

MICHAEL B. COLLINS is director of the Prehistory Research Project and research professor in the Department of Anthropology, Texas State University, San Marcos. For many years, Mike directed the investigations at Gault, the famous Clovis site. He specializes in Clovis culture, lithic technology, and the peopling of the Americas. He obtained his PhD in anthropology from the University of Arizona.

TOM D. DILLEHAY is Rebecca Webb Wilson University Distinguished Professor of Anthropology, Religion, and Culture and Professor of Anthropology and Latin American Studies in the Department of Anthropology, Vanderbilt University. He is also professor extraordinaire with honorary doctorate at the Universidad Austral de Chile, internal professor in the Programa de Estudios Andinos at the Pontificia Universidad Católica del Perú, Lima, and adjunct faculty at the Universidad Católica de Temuco, Chile. Known mainly for his outstanding work at the older-than-Clovis site of Monte Verde in Chile, Tom has carried out numerous archaeological and anthropological projects in Peru, Chile, Argentina, and other South American countries and in the United States. His main interests are migration, long-term transformative processes leading to political and economic change, and the interdisciplinary and historical methodologies designed to study those processes. He has been a visiting professor at several universities around the world, including the Universidad de Chile; Universidad Nacional Mayor de San Marcos, Lima; Universidade de Sao Paulo; Universidad Nacional Autónoma de Mexico; Cambridge University; University of Tokyo; University of Chicago; etc. He currently directs several interdisciplinary projects focused on long-term human and environmental interaction on the north coast of Peru and on the political and cultural identity of the Mapuche people in Chile. Professor Dillehay is a member of the American Academy of Arts and Sciences.

NORA VIVIANA FRANCO is principal researcher at CONICET (Consejo Nacional de Investigaciones Científicas y Técnicas) and Professor at the University of Buenos Aires. She holds a PhD in Archaeology, University of Buenos Aires, focusing on lithic analysis in the Upper Santa Cruz River, and has participated in excavation teams outside the country. She began her career as a fellow at CONICET, working first in the Pampas and afterwards in the south of Patagonia, and is currently leading projects that focus on hunter-gatherer early peopling, behavior, and mobility in the Santa Cruz and Chico river basins, Patagonia. She has taught postgraduate courses on lithic analysis at universities in Argentina and Uruguay and is also director and codirector of fellows from CONICET and the University of Buenos Aires.

JUAN LUIS GARCÍA, professor and researcher at the Instituto de Geografía, Pontificia Universidad Católica de Chile (Santiago), is a Quaternary geomorphologist whose main interest resides in past physiographic changes along the southern Andes. He has conducted research that includes mapping and dating (radiocarbon and cosmogenic isotopes) glacial landforms to uncover former glacial history. Current research projects include studies to determine the timing of maximum glaciation and deglaciation and associated environmental change in Patagonia, as well as uncovering environmental change during the early peopling of Patagonia. Professor García also conducts research on present-time geomorphic changes linked to the deglacial trend in the central Andes of Chile and paleodunes of coastal central Chile using optically stimulated luminescence (OSL) dating.

ASHLEY K. LEMKE is assistant professor of anthropology, Department of Sociology and Anthropology, University of Texas at Arlington. Ashley obtained her PhD in archaeology from the University of Michigan, Ann Arbor. Her research concerns hunter-gatherers and prehistoric underwater archaeology, specifically focused on Paleoindian lifeways in North America.

JUAN IGNACIO MACÍAS-QUINTERO is a Mexican archaeologist, with a PhD in anthropology from the Universidad Nacional Autónoma de Mexico (UNAM), Mexico City, currently working as a lecturer-researcher at the Universidad de Ciencias y Artes de Chiapas (UNICACH). His doctoral work concerned ancient nomadic societies in the deserts of the Mexican northern high plains, focusing on primary cultural traits and connections with sedentary groups, AD 900–1400. He holds a Master's degree in archaeology from El Colegio de Michoacán, Mexico (2009) and a Bachelor's degree in Archaeology from the University of Zacatecas (2006). He has participated in archaeological projects in many regions of Mexico. His main research interests are hunter-gatherer societies, cultural and natural heritage, landscape archaeology, and GIS archaeological applications.

ANTONIO MALDONADO, researcher at Centro de Estudios Avanzados en Zonas Áridas, Universidad de La Serena (La Serena, Chile), is a Quaternary palaeoclimatologist specializing in palinological studies of arid and semiarid environments across Chile. He has a particular interest in paleoclimatic and paleoecological changes and how these may have influenced human activity. Current research projects include the expansion and retraction of forests with relation to the steppe of central western Patagonia, the processes of post-glacier colonization by flora communities, and associated fire dynamics. Antonio Maldonado has also been working on reconstructing environments in the highlands of central Chile and studying water courses and agricultural systems over the last 2,000 years in the Atacama Desert.

FABIANA MARÍA MARTIN is a researcher at the Centro de Estudios del Hombre Austral, Instituto de la Patagonia, Universidad de Magallanes, Chile. She holds a PhD from Universidad Nacional de La Plata, Argentina. Her main interests are taphonomy, extinction of Late Pleistocene megamammals, and early human colonization. She is the director of FONDECYT projects at Ultima Esperanza, Chile, 2010–2014, and 2015 onwards.

CÉSAR MÉNDEZ, resident researcher at Centro de Investigación en Ecosistemas de la Patagonia (Coyhaique, Chile), is an archaeologist whose main interest is past interaction between human beings and ecosystems along the southern Andes. He has a particular interest in the early peopling of Patagonia, linking archaeology to the modeling of ancient landscapes and paleoclimatology. Current research projects include the influence of Holocene hunter-gatherers on central western Patagonia ecosystems, uncovering the transformational role of human beings on marginal environments. César Méndez has also conducted projects dealing with the earliest human peopling in coastal and inland settings in central Chile, studying mobility and settlement through lithic analysis.

FLAVIA MORELLO is a PhD candidate at the Université de Paris I, Panthéon-Sorbonne, and researcher at the Centro de Estudios del Hombre Austral, Instituto de la Patagonia, Universidad de Magallanes, Chile. Her main interests are lithic technology, hunter-gatherers, and the archaeology of Tierra del Fuego and Patagonia. She is the Chief Editor of the journal *Magallania*, as well as director of FONDECYT proj-

ects at Tierra del Fuego, Chile, 2006–2010, and 2014 onwards.

AMALIA NUEVO DELAUNAY, resident researcher at Centro de Investigación en Ecosistemas de la Patagonia (Coyhaique, Chile), is an archaeologist specializing in historical and culture contact studies. She has a particular interest in assessing late and contemporary human occupations framed within a long-term understanding of the peopling of Patagonia. Her studies include analyzing the signs of human/environment interactions during recent times through the archaeological record. Current research projects include studying the transformations of rural archeological landscapes in Santa Cruz (Argentina) during the twentieth and twenty-first centuries. In addition, Amalia has been working collaboratively in projects studying the early peopling of central Chile and the slopes of the Andes.

JOHN O'SHEA is professor of anthropology, and curator of Great Lakes archaeology in the Museum of Anthropological Archaeology, University of Michigan. He is active in archaeological work in both North America and Europe. His research is also split between conventional land-based archaeology and underwater investigations of submerged prehistoric sites and historic shipwrecks.

DAVID R. PEDLER has worked as an editor and illustrator for over 30 years, 25 of them for the Mercyhurst Archaeological Institute. Prior to that, he worked in similar positions at the Southern Methodist University and the University of Pittsburgh. He is also a former journalist and city magazine editor. His research interests include the peopling of the New World and the prehistoric archaeology of northeastern North America and the Great Lakes. He is a native of Hamilton, Ontario, Canada, and a graduate of the University of Toronto.

PATRICIA PÉREZ MARTÍNEZ first studied Law at the Universidad Nacional Autónoma de México (UNAM), then archeology at the Escuela Nacional de Antropología e Historia (ENAH), and holds a Master's degree in Anthropology from UNAM, Mexico City. She specializes in use-wear analysis and the recovery of micro-remains from lithic artifacts. Since 2004, she has collaborated in diverse research projects on early societies. She co-organized different symposiums on hunter-gatherers and contributed to diverse publications on this subject. Currently, she is in charge of the Laboratorio de Tecnología de Cazadores, ENAH, Mexico City.

MONICA G. PONCE GONZÁLEZ is a practical specialist in speleology and cave-exploration techniques. She holds a wide array of leadership positions in a variety of international speleological organizations in Mexico and worldwide. Her main interests are the exploration of caves with archaeological presence and the development of vertical exploration techniques. She took part in the initial exploration of the Chiquihuite Cave, Zacatecas.

FRANCISCO J. PREVOSTI holds a PhD from the Universidad Nacional de La Plata, Argentina. His main interests relate to Quaternary paleontology, especially extinct carnivores. He is director of the Centro Regional de Investigaciones Científicas y Transferencia Tecnológica de la Rioja (CRILAR) at the Universidad Nacional de la Rioja, Argentina. He is also affiliated with the Universidad Nacional de Catamarca (UNCa), Servicio Geológico Minero Argentino (SEGEMAR), and Consejo Nacional de Investigaciones Científicas y Técnicas of Argentina (CONICET).

OMAR REYES, associate researcher at Centro de Estudios del Hombre Austral of the Instituto de la Patagonia, Universidad de Magallanes (Punta Arenas, Chile), is an archaeologist specializing in human/environment interactions and bioarchaeology. He has a particular interest in the process of human occupation of the northern Patagonian channels and the broader adaptation to maritime lifeways of southernmost South America. Current research projects include studying the archaeological record at the Chonos archipelago, assessing geomorphological features conditioning location of early hunter-gatherers at island settings that indicate the rise of navigational techniques. In Central Patagonia and elsewhere, Omar has been studying the lifeways of bioarchaeological populations of Holocene hunter-gatherers, integrating paleopathological analyses and stable isotopes.

JOEL RODET holds a PhD from the University of Paris I, Pantheon-Sorbonne (1982), and Doctorat d'Etat from the University of Paris IV (1991). He is a CNRS Honorary Research Fellow and is also at University of Rouen, Department of Geology. His main interests are karstology, geomorphology, geoarchaeology, speleology, and geological heritage.

MANUEL SAN ROMÁN is a PhD candidate at the Université de Paris I, Panthéon-Sorbonne and a researcher and director of the Centro de Estudios del Hombre Austral, Instituto de la Patagonia, Universidad de Magallanes, Chile. His main research interests are the archaeology of maritime hunter-gatherers and zooarchaeology. He was director of a FONDECYT project in the southwestern archipelago of Chile 2008–2012.

THEODORE SCHURR is professor in the Department of Anthropology and consulting curator in the physical anthropology and American sections of the University of Pennsylvania Museum of Archeology and Anthropology. He is also director of the North American Regional Center of the Genographic Project and head of the Laboratory of Molecular Anthropology, University of Pennsylvania. He was deeply involved in the exploration of the genetic prehistory of Asia and the Americas through studies of mtDNA, Y-chromosome and autosomal DNA variation in Asian, Siberian, and Native American populations.

JEAN-LUC SCHWENNINGER has a PhD in physical geography with specialty in Quaternary science and geochronology, Royal Holloway, University of London (1997). Currently, he heads the Luminescence Dating Laboratory within the Research Laboratory for Archaeology and History of Art (RLAHA), University of Oxford. He has a particular interest in the development and application of luminescence dating techniques, especially with regard to optically stimulated luminescence (OSL) dating of sediments from archaeological sites. He has been deeply involved in a diversity of archaeological projects in the Old World, mainly Paleolithic contexts, but more recently has also collaborated in projects in the Americas.

MICHAEL SHOTT, a child of the Great Unwashed, has been in the public schools since 1961. He teaches archaeology at the University of Akron and conducts research on hunter-gatherers, lithic analysis, and how the archaeological record formed.

CHARLES STERN is professor in the Department of Geological Sciences, University of Colorado, Boulder. He is a geologist/volcanologist with a special interest in the genesis of the active Andean volcanoes of Chile and Argentina and associated potential risks and hazards. He also collaborates with archaeologists in the application of tephrachronology to constrain the age of occupational levels in archaeological sites of Patagonia, as well as the study of the sources and distribution of lithic materials, particularly obsidian, from these sites.

RAFAEL SUÁREZ is professor in the Department of Archaeology, Universidad de la República, Montevideo, Uruguay, and researcher within the Sistema Nacional de Investigadores (SNI) of Uruguay. He received a PhD in natural sciences (2010) from the Universidad Nacional de La Plata, Argentina. His main research focuses on South America's Paleoamerican hunter-gatherer lifeways and adaptations and the organization of lithic technology for the Late Pleistocene–Early Holocene in southeast South America. He has conducted over 10 research projects on the peopling of Uruguay, funded by the National Geographic Society, the Wenner-Gren Foundation for Anthropological Research, the British Academy, ANII and CSIC (Uruguay), and others.

DOMINIQUE TODISCO obtained his PhD from the Université Laval, Canada (2008). He is associate professor at the University of Rouen, Department of Geography, France. His main interests are geoarchaeology, geomorphology, archaeological site formation processes, and paleoenvironments.

XIMENA ULLOA MONTEMAYOR studied archaeology at the Escuela Nacional de Antropologia e Historia (ENAH) in Mexico City. Since 2008, she has been working within the Department of Prehistory and Human Evolution at the Instituto de Investigaciones Antropológicas of Mexico's National University (IIA-UNAM) and has participated in various projects in charge of zooarchaeological analyses, studying materials from projects in Chiapas and the Basin of Mexico.

ANTONIO URIARTE is a research technician at the Laboratory for Landscape Archaeology and Remote Sensing in the Institute of History of the Spanish National Research Council (Laboratorio de Arqueología del Paisaje y Teledetección, Instituto de Historia, CCHS-CSIC). His professional activity is focused on the application of information technologies and data analysis to archaeological research and cultural heritage management. Much of his work has been applied to landscape archaeology by means of Geographical Information Technologies (GIT) such as spatial analysis with GIS tools or archaeological survey, including the use of GPS georeferencing and database management systems for field data.

NANCY VELCHOFF is research associate with the Prehistory Research Project in the anthropology department, Texas State University, San Marcos. She specializes in Clovis lithic technology and debitage studies. She obtained her MPhil in archaeology from the University of Exeter, United Kingdom.

LUCAS VETRISANO is a fellow of CONICET, also holding a student fellowship from the University of Buenos Aires. His interests in archeology concentrate on lithic studies, primarily technological aspects and experimentation in relationship to cultural change. His current research is centered on blade technology related to raw material quality in the Santa Cruz and Chico River basins, Argentinean Patagonia.

JENNIFER WATLING was involved in the research published in this volume while still a PhD student in the archaeology department of the University of Exeter, United Kingdom. At the moment of the submission of this volume, she holds a postdoctoral position in the Institute of Geosciences, University of Sao Paulo, Brazil. She specializes in landscape reconstructions through phytolith analysis, especially in wetland environments, and has participated in a diversity of large projects principally in South America.

THOMAS WILLIAMS is a postdoctoral research associate with the Prehistory Research Project in the anthropology department, Texas State University, San Marcos. He specializes in blade technology and manufacturing sequences. He obtained his PhD in archaeology from the University of Exeter, UK.

Index

Page numbers in italic and bold font indicate figures and tables respectively.